British and Commonwealth
WARSHIP
CAMOUFLAGE
of WWII

Volume III

British and Commonwealth
WARSHIP
CAMOUFLAGE
of WWII

Volume III

MALCOLM WRIGHT

Cruisers, Minelayers and Armed Merchant Cruisers

Seaforth
PUBLISHING

DEDICATION

This book is dedicated to the memory of my late elder brother, James Albert Wright, to whom as a small child I looked up as my special hero. In later life we were the closest of friends. His encouragement for me to write, paint and illustrate, his help, and his confidence in me, always lifted my soul when the going seemed daunting. I miss his dry humour and how, even though fatally ill, he fought on, never giving in to despair, always ready to crack a joke and keep everyone laughing even at the worst of times. Two days before his passing in 2015 and desperately ill, he was still joking and died with a spirit and will that inspired all those around him. Rest well, dear brother, we will always miss you.

Copyright © Malcolm Wright 2016

First published in Great Britain in 2016 by
Seaforth Publishing,
An imprint of Pen & Sword Books Ltd,
47 Church Street,
Barnsley S70 2AS

www.seaforthpublishing.com

British Library Cataloguing in Publication Data
A catalogue record for this book is available from the British Library

ISBN 978 1 84832 420 6 (HARDBACK)
ISBN 978 1 84832 422 0 (EPUB)
ISBN 978 1 84832 421 3 (KINDLE)

Typeset and designed by Stephen Dent
Printed by Printworks Global Ltd, London & Hong Kong

CONTENTS

INTRODUCTION

Cruisers were vital to the function of the British Navy. They were seen by the Admiralty as performing three separate roles. There were the scout cruisers that operated with the fleet and, prior to the arrival of reliable aircraft, scouted ahead to locate and shadow an enemy fleet until the battle fleet was able to close and engage them. At first they were small, fast and lightly armed cruisers with a relatively short range, as the main fleets were expected to operate near bases. The second type were larger, more heavily armed, had a longer radius of action, and were intended to protect the sea-lanes by hunting down and destroying enemy raiders. The third group, which eventually melded into the second, were heavily armed ships that could spend extended periods on distant stations as part of the colonial empire of Great Britain. These latter ships were intended to be powerful enough to back up the middle group, while also acting as flagships for distant colonial stations.

In the early part of World War II, those operating with the fleet, mostly in home waters or in the Mediterranean, saw most of the action, therefore they were the first to adopt camouflage. Those patrolling the sea-lanes could do the same as soon as available to do so, some more quickly than others, and some not for quite some time. Those on far distant stations often wore traditional colonial styles of white hulls and buff funnels, etc. These, of course, had to be painted out, but the ships were often limited to what they had in their own paint lockers or what could be applied at the nearest base to their deployment area.

At the end of World War I, and up to the outbreak of World War II, the British Navy developed and stocked its overseas bases. As camouflage was not a consideration, the bulk of paint stocks were the three main shades of light, medium and dark grey. Black was important for waterline boot topping and on many stations white was needed in quantity, if that was the main hull colour of ships. There might be some Brunswick green, favoured for some special areas and internal passageways, and buff for funnels. In home waters, much the same applied, but nearby industrial capacity did enable some other pigments to be available to provide greens and blues. And, of course, in all stations, there was always plenty of red lead undercoat, which was also used on the lower hull.

Therefore it should not surprise the reader that the base of most camouflage schemes of the early World War II period would be set around those shades available. Hence, in 1940, when ships started to seriously apply camouflage, colours such as green or blue were rarely available and therefore seldom used. As you proceed through this book you will see certain styles seemed to arise in different theatres of war. The Eastern Mediterranean was distinctive for its sharp and heavily contrasting angles and curves, always using very dark shades on a very pale base.

Ships operating out of the UK relied a lot on dark grey during the first winter of World War II, and often used little more than a false bow wave, a stripe on a funnel and, inevitably, pale mast tops. A few did go for more elaborate schemes using black or light grey on a mid-grey base, for example. In 1940 there was a temporary rash of very dark brown and dark green, mostly for ships at Scapa Flow. But overall, dark grey or mid-grey prevailed, with or without a contrasting shade.

The main decks of cruisers were usually of wood, because it was more comfortable for the crew than metal, which could make the usually non-air-conditioned ships of the time too hot or too cold. In peacetime, these decks were well scrubbed and usually scraped to fresh wood by holystoning. Large flat stones of rough surface were rubbed all over the timber by the crew to virtually sandpaper the wood fresh, giving a new and smart yellow look. If a ship was on colonial duty, this was important, as many guests would be entertained when visiting various ports. It was also important in other areas if a ship was to look smart when being inspected by senior officers.

In peacetime, decks and paintwork were kept up to a high standard. On the outbreak of war old habits would die hard. Some captains wanted their ships to look smart and until at least the Norway campaign and then the fall of France, it was often felt that the war would be over very quickly, therefore it bred a reluctance to mess up those fine-looking wooden decks. But after the fall of France, things took on a deadlier tone. Many ships had already stopped the scrubbing of wood decks and allowed them to fade to a natural greyish shade brought about by contact with salt water. But by mid-1940 even the most fastidious captains saw that the survival of the ship was more important than the neatness of its decks, and the practice of holystoning was completely discontinued. Therefore, even if the decks were not actually painted, the reader can be assured they will have turned to the greyish shade untreated wood tends to take on.

During World War II, many ships did have their wood decks painted over. In general, this was with a medium shade such as 507b, and with some the darker 507a. In some cases, camouflage on the side of the vessel was carried across the decks. The details of this are not always recorded, but where known will be mentioned in this book.

As mentioned in the first two volumes, this work was inspired by friends and readers of my World War II *Convoy* series of wargame books, who felt that I should publish the hundreds of colour drawings of ships that I have made over the years, as well as my maritime paintings and cover art. They were gathered together over the past fifty years, sometimes from descriptions given by veterans, museum models, works of art, etc. Where I have remembered the sources, these have been included in the bibliography. Many were taken from a study of war art that I did some decades ago. There are some which, across half a century, I have simply forgotten the origin of. In these cases, where mistakes occur in the drawings I have produced, I accept full blame.

An analysis of colour photographs is helpful, but the film used in World War II is not necessarily true to shade, with many colours appearing darker or lighter than in real life, owing to poor quality film or just tricks of light. But black and white photographs can be quite helpful if you have access to the shades that were available, and which were probably used on the ship in question. With patient research, it is possible to reconstruct schemes; distorting the shades of a black and white photograph will often reveal areas that were too light to see in the original.

In this manner, and with a lot of detective work, I have assembled line drawings of the hundreds of ships that appear in this series. If any are wrong, then again I accept responsibility, but would point out that in some cases there are no hard references and therefore my deductions are probably as good as any. In some instances, I was able to use the work of earlier authors as reference, or to check my own research against theirs. I have not always totally agreed with some, and if my drawings vary from other sources, it is because that is my opinion based on the research of many decades.

Of considerable importance is that when ships had their paintwork touched up by the crew, or during a short dockyard visit, the original lines could be slightly overpainted and shapes altered. On occasion, a particular paint might not have been available and another shade was used instead, so that the scheme, whilst appearing the same overall, was actually different in detail. The reader should keep in mind, therefore, that the exact angle of a curve, or a line might alter, yet the scheme remains mostly the same as planned.

This book is intended as a quick reference source for people wanting to paint model ships as a hobby, for wargaming or art. Where possible, I have shown both sides of a ship if the camouflage differed, and more than one illustration if armament and equipment changes made the ship's appearance change. I have not listed them by camouflage scheme: rather, by ship class. This should enable the reader to go straight to the ship type wanted and find an appropriate

scheme. They are also listed by name, and in this volume every ship of every class is recorded. Where possible, every scheme of every ship is also shown. Sometimes these may start in World War I if the ship is old enough, continue through the between-wars era, and then into World War II. If the scheme was known to me, I have included it. This should give the reader the satisfaction of being able to see all appearances of each ship, and for modellers to choose the date for which they wish to paint their models.

Overhead views are included with some ships, as concealment from aircraft was important for much of World War II, even if it meant painting over wooden decks that had been kept holystoned for years by the sweat of sailors. However, if the overhead view is much the same throughout a class, then I have only shown an example here and there.

One of the very important issues for those of you painting models to remember is that sometimes there is no exact shade. There may well be a recommended shade, and even a paint guide with colour chips to go with it. But you must place yourself in the shoes of the sailors of the day. Imagine you have been at sea with a convoy for a week or two; you arrive back in harbour exhausted, in need of rest. But half the crew are sent off for a few quick days' leave, and the others remain behind to carry out maintenance. This inevitably meant touching up the paintwork, or preparing it for the half on leave to tackle when they returned. Laid out are instructions telling them to add this much of a certain pigment to that much white or grey, and the result will be the shade specified for a particular scheme. But after a period at sea, the men may be tired, or perhaps the ship was on standby to leave harbour on yet another mission. So the level of care when told to add a cup of this to a tin of that can be rather less than careful. The famous 'TLAR' comes into effect. The buffer puts in the pigment, a seaman stirs it, they look at the result and say, 'That looks about right.'

Veteran after veteran told me how arduous was the task of chipping rust and repainting. It was hated, even more so by tired men waiting for the rest of their shipmates to get back, so they could get a few days' leave themselves. So up until 1943 we must accept some of the official Admiralty shades with a pinch of salt. Even they accepted that a ship may not have the right amount of paint and recommended a scheme be as near as possible – I stress that they were to apply the shades *as near as possible*. In some cases, this meant the colours might not even be the same, in which instance, the recommendation was that they be of similar shade tone. Hence pale blue was often used instead of pale green, and vice versa. No ship was going to be held back from the vital role of war just because the paint scheme was not exact. MS4a may have been available in quantity, 507c was not, and so instructions to use the latter were over-ridden by what was actually able to be used. From 1943 onward this was eased: never fully overcome, but eased, because the Admiralty started to issue ready-mixed paint to the ships, along with full instructions for specific schemes. Thus in late-war photography we are more likely to see ships looking much the same shade when wearing various regulation schemes. Also, new ships coming from the shipyard would have been painted in the yard, using paint delivered for the purpose.

But I state 'never fully overcome', because there were often shortages, and a ship might have to make do with what was available to the crew to use. There were instances of there being insufficient of a particular shade to cover the amount of area intended, so that area was either made smaller than specified, or often the problem was solved by mixing some other spare paint to eke out the shade that was running short. Therefore you should never assume a ship is exactly one shade or another, regardless of what official records might state.

The most reliable paint jobs were those provided by the various yards while ships were in for refit or repair. The crew were usually not involved, and the work was carried out by workers under the supervision of a foreman painter. But even here, many were not familiar with naval requirements and, despite written instructions, could easily get things wrong under the pressure to get the job done and on to the next one. First, they had to mark out the areas of the ship to be painted. One of the gentlemen I met who had worked in a naval dockyard said they would take measurements from drawings provided and mark the areas with a large lump of chalk. On each side of those lines they painted a dab of the shade required and moved on to another area. The painters then got to work and filled in the marked-out areas. Sometimes there was an 'oops' moment, and a straight line now had a bend in it, or a curve was a bit flatter than originally intended. But in general it would be as marked. Of course, these markings depended on the accuracy of the measurements in the first place. Hence one foreman docker might get a few things wrong that another got right. From one ship to another ship supposedly in the same pattern, these human errors were likely to be present: it is very important to remember that. The accuracy of the pattern depended on the human who marked it out in the first place. The demand for workers in the dockyards meant inexperienced foreman painters, who added further to the possibility of errors.

Even shipyards ran short of paint and, rather than hold a vessel up from entering service, it would be sent to sea with whatever was available. This explains why the reader will see ships of exactly the same class, but on which, although painted similarly, the colours may not necessarily be the same.

Other issues effected how a ship looked. The sudden demand for masses of

paint was a crisis for all the nations involved. Even the USA, with its vast resources, ran short from time to time. This meant that sometimes the pigments accepted were below standard, and faded very quickly. Those who have looked at photographs of US warships in dark navy blue will realise how quickly that faded, often in patches. US shipyards were churning out ships at a prodigious rate and rather than delay the yards, new ships could be painted in what was available, and the task of providing the correct shades left to the dockyard where the ship had its first refit, or the crew to alter during the work-up period. Getting the ships completed and at sea was more important than the exact shade of paint.

In addition to pigments fading, there were at times difficulties in supplying particular colours. Green was in high demand by the army and the air force as part of their camouflage schemes. Many shades of khaki required green pigment too, as did olive drab. For this reason, green was often not available for warships, and other colours had to be substituted. Blue was in less demand by the other services and therefore pale blue often stood in for pale green in naval schemes. Indeed, there were many shades of blue and blue-grey used, although the designer of a particular scheme may have specified green of various hues.

Lastly, not only were paint schemes affected by shortage of pigments, the TLAR system, fading, and wrong colours available, there was also the effect of seawater on the paint itself. Ships at sea suffer salt corrosion and rusting. Paint can bubble up in rust patches and flake off, exposing previous paint colours. This was particularly the case if applied and dried, but not given sufficient time to truly set on the metal surfaces. When looking at photographs, if you see the loss of paint, around the bow and waterline in particular, this may well be because the ship had to put to sea before the paint had truly set. For some paint schemes this effect was very bad. White and other pale shades became much less effective once they became rusty. For larger ships with more crew available, touching up was much easier, but still affected by the TLAR principle.

It is up to the person painting a model as to how specific they are. But when using reference sources, just keep in mind that the very neat-looking ship in a photograph has probably just come from a refit or dockyard job. The ship that looks rather scruffy has probably been worked hard and had little time for the fancy touch-up jobs.

So, if your model-painting skills are not the best you can always claim your model ships have seen a lot of sea time. If you are a very discerning model painter who strives for total accuracy in shade, spare a thought that perhaps you may not be producing a realistic model after all, simply one that looks perfect. A more genuine approach would be to deliberately alter shades, change patterns slightly, and add a rust streak or two here and there. Then you can truly claim your model is very accurate. There could be an area that has been cleaned of rust and touched up, but the new paint is not exactly the same shade: close, but darker or lighter!

A final point: when working on this book I deliberately made contact with some ex-naval veterans and asked them their opinion of the TLAR attitude. Most responded that it was by far the most common way of mixing paint, especially when in a hurry. More than one pointed out that even in peacetime, when ships were painted to regulation and with crew who had time to do it, there was nothing at all unusual to see a group of sister ships tied up together, all resplendent in new paint straight out of the regulation tins, and all still somewhat different.

One ex-rating I interviewed told of how they had been rushed and pushed to get a particular paint scheme applied to their ship. Men were pushed to exhaustion in order to get the job done, as they had little time. He then told how, when only a few weeks later it was decided the scheme was unsuitable and should be painted out, there was considerable discontent among the men. Things like that could affect morale and, of course, an unhappy sailor is less likely to be particularly concerned if a new paint job is all that thorough.

SCALE

DRAWINGS ARE NOT TO SCALE. In order to give the reader a good view of the drawings, they have not been produced to a comparative scale, rather they are to best size for viewing presentation.

PHOTOGRAPHIC ANALYSIS

Black and white film varies in quality and did so even more during World War II with the shortage of quality film stock. The armed services used vast quantities, which left civilian photographers, and even military ones, at the mercy of what they could obtain. As a result, true shade is not always present. A scheme can look lighter or darker than it really was. Pale blue can come out quite dark grey and give the wrong impression of the real shade. Similarly, it can fade almost to nothing and look like there is no camouflage at all.

With diligent research, one can sometimes be lucky enough to come up with multiple photographs of the same ship from different sources and angles. Some may be in sepia and others a variety of faded or under-exposed film. But if one knows what the colour was supposed to be, it is possible to take these, analyse them, and come to a fairly reasonable conclusion as to the pattern and the depth of shade. This is helped if the collection includes the ship from different angles and one can work out the depth of shade from the sun, etc. It is not perfect, but in some cases where records have been lost, it is our best way of working out what a particular ship looked like.

I have used that technique many times. It is a case of using some detective work to gather a whole range of evidence and then from that come to a reasonable conclusion. It is something that requires great patience in finding the different sources to compare, but in this day of the internet that has become much easier. With patience, one can look up the memories posted online either by the veteran, or his family, along with some 'box brownie' photographs those people took, and compare them with more official sources.

I have touched on issues here that I have used for fifty years of my life during research. I have, of course, referred to official sources too. That is the easiest of all and does produce lots of 'what it should have been', as well as a lot of 'what it actually was'. The Imperial War Museum sources in London are excellent. But I am firmly of the belief, based on personal interviews over many decades, that what was supposed to be and what actually was, has not been recorded.

ACKNOWLEDGEMENTS

The author was greatly assisted in the completion of this book through the editing and research assistance of David Schueler and Sam Smith, my chief editing assistants. Without the patience and editing skill of David, I cannot see how this series of books could have got to print without a vast number of additional helpers. David seems able to understand my sometimes 'senior moments', correctly conclude what I meant to say, and put it all right.

Andy Doty and Ian Thompson, both of whom were kind enough to be proofreaders, are also thanked.

A very special thanks go to Mr Wes Olson for his assistance and freely given help from his extensive research into HMAS *Sydney* and other Australian World War II cruisers. Also Peter Cannon for help with HMAS *Perth*.

The members of the Shipbucket site are sincerely thanked. The knowledge of the members and their ability to come up with difficult-to-find information from obscure sources is very impressive.

Of great value in double-checking the pennants of RN ships was the unpublished PDF, 'Ships' Pennant Numbers: The Royal Navy Pennant Numbering System', by Jim Bryce.

The champion reference sources of them all, over years of research, were so many veterans to whom I owe thanks for their invaluable and willing help. We all owe so much for the sacrifice they made fighting World War II.

Mal Wright
2016

REFERENCE SOURCES

Numerous paintings by war artists: some were actually 'there' and I place a higher reliance on their work than some who painted later.

Admiralty, Confidential Admiralty Fleet Orders.

British Vessels Lost at Sea 1939–45 (Patrick Stephens, 1976).

Brown, Les, *Shipcraft 19: County Class Cruisers* (Seaforth, 2011).

Burton, Tom, *Warship Profile 38: Abdiel Class Fast Minelayers* (Profile Publications, 1973).

Campbell, John, *Naval Weapons of World War Two* (Conway, 1985).

Chesneau, Roger, *Conway's All the World's Fighting Ships 1922–1946* (Conway Maritime, 1997).

Friedman, Norman, *British Cruisers: Two World Wars and After* (Seaforth, 2012).

Gillett, Ross, *Australian and New Zealand Warships 1914–45* (Doubleday Books, 1987).

Gooden, Henrietta, *Camouflage and Art, Design for Deception in World War 2* (Unicorn Press, 2007). Some good technical discussion.

Hodges, Peter, *Royal Navy Warship Camouflage 1939–45* (Almark Publications, 1973). Long out of print, but an invaluable work.

Hreachmack, Patrick, *The Painter's Guide to World War Two Naval Camouflage* (Clash of Arms, 1996).

Jane's Fighting Ships, numerous editions.

Lenton, H T, and J J Colledge, *Warships of World War II* (Ian Allan, 1964).

Nicholson, Arthur, *Very Special Ships: Abdiel-Class Fast Minelayers of World War Two* (Seaforth, 2015).

Munsell, A H, *Munsell Book of Color* (Munsell, 1929).

Osborne, Richard, Harry Spong, and Tom Grover, *Armed Merchant Cruisers 1878–1945* (World Ship Society, 2007).

Preston, Antony (ed), *Camera at Sea, 1939–45* (Sydney: Bay Books, 1978).

————, *Cruisers* (AP Publishing, 1980).

Randall, Ian, *Conway's All the World's Fighting Ships 1906–1921* (Conway Maritime, 1997)

Raven, Alan, *Warship Perspectives*, vols 1–4 (WR Press, 2000–2003).

Raven, Alan, and H Trevor Lenton, *Ensign 2: Dido Class Cruisers* (Arms & Armour Press, 1973).

Raven, Alan, and John Roberts, *Man-o'-War 1: County Class Cruisers* (Arms & Armour Press, 1979).

————, *Ensign 5: Town Class Cruisers* (Arms & Armour Press, 1975).

————, *British Cruisers of World War Two* (Arms & Armour Press, 1980).

Warship: A Quarterly Journal of Warship History (Conway Maritime, 1977-1988)

Warships of World War II (Macdonald series).

Whitley, M J, *Cruisers of World War Two: An International Encyclopedia* (Brockhampton, 2001).

Williams, David, *Naval Camouflage 1914–45* (US Naval Institute Press, 2001).

Numerous other books were referred to, not specifically related to camouflage, but which contain colour photographs and illustrations, as well as those that show good quality black and white illustrations.

RECOMMENDED ONLINE RESOURCES

Axis History Forum (forum.axishistory.com/index.php?sid=32afc71cc4e036a37e2f9d1380df1662)

Finewaterline.com (www.finewaterline.com/pages/gallery/modelgallery.htm)

Old Ship Picture Galleries (http://www.photoship.co.uk/Browse%20Misc%20Galleries/?Naval)

Shipbucket: A valuable resource for information and to make contact with naval researchers and enthusiast (www.shipbucket.com/)

The-Blueprints.com (www.the-blueprints.com/blueprints/ships/)

The U-Boat Net (www.uboat.net/allies/warships/)

The Wars at Sea AD to BC on Facebook, the site of author and maritime research friend, Trevor Powell

Tworzymy najlepsze plany okre?tów dla modelarzy[ship plans for modellers] (profilemorskie.home.pl/PlanyPDF.htm#RZP)

Weapons of the World From 1880 to Today (www.navweaps.com/Weapons/index_weapons.htm)

World War II Cruisers (www.world-war.co.uk)

PAINT TYPES AND SCHEMES

At the commencement of World War II, there were no official Admiralty-approved designs for the camouflage of a warship. The commanding officers of ships were left to decide if this would be done, and how, depending on the available paint supply. On occasion, they may have consulted the senior officer of the squadron or fleet to which the ship was attached. In some areas, ships thus applied quite similar schemes, even though they were actually unofficial. Examination of photographs from the era can therefore mislead modern researchers into thinking there was a standard scheme, when it fact it was just ships' crews applying similar ideas – perhaps copying others. Such schemes used the paint that was available to each ship. It requires a lot of paint to repaint an entire ship, and this was not usually available on board, as it would not only require a lot of room, but would also be a fire hazard.

UNOFFICIAL CAMOUFLAGE SCHEMES

In the pre-war era, cruisers were usually painted when in dock or when undergoing a refit. Ships tended to carry enough in their paint lockers as would be required during the removal of rust and general touch-up work in between refits. Therefore, if a ship was to be camouflaged, it was limited to what was available. That could be black, white, and the two main shades of the fleet: MS4a Home Fleet grey, and 507c Mediterranean grey; 507a dark grey was another shade commonly available. There may have been a small amount of primrose, Brunswick green or buff carried by a ship on some stations and, as quartermasters do not like throwing things away, ships that had previously been on those stations might still have some stored in their paint lockers. Naturally, this meant that the range of shades able to be produced by an individual ship would be limited. Captains might also resort to paint available for purchase from sources ashore. These were referred too by the Admiralty as 'local procurement shades'.

The examination of early schemes leaves little doubt that local procurement was understandably common under the pressure of war. In all cases, a scheme not designed by the Admiralty, but worn by a warship of the RN, would be referred to as 'unofficial', even if the Admiralty had given approval to actually camouflage the ship. However, when it was realised that the war was likely to drag on for years, the wheels of Admiralty turned toward official schemes which would use certain colours, thus providing a predictable supply requirement. Green was always in short supply during the early years, as priority for

its use was understandably given to the army and for use on aircraft.

Once a range of suitable colours had been designed, based around pigments that could be reliably obtained, it made supply to ships much easier. Repair ships, depot ships, dockyards and naval stores dumps could be stocked accordingly. The Admiralty could then also issue instruction books on how to apply these paints and provide designs drawn up for specific ships. However, it must still be remembered that all of this was subject to where the base was, how easy it was to resupply, and what priority paint had over other material.

MEDITERRANEAN SCHEMES

The British base at Alexandria was somewhat isolated due to enemy interdiction of its supply line. War priorities meant that other items could be far more vital to the local war effort than paint. However, the base at Alexandria and, to some extent, Malta, seem to have had a rather plentiful supply of the standard paint supplies. Hence camouflage schemes applied there tended to use high contrast shades such as 507a on 507c, or variants of 507b, or white, or even black. In some instances, these were applied with an outline of a lighter colour than the darkest, yet darker than the lightest. For example, a ship might have black on 507c, but with a dividing line of 507b. In other cases, it might have no outline at all and just utilise the main shades. Blue and green were not available in any quantity, and therefore did not feature in any of the schemes devised in the Eastern Mediterranean.

To some extent, the situation was the same regarding camouflage applied in Bombay and South Africa when ships from the Mediterranean went there for repair or refit. I have not encountered any examples of paint other than standard pre-war type used by any of those dockyards until after 1943. Singapore was another location used until its loss to the Japanese, and again there seems to have been only standard RN paint available. The sole exception to this rule seems to have been in the application of Mountbatten pink, which was achieved by using common red lead undercoat, mixed with grey, to achieve its distinctive look.

ADMIRALTY SCHEMES

To suit this supply situation, the Admiralty devised three basic disruptive designs. These were 'light', 'intermediate', and 'dark'. The intermediate was often referred to as 'medium'. They were designed to meet the average light conditions in the various operational zones. The intent in all instances of disruptive schemes was to break up the normal view of the ship, in other words, disrupt what the eye was seeing.

ADMIRALTY LIGHT DISRUPTIVE

The tones of these designs were best suited to dull conditions where direct sunlight might be less common. Pale shades have a tendency to blend in with a light background and with a mix of colours; the blend can make a ship almost invisible. It did require careful counter-shading. There are always areas of over-hang that provide shadow and the use of high gloss instead of matt in the shade meant a greater reflection of light and thus such an area might match that in full light. This type of scheme was favoured for the North Atlantic, convoys to Russia, etc. The colours used were often quite close to each other in shade and only a certain amount of high contrast would be present. It was not unusual for several colours to be applied, even as many as six on some ships, but this was unpopular, not only because of the amount of touch-up paint needed to be carried, but also because it took a lot of work to keep each shade up to standard.

ADMIRALTY INTERMEDIATE OR MEDIUM DISRUPTIVE

Naturally, not all areas suited the light schemes. The central and southern Atlantic for example tended toward much brighter conditions. Therefore, the shades chosen were stronger, even though the actual pattern of the camouflage in layout and style may resemble the lighter type. The number of shades used were usually less, but as all things were continually experimented with, it was not always the case. Achieving an intermediate scheme could simply be a matter of applying new medium-shade paint over a light one. Ships often changed stations and this would require the camouflage to be suited to the new area. Adjusting the intensity of colour was easier than repainting the entire ship, and photographic evidence would seem to suggest that many ships changed back and forth between the grades of disruptive colours.

ADMIRALTY DARK AND ADMIRALTY DARK DISRUPTIVE

Bright sunlight can cause highly contrasting shades to confuse the eye. In the Eastern Mediterranean, the Red Sea and the Indian Ocean, black and white can very effectively break up the outline of a ship, and while the viewer can clearly see that it is indeed a ship, the confusion of light reaching the eye will hinder observing exactly what ship is being seen, its size and type, etc.

Therefore, in this instance, disruption to the eye is important, resulting in the use of darker shades upon very light. Matt white areas would become detached from areas of black. Counter-shading light or white areas in high gloss was important. For dark colours, counter-shading was less important because shade simply added to the contrast. With such a scheme, very dark grey on pale grey would be successful, as would black on white. If an intermediate colour was used, this might spoil the effect of contrast.

THE WESTERN APPROACHES SCHEME

Although one of the most widely adopted for ships operating on the Atlantic convoys, it was generally not used on large warships. Some ideas were taken from it for a few cruisers, and some of the old light cruisers used to escort fast troopships.

MOUNTBATTEN PINK

When commanding the 5th Destroyer Flotilla in the Mediterranean, Lord Louis Mountbatten designed a camouflage which ultimately used three shades of a pinkish grey. It required the mixing of red lead undercoat with various shades of grey. It was not used on capital ships, but it is probably the most argued over and contentious of all shades, as there seem to be many opinions about its actual colour. Belief in its magic properties even resulted in many cruisers using this paint, but the magic only lasted around twelve months before it was realised that at dawn and dusk it was more visible than other colours, and it fell out of use.

ADMIRALTY STANDARD LIGHT SCHEME

From the mid-war period onward, the increasing use of radar meant that ships were often detected at long range, regardless of camouflage. Once detected by radar, a keen observer would soon see through the effects of schemes intended to confuse and thus be able to use those contrast shades to identify the target. The solution was to make it very hard to distinguish the most common or prominent details of the ship. The scheme was only effective in areas of bright light, and was therefore most commonly found on ships sent to the Indian Ocean or the Pacific. The idea was to take a leaf from the Western Approaches book and paint the ship overall in very pale grey with heavy counter-shading of shade areas. This made it difficult for an observer to pick out detail, so that although the ship could be seen, it was not always able to be identified. To increase the problem of observation, a blue panel was added on the hull. This was instructed to be painted from the forward breakwater to the end of the muzzles of 'Y' gun but, in practice, varied a lot. Its intent was to give an illusion of the ship being shorter than it actually was and thus probably further away. There were instructions for the forward edge of the panel to be sloped forward at the top, to create a false bow, but this too was often ignored. For the Eastern Fleet, mostly operating in the Indian Ocean, the blue panel was to be a very pale blue. For the British Pacific Fleet, it was to be dark blue. However, once again there was considerable variation, especially as ships often changed station.

ADMIRALTY SPECIAL SCHEMES

From time to time, the Admiralty camouflage department issued designs of specific type for particular ships. These were often experimental and exclusive to that vessel. A vessel might have a scheme applied, then other ships that went to sea in company were requested to put in a report on its effect. This came about because it was not possible for the Admiralty's own designers to go to sea and actually observe the value, or lack thereof, of the many ideas they came up with. Essential additions to equipment meant an increase in crew numbers. Berths for passengers doing nothing more than observe the effect of camouflage schemes was not a high priority. Hence most ideas were tested using models in rooms with varied lighting conditions and backdrops.

By the end of World War II, other Admiralty schemes were being issued and these included a darker version of the light system discussed for the Indian Ocean and Pacific combat regions. Various colours were now available and tried out experimentally, although by this time they were no longer unofficial, being instead applied to see how various things worked. Hence near the end of World War II, duck egg green and duck egg blue appeared, along with various other combinations of green, which was now, finally, in plentiful supply. Some such as duck egg blue continued into the post-war era before falling out of favour. There were so many of these experiments that it is not possible to sort them into any specific recognisable group.

ADMIRALTY STANDARD SCHEME

This was introduced in mid-1944 and was intended to replace all other camouflage schemes; however, the influence of war meant this never completely happened. It was intended to limit the colours to only two. A dark shade was applied as a panel on, or to the whole hull, with a lighter shade for the rest of the ship. Masts were ordered to be white. In most cases the shades were various types of dull green with much darker green on the hull, or a very dark blue panel on green.

MISTAKES

The demands of war meant that many dockyards not normally given naval work had to be used. But even those that were could suffer manpower shortages or have to use less-skilled workers than they might normally have done. When a camouflage scheme was applied, a plan was supplied to the dockyard and, under the supervision of a foreman painter, it would be marked out in chalk on the side of the ship. The measurements could vary according to the skill of those doing the work; hence a patch of a particular colour could be applied in a proportion not part of the plan, or to a wrong shape and so on. These variations of official patterns were merely mistakes due to human error. The reader should not necessarily conclude the Admiralty intended it that way.

PENNANT NUMBERS

Many cruisers had a number without a flag superior, but there were exceptions, particularly for ships manned by Commonwealth navies. Apart from one instance shown in this book, it was not normal for pennants and flag superiors to be painted openly on the hull during World War II. However, with the forming of NATO, the display of these for ship recognition did become general.

TURRET LETTERS

Letters abbreviating names were sometimes placed on top of one or more turrets on larger cruisers to allow them to be identified. Where this was carried out, it is mentioned in the text for that ship. Generally, the letters were arranged so that an aircraft flying over from stern to bow would be able to read the letters. In other words, they ran from port to starboard. These letters always formed groups that were easily able to be distinguished as an abbreviation for that vessel. For example, 'EX' for HMS *Exeter*, 'AU' for HMAS *Australia*.

BRITISH AND COMMONWEALTH WARSHIP PAINTS DURING WWII

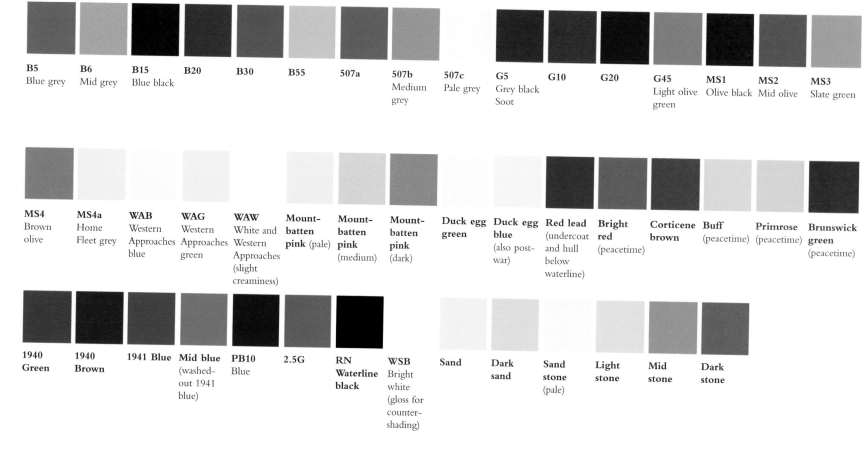

B5 Blue grey

B6 Mid grey

B15 Blue black

B20

B30

B55

507a

507b Medium grey

507c Pale grey

G5 Grey black Soot

G10

G20

G45 Light olive green

MS1 Olive black

MS2 Mid olive

MS3 Slate green

MS4 Brown olive

MS4a Home Fleet grey

WAB Western Approaches blue

WAG Western Approaches green

WAW White and Western Approaches (slight creaminess)

Mountbatten pink (pale)

Mountbatten pink (medium)

Mountbatten pink (dark)

Duck egg green

Duck egg blue (also post-war)

Red lead (undercoat and hull below waterline)

Bright red (peacetime)

Corticene brown

Buff (peacetime)

Primrose (peacetime)

Brunswick green (peacetime)

1940 Green

1940 Brown

1941 Blue

Mid blue (washed-out 1941 blue)

PB10 Blue

2.5G

RN Waterline black

WSB Bright white (gloss for counter-shading)

Sand

Dark sand

Sand stone (pale)

Light stone

Mid stone

Dark stone

NOTE: Unofficial paint colours were known as 'local procurement shades'. These were very common in the early years of World War II on ships in areas where official paints were not available. In these cases, it was expected that an attempt would be made to obtain the nearest possible official or appropriate shade. However, through human intervention, official shades were often badly mixed and were not exactly as intended. In some areas, such as the Eastern Mediterranean and India, there were large stocks of the standard RN colours of 507a, 507b, 507c, black and white. Some stations may have had small amounts of Brunswick green, buff and primrose, plus, of course, red lead undercoat. Therefore local procurement was discouraged, to save money, and camouflage schemes were designed around the standard colours. Some hues came and went at various times of the war, while others remained throughout.

Since volumes I and II there are some shades in the in the above chart that have been slightly changed in response to reader input. G10 and 507a have been separated to show the individuality of each, even though many colour charts show them so close as to be indistinguishable. B30 has also been changed and the three shades of Mountbatten pink made more grey. These last three are particularly difficult to get to appear correctly in print, but I hope that the alteration will assist getting the printed version to render their appearance more accurately. 2.5G was a special one-off shade.

Cemtex (Semtex) is not shown because its colour depended on age, and wear and tear. It started out as mid- to light grey, but could fade to a creamy grey. Pigments could be added to the mix to colour Cemtex, and there were many varied results. It could, for example, be made to appear green or various shades of grey. In the late-war period, and post-war, it was common for Cemtex to be dyed Brunswick green, or, if already laid, overpainted in that shade.

SYMBOLS AIRCRAFT, WEAPONS AND ELECTRONICS IN THIS VOLUME (markings and colours may vary)

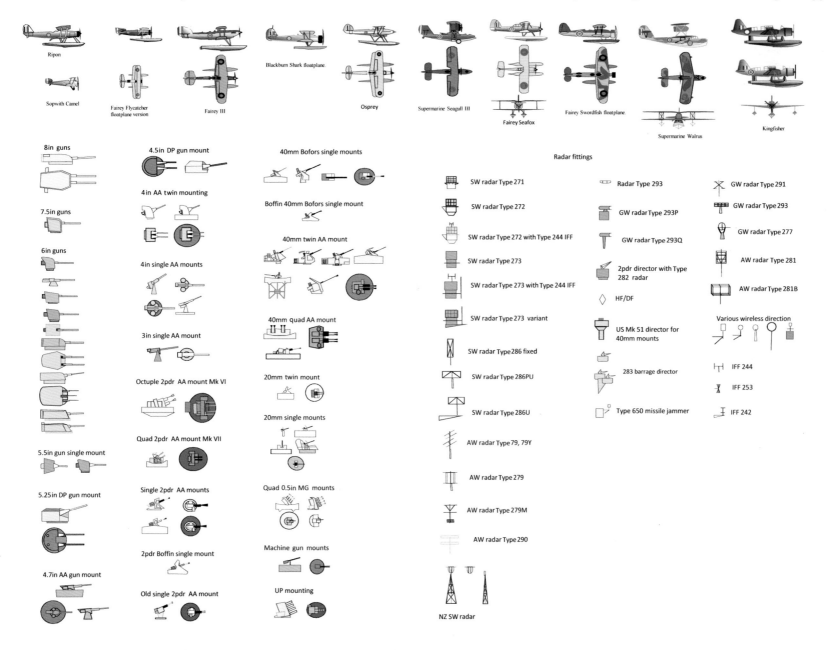

Ripon

Sopwith Camel

Fairey Flycatcher floatplane version

Fairey III

Blackburn Shark floatplane.

Osprey

Supermarine Seagull III

Fairey Seafox

Fairey Swordfish floatplane.

Supermarine Walrus

Kingfisher

8in guns

7.5in guns

6in guns

5.5in gun single mount

5.25in DP gun mount

4.7in AA gun mount

4.5in DP gun mount

4in AA twin mounting

4in single AA mounts

3in single AA mount

Octuple 2pdr AA mount Mk VI

Quad 2pdr AA mount Mk VII

Single 2pdr AA mounts

2pdr Boffin single mount

Old single 2pdr AA mount

40mm Bofors single mounts

Boffin 40mm Bofors single mount

40mm twin AA mount

40mm quad AA mount

20mm twin mount

20mm single mounts

Quad 0.5in MG mounts

Machine gun mounts

UP mounting

Radar fittings

SW radar Type 271

SW radar Type 272

SW radar Type 272 with Type 244 IFF

SW radar Type 273

SW radar Type 273 with Type 244 IFF

SW radar Type 273 variant

SW radar Type 286 fixed

SW radar Type 286PU

SW radar Type 286U

AW radar Type 79, 79Y

AW radar Type 279

AW radar Type 279M

AW radar Type 290

NZ SW radar

Radar Type 293

GW radar Type 293P

GW radar Type 293Q

2pdr director with Type 282 radar

HF/DF

US Mk 51 director for 40mm mounts

283 barrage director

Type 650 missile jammer

GW radar Type 291

GW radar Type 293

GW radar Type 277

AW radar Type 281

AW radar Type 281B

Various wireless direction

IFF 244

IFF 253

IFF 242

1 THE OLD CRUISERS

CONTENTS

AUSTRALIAN TOWN CLASS LIGHT CRUISERS

HMAS ADELAIDE Pennant I47
Australian Town class light cruiser 1922

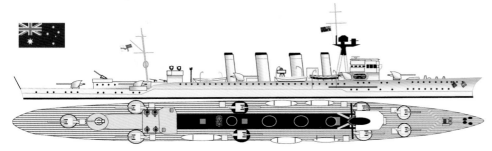

Adelaide was the last of the World War I Town group of cruisers based around the *Chatham* class. Three ships were ordered from UK shipyards and it was decided that the fourth vessel would be constructed in Australia. Although laid down in 1915, her construction became a disgrace. Owing to industrial action and delays in delivery of equipment, it took seven years and four months to complete *Adelaide* for service. By that time the war had ended and her design was obsolete. Newspapers gave her the nickname 'HMAS *Long delayed*'. The bridge usually had canvas over it in hot conditions. A 3in AA gun was placed aft on the centreline. She carried nine 6in guns, with the two forward being abreast in front of the bridge. During her early career the ship was painted in a very pale grey, but the top section of the tripod foremast, fighting top and director were black. Decks were holystoned wood. However, it was a practice of the day to paint vertical metal surfaces matt black in areas where coal was handled. *Adelaide* was the first RAN ship to transit the Caribbean after passing through the Panama Canal. She was very active on colonial duties, including putting down a native uprising in the Solomon Islands at Malaita.

HMAS ADELAIDE Pennant I47
Australian Town class light cruiser 1939

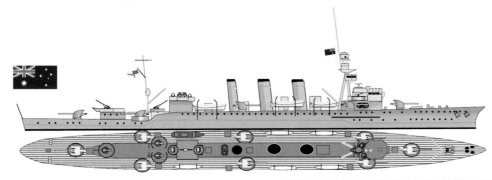

This ship was not disposed of prior to World War II, as had been her British-built sisters, because her very late, delayed construction meant she was in a much better condition. However, it was realised that modernisation was required. Owing to the conversion from coal and oil fuel to oil only, the number of boilers was able to be reduced and the fore funnel removed. One of the forward 6in guns was removed and the other placed on the centreline. Her fighting top was increased and rearranged. The aft 3in AA was replaced by a single 4in on the centreline and two more singles were added port and starboard at the break of the hull. Machine guns were added to the bridge wings and others could be mounted if required. The searchlight structure was increased in size and a secondary director added. The old gun shields were retained on her main armament. Initially, she adopted a grey similar to MS4a overall and the decks remained unpainted wood. The previously black painted fighting top area was now grey. In this form, the ship was intended mostly for training duties and was not expected to deploy outside home waters, but the coming war would see her on active service.

HMAS ADELAIDE Pennant D47
Australian Town class light cruiser 1940

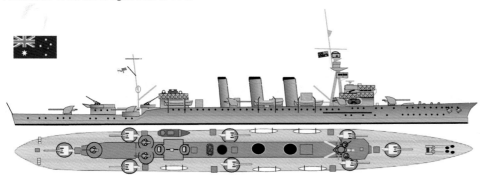

A more warlike scheme approximating B6 seems to have been adopted by 1941, although some sources say 507c was the actual shade used. The decks were still unpainted, but permitted to gradually fade to pale grey from the action of salt water. Splinter mats were placed around areas of the bridge and searchlight platform aft. A crow's nest was added above the fighting top. As the war was being fought far away in Europe and North Africa, there had as yet been no attempt to increase the AA armament. She remained little altered from her major rebuild. The searchlights between the funnels were removed during, or very shortly after, her rebuild. The flag superior of this ship was changed from I47 to D47 in late 1940. With Japan having entered the war and some of the more modern Australian cruisers lost, *Adelaide* was called on to perform duties around New Guinea and other places, as the RAN was pressed for warships. She was present in Sydney Harbour during the midget submarine attack, but was not damaged. Some depth charges were provided on the quarterdeck in racks, but no throwers were fitted at this time.

HMAS ADELAIDE Pennant D47
Australian Town class light cruiser 1941–2

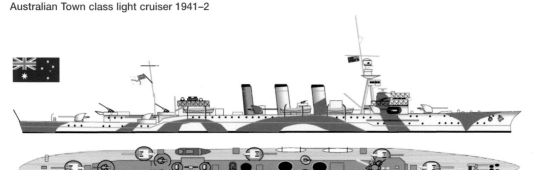

Adelaide was given a disruptive camouflage scheme in 1941 utilising B6 and G10. This scheme was applied the same on both sides of the ship. The decks still remained wood, but were no longer polished and became a natural sea-stained grey. One anchor was removed to save weight. Light AA guns were added each side between the first and second funnels. Although stated in most sources to have been 20mm singles, photographic evidence seems to show them as single 2pdr pom-pom mountings. Depth-charge racks were added on the quarterdeck port and starboard aft of 'Y' gun. This was increased later since *Adelaide*'s main duty was convoy escort. It was expected that German raiders would attack coastal shipping and the ship would be involved with protection of the sea-lanes and covering convoys. After the fall of France, *Adelaide* was sent to New Caledonia to deliver a Free French governor to replace the Vichy French one. There was a stand-off with the heavily armed French colonial sloop *Dumont d'Urville*, but eventually the mission was completed. In November 1942 she sank the German blockade-runner *Ramses* while escorting a convoy in the Indian Ocean, scoring hits from her third salvo onward.

HMAS ADELAIDE Pennant D47
Australian Town class light cruiser 1943–4

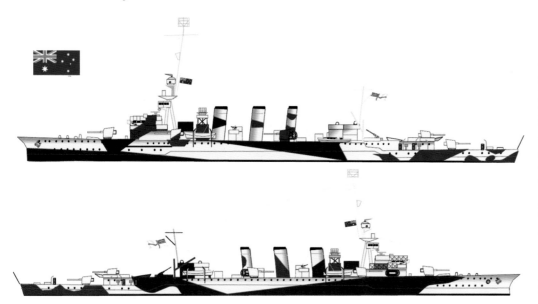

In 1943 *Adelaide* received her last major refit. The original gun shields were replaced by a square type and could indeed have been provided from those removed from the Royal Navy 'C' class cruisers when they were refitted for AA duty. The main guns on each side of the aft deckhouse were removed and a single gun was mounted on the centreline in place of the aft 4in AA gun. This gave the ship the same broadside as before but with a weight saving, which could be used in other ways. Type 285 radar was fitted to the forward director, a Type 281 air-warning set to the foretop and a Type 271 lantern surface warning radar was fitted where the original fore funnel had been. A well-designed camouflage scheme, utilising B15 or G10, was added. The scheme was different on each side as shown. At this time the light AA armament still comprised four single 20mm, with one each side of the bridge front and two between the fore and central funnels. Some additional 20mm were added in 1944. Depth-charge throwers and racks were placed each side of the aft deckhouse, now that this space had been vacated by the removal of the waist guns. The side 4in guns were retained. On completion of the 1943 refit *Adelaide* returned to Fremantle in Western Australia for more patrols and convoys in the Indian Ocean. Much of this was carried out while also training new recruits.

HMAS ADELAIDE Pennant D47
Australian Town class light cruiser 1944–5

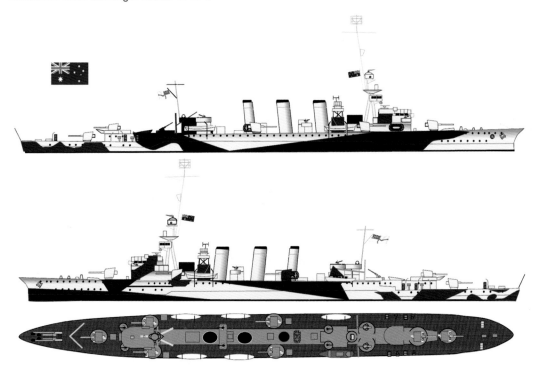

In late 1944 the camouflage on the funnels was painted out. The reason for this is unknown, but the same paint shades were used. The decks may have been painted in 1943 or had simply become much darker due to fading. Type 244 IFF was fitted to the radar lantern and the set may have been upgraded to a Type 272 radar. One of the aft searchlights was replaced by a single 20mm AA and others were also apparently fitted, for a total of up to ten guns. By late 1944, *Adelaide* was confined to training duties only. She was paid off into reserve in February 1945 in order to free up crew for the large number of newly built warships then coming into service. *Adelaide* remained in reserve until 1947, when she was finally sold for scrap. She was the oldest cruiser design to serve in the British and Commonwealth navies during World War II.

CALEDON CLASS LIGHT CRUISERS

HMS CARADOC Pennant I60
Caledon class light cruiser 1917

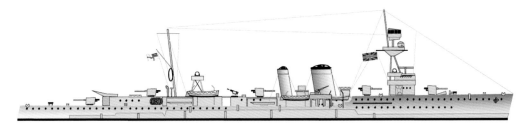

The *Caledon* class cruisers were a further improvement on the famous 'C' classes produced in World War I. The appearance of this ship was standard for the class, all of which were in service by 1917–18. *Cassandra* was mined and sunk in 1918 during the Russian Revolution. The remaining three were little altered before World War II. *Caradoc* is shown in standard World War I mid-grey. The decks were unpainted wood, but in the post-war period were brightly holystoned. The Union Jack was flown during World War I because of the similarity of the German naval ensign to the Royal Navy white ensign. It was placed either on a hoist or even higher on the foremast.

HMS CARADOC Pennant I60
Caledon class light cruiser 1934

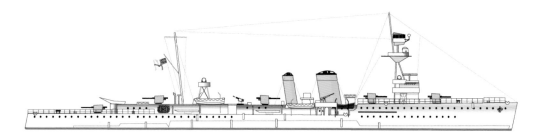

Caradoc served in the China and Far East squadron from 1930 until 1934, during which she was painted in the traditional style for ships in the region: hull and upper works in white, with funnels and gun shields in buff. Gun barrels were painted black, and some ships also had the shields in black. The waterline was red, which was extended to most of the boats. However, one, as shown here, was normally stained wood. The motor launch, which is not visible here, would also have been stained wood, with lots of polished brass. It was the intention to impress the local population and leaders through the smartness of each ship. In addition to the normal crew, there would have been many Chinese from Hong Kong serving in auxiliary roles, as well as many others as servants working in the wardroom, galley, washing clothes and doing other tasks.

HMS CARADOC Pennant D60
Caledon class light cruiser 1939

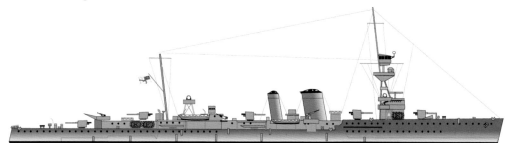

At the start of the war, *Caradoc* was painted overall mid-grey. The area under the 3in gun mounts was plated over to provide more accommodation. A single 2pdr AA gun was added at the end of the aft deckhouse and single machine guns on the bridge wings. Other rifle-calibre machine guns could also be mounted. Extra Carley rafts were carried, but in general the ship is little altered from her pre-war appearance. Type 128 Asdic was fitted, but usually only six depth charges were carried by unconverted ships. The flag superior of her pennant number was changed from I to D. *Caradoc* had been placed in reserve in 1934 and on recommissioning in 1939 was sent to the East Indies Squadron. During this period *Caradoc* intercepted two German blockade-runners.

HMS CARADOC Pennant D60
Caledon class light cruiser 1940

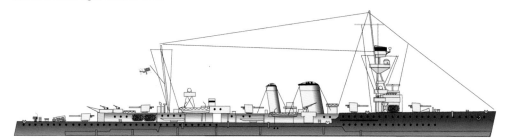

In mid-1940 *Caradoc* was repainted with 507c pale grey upper works and a 507a dark grey hull, and remained in this scheme until her US refit commenced at the end of that year. Although on the East Indies Station, she continued to be used for ferry duty, transporting gold reserves from the UK to Canada. Note that she carried two single 2pdr AA guns on the aft shelter deck, in addition to machine guns in the bridge wings. Her areas of operation were such that the risk of air attack was very slight. Depth-charge capacity was raised to sixteen about this time, with most on the rack or stored by throwers.

HMS CARADOC Pennant D60
Caledon class light cruiser 1943–5

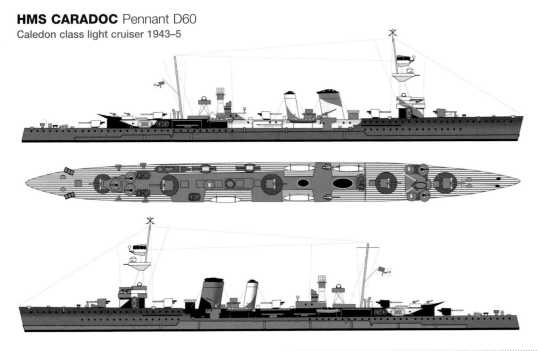

Caradoc received a refit in the United States from late 1941 until early 1942. During that time she was repainted in three colours, which appear to have been white, dark grey and dark blue or black. The decks remained unpainted wood. As no records exist, it is entirely possible that the colours used were of USN type, which would have been readily available. The light AA was altered to five single 20mm Oerlikon guns, two forward on the bridge and three at the rear of the aft deckhouse. She retained the 3in AA guns to the last. She was fitted with Type 290 radar at the masthead and a Type 271 lantern amidships. As the Type 290 was not very successful, it was probably later swapped for the improved Type 291. ASW equipment was carried at the stern, because ships of this type often operated in waters away from smaller escort vessels, but where longer range U-boats might be encountered. It is possible her Asdic was upgraded to Type 132. She went to the Eastern fleet in 1943, where she was first a gunnery training ship operating out of Durban and later as a base ship at Colombo until the war ended. She was scrapped in May 1946.

HMS CALYPSO Pennant I61
Caledon class light cruiser 1917

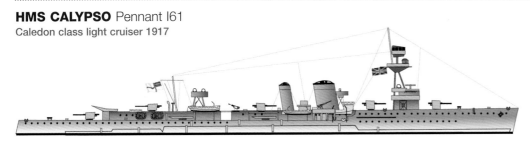

Calypso saw service near the end of World War I and was badly hit on 17 November 1917 during the Battle of Heligoland Bight. After repairs she was posted to the 3rd Cruiser Squadron in the Mediterranean in 1919, where she spent much of her post-war service, before going into reserve for seven years. While serving in the Mediterranean, she may have been painted in white and buff, similar to *Caradoc* while on colonial service. Note that *Calypso* had four searchlights amidships, a further pair in front of the fore funnel and two on the rear of the bridge.

HMS CALYPSO Pennant I61
Caledon class light cruiser 1939

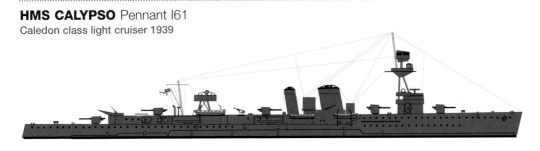

Calypso was assigned to the 7th Cruiser Squadron on the Northern Patrol and captured two German blockade-runners near the end of 1939. During this time, which was mostly winter, she was painted in 507a battleship grey, which would have provided good concealment in the dull winter conditions. Note that the radio cabin between the funnels was enlarged, the aft searchlight platform was enlarged to include a director, and that machine guns were mounted on the aft deckhouse. The midships walkway had been filled in to provide more accommodations, as had the area under the 3in gun mounts.

HMS CALYPSO Pennant I61
Caledon class light cruiser 1940

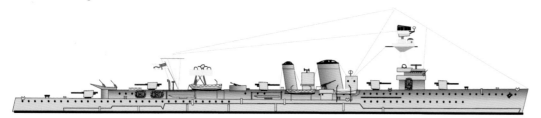

In 1940 *Calypso* was sent to reinforce British naval forces at
Alexandria. For this deployment, the previous dark scheme was painted
out and MS4a adopted instead. The fighting top and masts were pale
grey or white. There was little time for modifications. Extra machine
guns were added on the aft deckhouse and a zareba was placed around
the 2pdr mounts amidships. No radar was fitted. Her service was brief
as she fell victim to the Italian submarine *Bagnoli* south of Crete on 12
June 1940. She was the only one of her class lost in World War II. The
flag superior of her pennant number was not changed to D, as with
her sister ships, since she was sunk before that change was ordered.

HMS CALEDON Pennant I53
Caledon class light cruiser 1917

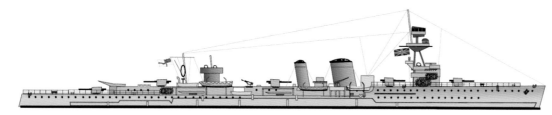

Caledon became flagship of the 1st Light Cruiser Squadron in 1917.
On 17 November 1917, during the Battle of Heligoland Bight, she
was hit by a German 12in shell, but survived. After repairs, she
remained flagship of the 1st Light Cruiser Squadron until 1919. She
is shown wearing typical World War I mid-grey with black waterline. She
differs from others in this class by having a searchlight platform on the
back of each rear leg of the tripod mast. Additionally, her aft searchlight platform is more substantial, with two lights per side. There are
large and small Carley rafts carried and she has more boats. The
rounded object on the stump mainmast was a range clock, to enable
following ships to know the bearing of a target if they were unable to
see it.

HMS CALEDON D53
Caledon class light cruiser 1941–2

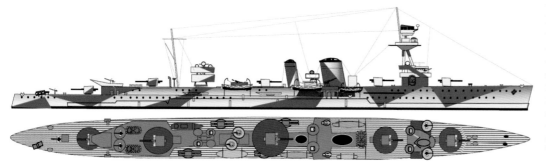

Caledon came out of reserve in 1939 and served for a time with the
Northern Patrol as part of the 12th Cruiser Squadron, with the same
paint scheme as *Calypso*. In mid-1940 she was deployed to the
Mediterranean Fleet for convoy escort, but by August was operating in
the Red Sea. At one point there was consideration about using her as a
block ship against an Italian port in North Africa, but this operation
was never carried out. In 1941 she received a refit at Colombo, where
the camouflage scheme shown is believed to have been applied. It is a
simple, and almost certainly unofficial, scheme using 507c and 507a.
However, it is similar to the schemes used on other ships serving in the
Indian Ocean and Eastern Mediterranean. The port side pattern was
identical. As *Caledon* was now to be assigned to the Eastern Fleet, she
was given five single 20mm AA guns: one on the quarterdeck, two at
the aft end of the rear deckhouse and two on each side of the bridge.
The old single 2pdr AA guns were retained. This was still a very weak
AA for a ship in an area with a high risk of air attack. The decks
remained unpainted wood and the areas of brown Corticene around
the guns were retained. Two searchlights were moved to between the
funnels, so a small director could be placed on the original searchlight
platform. Type 128 Asdic and six to fifteen depth charges were added
as part of her armament, owing to one of the ship's duties being
convoy escort.

HMS CALEDON Pennant D53
Caledon class light cruiser 1944

Caledon returned to the UK and was extensively rebuilt as an AA ship between September 1942 and 7 December 1943. She was the last of the old cruisers to receive such a rebuild. On her return to service she was painted in an Admiralty-designed scheme using G45 green as a base, with areas of G10 dark grey and B15 blue black. Although information is lacking, it is almost certain her decks and horizontal metal surfaces were painted mid-grey, similar to the 507b. The armament change was considerably altered. The main armament became three twin 4in AA mounts. Amidships were two of the new twin 40mm Hazemeyer mountings with radar control. Type 273 radar in a lantern was mounted amidships, with Type 244 IFF on top, as well as Type 242 IFF on the bridge front. Type 281B radar was at the mast tops and Type 285 on the main gun director. Type 282 was fitted for light AA control. Type 253 IFF was added on the mainmast along with Type 650 missile jammers. This very extensive range of electronics was necessary to combat some of the sophisticated German radio-controlled bombs then entering service. Asdic was upgraded to Type 129 or 132 and a maximum of sixteen depth charges were carried.

HMS CALEDON Pennant D53
Caledon class light cruiser 1944–5

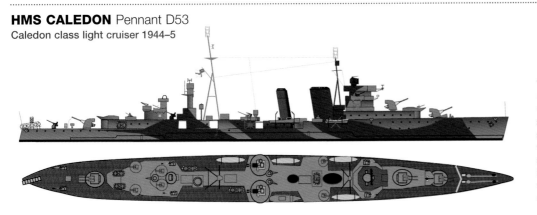

The AA armament was further strengthened in 1944, and by October *Caledon* was carrying six single 40mm AA guns and a single 20mm Oerlikon gun. She was involved in the Operation Dragoon landings in the south of France and later moved to the waters of Greece. However, the ship was showing more and more signs of being worn out owing to heavy wartime service. Thus, in April 1945, she was decommissioned in the UK, so her crew could man the numerous new vessels entering service. She was in disarmed reserve in 1946, and finally sold for scrap in 1948. Note the use of Corticene on the bridge areas where those on watch stood in the open for long periods.

CERES CLASS LIGHT CRUISERS

HMS CARDIFF Pennant I58
Ceres class light cruiser 1917–18

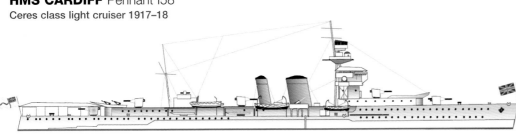

Cardiff joined the fleet in late 1917, becoming the flagship of the 6th Light Cruiser Squadron, and was the ship that led the German High Seas Fleet into internment after the Armistice. She went to the Baltic in 1919 during the Russian Revolution, but soon after was sent to join the Mediterranean Fleet as flagship of the 3rd Cruiser Squadron. She is shown here in typical late World War I mid-grey, similar to MS4a. The decks were scrubbed wood. Note that, unlike her sister ships, she did not initially carry the two 2pdr AA guns originally allocated. These were fitted on the aft deckhouse after the war. She carried a platform and aircraft for a time but it was soon removed.

HMS CARDIFF Pennant I58
Ceres class light cruiser 1931

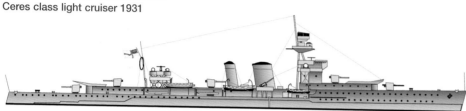

After service with the Mediterranean Fleet, *Cardiff* was sent to the African Station in 1931 as flagship of the 6th Cruiser Squadron. She is shown here in colonial colours of white hull and buff funnels. In some cases, the gun mounts were also painted buff (see *Caradoc*). I have shown her with awnings rigged aft over the quarterdeck and the bridge. Much of a flagship's time was taken up with entertaining guests, government officials and various dignitaries, and quarterdeck parties were part of that duty. Note also that the guns have white canvas bags to add to the smartness of the flagship. The two 2pdr AA guns were eventually mounted in 1923 and placed right aft on the blast screen of the after deckhouse.

HMS CARDIFF Pennant D58
Ceres class light cruiser 1942–3

Cardiff was at Hong Kong on the China Station when war clouds loomed. She was returned home, with the possibility of conversion to an AA ship, and spent a few months in reserve. However the conversion was not carried out, and she was recommissioned with the 12th Cruiser Squadron on the Northern Patrol. By 1941 the ship was showing the effects of a more extensive peacetime service than her sisters, and it was decided to allocate her as a training ship, stationed in home waters. The camouflage scheme shown was applied in 1942 and suited her training area, which was mostly in the Western Approaches. The colours are 1941 blue, B5 and MS4a. It was the same on both sides of the ship. The decks were probably unpainted and allowed to fade to grey wood. Type 128 Asdic had been fitted pre-war, but only six depth charges were usually carried. She had two throwers, but no racks.

HMS CARDIFF Pennant D58
Ceres class light cruiser 1944–5

Cardiff adopted the official home waters scheme some time in 1944 and carried it until the end of her service. This comprised an overall coat of B55 grey with a central panel of B30. She remained a training ship until her decommissioning in 1945. The ship was sold for scrap in 1946. Note that, in addition to the 20mm AA guns, there are still 2pdr guns on the aft blast shield. This was no doubt because, as a training ship, it would be required that she prepare gunners for all kinds of weapons. The single 40mm Bofors shown on the quarterdeck comes from the recollections of one of the crew, who stated the weapon was put aboard for training purposes. I can find no official record of this, but it is quite probable that could have been done. The same source stated that a quad 0.5in machine gun (MG) mount was carried for a time, for the same purpose, until the weapon was no longer in use at sea. Apparently, it was also on the quarterdeck, where it was replaced by the single Bofors gun.

HMS CERES Pennant D59
Ceres class light cruiser 1941

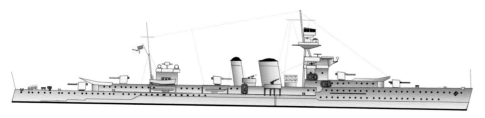

Like her sisters, *Ceres* spent much of the time before World War II on peacetime duties away from the UK and was placed in reserve. She returned to service in 1939 and took part in the Northern Patrol and Channel Force, during which she was probably painted in a similar fashion to the 1940 scheme worn by *Caradoc*. In early 1940 she was posted to Singapore, where the above scheme of overall very pale grey was adopted. Note that the 2pdr AA guns are mounted between the funnels, not aft, and there are machine guns on the bridge wings. The decks remained scrubbed wood. Her previous flag superior had been the letter I, but this had changed to D in mid-1940.

HMS CERES Pennant D59
Ceres class light cruiser 1943

Ceres received four 20mm AA guns during 1942 and then underwent a more extensive refit at Simonstown. The exact colours of the camouflage scheme applied are unknown. But from the little photographic evidence, I would suggest the above pattern is rather likely, as it utilises the various paints then being used on Royal Navy warships and that probably would be available at an overseas station. The colours I have used are 507a, 507b and 507c. In general, ships had to make do with whatever stocks they themselves were carrying, or what was available at the yard carrying out the refit. The basic shades of Royal Navy grey were usually plentiful and could be darkened or lightened as required. As completed, all torpedo tubes were removed and six single 20mm AA guns were added. The 2pdr and 3in guns were also retained. She served in the Mediterranean for a time before returning to the UK in 1944. She is shown here with her initial radar fit of Type 286 at the mastheads and Type 271 on the searchlight platform. The Type 286 set was removed in the Mediterranean and replaced by Type 290, while the Type 271 became Type 273 by modifying the lantern. Type 128 Asdic was carried, along with six depth charges.

HMS CERES Pennant D59
Ceres class light cruiser 1944

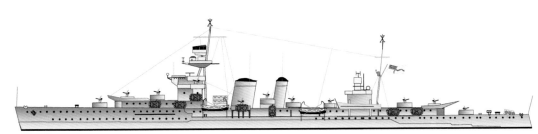

On return to the UK, it was decided that Ceres was not worth further repair. However, she still had a useful task to perform. All her original main guns and 3in AA guns were removed and replaced by a large number of 20mm AA guns. In this guise she became a HQ and support ship for landing craft during the Normandy landings. On D-Day in 1944, she was flagship of the service squadron off Omaha Beach, operating with the US Army. Note that there were whip antennae added to allow communications with landing craft and shore parties. Her previously fitted Type 273 and Type 290 radars were retained, but various IFF antenna were fitted, along with Type 650 missile jammers, in case she was attacked by German controlled rocket bombs. The ship was painted plain grey, which may have made her more visible to the small craft she was operating with, as so many other ships were camouflaged. After the Normandy landings, she returned to the UK, where she was used as an accommodation ship, before being discarded for breaking up in mid-1946.

HMS CURACOA Pennant D41
Ceres class light cruiser 1940

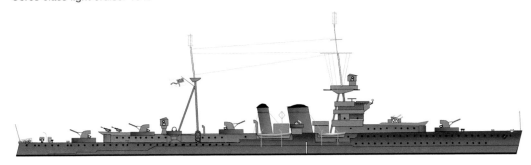

Curacoa's early appearance was almost identical to that of her sister ships. However, just prior to World War II, it was decided to convert her to the role of AA cruiser, following similar alterations to her sisters Coventry and Curlew. However, the conversion was revised to have twin 4in AA gun mounts replace all 6in guns, except in 'B' position, which was replaced by a quad 2pdr mount. Radar 279 was fitted shortly after conversion. This type of radar needed one aerial to send and one to receive, thus it was on both masts. This made her a valuable asset during the Norwegian campaign, where she was badly damaged. The ship was given an overall cover of 507b. The decks were wood, but apparently allowed to fade. All torpedoes were removed. Prior to mid-1940 this ship carried the flag superior 'I', but it was changed to 'D' at this time.

HMS CURACOA Pennant D41
Ceres class light cruiser 1941

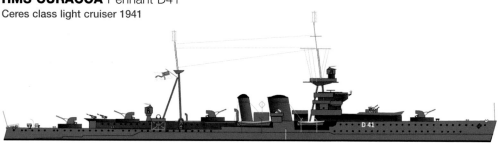

After repairs from the Norway campaign, *Curacoa* was painted in overall 507a. It is not known if the decks were painted as well, but with the new awareness of the danger of air attack, it is possible that they were. Type 282 radar for control of 2pdrs was mounted either side of the bridge and Type 285 was fitted to the directors. No light AA changes took place at this time. She was stationed in UK home waters, mostly escorting fast, high-value ships in and out of the air danger zone of the Western Approaches. The application of her flag superior and pennant number in white was very unusual for a cruiser. However, as she was mostly operating with escort vessels which did have these displayed, it was possibly done to prevent her being misidentified as hostile. Type 128 Asdic had been fitted prior to conversion and depth charges were increased from six to fifteen.

HMS CURACOA Pennant D41
Ceres class light cruiser 1942

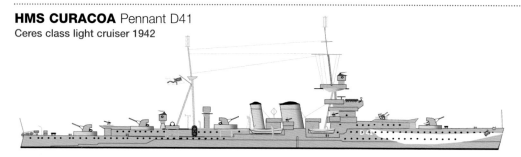

Just before her tragic loss, *Curacoa* had been given a coating of pale Mountbatten pink, which was very popular. The shade appears to have been the medium version. Because of the flare of the bows, the shade tended to take on a darker reddish tinge, so this was counter-shaded with gloss white. Type 273 radar had been added amidships. The single 2pdr guns and quad machine guns were replaced by five single 20mm AA guns. Unfortunately, while carrying out high-speed escort duty, she cut across the bows of the liner *Queen Mary* and was lost with heavy casualties. The impact rolled the small cruiser over as she broke in half. The liner suffered surprisingly minor damage and continued on unaided. The danger of escort duty at high speed was always a risk.

HMS COVENTRY Pennant I43
Ceres class light cruiser 1920

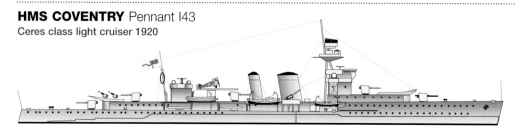

Coventry was the only ship of her class to carry an aircraft. It was not on a catapult, but a revolving version of the flying-off platforms used in World War I. The aircraft was a Sopwith Camel. Plans to carry aircraft on the rest of the class were abandoned. The aircraft was soon discarded, but the platform remained until removed during a later refit in 1928. She is depicted here in 507c grey, which she wore while flagship of the commodore (D) in the Mediterranean. The decks would have been well-scrubbed wood.

HMS COVENTRY Pennant I43
Ceres class light cruiser 1936–7

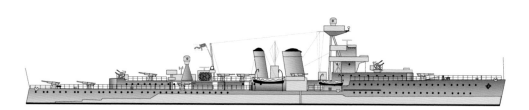

When converted to an AA cruiser, *Coventry* and her sister *Curlew* carried ten single 4in AA guns that were already available, as major ships were having their single mountings replaced by twins. Quad 2pdr AA guns were mounted one in front of the bridge and one at the rear of the aft deckhouse. Positions were fitted for 2pdr directors, but they were left empty, as none were actually available at that time. The forward 2pdr director position was on an extension of a bridge platform, rather than a separate pedestal. Note that her forward 2pdr mounting was closer to the bridge than her sister ship *Curlew*. Also note that all torpedo tubes were removed. MS4a Home Fleet grey was adopted for her overall scheme. The decks remained unpainted and would have been holystoned to a yellowish wood. The general appearance was of the peace-time navy. Had the crises of pre-1939 led to war, this would have been the configuration in which she would have gone to war.

HMS COVENTRY Pennant D43
Ceres class light cruiser 1940

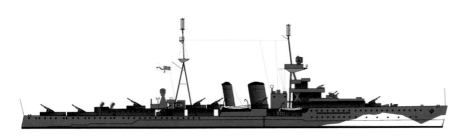

Coventry is shown in a very dark scheme of 507a/G10 with a white false bow wave. False bow waves were common on ships in the early part of World War II. The decks were still wood but no longer holystoned, which would have led to them fading to a pale grey. The scheme was the same on both sides of the ship. Due to a shortage of quad 2pdr mounts for other ships, the aft mount was removed and replaced by two quad 0.5in MG mountings, which was a very poor swap indeed. A 2pdr director has been added in front of the bridge. No other light AA had been added by this time, but Type 279 radar was carried at the mastheads and there had been other alterations to her masts. Although she started the war in the Mediterranean, the ship took part in the Norway campaign, then to Gibraltar and the Eastern Mediterranean for Crete and other operations in that region. She gained an excellent reputation for her AA accuracy, although no Type 285 radar was fitted to her directors. Note that by this time zareba protection was added around the gun mounts. A large wireless hut and radio direction-finding office was built in between the fore funnel and the bridge.

HMS COVENTRY Pennant D43
Ceres class light cruiser 1941

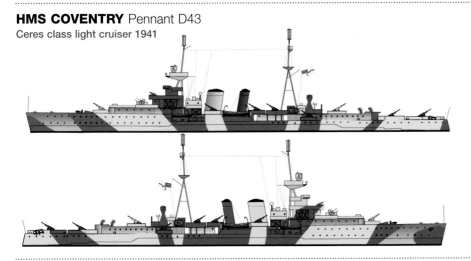

By the beginning of 1941 *Coventry* had changed her camouflage. The dark grey 507a/G10 was retained, but areas were over-painted with B55 grey. The decks were probably still faded wood, but horizontal metal surfaces were the same dark grey as the sides. Port and starboard were similar, but differed as shown in the illustrations above. Type 279 radar was still carried at the masthead. There had been no changes to her armament at this time. Not only due to shortages, but probably because the ship had a high reputation for AA fire with the weapons she already had and may have been on a lesser priority. *Coventry* survived being torpedoed by the Italian submarine *Neghelli*. Her service was arduous and she was frequently called on for duty in the Eastern Mediterranean. Repairs and refits were usually at Bombay, away from the danger of air attack. She was equipped with Type 128 Asdic, but only carried six depth charges in a single rack with no throwers.

HMS COVENTRY Pennant D43
Ceres class light cruiser 1942

After a refit at Bombay, *Coventry* appeared with an altered camouflage, which was similar on both sides. The two shades of grey previously carried were retained. It is possible that during a Bombay refit her wooden decks were painted grey. Her horizontal metal surfaces had been painted dark grey for some time. The last alterations to this ship took place at Alexandria when the quad 0.5in machine guns were removed. Three single 20mm AA guns were placed on the end of the aft deckhouse and two more on the bridge wings, for a total of five. It is possible that another would have been fitted right at the stern as soon as a weapon became available, since a gun tub was fitted, but was empty, when the ship was lost. Note that, according to records, no Type 285 radars were fitted to the directors of this ship, despite most AA cruisers having received that equipment. *Coventry* retained this scheme until her loss in September 1942. While covering ships involved in a raid on Tobruk, she was badly damaged by an air attack. Efforts were made to save her, but eventually she was abandoned and scuttled.

HMS CURLEW Pennant I42
Ceres class light cruiser 1925

Curlew served with the 8th Light Cruiser Squadron on the West Indies Station from 1922 until 1927. The ship is painted in the station colour of a grey so pale that it is almost white. Horizontal metal surfaces were probably also painted the same colour to keep the ship cool. The decks would have been brightly holy-stoned wood. On such a station, the peacetime crew would have been kept busy polishing brass and keeping the ship extremely tidy, to impress the many visitors she would have received as she showed the flag in the Caribbean. *Curlew* was one of the ships to receive two single 2pdr AA guns aft on completion and, for reasons unknown, these were painted black.

HMS CURLEW Pennant I42
Ceres class light cruiser 1939

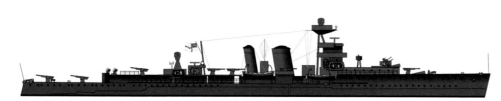

Curlew, along with her sister *Coventry*, was converted to an AA cruiser. Having ten 4in AA guns added and a director mounted high over the bridge required almost a hundred tons of concrete ballast to be added, but after this she proved a better sea boat than as originally designed. A point of recognition from her sister was that the quad 2pdr mounting was further forward and the director tub for it was free-standing, instead of part of the bridge. This gave the mounting a greater arc of fire aft, but the position was also much wetter at sea. She is shown here in the dark grey of 507a/G10 in the winter of 1939–40. She had previously been painted in MS4a Home Fleet grey when first converted to an AA ship.

HMS CURLEW Pennant I42
Ceres class light cruiser 1940

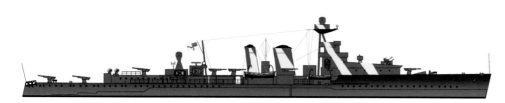

Curlew is depicted at the time of her loss with 507c pale grey areas over the 507a/G10 dark grey she wore previously. This was almost certainly an unofficial pattern, but one can find similar versions of this general idea. The decks remained unpainted wood at this time. She was sunk by German aircraft off Norway in May 1940 while engaged in the Norway campaign. This ship was sunk before her flag superior could be changed from 'I' to 'D'. Experience with the ship at sea resulted in bulwarks on the forward deckhouse being raised somewhat to improve dryness. Type 128 Asdic was fitted to this ship in the 1930s and was retained after conversion. However, only six depth charges were carried.

CAPETOWN CLASS LIGHT CRUISERS

HMS CAPETOWN Pennant I88
Capetown class light cruiser 1934

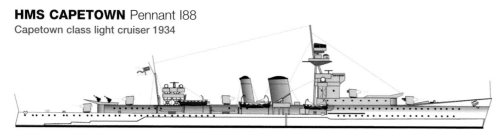

Capetown is depicted showing off another version of colonial appearance. The hull is white, as are the gun barrels and their blast covers. But all superstructure and both funnels are in buff. Horizontal metal surfaces were also buff and the decks holystoned wood. Note that the ship's boats were dark stained wood. This class was a repeat of the previous *Ceres* group, with the bow raised to improve wetness forward, experienced with the earlier ships. This required a prominent knuckle in the hull, but it proved very successful and most Royal Navy cruisers from this class onward used this feature, rather than a flared bow.

HMS CAPETOWN Pennant D88
Capetown class light cruiser 1940

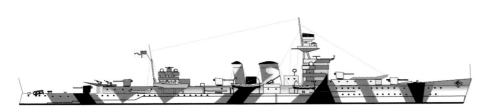

Capetown had her flag superior changed to 'D' in mid-1940. The camouflage scheme shown here is from late 1940 and comprises a combination of 507c pale grey and 507b medium grey with black. Decks were wood. Metal deck areas had been painted medium grey. This was a typical early application utilising paints that would have been readily available at any naval dockyard. At this time the ship had no extra AA armament added, although operating in the dangerous East Mediterranean and Aegean Sea. According to a crew recollection, backed by photographs, she was in this camouflage when towed to Port Sudan for repairs after being torpedoed by the Italian motor torpedo boat *MAS-23* in April 1941. Damage was severe and she was lucky to survive.

HMS CAPETOWN Pennant D88
Capetown class light cruiser 1941

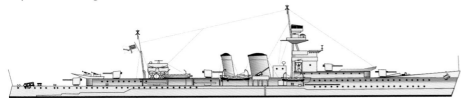

It took almost a year for *Capetown* to be repaired after being torpedoed. She returned to service in 507c with the previous camouflage painted out. The decks were almost certainly left unpainted wood, with metal decks as previously. A light AA armament of six single 20mm Oerlikon guns was added, one each side of the bridge and a cluster of four on the searchlight platform. Type 290 radar was added at the mastheads. It is possible, but not confirmed by records, that this ship had a dark green or dark blue panel on the hull by 1944. She was scrapped in 1948 in the UK.

HMS CAIRO Pennant I87
Capetown class light cruiser 1939

As built, *Cairo* resembled her sister *Capetown* and her pre-war experiences were similar, including paint schemes. In 1938 she was converted into an AA cruiser with improvements over *Coventry* and *Curlew*. All 4in AA guns were twin mounts on the centreline. A quad 2pdr AA mount was placed forward and the old singles removed from aft. Quad 0.5in MG mounts were placed each side of the fore funnel and the previous 3in AA guns removed. The ship apparently appeared in this 507a dark grey scheme during the 1940 Norway campaign. Note the lack of zareba tubs around the main guns. Six depth charges were carried on a rack that dropped them over the starboard side and Type 128 Asdic was used.

HMS CAIRO Pennant I87
Capetown class light cruiser early 1940

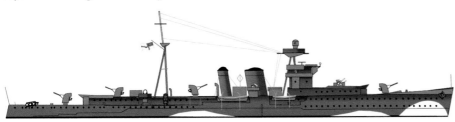

By 1940 a false bow wave, in white, was added to give the impression of high speed. The wave was continued along the waterline twice, as might be expected on a fast-moving cruiser. The main colour remained 507b. This was a deception scheme and not necessarily intended to hide the ship. Its main value would have been against U-boat attacks. The same style was used on both sides. Note there is only a single AA director above the bridge. The limits of a single director were soon discovered from war experience. This ship had to carry concrete ballast to compensate for so much weight up high, but it actually improved the performance of the ship rather than spoiling it. The ship has no extra light AA added. Flag superior changed to 'D' later.

HMS CAIRO Pennant I87
Capetown class light cruiser mid-1940

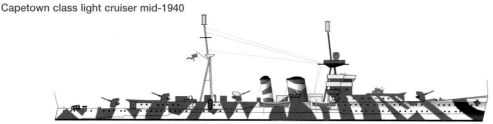

The Admiralty issued orders to all ships to adopt camouflage. However, at this time, it was not specified how this was to be done. As a result, there were many schemes thought up by the wardroom and this was typical of those ideas. Many incorporated a bit of World War I dazzle into them, but, of course, were limited to what paint was available. Hence there were a prolific number of black and white, or dark grey and pale grey, schemes, as shown here. The dark shade was probably 507a, with some black added to produce an effect similar to G5 issued later, and 507c. A higher mast was stepped on the top of the director platform. Type 290 radar was added to the mast tops at this time, but no changes to the light AA were made. As previously, the same pattern was used on both sides of the ship.

HMS CAIRO Pennant D87
Capetown class light cruiser mid-1941

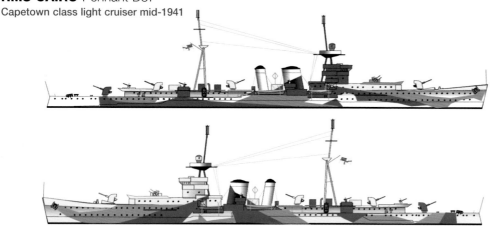

An Admiralty-designed disruptive scheme was applied to *Cairo* in mid-1941. The scheme used 507c, MS3 and 507a. Decks were allowed to fade to a greyish shade and were no longer holystoned. The director was not fitted with Type 285 radar and no other radar was installed, except for the already carried Type 290. The director intended for aft of the mainmast was not fitted. Five single 20mm Oerlikon guns were added. One each side of the fore funnel, two more just aft of the mainmast and one on the aft deckhouse. The director for the 2pdr mounting was on top of the bridge. As usual, there was a Type 128 Asdic set and six depth charges carried on the stern. However, some ships increased this to fifteen or more, depending on the escort role they were expected to carry out.

HMS CAIRO Pennant D87
Capetown class light cruiser 1942

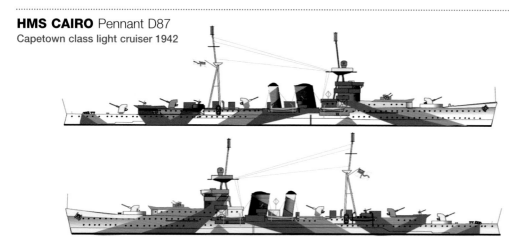

The Admiralty-designed disruptive scheme was modified during *Cairo*'s last refit, but it retained the same colours as before. Although this refit was supposed to see the fitting of a Type 273 radar lantern ahead of the main-mast and a second gun director, I have been unable to find any photo-graphic evidence of this, and most records state these were never actually fitted. Note that zareba protection was finally added to forward and aft gun mounts. She was torpedoed and sunk by the Italian submarine *Axum* while covering the Pedestal convoy to Malta, but had seen very hard service in the Mediterranean covering other major convoy operations and missions. Like many ships in that region, it is probable that, in addition to her official armament, she may have had various captured Italian AA weapons of machine-gun calibre as well.

HMS CALCUTTA Pennant I82
Capetown class light cruiser 1930

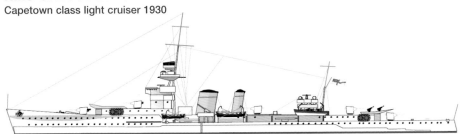

Calcutta served on the Africa Station from 1929–31 and is shown here in overall white with buff funnels. Note the blue motor launch with red waterline. When applying camouflage, it was necessary to use a lighter tone and gloss paint in the areas of shade in order not to ruin the effect, but that was not done in peacetime. At this time, *Calcutta* carried her standard, as-built, armament of five 6in guns, two 3in AA guns and two 2pdr light AA guns plus four twin banks of torpedo tubes. From 1931 she was mostly in reserve until taken in hand for conversion to an AA cruiser in 1938. She joined the Home Fleet in July 1939, just in time for World War II.

HMS CALCUTTA Pennant I82
Capetown class light cruiser 1939–40

A false bow wave, in white, was often added to give the impression of high speed in the early part of World War II. The main colour was 507b. The decks were unpainted wood. The ship has a quad 2pdr AA mount forward and quad 0.5in MG mounts on each side of the fore funnel. The main armament comprises four twin 4in AA mounts. This conversion was completed as World War II started, and the ship took part in the Norwegian campaign and evacuation of Dunkirk, as well as other areas as France fell to the Germans. There was a director for the 2pdr quad on top of the bridge as shown. Six depth charges were carried at the stern, but no throwers.

HMS CALCUTTA Pennant D82
Capetown class light cruiser 1941

Calcutta adopted a more complicated camouflage scheme just prior to her loss in 1941. This was Mediterranean-inspired, but most were unofficial designs of the wardroom when the Admiralty instructed ships to adopt camouflage. The shades used would have been readily available from most dockyards with pre-war stocks on hand. This was the great advantage of the Mediterranean scheme, in that it did not require special paints. The colours appear to be 507a, 507b and 507c. There are suggestions that blue shades were involved, but this would have needed special dyes and tints, which would have been contrary to the entire idea of simplicity in using what was easily available. Note the aft director was not fitted prior to loss. It would seem some radar type was fitted, but records are lacking. I have shown her with Type 286 radar, as it was a common set being hastily issued just before this ship was lost to air attack off Alexandria after the evacuation of Crete.

HMS CARLISLE Pennant I67
Capetown class light cruiser 1918

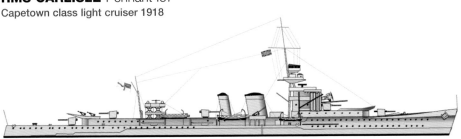

Carlisle was completed five days after the World War I Armistice was signed. She is shown here in the standard grey that would become known as MS4a Home Fleet grey. Decks were scrubbed wood. The fighting top was pale grey. As completed, she carried an aircraft forward of the bridge with a collapsible hangar. Take-off was via a flying platform that extended out over 'B' gun. The arrangement required that the bridge be raised one level, so the compass platform was over the hangar. But even by the time of her completion, it was realised that aircraft were becoming more powerful and such an arrangement was not satisfactory. By 1920, the hangar, flying-off platform and other arrangements were removed, and the bridge lowered to the same level as her sister ships.

HMS CARLISLE Pennant I67
Capetown class light cruiser 1940

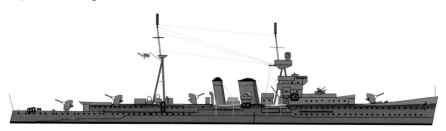

Carlisle just missed World War I and was still under conversion to an AA cruiser when World War II commenced. Unlike her sisters, she entered service with Type 279 radar fitted, which in 1940 made her a very valuable asset for any admiral to have in his force. She was thrown straight into action on completion, taking part in the Norway campaign, where she sank a German troop transport. The ship is shown painted overall 507a, but the decks were left unpainted. Although she had Type 128 Asdic fitted, only six depth charges were carried. It was quite normal for the older British cruisers to carry this type of Asdic in the pre-war era and the six depth charges allocated were not carried in peacetime.

HMS CARLISLE Pennant I67
Capetown class light cruiser late 1940

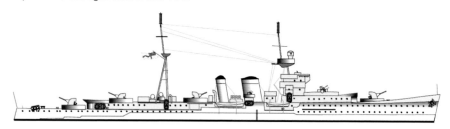

From extreme cold to extreme heat, *Carlisle* was sent to the Red Sea after Norway. Before reaching her new operations area she was painted 507c pale grey. The decks were wood and unpainted, but allowed to fade to grey with the action of salt water. Note that the searchlights have been placed each side of the mainmast legs at a lower level than previously. There is a 2pdr director on the bridge and this later received Type 282 radar. Note also that zareba protection was added around the gun mounts after the experiences of Norway and Dunkirk.

HMS CARLISLE Pennant D67
Capetown class light cruiser 1941

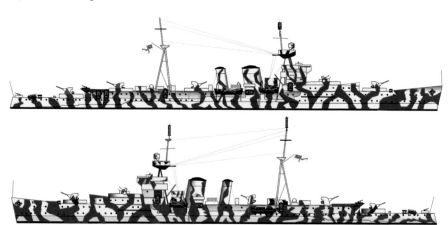

Carlisle had an unofficial camouflage applied, with a somewhat Alexandrian touch while in the Mediterranean. It was a quite complicated pattern that would have been difficult to maintain. As usual for the period, it made use of 507a and 507c, standard paint available in quantity at any Royal Navy dockyard. It is possible that the 507a was further darkened by the addition of some black. The wood decks were apparently unpainted, but would no longer be holystoned to a bright new wood colour. She started this period with Type 279 radar, as shown in the lower illustration, but exchanged it for Type 281 as in the upper illustration. Two single 2pdr AA guns were added, one on the stern and one at the rear of the aft deckhouse.

HMS CARLISLE Pennant D67
Capetown class light cruiser 1942

The camouflage of *Carlisle* was simplified early in 1942, most probably to ease maintenance. Crews returning to harbour from a tiring combat cruise needed rest, not endless work touching up paint. The earlier scheme was probably effective enough, certainly confusing to the viewer, but for the crew it was probably a continual task to keep it free of rust. The colours of the simpler version remained the same, 507a and 507c, and the decks probably remained unpainted, unscrubbed wood. According to sources such as Alan Raven, the pattern was the same on both sides. Although the two single 2pdr guns aft were retained, an additional seven single 20mm guns were added: one aft of 'X' mount, one on each side of the mainmast, one each replacing the quad machine guns abreast the fore funnel and one each in the bridge wings. It is probable that there would be rifle-calibre machine guns ready to place about the ship when air attacks threatened.

HMS CARLISLE Pennant D67
Capetown class light cruiser 1943

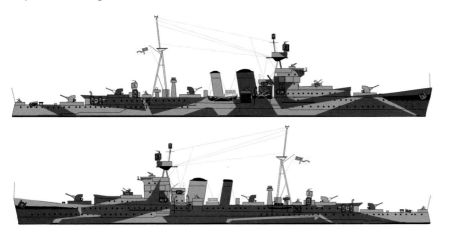

At this time *Carlisle* had an Admiralty-designed camouflage of Admiralty disruptive design. The colours were G10 and B55 – however, it is possible that the G10 was darkened and rather more like G5. Wood decks were unpainted wood and all horizontal metal surfaces G55. The ship carried seven single 20mm AA guns after her April 1942 refit, but in November of the same year these were replaced by five twin 20mm guns on powered mounts as shown. There were two on each side of the fore funnel, two forward of the aft director and one mount at the stern. Type 285 radar was added to the director and another director with Type 285 added aft. A lantern Type 271 radar was added just before the mainmast, and the 2pdr director on the bridge was fitted with Type 282 radar. The Type 281 radar was retained. *Carlisle* was badly damaged in 1943 and became a base ship for the rest of the war, before being scrapped.

HMS COLOMBO Pennant I89
Capetown class light cruiser 1932

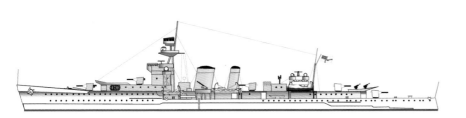

All dressed up for a party, *Colombo* is shown on the East Indies Station during the summer of 1932. Colonial schemes could vary according to the admiral on station, and here we see some variations. The rear section of the aft deckhouse is white, as are the two aft guns. This may have been so that the many guests ships entertained on a colonial station could be more impressed with a white reception area, which would be covered with gleaming white canvas awnings. The 2pdr AA guns have been left a menacing black, possibly to give young officers something to impress the ladies with. Additional deckhouses have been added forward of the searchlight position and the gallery chimney projecting from one may have been to cook up fine fare to impress important guests. Note that the torpedo tubes are white, to make them stand out, and the admiral's motor boat has a fine white canvas cover and stained wood hull. The rest of the boats are in buff with white canvas as well. Gun barrels are black. Decks would be gleaming wood, brightly holystoned. The horizontal metal surfaces would be white to reflect the heat of the East Indies.

HMS COLOMBO Pennant D89
Capetown class light cruiser November 1941

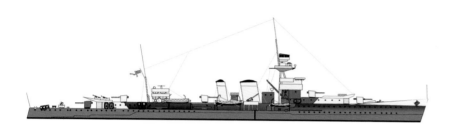

Looking more warlike, *Colombo* is shown around the time of the invasion of Madagascar. There is some similarity to French schemes of the period, and this may have been deliberately applied for that reason. However, it is to an unofficial style, certainly not designed by the Admiralty. The hull is in very dark grey, 507a with a touch of black probably, and this extends to some of the superstructure. The rest of the ship is in 507c pale grey, with each end of the forward and aft deckhouses the same. Prior to this, *Colombo* had worn MS4a for service in home waters, but adopted 507c when sent to the Far East. After this operation she became part of the Far Eastern Fleet and returned to 507c as the main tone; however, it is possible that she had a blue hull patch of some sort for a time. This was the last of the group to be converted to an AA cruiser and she returned to the UK for this work in 1942. Note that while her basic armament remains unchanged, she seems to have acquired a quad 0.5in MG mount on the quarterdeck, which is not listed in records. That was not unusual, as the pressures of war and lost records meant incomplete files were kept, to the puzzlement of later researchers.

HMS COLOMBO Pennant D89
Capetown class light cruiser 1943

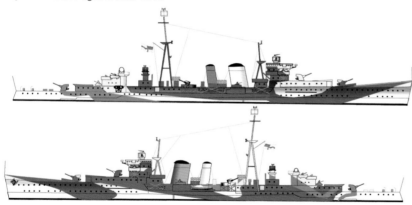

Colombo is shown after conversion to an AA cruiser. The colours used were white, B5, and MS2. The decks were very dark grey, probably 507a. After much wartime experience, this ship was altered in a manner that placed a greater emphasis on light and medium AA. There were only six twin 4in AA mounts to save weight, but also because radar and better control enabled the fitted mountings to be more effective. Amidships, twin Hazemeyer radar-directed twin 40mm mounts were fitted. There were six twin 20mm powered mounts and two single manual 20mm guns as well. Type 281B radar was fitted at the head of the mainmast and Type 285 on the main director. Surprisingly, only one director was supplied. A short tower with a Type 272 radar lantern was placed aft of the mainmast. The old searchlight platform was reconstructed to retain a single light, two single 20mm guns and a light AA director. The latest electronic devices fitted included Type 242 and Type 244 IFF systems, along with a Type 650 missile jammer.

HMS COLOMBO Pennant D89
Capetown class light cruiser 1945

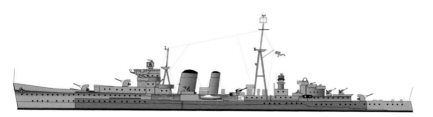

Colombo is shown here as she appeared toward the end of World War II, probably while serving in the Aegean. A standard Admiralty scheme 'B' is worn. The upper works are B55 and the hull, B30. Mast tops were white. Decks were probably faded wood, but horizontal metal surfaces were B55. As shown, the ship has had two of the twin 20mm mounts removed and four single 40mm added. These are the type known as Boffins, and were mounted on the same power mounts on which the twin 20mm had previously been mounted. The ship saw service during Operation Dragoon, and later in the Aegean Sea. She was decommissioned near the end of the war and sold for scrap in 1948.

'D' CLASS LIGHT CRUISERS

HMS DANAE Pennant I44

'D' class light cruiser 1918

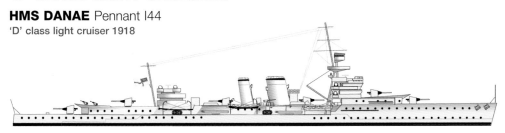

Danae is shown as first completed in 1918, in a grey the equivalent of MS4a. The decks were scrubbed wood and the horizontal metal surfaces grey. Unlike the rest of the class, this ship was never fitted to carry aircraft. She saw a brief war service as part of the Harwich Force, then went to the Baltic during the Russian Revolution. She was armed with six 6in guns on the centreline, two single 3in AA guns port and starboard amidships, and two single 2pdrs on the aft deckhouse. The torpedo armament of four triple 21in tubes was exceptional for her time, and not exceeded until the 'E' class were completed.

HMS DANAE Pennant I44

'D' class light cruiser 1936

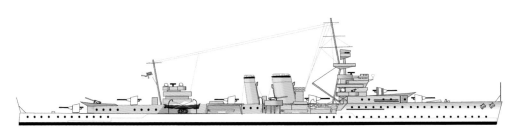

Danae on the China Station during the Sino-Japanese war: the retention of colonial colours enabled non-belligerents to be very clearly identifiable, at a time when there were frequent bombings of European warships in the region. Note that this is yet another variation of the scheme with all gun shields white. Torpedo tubes were painted white and, if covered, had white canvas. The masts are buff, as is most of the superstructure, and the decks are scrubbed wood. Horizontal metal surfaces are probably buff. Note the red, white and blue neutrality markings on 'B' gun mount. These were worn off China to avoid attacks from either side in the Sino-Japanese war. The original single 3in AA guns have been removed and replaced by single 4in AA guns. The 2pdrs on the aft deckhouse have been moved to the bridge wings and a single 4in AA gun replaced them.

HMS DANAE Pennant D44

'D' class light cruiser 1941

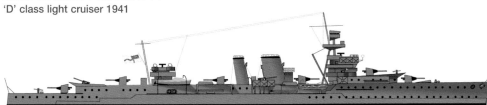

Danae as part of the British Malaya force in 1940–1: the ship is painted in overall 507b, which was also used for the horizontal metal surfaces. The decks were probably unpainted wood and allowed to fade. Note that additional single 2pdrs were added on the aft searchlight platform. There are two single Lewis guns on the quarterdeck, side by side, and another two forward of 'B' gun mount. These were mounted behind a curved shield similar to those on most of the Flower class corvettes. No radar was fitted, as ships on distant stations had a low priority for such fittings. Note the splinter mats added to bridge and around the amidships 4in guns.

HMS DANAE Pennant D44

'D' class light cruiser 1942

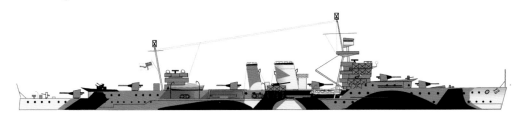

Camouflage was applied sometime in 1942 and, as expected, appears to be the usual application of paint available on station: 507b, 501c and black. Apparently, this scheme was carried up across the decks and was the same on the port side. This means that at least part of the wooden deck was painted. The rest was probably faded wood. Note that the 4in AA gun aft has been replaced by a quad 2pdr AA mount. Apart from that, her armament is little changed. There are some reports she had radar fitted in 1942, so I have shown her with Type 286 radar at the mastheads. What is known is that more advanced radars were fitted in 1943. Type 128 Asdic was never actually fitted, although planned, but six depth charges were carried.

HMS DANAE Pennant D44
'D' class light cruiser 1942–3

ORP CONRAD Pennant D35
'D' class light cruiser 1944

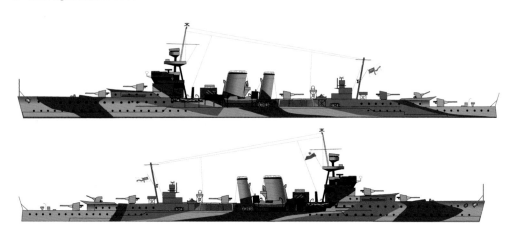

By 1943 *Danae* had a new camouflage based on G5, B30 and B55, along with other changes. It is not known if the camouflage was carried up over the decks, as with her previous scheme, but any unpainted wood should have faded to a dirty grey after several years of exposure to salt water and no longer being holystoned. As can be seen, the port and starboard patterns were different. The quad 2pdr mounted on the aft gun deck has been moved to slightly ahead of the fore funnel on one side of the ship and another added to the opposite side. The previous position was taken up by a twin 4in AA gun mount. All single 2pdr guns have been removed and replaced by four powered twin 20mm mounts. Two were forward of the new radar tower and the other two were each side of the bridge at a low level, but are difficult to see because of the dark camouflage. The 6in gun aft of the bridge was removed to save weight. Although still carried in 1943, her torpedo tubes were removed in 1944, again to save weight. She also received a Type 273 radar forward of the short mainmast and Type 291 at the head of the foremast. The ship was present at the Normandy landings, providing bombardment support. After the loss of the Polish manned cruiser *Dragon*, this ship was handed over to the Free Polish Navy in October 1944 and renamed *Conrad*.

ORP CONRAD Pennant D35
'D' class light cruiser 1945

This ship was of somewhat advanced age and had seen extensive war service. Early in 1945 she suffered extensive turbine damage and repairs kept her out of service until May 1945, but she then went to Wilhelmshaven after the German surrender. Her remaining service was mostly running Red Cross supplies to Scandinavian ports, but she then spent a short time with the British Home Fleet. There was never any question of such an old ship taking part in the war against Japan, and Poland was not obliged to do so.

ORP CONRAD Pennant D35
'D' class light cruiser 1946

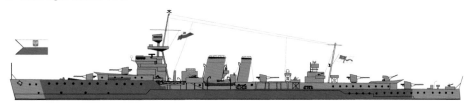

The final scheme worn by this ship was the standard one for ships of the British Home Fleet in 1946. It seems to have been applied only just before the decision was taken to hand her back to the Royal Navy, where she reverted to her old name. No other changes were made. However, her age and repaired engines ensured that she was not to see any further service. She was put into reserve and then sold for scrap in 1948.

HMS DAUNTLESS Pennant I45
'D' class light cruiser 1919

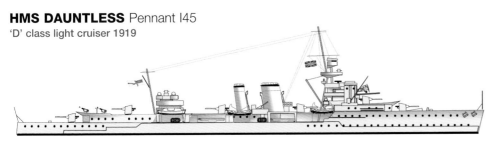

Dauntless is shown as first completed in 1919 in a grey, equivalent to MS4a. The decks were scrubbed wood and the horizontal metal surfaces grey. She was fitted to carry a single aircraft with a folding hangar placed in front of the bridge, which required raising the bridge one level. The aircraft used a flying-off platform, with the ship steaming at full speed, to get airborne. This proved to be a clumsy arrangement, so the hangar was removed during the 1920s and the bridge altered to match the rest of the class. She went to the Baltic during the Russian Revolution. Her service was much like that of most of her sisters with colonial and Home Fleet deployments. However she ran aground off Nova Scotia in 1928 and could not resume service until 1930.

HMS DAUNTLESS Pennant D45
'D' class light cruiser late 1941

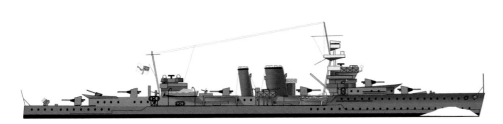

This ship came out of reserve and joined the South Atlantic Squadron at the start of World War II. The squadron later went to China and then joined the Malaya force in 1941. However, she was damaged in a collision with HMS *Emerald*, was repaired at Singapore, and then returned to the UK before war with Japan commenced. While in transit she carried a false bow wave over her 507b grey. Note that the upper bridge and fighting top were painted very pale grey, or possibly white. Because of the danger of German air activity near home waters, she has an emergency AA armament. On the quarterdeck there is a quad 0.5in MG mount, behind 'X' gun mount are shielded Lewis guns and aft of 'Q' gun mount are single 20mm Oerlikon guns. More substantial changes were made when she reached Portsmouth. Light paint areas and emergency AA credit to the late J Fremont (RN), who took passage home on *Dauntless* from Singapore. The original 3in AA guns had been replaced by 4in guns much earlier. The bow wave area is estimated. As with many other ships, her flag superior was changed to 'D' from 'I' in mid-1940.

HMS DAUNTLESS Pennant D45
'D' class light cruiser 1942

Dauntless received a small refit on return to the UK in early 1942 and was then sent back to the Eastern Fleet, previously known as the Malaya Squadron. The paint scheme followed a basically Alexandria style and, unlike earlier versions, was relatively simple, which would have made the job of keeping it freshly painted easier for the crew. Only two colours were used: a base of 507c with 507b over that. It is presumed the pattern was the same on both sides. The colour of the wood deck is unknown, but in an aerial photograph it appears to be dark, and may have been painted with 507b. Armament changes comprised the replacement of the emergency AA with eight single 20mm AA guns. Note that the single 4in guns were retained, but given shields. Type 273 radar was added atop the searchlight platform and Type 290 at the mastheads. She returned to the Eastern Fleet in this form.

HMS DAUNTLESS Pennant D45
'D' class light cruiser 1944–5

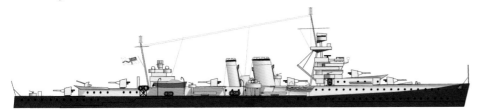

By the end of 1943, the wear and tear of heavy use was starting to tell on *Dauntless* and her sisters. As newer units were joining the Eastern Fleet, she was sent back to the UK and became a training ship in 1944. The 4in AA guns on each side amidships were replaced by quad 2pdr mounts, but no other major alterations were made. Her camouflage scheme was rather unique because of an unusual interpretation of the dark hull/light upper works instructions then being used. Instead of a dark panel, the area of dark grey extended from bow to stern. However, it curved up from the break in the deck to the bow, instead of continuing on in a straight line. The colours used seem to be G10 and MS4a, but Admiralty instructions for the period were B30 and B55 for home waters, with G10 decks. The ship was so worn out that she was decommissioned in early 1945 and scrapped the following year.

HMS **DURBAN** Pennant I99
'D' class light cruiser 1921

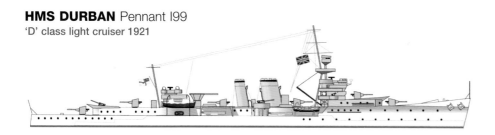

Durban was completed in 1921 and went straight to the China Station. She is shown in a colonial paint scheme, often referred to as Victorian livery. Note that she differs from her sister *Danae* when she was on the same station. The hull and deckhouses were white, but all guns and upper works were buff. Even the canvas gun dodgers are in buff. Note also that the new-style raised bow meant that the upper part was not in shadow, while that below was. The ship has the standard armament for her class. She carried the flying-off platform amidships, as did others, and because of her station it was not removed until 1928. As far as I can determine, she never actually carried an aircraft for the platform.

HMS **DURBAN** Pennant D99
'D' class light cruiser 1942

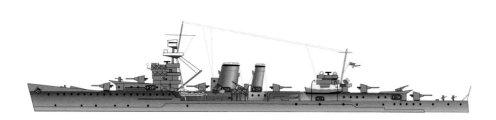

Durban was an escort for the last convoy out of Singapore before it fell to the Japanese in 1942. She was apparently dressed overall in 507b, with some decks painted dark green. Her fighting top was white. One woman evacuee said, 'She was dull grey, but to us she was a golden ship.' *Durban* was badly damaged during the evacuation and needed emergency repairs at Colombo, after which she proceeded across to the United States for the work to be finished. At the time, the last convoy was preparing to leave, most of the naval base was being demolished, and ships took the opportunity to grab what they could, especially AA guns. In this case, *Durban* was able to 'unofficially acquire' three quad 0.5in MG mounts, which were placed either side of the fore funnel and on the rear of the searchlight platform. She also had several shielded Lewis guns mounted wherever space could be found. There were reportedly many other weapons, such as army Bren guns, placed about the ship. There are two Lewis guns shown here on the quarterdeck and one ahead of 'B' gun mount. The Japanese air attacks were relentless and she was lucky to survive.

HMS **DURBAN** Pennant D99
'D' class light cruiser 1943

This ship underwent an extensive repair at New York in the United States, during which time a disruptive camouflage scheme was applied. The colours used were 507c as a base, with MS3 and B5. It is possible similar USN paints were used. Her full main armament was retained, along with three single 4in AA guns and two single 2pdr AA guns. Eight single 20mm guns were also added. Between June and August, further changes were made at Portsmouth in the UK, at which time the single 4in guns were given shields as shown. She joined the Eastern Fleet after the work was completed, but was returned to the UK in 1943. The ship seems to have never got over the bomb damage and her age was causing her to be increasingly unserviceable, so she was paid off and disarmed. In 1944 she was scuttled as part of the breakwaters off the Normandy beachheads and the wreck scrapped after the war.

HMS **DIOMEDE** Pennant I92
'D' class light cruiser 1925–35

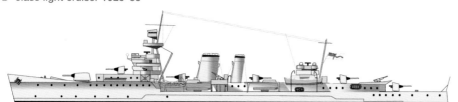

This ship was completed with the 'A' gun in a fully-enclosed mounting as an experiment in weatherproofing. The idea would be adapted by later ships. *Diomede* spent some time on the China Station after she was commissioned, then went to join the New Zealand Squadron until 1936, when the modern cruiser *Achilles* relieved her. She is shown here in an overall scheme of 507c. The decks would have been holystoned wood. During this period, most of the crew were New Zealanders, but the ship remained the property of the British Admiralty, as the squadron country only maintained a naval reserve at the time. New Zealand paid the British government a subsidy for a naval force to be stationed there. The largest ships were cruisers, but there were also some sloops deployed with the squadron.

HMS DIOMEDE Pennant D92
'D' class light cruiser 1943

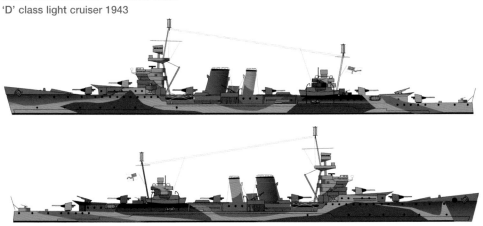

During the early part of the war, *Diomede* was painted in a similar manner as the 1942 illustration of *Durban*. In 1943 she wore the scheme shown in 507a, MS2 and MS3. *Diomede* served in the South Atlantic and West Africa after a period with the Home Fleet on blockade patrols. She intercepted a German blockade-runner off Mexico, but otherwise saw little action. *Diomede* landed her special 'A' gun mounting in 1942 to save weight. It was replaced by a standard 6in gun mounting. The original two single 2pdr guns were replaced by single 20mm and six more 20mm guns were also added. In 1943 two of the singles were landed and replaced by twin 20mm mounts. Apart from that, the ship retained her main 6in armament and secondary 4in AA guns. Type 273 radar was placed on the old searchlight platform and Type 290 at the mast tops. Her role for the rest of World War II was as a training ship, before being paid off in 1945, and scrapped in 1946.

HMS DRAGON Pennant I46
'D' class light cruiser 1918

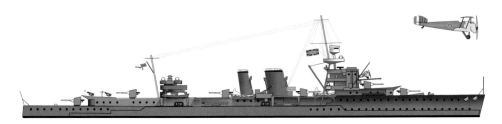

Dragon was completed in time to see some short war service with the 5th Light Cruiser Squadron of the famous Harwich Force. The ships of this force seem to have been painted in a mid-grey similar to 507b. The fighting top was white. The decks would have been brightly holystoned wood, with horizontal metal surfaces the same grey as the rest of the ship. She was one of two of this class to be completed with an aircraft hangar in front of the bridge and an aircraft flying-off platform. She flies the British Union Jack and a reasonably large White Ensign because of the difficulty in telling British and German ships apart. The aircraft arrangements were unsatisfactory and were removed around 1920, but the Japanese copied the idea and many of their light cruisers had flying-off ramps forward for some years.

HMS DRAGON Pennant D46
'D' class light cruiser 1942

Dragon is shown wearing the scheme applied while she was serving with the Eastern Fleet. The style is typical of that area in the early part of World War II, when ships used local paint supplies for camouflage. 507c forms the base, with 507a and 507b making up the disruption areas. When camouflaged, ships were not supposed to show a black waterline and this has been kept to a minimum. Decks were unpainted wood. The ship had no radar at this time and her light AA is restricted to two single 2pdr AA guns on either side of the bridge, a single 20mm at the stern and two more forward of the searchlight platform. Ships on far stations were slow to receive light AA guns until the war with Japan broke out, because the demand for European and Mediterranean waters was much more urgent. The ship was still fitted with a full complement of torpedoes at this time.

ORP DRAGON Pennant D46
'D' class light cruiser 1943

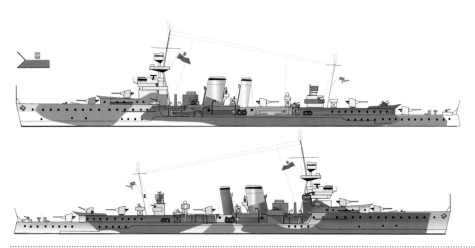

Dragon was manned by the Free Polish Navy in January 1943, but did not complete refitting until August. Her armament at that time was five 6in guns, three quad 2pdr mounts and eight single 20mm guns. She still carried her original torpedoes. All the 4in AA guns had been removed, which left her with close-range AA only, although it was planned to correct this at her next refit. In March 1943 the aft 2pdr mount was removed and a twin 4in AA mount installed in its place. The illustration of the port side shows her with that armament. The light AA was then altered to four twin and four single 20mm AA guns, with the two amidships, the quad 2pdrs, retained. All torpedo tubes were removed during this refit. The ship covered two Russian convoys and the camouflage, as shown here, would have been quite effective. The base colour is 507c with B6 and B5 areas. It is believed this scheme was carried throughout her service with the Polish Navy. Type 273 radar was fitted on the previous searchlight platform, most of which was removed. Type 286Q radar was added at the mastheads and Type 282 radar to the 2pdr directors. For the invasion of France, she was allocated to bombardment duty of Sword Beach with HMS *Warspite* and others. *Dragon* continued in gunnery support roles until 8 July, when she was attacked and hit by a German Neger one-man torpedo. The torpedo hit detonated the 'Q' magazine and, although casualties were heavy, the ship did not sink. However, damage was so extensive that the ship was declared a total loss and evacuated by most of the crew. On the following day she was scuttled as part of the breakwater system for the Mulberry 'B' Harbour. The Poles asked for a replacement and a sister ship was provided (see *Danae/Conrad*).

HMS DUNEDIN Pennant I93
'D' class light cruiser 1919

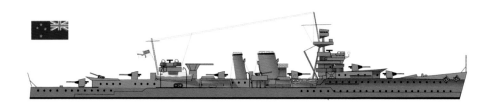

Dunedin was completed in September 1919, the urgency of work on her having slowed when World War I ended. Note the new raised bow similar to that on the later 'C' class cruisers. This was often referred to as a trawler bow. It proved better at sea than the flat bow, the distinctive knuckle deflecting water outward rather than washing out the 'A' gun mount on the earlier ships. She was painted in overall dark grey for all metal surfaces, but the decks were scrubbed wood. In May 1924 she was loaned to the New Zealand division of the Royal Navy and stayed there until relieved in 1937, although she did return to the UK for a refit in 1931. There was no Royal New Zealand navy at this time and ships on that station retained HMS before their names, even if mostly manned by crew from New Zealand. The prominent aircraft flying-off platform was removed before 1924. Her 3in AA guns were not replaced until the refit of 1931.

HMS DUNEDIN Pennant D93
'D' class light cruiser 1941

Dunedin was part of the Northern Patrol at the start of World War II, but in 1940 was sent to the West Indies, where she captured several German and Vichy French merchant ships, the most important being *Hannover*, which was then selected by the Royal Navy for conversion to the first escort carrier, HMS *Audacity*. She had a close call with the German cruiser *Admiral Hipper* when it attacked convoy WS5a. *Dunedin* was escorting the convoy, but could not get into range before the enemy ship turned away. The camouflage shown here was applied in 1941 and comprised 507c and 507a. The scheme was probably the same on both sides of the ship. Her decks remained unpainted wood. She was torpedoed and sunk by U-boat *U-124* on 24 November 1941. Her armament remained the same as when built, except for the addition of two quad 0.5in MG mounts side by side on the quarterdeck. The ship carried Type 286M radar with aerials at both mast tops.

HMS DESPATCH Pennant I30

'D' class light cruiser 1931

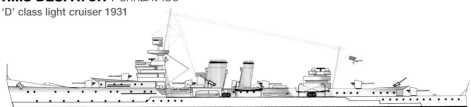

Despatch was not completed until mid-1922. She went to the China Station and then later to the West Indies. This illustration, showing her West Indies colours, depicts her in almost overall white, with only the funnels and masts in buff. Her boot topping is black, but fairly shallow in depth. This ship was apparently never fitted with the amidships flying-off platform.

HMS DESPATCH Pennant D30

'D' class light cruiser 1939–40

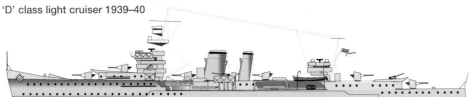

Despatch went to the South Atlantic in 1939 and, other than a brief service with Force H, remained in the area until 1942. She is shown in MS4a grey with white masts and fighting top. The two old 2pdr guns on each side of the bridge were removed when she came out of reserve for war service and replaced by quad 0.5in MG mounts. Apart from that small change and lower masts, the ship had almost the same profile as when built.

HMS DESPATCH Pennant D30

'D' class light cruiser 1942

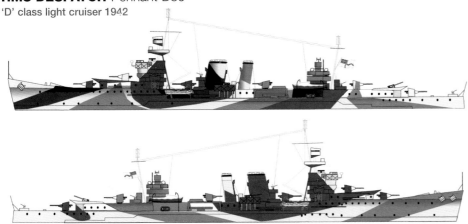

Despatch was given a large refit in 1942 and emerged in an Admiralty disruptive scheme. The colours used were a base of 507c with B5 and 507a areas. The decks were unpainted wood, and metal areas were the colour of the camouflage in that area. The previously mounted quad 0.5in MG mounts were removed and eight single 20mm AA guns added. Type 273 radar was fitted in a lantern on the search-light platform, with a Type 244 IFF aerial on top. At the mastheads were aerials for Type 290 radar. The torpedo tubes were retained. The ship returned to the South Atlantic Command. Despite her refit, maintenance levels were high and breakdowns frequent. As a result she was sent back to Portsmouth and allocated to training and special duties.

HMS DESPATCH Pennant D30

'D' class light cruiser 1944

Despatch had all her main guns and torpedo tubes removed in May 1944 for conversion to a headquarters ship, to be used as part of the Normandy landings. A total of sixteen single 40mm Bofors guns and two single 20mm guns were added. Numerous whip aerials were placed about the ship, along with additional IFF types and Type 650 missile jammers. Her services were no longer required by the end of 1944, and the ship was placed in reserve and then sold for scrap in 1946. Note that the camouflage scheme remained the same, but her appearance was altered by the absence of main armament and a multitude of light AA guns. Two small landing craft were carried to enable ship-to-shore personnel movement.

HMS DELHI Pennant I74
'D' class light cruiser 1939

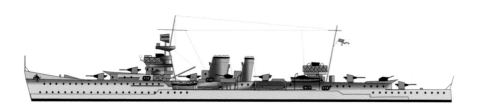

Delhi is shown here in a standard MS4a, but I have illustrated the effect of strong sunlight, which can highlight shadow to a much darker hue, giving the impression of being a different colour. As the ship changed course and the sun moved across the sky, so too the effect could change. At the start of World War II, the ship was armed similarly to her sisters, with six 6in guns, three 4in AA guns and two single 2pdr AA guns. In late 1939 there were still some peacetime touches, such as the brown motor launch, and wood davits and booms. The 4in guns have black canvas covers and the main guns also have black canvas hoods. At this time, she was serving with the 12th Cruiser Squadron of the Home Fleet, before joining Force H at Gibraltar in 1940.

HMS DELHI Pennant D74
'D' class light cruiser 1941–2

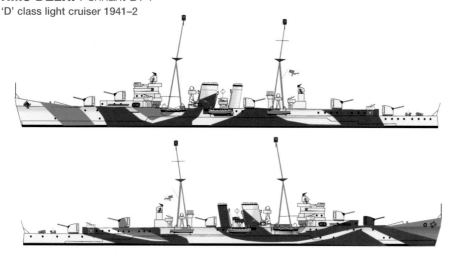

From May to December 1941, *Delhi* was completely rearmed at the New York navy yard. Five single US pattern 5in/L38 gun mounts were added to convert her into an anti-aircraft ship. This included the installation of two US Mk 37 gun directors. British quad 2pdr AA guns were added on either side of the fore funnel, along with eight single 20mm AA guns. All torpedo tubes were removed at the same time. The ship was not fitted with radar, but instead preceded to the UK where radar was added. Type 271 radar was added to the mainmast, Type 281 at the mastheads and Type 285 radar was fitted to the directors. The 2pdr directors received Type 282 radar. The scheme chosen for the ship was a three-colour disruptive scheme using 507c as the base, with areas of B5 and heavily contrasting areas of 507a. It was a very striking scheme and the ship seems to have been particularly well photographed. Decks were mid-grey.

HMS DELHI Pennant D74
'D' class light cruiser July 1943

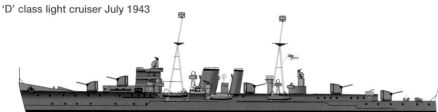

Delhi was damaged by air attack at Algiers and went to the Tyne for repair. By July 1943, she was in a plain 507b overall. During the repairs, two single 20mm AA guns were removed and replaced by twin 20mm guns. The decks were grey, possibly 507b. There were no other armament changes.

HMS DELHI Pennant D74
'D' class light cruiser 1943–4

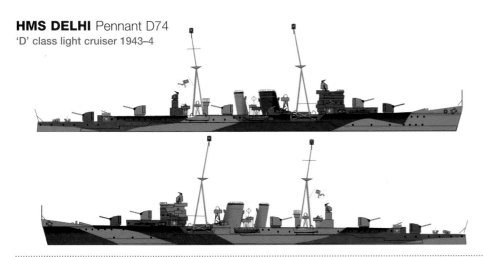

In mid-1943 *Delhi* was once again painted in an Admiralty disruptive scheme, but using two colours instead of three. These were MS3 and G10. The decks remained mid-grey. This scheme marked the use of more green in British schemes than had been possible earlier in the war, when green pigment was needed for the British Army and Royal Air Force.

HMS DELHI Pennant D74
'D' class light cruiser late 1944

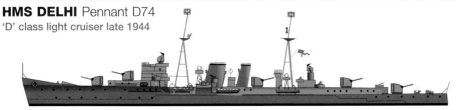

During the 1944 refit at Gibraltar, *Delhi*'s camouflage scheme was changed to the new standard colours issued by the Admiralty for ships in home waters or the Mediterranean. The hull was darkened to MS2 and the upper areas were MS3, with grey decks, possibly MS2. Type 659 missile jammers were added, along with Type 253 IFF. Two twin 20mm AA guns were also added.

HMS DELHI Pennant D74
'D' class light cruiser March 1945

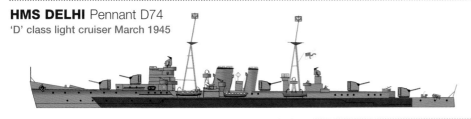

Delhi was severely damaged by an explosive motor boat in February 1945 off Yugoslavia. Emergency repairs were carried out on-site and the ship then went to Malta, where more work was done. However, major repairs were required, so the ship returned to the UK. Because the war in Europe was ending and *Delhi* required so much repair work, it was decided to patch her up for target trials. She was sold for scrap in 1948.

'E' CLASS LIGHT CRUISERS
HMS EMERALD Pennant I66
'E' class light cruiser 1927

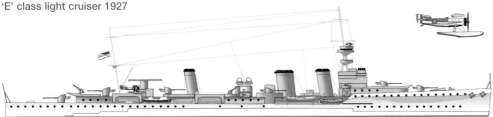

Emerald went to the West Indies Station on her first commission and is shown here as completed, with short funnels and a flying-off platform aft. A single Fairey Flycatcher aircraft was carried. The superstructure is buff, as are the funnels, masts and so forth. The hull is white with a red boot topping. The torpedo tubes are the triple-tube mounts originally fitted, giving total of twelve torpedoes. The main armament was seven 6in guns, three 4in AA guns and a single 2pdr AA gun on each side of the bridge. The 'E' class cruisers were large and very fast. Their intended mission was to hunt down enemy raider-cruisers. Although they had the same broadside as the smaller 'D' class, they were better protected and could absorb more damage owing to their larger size. The ships of the 'E' class spent the vast majority of their time on overseas stations.

HMS EMERALD Pennant I66
'E' class light cruiser 1937

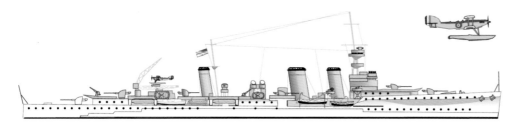

After refit, *Emerald* returned to the West Indies, but this time adopted a more modern form of the colonial paint scheme. Not only was the hull white, but also the area up to the level of the forecastle deck. Even 'Y' gun was painted white. The boot topping was black, instead of the older red style. During the refit, there were a number of changes to the ship. The funnels were raised due to problems with smoke on the bridge, and the mainmast lowered and moved to forward of the third funnel to clear the aircraft facilities. A SIIL catapult was added aft, along with a crane to handle the single Osprey aircraft. Just forward of the third funnel, a new HACS Mk 1 director was added to control the 4in AA guns. Quad 0.5in MG mounts were added on each side just aft of the fore funnel. The triple torpedo tubes were replaced by quad mounts, giving her sixteen tubes, the most of all British cruiser classes.

HMS EMERALD Pennant D66
'E' class light cruiser 1940

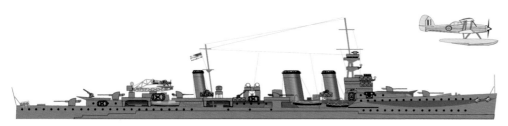

Emerald joined the 12th Cruiser Squadron on the Northern Patrol in 1939. However, within a month she was sent to Halifax, Nova Scotia, because of the danger of German raiders intercepting British merchant shipping. She escorted many convoys, but also took part in the transfer of £58 million of gold to Canada, keeping it safe from any possible invasion, and also to pay for war material from the USA under an agreement reached with the US government. During this time she was painted in a very dull 507b without a black boot topping. The decks were unpainted, except for horizontal metal surfaces, which were also 507b. Just before the outbreak of war, her AA armament was strengthened with the addition of two quad 0.5in MG mounts by the aft funnel. The 'E' class were the fastest cruisers in the Royal Navy and carried the most torpedoes. They remained fast and in quite good repair right up to their end of service. Flag superior changed from the letter 'I' to the letter 'D' in 1940. These ships were fitted with Type 128 Asdic and six, later fifteen, depth charges.

HMS EMERALD Pennant D66
'E' class light cruiser 1941

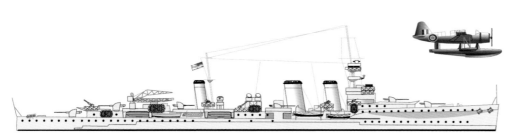

In 1941 *Emerald* was sent to the Indian Ocean to escort troop convoys and took part in operations around the invasion of Iraq. During this period she was painted in the Royal Navy hot climate style of overall 507c. The decks were unpainted wood and it is possible the horizontal metal surfaces remained in 507b. The AA armament did not change, although there are more splinter mats protecting various areas. In descriptions of the general emergency situation after Japan entered the war, there are mentions of all ships fitting any machine guns they could 'find', especially if the army left them unguarded! One of my uncles, who served in the area, related that as the British were forced back from Singapore and Burma, lots of panicking British and Indian troops left weapons lying about, which were promptly seized and placed aboard warships. Although usually only of rifle calibre, he stated that one of the first things ships did when they pulled in to evacuate troops was to look for abandoned weapons and ammunition suitable for them. In this way, many ships had quite a lot of unofficial weapons aboard. It is therefore likely that *Emerald*, which was in the thick of it, took part in this unofficial increase in AA armament. In 1942 this ship became the flagship of the 'Fast Squadron' of the Far Eastern Fleet. Her original aircraft was replaced by a USN Kingfisher floatplane.

HMS EMERALD Pennant D66

'E' class light cruiser 1943

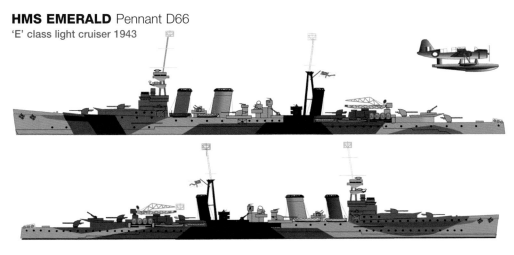

Emerald had a major refit from August 1942–April 1943. The foredeck was extended aft to create more accommodation, which also kept the ship drier aft. Some sources state that the aft gun was removed but this is disproved by photographs showing the gun right to the end of service. 507a, B15, B30 and B55 provided a disruptive scheme that was rather dark. Four-colour schemes were difficult to maintain, but were often applied mid-war. 507a and B15 are very close in shade and blend together as one at long ranges, but were sufficiently different to make the eye of a viewer uncertain at medium ranges. The use of B30 was intended to further confuse. Wood decks were no longer scrubbed. Being an older ship, there was still quite a lot of brown Corticene in use on the bridge. Her AA armament was improved. Quad 2pdr mounts were placed between the first and second funnels. Six power-operated twin 20mm AA gun mounts were added. Type 285 radar was provided on a director amidships. Type 273 radar was added on the bridge and Type 281 at the head of both masts. Type 282 radar for the quad 2pdrs was added. The Kingfisher floatplane was given markings that eliminated the red centre of the British roundel, to avoid being shot at by US gunners.

HMS EMERALD Pennant D66

'E' class light cruiser
January 1944

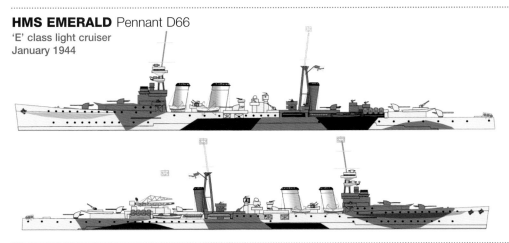

The previous four-colour disruptive camouflage scheme was simplified to two colours. The grey became 507c, the olive was lightened to MS3 and the dark area to MS1. Greens seem to have become popular towards the end of World War II, when the shortage of pigments was overcome. The starboard view is shown with her catapult and crane still fitted, while the port side shows the ship after it was removed in April 1944 to save weight. The crane removal allowed the fitting of six more single 20mm AA gun mounts. This ship remained very fast and could show clean heels to most of the newer cruisers. After the major refit she returned to the Eastern Fleet and remained there until being called back to the UK for the Normandy landings.

HMS EMERALD Pennant D66

'E' class light cruiser 1944–5

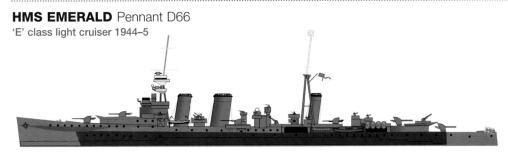

Prior to being paid off into reserve, *Emerald* was painted with the new standard Home Fleet pattern. It is doubtful she saw much service in this camouflage, which was overall MS3 with a panel of MS2. The ship was paid off in January 1945 when the Royal Navy was going through a crew shortage crisis, owing to all the newly constructed ships joining the fleet. In 1947 she was earmarked as a test bed to establish the limitations of damage from underwater detonations, such as those experienced by near-misses from bombs. All of her armament was stripped off and she underwent several major detonations. These caused her to sink to the bottom of Kames Bay, Rothesay, with only her upper decks above water. She was raised and carefully examined before being sent for scrapping in 1948.

HMS EMERALD Pennant D66
'E' class light cruiser 1944–5

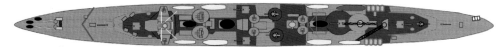

The overhead view shows the late-war armament layout with the crane in place, but the decks probably would have faded to a much duller and rather grey look. This view shows how the decks would have looked pre-war, when daily holystoned. There are large areas of brown Corticene, a linoleum-type product that helped crews withstand the cold from uncovered steel deck.

HMS ENTERPRISE Pennant I52
'E' class light cruiser 1937

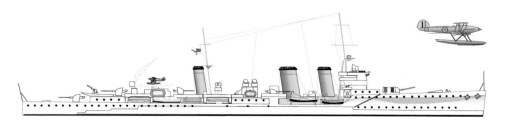

Although laid down five months earlier than her sister ship, *Enterprise* was delayed during construction in order to fit her with an experimental twin 6in gun turret forward. This turret style would become standard for new British cruisers. As first completed, she had a flying-off platform aft of the third funnel and the mast stepped aft as well. However, this was soon changed in order to install a SIIL catapult, along with an aircraft handling crane. This was slightly different from the SIIL fitted on *Emerald*. The bridge was also modified to place the main director on top, removing the need for a fighting top. These various arrangements proved to be a success and were carried forward in new designs. The ship is shown here in colonial cruising colours – in this case, virtually a white ship with buff funnels and masts. The red, white and blue markings on the forward turret distinguish her as a British cruiser, at a time when the Spanish Civil War and the Sino-Japanese War were raging.

HMS ENTERPRISE Pennant D52
'E' class light cruiser 1940

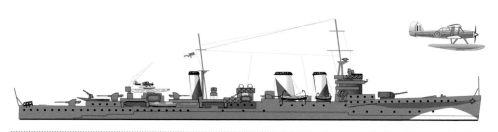

Enterprise was given a typical early-war camouflage in 1940. The white false bow wave was common, but the funnels have been given angled areas of 507c. The rest of the ship was 507b, but the wood decks remained unpainted. Although the foredeck was extended aft to provide more accommodation and prevent areas aft from being washed out in high seas, there were few other changes. Her AA armament remained three single 4in guns, with single 2pdr guns on each side of the bridge. During this period she took part in the Norwegian campaign and was involved in escorting convoys to and from the UK across the North Atlantic. Apart from Norway, she was not at great risk of air attack, but note that there were various areas protected by splinter mats. However, *Enterprise* was at a greater risk of submarine attack and was lucky to be missed by *U-65* on 19 April 1940.

HMS ENTERPRISE Pennant D52
'E' class light cruiser March 1942

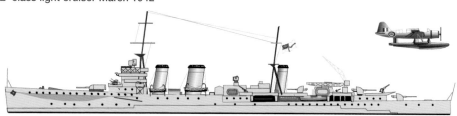

As a temporary measure, the two amidships 6in guns and the aft torpedo tubes were removed to save weight. A quad 2pdr mount was added forward, along with four single 20mm AA. The old single 2pdr was removed. The scheme carried seems to have been MS4a. The ship proceeded home to the UK for a major refit. At this time she was carrying a US Kingfisher-type aircraft, the only British cruiser to do so. As she was not operating with US forces anywhere in the Far East, the aircraft retained the red spot in the centre of the insignia. *Enterprise* was fitted with Type 128 Asdic and carried six depth charges. This was later increased to fifteen depth charges.

HMS ENTERPRISE Pennant D52

'E' class light cruiser 1943–4

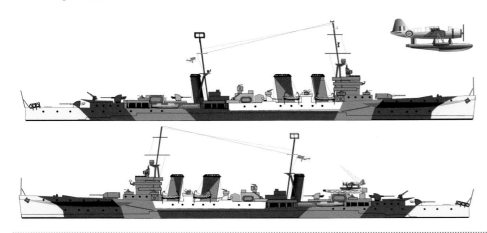

Enterprise emerged from her major refit with many changes, one of which was her four-colour camouflage. By 1944 this was unusual, as there had been a move to simplify schemes to use fewer shades. However, she had 507c at bow and stern, a panel of white amidships at deck level, plus areas of 507b and 507a. There were major changes to armament as well. The amidships 6in guns were reinstalled and quad 2pdr AA mounts were placed on each side between the first and second funnels. The one forward quad 2pdr mount was removed. Also, six powered twin 20mm AA guns were installed. Directors for the 2pdr mounts, equipped with Type 282 radar, were placed on each side aft of the middle funnel. The director on the bridge was given Type 284 radar and the AA director amidships was given Type 285 radar. Type 281B radar was placed at the masthead, with Type 272 at the head of the forward tripod. All torpedoes were removed. For a time, the catapult, along with its crane and aircraft, was retained, as shown in the port side illustration. The starboard illustration shows the ship after the crane was removed and with various other electronics added, as was done to most ships in the late-war period. The illustration shows Type 650 missile jammer on the mainmast, just forward of the aft funnel, and Type 242, 244 and 273 IFF systems on the foremast. This was how the ship appeared during the action on 28 December 1943 in the Bay of Biscay, when a German destroyer and two torpedo boats were sunk. *Enterprise* provided gunfire support at Utah Beach during the D-Day landings.

HMS ENTERPRISE Pennant D52

'E' class light cruiser 1944–5

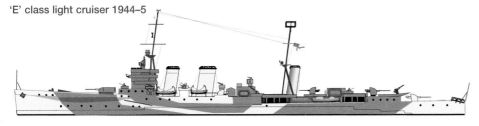

The previous camouflage scheme was simplified to 507c and 507b after Normandy. This was more normal for the period, when maintenance of paintwork was reduced for the benefit of crews and to save paint. The ship was sent to reserve on 5 January 1945. But she was not totally inactive, and engaged in some training duty and minor movements. Later that year, when World War II ended, she was reactivated for use in repatriation of troops from overseas stations, which was a huge operation as so many military personnel were serving abroad. *Enterprise* was again put out of commission in January 1946. This time there was no reprieve, and she was sold for scrap a few months later.

HAWKINS CLASS CRUISERS

HMS HAWKINS Pennant I86

Hawkins class cruiser 1919

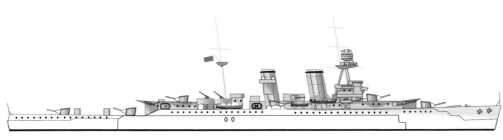

This class were the first of what would become known as heavy cruisers. They carried 7.5in guns of a new pattern, giving these large ships enough firepower to overwhelm enemy raiders, which was the intention behind the design. *Hawkins* went to the China Station upon completion as flagship of the 5th Light Cruiser Squadron. She is shown here in her original colonial colours. There are low-angle 3in guns mounted behind flaps in the forward deckhouse, under the bridge, and between the funnels. There were four single 3in AA guns aft near the mainmast. These all fired the same ammunition, despite some being low-angle. It is presumed the low-angle guns were provided to engage submarines and torpedo boats, although, based on war experience, the 3in guns were already deemed to be too small for the latter. The low-angle 3in guns were not retained for long. *Hawkins* was a large and comfortable ship. My friend, the late A E Charlton RN, served on this ship for a time during World War II and declared that of the many ships he was on, this was easily the most comfortable in a seaway, and an extremely steady gun platform. He also remarked that they could maintain the top speed for long periods in sea states that had more modern cruisers struggling.

HMS HAWKINS Pennant D86
Hawkins class cruiser 1939–40

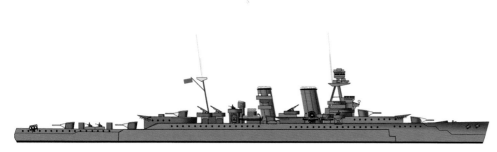

At the outbreak of World War II, *Hawkins* was in reserve in a disarmed state, waiting to be converted to be like her sister *Effingham*. Due to the lack of dock space, all of her seven 7.5in guns were remounted. She was equipped with four 4in AA guns, three in a cluster around the mainmast and one between the funnels. Four single 2pdr guns made up her light AA, with one in each bridge wing and one on each side of the amidships HA director. Two single 2pdr guns were later added on the quarterdeck. These appear in photographs, but are not recorded. *Hawkins* is shown in overall 507b, with the decks left unpainted. Black boot topping is worn, but the overall effect is to produce a very dull ship when viewed from a distance. It is often forgotten by ship enthusiasts that grey is in itself a camouflage. The emergency of war and heavy losses meant that this ship was not given any serious modifications, merely rearmed and sent off to war. No radar was fitted at this time. She was sent urgently to the South American Squadron to hunt raiders and enemy blockade-runners, the role for which she had originally been designed. Type 132 Asdic was fitted and six depth charges were carried.

HMS HAWKINS Pennant D86
Hawkins class cruiser 1941–2

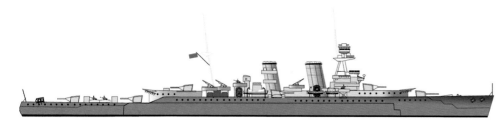

As a result of the growing crisis in the Indian Ocean, *Hawkins* was sent to join the Eastern Fleet. Her scheme was altered to retain the dark 507b hull and her upper areas were painted in MS4a or 507c. The decks apparently remained unpainted. Masts were painted white, as was the fighting top and upper bridge. While in this region, she took part in the attack on Italian-held Mogadishu and captured an Italian merchant ship. The armament remained unchanged but, as with other ships, it was not uncommon for special shore parties to 'find' lost army weapons, as long as the owners were not looking, and 'capture' abandoned enemy weapons. Ships in these areas were too far from the normal supply lines and shipbuilding was still catching up with weapons needed for new ships and those under refit. So having a few clever thieves and a good bosun aboard could be of great help. Note that the searchlight platform on the aft funnel and the AA director amidships were carried higher than her sister ships, which is a point of recognition.

HMS HAWKINS Pennant D86
Hawkins class cruiser 1943

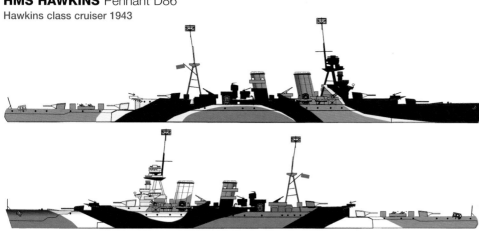

In December 1942 *Hawkins* underwent a major refit, which lasted until May 1943. During the refit, the AA defences were improved. The 7.5in and 4in AA guns remained the same, but quad 2pdr AA mounts were fitted on either side of the bridge and seven single 20mm AA guns were added. Two of the original four single 2pdr guns were removed, but the two on her quarterdeck were retained. She is shown wearing a four-colour scheme typical of Admiralty ideas at the time of her refit. The decks apparently remained unpainted wood, but, as usual, were no longer holystoned to a bright new wood look. The colours used were MS1, B5, B6 and 507c. The ship served with the Eastern Fleet in this scheme and returned home in early 1944 to take part in the Normandy invasion, where she provided gun support for Utah Beach. There are considerable recognition errors in many books, even some of the best, between this ship and her sister *Frobisher*. *Frobisher* is easy to pick out, because she did not have the 7.5in guns in the waist restored during rearmament, receiving quad 2pdr mounts instead. But the easiest and simplest way to tell them apart is that *Hawkins* did not have the rows of Carley floats along the side and her sister did. Those on *Hawkins* are hard to see, while those on *Frobisher* are very prominent and numerous. Keep this in mind and you will soon see all the mistakes in books and online where the two are misidentified.

HMS HAWKINS Pennant D86
Hawkins class cruiser August 1944

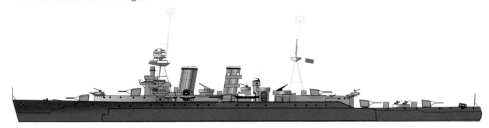

Hawkins received this final scheme of B55 and B30, the standard Home Fleet colours, with white masts in late 1944. At this time her quad 2pdr AA mounts were replaced with octuple mounts and two more single 20mm AA guns. However, from this time on her main role was as a training ship. She was used as a bombing target by the RAF in 1947, and then sold for scrap the same year.

HMS FROBISHER I81
Hawkins class cruiser 1927

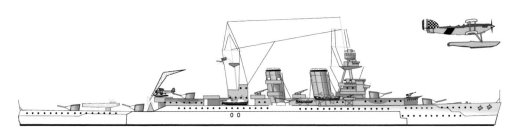

In 1927 *Frobisher* was fitted with a RAE model catapult and an aircraft crane. The catapult was on the centreline, but the crane was offset to starboard. This displaced the 4in AA gun, which in turn was moved up between the funnels, and a four-gun arrangement used. Two single 2pdrs were placed in the bridge wings as with her sisters, but two more were placed on the forward blast screen. There are two above-water torpedo tubes in the side of the ship below the mainmast. She is depicted here on colonial duty, in white and buff, something that was to occupy ships of this type for most of their naval service. Note that at this time the 7.5in guns in the waist were still carried. The object in front of it was a drop-down platform to allow gunners to move around the mount more easily when cleared for action.

HMS FROBISHER Pennant D81
Hawkins class cruiser 1942

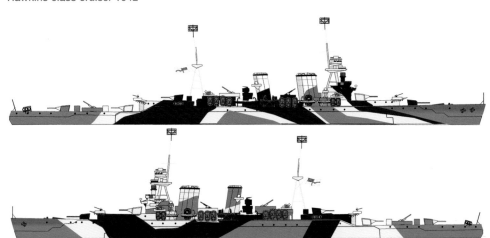

Just before World War II, this ship was disarmed, to be rebuilt and armed as was her sister ship, *Effingham*. But this was cancelled when war broke out. As a result of emergency war work, *Frobisher* sat unarmed during the first part of the war until dockyard space could be found to rearm and refit her for service. Five of her original 7.5in guns were reinstalled, but the wing guns were omitted. Five single 4in AA and four quad 2pdrs were added with seven single 20mm. She re-entered service in a three-colour Admiralty disruption scheme based on 507c, MS1 and B5. In photographs, one can observe minor variations in this paint scheme, which probably came about from the way the camouflage was patched up from time to time. The major recognition elements are the rows of Carley rafts along her sides, and the lack of the sided guns amidships. On resuming service, she had radar Type 281 at the mastheads, Type 273 on the bridge, and Type 285 on the AA director, but Type 282 for the quad 2pdrs does not seem to have been installed. Her role as a gunfire support ship off Sword Beach at the Normandy landings has been well recorded on film and is often shown. All too often, the film and still photographs are also labelled as HMS *Hawkins*, although the large number of Carley floats made her easy to pick out from her sister ship. *Frobisher* was badly damaged by a German Dakel torpedo in August, and, while in dock for repairs, it was decided to turn her into a training ship.

HMS FROBISHER Pennant D81
Hawkins class cruiser 1944–5

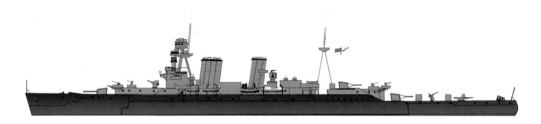

In August 1944 the RN wanted a training ship that could take 150 cadet officers to sea and, reluctant to use any of the newer ships, turned to *Frobisher*, which had performed the role pre-World War II. All but three of her 7.5in were removed, and the twin 4in AA replaced by a single 4in AA mount in 'B' position. All 2pdr mounts were removed, but she carried thirteen 20mm. The aft gun was replaced by a quad torpedo mounting. Although not listed, a very clear broadside photo of her on 1 May 1945 shows a single 40mm Bofors between the remaining main gun aft, and the torpedo tubes. The Type 281 air-warning radar was removed, but all other radars were retained. Asdic Type 132 was retained and six depth charges. As a training ship, it was intended that she would only operate in home waters and is shown here in the appropriate Admiralty standard scheme with upper works in MS3 and the hull in MS2. Deck colour is not known. She was not broken up until 1949.

HMS EFFINGHAM Pennant I98
Hawkins class cruiser 1930

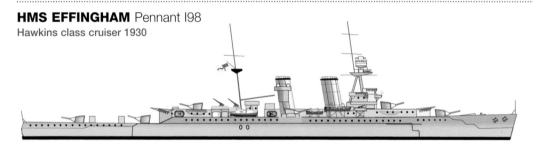

Effingham is shown here as she was just before being disarmed for reconstruction as below. The casemate guns had been removed as ineffective and the space better used. She is painted over all in MS4a, but the wood decks are almost certain to have been very well holystoned to a whitish, new-timber look. Some of the masts and spars are in brown wood for a smart appearance. The fighting top and director were painted white.

HMS EFFINGHAM Pennant I98
Hawkins class cruiser 1940

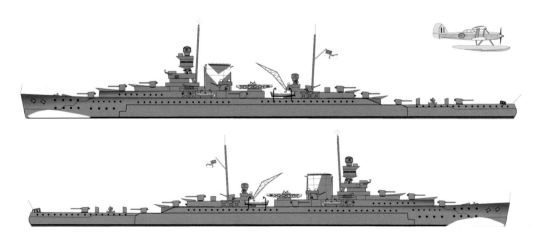

Effingham was originally the same as *Frobisher* and *Hawkins*, but prior to World War II a decision was taken to turn her into a light cruiser, because the terms of the international treaties were causing difficulty for the RN with its permitted heavy cruiser numbers. The other two were disarmed ready for this rebuild, but the outbreak of World War II prevented this. *Effingham* is shown in a typical 1940s scheme of false bow wave, but care has been taken to disguise her rather large and distinctive single funnel. The main shade is 507b with, of course, white areas. During the rebuild, her previous two funnels were trunked into one and all the armament removed. A three-tier arrangement fore and aft was adopted for the 6in guns on the centreline. In addition, there were two each side amidships and one on the quarterdeck, giving her a broadside of eight. At first there were four single 4in AA, but these were replaced by twin mounts by the outbreak of war. Abreast the bridge she was fitted with tubs for octuple 2pdr AA mountings and, although completed without them installed, they too were fitted in time for the war. There were also quad 0.5in MG mountings either side of the amidships AA director, and another on the quarterdeck. There was an EIVH model catapult amidships with a crane to handle aircraft. Asdic Type 132 was fitted and she carried six depth charges. The resulting reconstruction was considered very satisfactory, but unfortunately the ship had a short life in this form: she was lost during the Norwegian campaign after striking a rock and was unable to be saved.

HMS **VINDICTIVE** Pennant I36
Hawkins class cruiser 1918

This is an approximation of the camouflage scheme worn by *Vindictive* when she joined the Grand Fleet in 1918. It was derived from a black and white photograph, but based on reports of her colours. While it is not clear that this is accurate, the colours are common to those used in other schemes at this time. The intent behind such dazzle schemes was to confuse attacking submarines as to the range, speed and angle of a target. The flight deck aft was intended for landing aircraft and had a hangar beneath it. Aircraft were transferred to the front take-off area by a path along the port side.

HMS **VINDICTIVE** Pennant I36
Hawkins class cruiser 1919

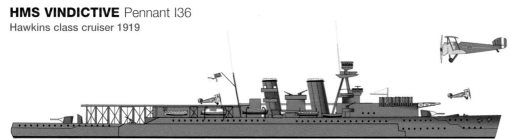

Vindictive from the starboard side in battleship grey. The foremost and aft guns were retained, along with those each side in the waist. Besides the four 7.5in guns, she had four low-angle 3in guns and four 3in AA guns. Aircraft carried were mostly Sopwith Camels. Four of these could be accommodated in the hangar under the aft landing deck and brought up by lift.

HMS **VINDICTIVE** Pennant I36
Hawkins class cruiser 1927

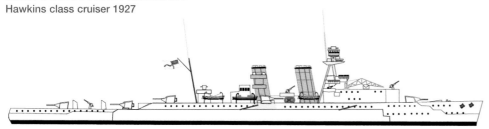

During the late 1920s, it was decided that *Vindictive* was too small to be an aircraft carrier and the ship was converted back to cruiser status. However, the hangar forward was retained and surmounted by a 4in AA gun instead of a 7.5in gun. In this form she had six 7.5in guns, four 4in AA guns and two 2pdr AA guns. Retaining the hangar allowed the ship to be used for cruising with cadet officers. The ship is dressed in white with buff funnels during a cruise in the Mediterranean. *Vindictive* was not officially a training ship at this time, but undertook some of those duties.

HMS **VINDICTIVE** Pennant I36
Hawkins class cruiser 1937

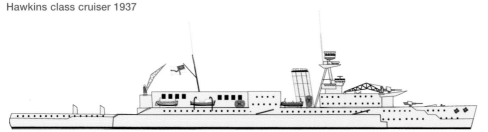

During the 1930s, it was decided that *Vindictive* would officially become a training ship, which freed up tonnage under the naval treaties then in force. Her only armament was a pair of old 4.7in guns and some saluting guns. The old hangar area was turned into accommodation, and a large classroom and training facility was added. This was extended forward with the removal of the aft funnel and reduction in boilers and machinery. As a training ship, she was not required to be capable of more than 18 knots, which also fitted in with her status as a demilitarised ship. She is shown dressed overall in MS4a. The wood decks were no doubt thoroughly holystoned, and therefore appeared as gleaming fresh wood.

HMS **VINDICTIVE** Pennant I36
Hawkins class cruiser 1940

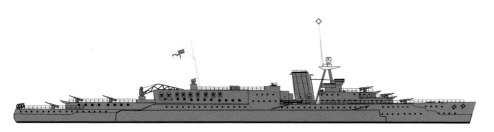

When it was decided to convert the ships of this class as per *Effingham*, consideration was given to giving this ship the same rebuild. However, reinstallation of machinery and changes in general made the conversion too expensive. The idea was then put forward to turn her into a forward repair ship. This meant she would need a good AA armament, if she was to repair damaged ships in combat areas. As a result, she returned to service with a three-tier arrangement of 4in AA guns forward, not unlike the three layers of *Effingham*. Three more single 4in AA guns were placed aft. On top of the superstructure, just aft of the remaining funnel, quad 2pdr mounts were added port and starboard, with quad 0.5in machine guns on the bridge wings. Type 132 Asdic was fitted, and six depth charges carried at the stern. In this form she went to war during the Norway campaign, but because of the open workshops, she was utilised as a troop transport and for carrying heavy equipment that her crane proved useful in unloading. *Vindictive* is shown here in a dull grey colour that was probably 507b, but could have been darkened slightly. The fighting top and masts are white. No radar was fitted at this time, but there is a HA/LA director on the fighting top and another aft, forward of the crane. The triangular HF/DF at the foremast head was for intercepting radio transmissions, but not the same as the type used by escorts for the detection of U-boats.

HMS **VINDICTIVE** Pennant D36
Hawkins class cruiser 1943

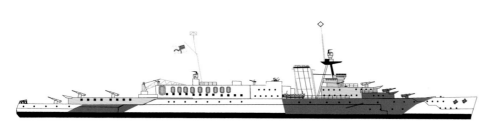

As a forward area repair ship, *Vindictive* saw wide service and is shown here as she appeared in the Mediterranean during 1943. Her scheme is mostly white, with areas of MS4a and panels of B5. The scheme appears to be unofficial, but may have been a special one-off design. Deck colours are not known. Along with her previous armament, she now carries six single 20mm AA guns, while the quad 0.5in machine guns were removed. There is an arrangement of one large and nine small Carley floats on her sides, as opposed to the two large and seven small in 1940. Type 286 radar aerials are carried at the aft masthead and Type 285 radar has been installed on the HA/LA directors. *Vindictive* continued to perform valuable service in this role right until the end of World War II. By then, newly built repair ships were available. She was paid off in late 1945 and sold for scrap in 1946. As with all ships with the flag superior 'I', she changed to 'D' in late 1940. Surprisingly, she does not seem to have adopted a flag superior and number suitable for a repair ship, and instead retained that of a cruiser. The radar Type 286 would almost certainly have been replaced by late 1943 or early 1944, when the Admiralty realised that it was too easy for U-boats to detect and could give away the position of the user. However, there are no records I could find that indicate what replaced it. I would suggest the most likely replacement was radar Type 281 on both masts, as this was being replaced by 282B and spare sets were becoming available.

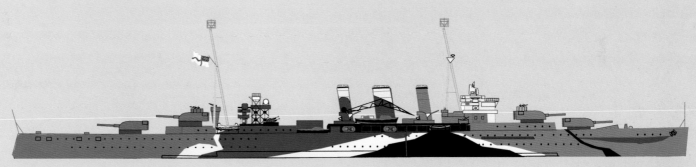

CONTENTS

KENT CLASS HEAVY CRUISERS
HMS BERWICK Pennant 65
Kent class heavy cruiser 1927

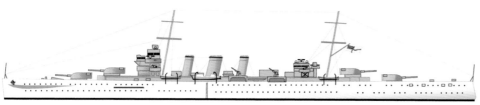

Berwick was completed with low funnels as shown. Her first deployment was to the China Station, and she is shown in the buff and white worn on that duty. Note that the base of the catapult is present, but not fitted. This was done later on station. Her main armament of four twin 8in guns was distinctive, because at the time most cruisers had guns in single open mountings. There were only four single 4in AA guns on board at this time, along with four single 2pdr AA guns. Provisions were made to install quad 2pdr mounts, but these were not yet ready. The very high free-board made these ships quite easy to identify. Officers and men reported that they were far more habitable than earlier ships, and comfortable in hot or cool climates. Protection was poor, but the ships were intended to patrol distant colonial stations, for which they needed long range and habitability. When the catapult was fitted, a crane was mounted on the starboard side and a Fairey IIIF aircraft carried. The low funnels proved incapable of keeping smoke from the bridge when there was a following wind.

HMS BERWICK Pennant 65
Kent class heavy cruiser 1927

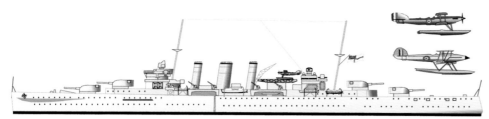

Berwick had her funnels raised by 15ft and an aircraft catapult fitted. Secondary armament was increased to eight single 4in guns and two quad 0.5in machine guns were fitted each side of the bridge at the level of the 4in guns. She is shown here in 507c while serving in the Mediterranean, just before she went back to the UK for a major refit. At the time there were rumblings of war with Italy over Abyssinia, and the old cruising colours of white and buff had been discarded for plain grey. Note the heavy black boot topping on the hull, which was common on many ships at this time. The bridge has also been modified to carry a HACS on each side and an improved director. There is also a HACS on the aft superstructure and a reserve main gun director. Also note that small rangefinders were carried on each side of the bridge. These were used to keep track of the distance between other warships, in order to help with the battle plot that was part of Royal Navy practice at this time. Fairey III aircraft were originally carried, but later replaced by Osprey aircraft.

HMS BERWICK Pennant 65
Kent class heavy cruiser 1940

In 1939 *Berwick* was painted overall 507b. However, as with some of the other ships involved in the Norwegian campaign, an attempt at camouflage was made by using 507c to lighten areas of the upper works. The application of this would have been easy, as it only required the use of paint readily available. In some cases, a false bow wave was added, but *Berwick* does not seem to have carried one. The camouflage scheme would have been unofficial, but as several ships did this sort of thing, there may have been some consultation between units of the Home Fleet, where this scheme was usually seen. Note that during the immediate pre-World War II period she was modernised in a manner that considerably altered her appearance. The original catapult and aircraft facilities were removed, along with the aft control tower, and a large hangar was installed. An athwartships DIH catapult was installed. The hangar could accommodate three of the smaller TSR aircraft or one Walrus, but two could be carried if necessary. The original single 4in AA guns were replaced by four twin mountings. Octuple 2pdr mounts were added either side of the fore funnel. Quad 0.5in MG mounts were added on top of the new aircraft hangar. The torpedo tubes were removed to save top weight for the hangar, but as this ship had sufficient reserve, the quarterdeck was not cut down as with two of her sister ships. Note the ships of this class carried Type 132 Asdic and up to six depth charges. This equipment was purely defensive.

HMS BERWICK Pennant 65
Kent class heavy cruiser November 1940

Berwick was sent to the Mediterranean after Norway, and some alterations to her scheme took place. The entire hull was repainted in 507c and all the turrets were 507b. There were minor changes to the position of some camouflage and, as usual when repainting took place, the lines and angles changed slightly in some places. The ship was damaged by Italian cruiser gunfire during the Battle of Cape Spartivento and also took part in the evacuation of Greece. Note that the armament had not changed at all, although rifle-calibre machine guns were probably mounted on the initiative of the crew and when available. The wooden decks had not been painted at this time. Turret tops were probably the same colour as the sides.

HMS BERWICK Pennant 65
Kent class heavy cruiser December 1940

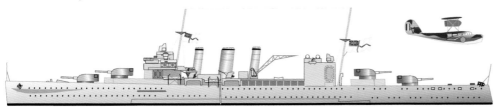

While repairing at Malta from damage sustained in her action against Italian cruisers, the ship was repainted to overall MS4a and appeared this way at the time of her clash with the German cruiser *Admiral Hipper* on 25 December 1940. There were no armament changes and no radar was fitted. She is depicted with battle ensigns flying.

HMS BERWICK Pennant 65
Kent class heavy cruiser May 1941

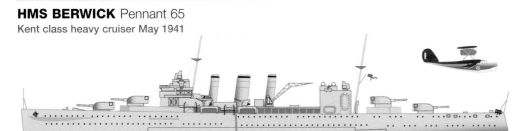

After repair of damage at Portsmouth, *Berwick* emerged in the then-popular camouflage of pale Mountbatten pink overall. This was usually reserved for the Mediterranean and was not a colour favoured for the Home Fleet, so perhaps the intent had been to send her back to that region. Decks and turret tops were dark grey. Note that there is no black boot topping with this camouflage scheme. The scheme was only worn for a few months. Armament had not yet changed and no radar had been added. This was rather late for a major ship still to be carrying the quad 0.5in MG mounts, but the shortage of newer and better light AA weapons was critical until mid-1943.

HMS BERWICK Pennant 65
Kent class heavy cruiser July 1941

The venture into complete Mountbatten pink did not last long, and by July 1941 large areas of dark grey, most probably 507a, had been added. The port side was the same. *Berwick* served with the Home Fleet in the second half of 1941 wearing this camouflage scheme, which was unique in that it combined dark grey 507a with the pink. This was an Admiralty disruptive scheme exclusive to this particular ship. However, it was not really suited for operations in northern waters and was looked upon unkindly by senior officers of the fleet. Note that Type 281 radar has been placed at the mast-heads. This set required two aerials, one for sending and one for receiving. Type 284 radar for gunnery has been added to the forward director, but Type 285 has not been fitted to the HACS. The original pole masts have been replaced by tripods to handle the growing weight of electronics carried high in the ship.

HMS BERWICK Pennant 65
Kent class heavy cruiser October 1941

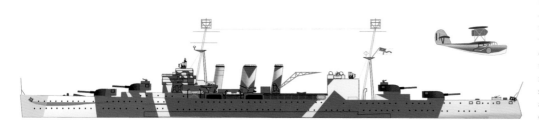

Mountbatten pink was reduced to panels at the bow and stern by October 1941, with 507c and 507a having become the predominant colours. There were minor changes in the boundaries of the dark scheme, but in general they were the same as previously carried. The changes were the same on both sides. The ship continued to serve with the Home Fleet, which entailed operations in northern waters so would almost certainly have led to the reduction of pink. The V-shape light grey 507c on the funnel seems to have changed slightly at various times in photographs, sometimes being deep and with sharper angles. This would be typical of the way in which a touched-up scheme could vary at the hands of the crew carrying out maintenance. At this time, the ship was carrying five 20mm AA guns and still retained its quad 0.5in MG mounts. The 20mm appear to have been arranged with one each on top of 'B' and 'X' turrets, one on the quarter-deck and one each side of the bridge.

HMS BERWICK Pennant 65
Kent class heavy cruiser January 1942

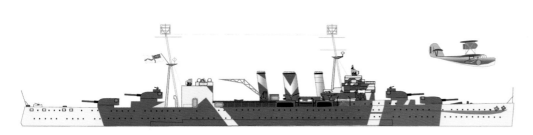

By January 1941, all traces of Mountbatten pink had been removed. The ship was camouflaged simply, but effectively, in 507a and 507c. The star-board side used the same pattern. The deck is believed to have been painted dark grey, as were the turret tops. Masts were white. Note that there was only a very narrow black boot topping, in keeping with camouflage instructions. The hangar and aircraft were still carried. Note also that as late as January 1942, this ship still had no dedicated surface search radar, as the Type 281 had no surface search capability. Note there is a HF/DF aerial on the cross arm of the tripod mast. These ships did not hunt submarines, although they carried Type 132 Asdic and six depth charges. However, the HF/DF helped determine the position of enemy U-boats, especially if triangulated with another ship, and thus allowed major ships to avoid threats.

HMS BERWICK Pennant 65
Kent class heavy cruiser August 1942

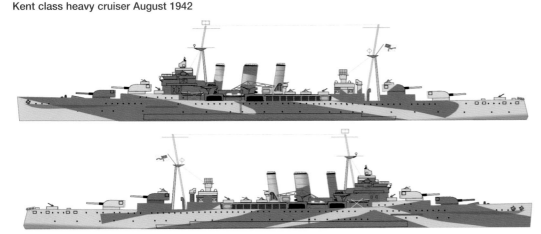

Berwick entered refit in May 1942, emerging in August with the large hangar and the catapult removed. However, the aircraft cranes had proved so useful that they were retained. A new aft control position was fitted and the ship emerged in yet another camouflage scheme of Admiralty design. This time the base colour was MS4a grey, with MS4 forming a disruptive pattern. The decks were painted dark grey, as were the turret tops. The newly rebuilt aft control position had searchlights installed and between them a lantern and tower Type 273 radar. The previous Type 281 radar was replaced by Type 281B, which required only one aerial and also had some surface detection capability. The aft director was now on a free-standing tower of its own. Six twin 20mm mounts were added and seven singles removed. This gave a 20mm armament of six twin and five singles. Note that as the war progressed the number of portholes were reduced by plating them over. This was because damage reports from many ships had shown the portholes were vulnerable to popping under pressure if a ship was listing, which caused additional flooding.

HMS BERWICK Pennant 65
Kent class heavy cruiser December 1943

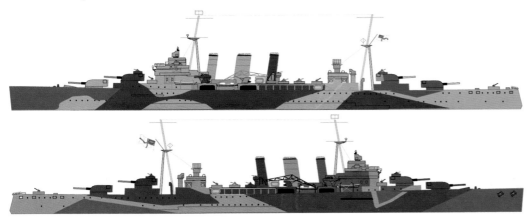

Berwick seems to have had a different paint job each time it came out of refit. By December 1943, *Berwick* was wearing an Admiralty scheme based on B55, B30 and MS1. This form of camouflage became common in 1943.

HMS BERWICK Pennant 65
Kent class heavy cruiser mid-1944

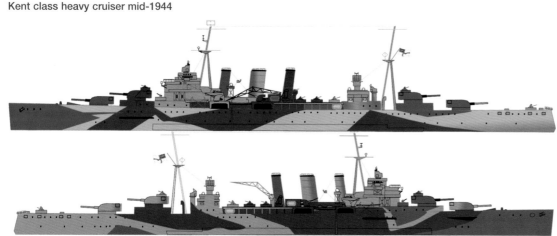

This *Berwick* scheme was similar to the previous scheme and the same colours were used, but the boundaries of the areas changed. This sort of thing was not uncommon. It could be deliberate, or simply a case of having more of one paint available than another, or someone overstepped the original boundaries and made a mistake. What is clear is that this ship had a lot of paint used on it over the years, and one would hope it was chipped off after a while. Paint is surprisingly heavy, and can cause stability problems if not taken into account after repeated repainting. Note that both main directors mounted Type 284 radar by this time and, although records do not show it, photographs seem to show that the HACS also received Type 285 radar. The radar lantern of the Type 273 set has Type 244 IFF mounted on it. Type 242 IFF is also on the foremast. Towards the end of World War II, there were a growing number of electronic signals from friendly to hostile, and it was important that these were able to be analysed to determine their source.

HMS BERWICK Pennant 65
Kent class heavy cruiser 1945

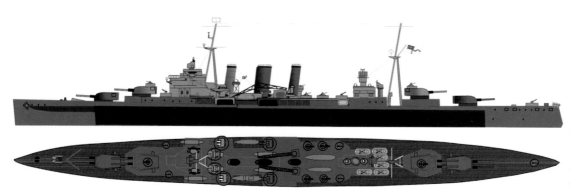

Near the end of World War II, *Berwick* adopted a version of the standard Home Fleet scheme. However, this used three colours instead of the usual two. G20 formed a dark green panel on an MS2 hull, with MS3 on the upper superstructure and fore funnel. 'B' and 'X' turrets were MS3, while 'A' and 'Y' turrets were MS2. This could have been an experiment to see if variations of the green style could produce better results. At the time, the ship was involved in operations with the Home Fleet and covering convoys to Russia. Although several sources say that by 1944 this ship only had two single 20mm guns remaining, with all the rest having been replaced by twin mountings, a photograph of the ship in this camouflage scheme clearly shows that the 20mm guns abreast the front of the bridge, as well as on 'B' and 'X' turrets, were singles. The ship went into reserve immediately after the war ended and was sold for scrap in 1948.

HMS CORNWALL Pennant 56
Kent class heavy cruiser 1934

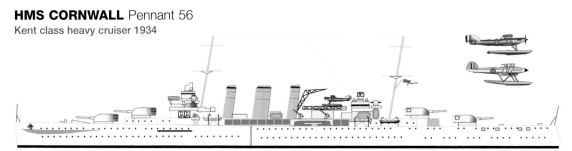

Cornwall spent most of her pre-World War II service on the China Station, until she came home for a rebuild in 1936. While in the east she received a catapult and HACS. A crane was placed on the starboard side of the ship near the aft funnel to handle the aircraft. There were only four single 4in AA guns, although quad 0.5in MG mounts had been fitted on either side of the bridge. The decks were scrubbed wood. At various times she had a buff super-structure and, towards the end of her service before rebuild, prim-rose yellow funnels. She appears to have returned to the UK in this scheme. It is probable, but not certain, that the turret tops were also white.

HMS CORNWALL Pennant 56
Kent class heavy cruiser 1941

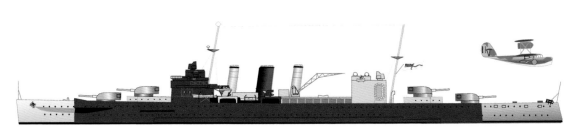

After reconstruction, *Cornwall* emerged with a large hangar and two cranes. She carried one Walrus aircraft, and the catapult was placed athwartships. On completion, she was in an overall grey, possibly MS4a, but was sent back to the China Station in 1938, and again adopted white and buff. However, upon the outbreak of World War II she was painted in a medium grey similar to 507b. At some time in early 1941 a rather unique camouflage scheme was applied, using MS4a and 507a. The intent behind this was to give the appearance of a single-funnel, bluff bow ship, which at a distance could be mistaken for a freighter. It was the same both sides. The scheme was intended to fool raiders and blockade-runners that she was hunting in the Indian Ocean. Note that when rebuilt there were two medium-size Carley floats on the side of the hangar, hanging on their sides rather than horizontal. The hangar normally had one Walrus, but could fit two if needed. The previous single 4in guns were replaced by twin 4in AA mounts. After moving to the South Atlantic and participating in the Dakar campaign, *Cornwall* was sent back to the Indian Ocean and was wearing this scheme when she intercepted and sank the German raider *Pinguin*. No armament changes had been made since her major refit and no radar was fitted. However, she appears to have HF/DF and WDF, both of which would have been important for her role seeking enemy ships in such a vast ocean.

HMS CORNWALL Pennant 56
Kent class heavy cruiser 1942

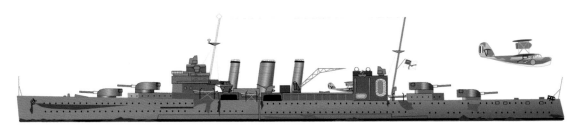

At the time of her loss, *Cornwall* had been repainted in a 507a dark grey, which had apparently faded rather a lot and was badly in need of a touch-up. She had seen continual service on patrols of the Indian Ocean, as well as escorting troop convoys back and forth. With the entry of Japan into the war, her duties became even more arduous and the ship was worked hard. The dark grey had faded so much in the hot conditions of her operational area that it was no longer a consistent shade, and much of the ship appeared to be medium grey. The illustration here is not to be taken as a camouflage scheme as such. It is merely a representation of how the ship may have looked at the time of her loss, with areas of faded paint and rust.

HMS KENT Pennant 54
Kent class heavy cruiser 1929

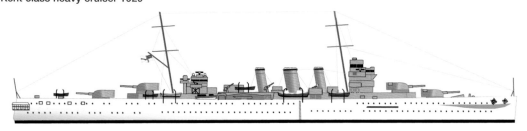

Kent as completed went out to the China Station, where she became flagship of the 5th Cruiser Squadron. She is shown here in buff and white. Her funnels were low at this time and there are only four single 4in AA guns as secondary armament. As the multiple 2pdr mounts were not ready, she was temporarily given four singles. Note there was no HACS at this time. But there are rangefinders on the side of the bridge and top of the searchlight platform. The wood decks were scrubbed wood.

HMS KENT Pennant 54
Kent class heavy cruiser 1932

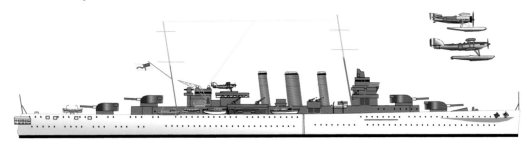

Kent was fitted with a folding catapult while on the China Station and by 1932, with Japan and China engaged in fighting, had changed her overall colour to a white hull and mid-grey superstructure and funnels. The fitting of a crane required the movement of the aft single 2pdr guns and they were newly arranged in a rather crowded, offset fashion between the fore and centre funnels. The 8in guns of this class were very powerful and most of the class served on this station to hopefully overawe the Japanese. The boats were still in various peacetime colours and, strangely, the bridge windows had buff frames. A single Flycatcher aircraft was carried at first, but changed to a Fairey III when it became available. This colour scheme was taken from a detailed model built by a Royal Marine while serving aboard *Kent*.

HMS KENT Pennant 54
Kent class heavy cruiser 1934

Kent adopted overall 507c around 1934, after some alterations in Hong Kong. The decks remained as before. Extra single 4in AA guns were placed opposite the fore funnel and a HACS installed on the aft super-structure. She was also fitted with quad 0.5in MG mounts either side of the bridge at the 4in deck level, but this was only temporary. The single 2pdr guns seem to have been landed, but the multiple-barrel versions not yet fitted. This ship carried an admiral's stern walk, because she was intended to operate as a flagship on distant stations. Flag accommodation was included and she had less available spare weight than her sisters, which would affect the plans being prepared for her further upgrade. She carried a Fairey III aircraft during this period and retained the folding catapult. Note that the large base around the catapult gave an amount of working area around an aircraft. As with her sister ships, the Fairey III was later replaced by an Osprey.

HMS KENT Pennant 54
Kent class heavy cruiser 1939–40

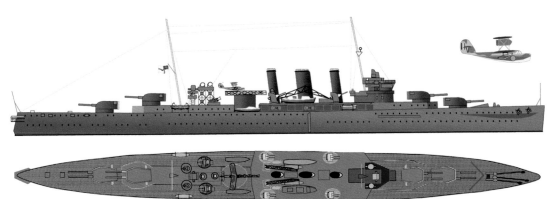

At the outbreak of World War II, *Kent* adopted a colour scheme of 507b and retained that shade for some time. The black boot topping was reduced in height along the waterline, as well. The wood decks remained natural scrubbed wood and were probably not allowed to fade until after 1940, as the danger of air attack was not fully appreciated until later. She had received a major refit between 1937 and 1938, during which many changes took place. The main armament was unaffected, but her torpedo tubes were removed and the single 4in AA guns were all removed. In their place were four twin 4in AA mounts, but they were more widely spread apart than in most ships of this type. An octuple 2pdr mount was placed on each side of the much reduced aft control position, and quad 0.5in MG mounts were added abreast the aft gun director. The HACS was removed and replaced by one on each side of the bridge. The bridge itself was lowered as well. New cranes replaced the single one fitted in Hong Kong, and these were placed inboard of the aft twin 4in mounts. At the waterline, the ship was given an armoured belt to overcome the lack of protection this class had experienced for the main machinery and magazines. Because she did not have sufficient spare weight to remain within treaty limits, this ship did not receive a large hangar and was not cut down aft. She had an EIVH catapult and only a single Walrus aircraft. After initial anti-raider and blockade-runner patrols, she covered troop movements in the Indian Ocean before transferring to the Eastern Mediterranean to lead the 3rd Cruiser Squadron. The ship was torpedoed and badly damaged by Italian aircraft off Bardia in September 1940.

HMS KENT Pennant 54
Kent class heavy cruiser September 1940

With repairs partly completed at Alexandria, *Kent* emerged in a disruptive scheme using 507a, 507b and 507c. Using these three shades was common for ships repaired or refitted at Alexandria. The outline was popular for a time, up until after the battle for Crete, but seems to have been discontinued after that. However, the damage suffered by the torpedo hit off Bardia was so extensive that *Kent* was forced to sail for the UK and more permanent repairs. She wore this camouflage as she returned via the Indian Ocean, Cape Town and up the Atlantic. The state of the decks is unknown, but the scheme applied was the same on both sides of the ship. Once again, we are seeing a scheme that would have used paints available in large quantities on station, as the colours preferred later were not yet supplied. There may have been some 20mm guns added temporarily for the voyage home.

HMS KENT Pennant 54
Kent class heavy cruiser 1941

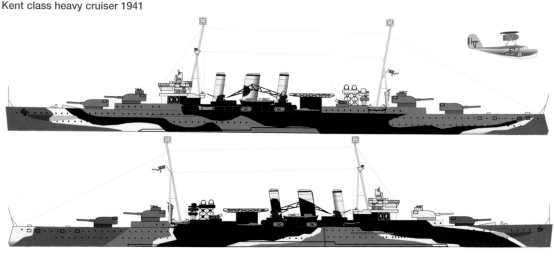

With repairs completed, *Kent* emerged in an Admiralty disruptive scheme using four colours: 507c, B5, MS1 and MS2. This particular application appears to have been to confuse the eye as to the ends of the ship and draw attention to the dark colours of the centre, thus making it hard to tell what the ship was. During the repairs she was fitted with aerials for Type 281 radar at each masthead, Type 284 on the main director for gunnery control, and Type 285 on the HACS directors each side of the bridge. She did not receive Type 273 radar, as it was in short supply at the time. The ship retained the quad 0.5in MG mounts and added six single 20mm guns, with two on 'B' and 'X' turrets, and two more on the gun deck opposite the bridge. The masts have been altered to tripods to take new electronics. The problem with four-colour schemes, such as this, was upkeep and availability of the right colours. Therefore, patch-up work might well be done in a different colour, if the first was not available, and from 1942 the colours shown here did change.

HMS KENT Pennant 54
Kent class heavy cruiser 1943–4

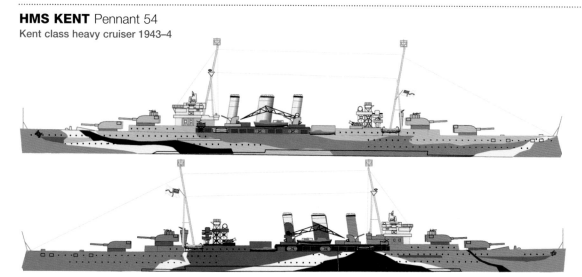

Kent gradually lost her more colourful scheme during service with the Home Fleet. According to Alan Raven (*Warship Perspectives*), more normal grey colours were substituted. This was probably because of what was available for touching up, rather than any other reason. These illustrations are speculative. I have allowed for some MS3 because it was available in quantity and used on many ships involved in covering convoys to Russia, plus some areas of MS1. Apart from those, I have shown her in 507c with 507b and areas of 507a. Type 272 radar was fitted on the searchlight platform, displacing one light. The 0.5in MG mounts were removed and replaced by single 20mm guns. The catapult and aircraft facilities were removed in 1942.

HMS KENT Pennant 54
Kent class heavy cruiser 1944–5

As shown above, *Kent* is wearing the late-war Admiralty standard pattern for the Home Fleet. The overall colour is MS3 and she has a central dark panel of MS1. She spent most of her time in northern waters, protecting the route to North Russian ports and in raids on German facilities in Norway with the fleet. During this period, she had a total of twelve single 20mm AA guns, but in 1943 six of these were removed and replaced by six twin powered 20mm mounts. However, she was becoming worn-out and was never quite the same after the repairs of the damage caused by the 1940 torpedo hit. So in January 1945 she was decommissioned and her crew sent to new cruisers entering service. She was not brought back into service again and was sold for scrap in 1948, after having been used for fleet target trials.

HMS CUMBERLAND Pennant 57
Kent class heavy cruiser 1934

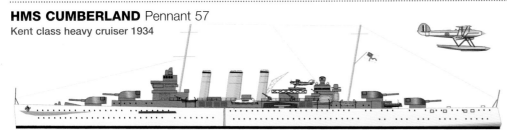

White hull, 507b superstructure and guns, with primrose yellow funnels and masts, was one of the combinations of the colonial scheme worn by *Cumberland* on the China Station. The SIIL catapult was installed in Hong Kong during 1932, while she was on station, but the HACS on her aft superstructure was installed at Chatham in 1929. There were only four single 4in AA guns fitted and, because the multiple 2pdr mounts were not available, four single guns were carried as a temporary measure.

HMS CUMBERLAND Pennant 57
Kent class heavy cruiser 1938

After an extensive rebuild, *Cumberland* went back to China. Her aft deck had been cut down to save weight for the addition of a large aircraft hangar and two quad 2pdr AA mounts aft of the bridge. A quad 0.5in MG mount was fitted on the top of the hangar. The single HACS aft was replaced by one on each side of the bridge, along with directors for the 2pdr mounts. There were two single, shielded 4in AA guns, but the aft mounts were twin 4in. The torpedo tubes were removed and a Walrus aircraft was provided as soon as one became available. However, *Cumberland* is believed to have operated at least one Seafox initially. The hangar could hold three to four of the smaller shipborne floatplanes of the time, as an alternative. The boot topping at the waterline is consistent with peacetime cruising. The main paint shades are once again 507c and 507b. Decks would be natural wood with metal areas in 507b.

HMS CUMBERLAND Pennant 57
Kent class heavy cruiser 1939

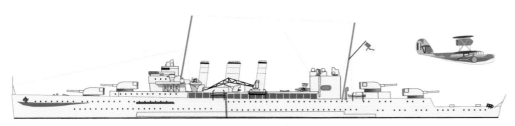

Cumberland adopted an overall scheme of 507c upon outbreak of war, and was sent to South America to reinforce units searching for a German pocket battle-ship known to be in the area. She arrived just too late to be involved in the Battle of the River Plate, when the South Atlantic Squadron engaged *Admiral Graf Spee*, but was present when that ship was scuttled. Note that the black boot topping has now been reduced, because when viewed this can give away the length of a ship and therefore its probable range, if the dimensions are known. Later, when camouflage was adopted, it was stipulated that ships should not have a black waterline at all. However, this was often ignored by captains, who felt it gave the ship a look of smartness. As far as is known, the wood decks were not painted. Horizontal metal surfaces were probably painted 507c to match the rest of the scheme. She remained in the South Atlantic and, along with the cruiser *Ajax*, intercepted the German blockade-runner *Ussukuma*. The single 4in AA guns were removed and replaced by twin mounts in 1939 prior to hostilities.

HMS CUMBERLAND Pennant 57
Kent class heavy cruiser 1940

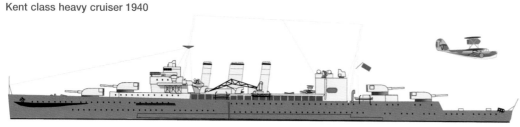

In mid-1940 *Cumberland* adopted a scheme based on a 507b hull, but retained her 507c superstructure and guns. The masts were white. Wood decks probably remained unpainted, but were no longer holystoned to a light colour. During this period, she was engaged in covering various troop movements. She was also present for the abortive Dakar operation and sank the Vichy ammunition ship *Poitiers*. Shore batteries scored a hit on her off Dakar, but she was soon repaired and back on station. Her light AA remained unchanged during this period, although rifle-calibre machine guns may have been added.

HMS CUMBERLAND Pennant 57
Kent class heavy cruiser 1941

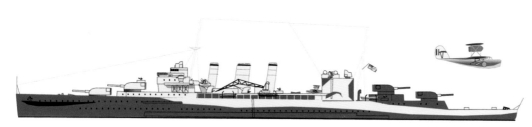

This very unusual camouflage was adopted in early 1941, and used 507a and 507c. Such a scheme was either experimental or, more likely, was unofficial. The general idea of the scheme sweeping down from the bow to the stern could have been to confuse the class of ship at long range, or give the appearance of a destroyer. The decks were apparently left unpainted, and I would suspect that the turret tops would have been the same colour as the rest of each turret. Flat metal surfaces were also probably the same colour as the horizontal areas around them. During this time, she was with the Home Fleet and serving on runs to Russia and general patrols of northern waters. At least some 20mm AA guns may have been fitted and the quad 0.5in MG mounts were retained. Note that depth charges are carried aft. The normal number would be six and the ship carried Type 132 Asdic.

HMS CUMBERLAND Pennant 57
Kent class heavy cruiser October 1941

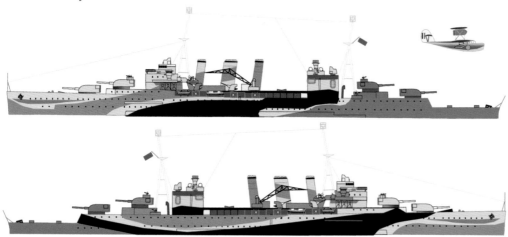

Cumberland went into refit at the beginning of July and returned to service on 11 October 1941. She emerged in an Admiralty disruptive scheme of light tones combined with a dark. The colours used were MS4a, MS1, B5 and B6. The effect was to draw the eye of an observer to the dark central colour, to give a shortening effect, while the pale shades blended with the background to make identification difficult. The turret colours matched the paint on their sides and the wood decks were unpainted. The horizontal metal surfaces probably matched the nearest vertical colour. Five 20mm AA guns were added and the quad 0.5in MG mounts were once again retained. The 20mm were arranged with two on 'B' turret, one on 'X' turret, and the remaining two on deck alongside the deckhouse of 'X' turret.

HMS CUMBERLAND Pennant 57
Kent class heavy cruiser February 1943

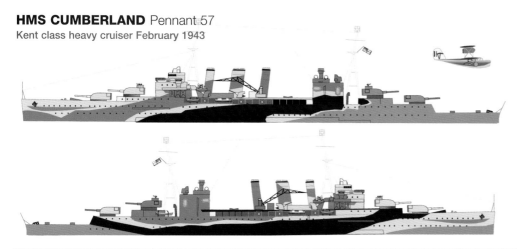

Cumberland underwent a brief eleven-day refit in February 1943, during which she was repainted. The previous pattern was retained, but the shades used were rearranged and the borders slightly altered. The decks were painted grey, possibly B6. According to Alan Raven, turrets 'B', 'X' and 'Y' were dark grey, while 'A' was camouflaged. There is no record of what that was, but possibly MS1 and MS4a, as they would be the colours closest on the side camouflage. The radars remained unchanged, but the light AA was improved, with the removal of the useless quad 0.5in MG mounts and a single 20mm guns. Twin 20mm AA mounts were then added to supplement the other singles. This gave a total of six singles and five twins. Her duties remained with the Home Fleet, during which she was usually employed providing cover for convoys to north Russia.

HMS CUMBERLAND Pennant 57
Kent class heavy cruiser March 1944

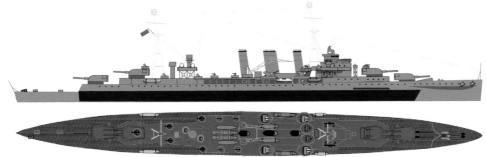

Cumberland was considered to be in the best shape of all the *Kent* class, and was despatched to join the British Eastern Fleet in 1944, operating in the Indian Ocean. There she wore the typical scheme of MS3 with a dark G20 panel on the hull. Her decks were dark grey at this time. Her large hangar and all other aircraft fixtures had been removed. There was a barrage director on a lattice in front of the bridge, and her light AA had been altered to five powered twin 20mm mounts and six singles. The two single 20mm guns on 'A' turret remained, although those on 'X' turret were replaced by a twin mount. Her 8in guns, 4in AA guns and 2pdrs remained. She did not have 'X' turret removed, as some other County-type cruisers did. The Type 273 radar was given the improved lantern. She proved to be a very efficient ship and was in such good condition that she was retained for some time post-war as a training ship and test platform for new weapons. As such, most of her existing weapons were removed and replaced at different times with a wide variety of mostly lighter types.

HMS CUMBERLAND Pennant 57
Kent class heavy cruiser post-war

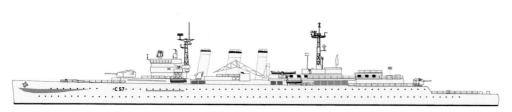

Post-war, *Cumberland* had her 8in guns, 4in AA guns and 2pdr mounts removed, along with all 20mm weapons. She was then rearmed as a trials and training ship. A twin 6in mount was placed forward in 'B' position and a 3in twin mount in 'Y' position. These weapons were intended for the *Tiger* class cruisers. In addition, she mounted 4.5in single guns for training purposes, with at times four, and later two, guns. Amidships were 40mm STAAG mounts (partially hidden by the motor launch in this illustration), and from time to time carried single Bofors 40mm guns for training purposes. The radar arrays and other electronics changed frequently, and it is difficult to give an accurate illustration, as she varied so often to suit tests. The ship was in quite good condition compared to the other heavy cruisers, and she was retained until 1958 before being scrapped. She appeared as herself in the movie *Battle of the River Plate*, and she is shown here wearing her post-war pennant C57.

HMS SUFFOLK Pennant 55
Kent class heavy cruiser 1939

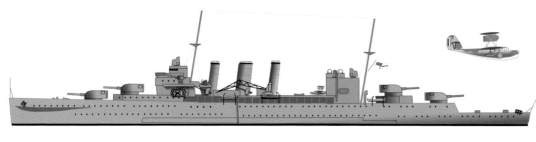

Suffolk wore the buff and white when first built and was of much the same configuration as *Cornwall*. Like that ship, she was taken in hand for reconstruction, and emerged in 1938 with a large hangar, athwartships catapult and two cranes. To save weight and remain under the treaty limits, the quarterdeck was cut down. She was fitted to carry a Walrus reconnaissance aircraft. The torpedo tubes were removed to save weight. She is shown here in a mid-tone grey at the time of the Norwegian campaign. This could be a faded 507b, but is more likely to be a mix of two standard greys to produce something between MS4a and 507b. Horizontal metal surfaces were the same colour, and the turret tops were probably the same. A black boot topping is still carried at the waterline. The wood decks were unpainted and there was Corticene on the bridge. During the refit, she had quad 2pdr AA mounts added on either side between the bridge and fore funnel, instead of the octuple mounts carried by some of her sister ships. There are quad 0.5in MG mounts and the second main gun director on top of the hangar. There are HACS directors on each side of the bridge. Unlike her sisters, she did not receive twin 4in AA mounts, and those shown were singles mounted in a shield of a similar type to the twins.

HMS SUFFOLK Pennant 55
Kent class heavy cruiser 1940

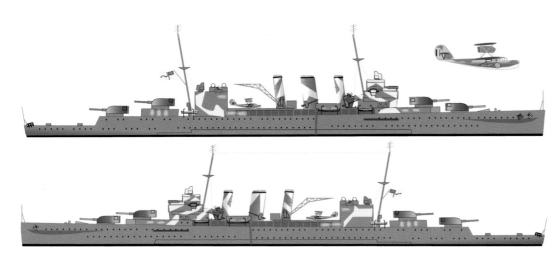

In the very early part of World War II, the Admiralty gave orders for ships to be camouflaged, but no details. In general, it was up to the captain and officers to decide. However, there does seem to have been a certain amount of following a similar idea within the Home Fleet. This could have been the admiral issuing instructions, or ships copying an idea. But however it came about, there was a trend towards using areas of light grey applied on a dark grey ship to produce the effect shown. The light pattern was only used on the upper works and funnels and was most likely 507c over 507b, as these would have been readily available in ships' paint lockers and at all naval port facilities. No doubt large stocks were carried by naval dockyards, etc. Despite the haste with which camouflage was applied, especially after the Norwegian campaign, there seems to have been a lack of enthusiasm for painting over the wood decks that many a sailor had scrubbed to brightness with holystones. Perhaps it was felt that the war would indeed be over 'by Christmas', and it would be a shame to spoil them with paint. However, the practice of holystoning did stop on most ships and the wood was allowed to fade. That probably applied to this ship, as well.

Suffolk was severely damaged by bombing off Norway and was very lucky to make it home to the UK. The cutting down of her stern during the rebuild almost caused her loss, as there was less internal buoyancy. The ship had to be beached at Scapa Flow to prevent her sinking. Repairs took many months. *Suffolk* is shown here carrying the aerials for Type 79Z radar, with which she was fitted in September of 1939. This set was mostly intended for air warning, but had some surface search capability which was valuable for patrols in places like the Denmark Strait. Its range was actually slightly better than the Type 297 that replaced it, but it was far less reliable than the later set.

HMS SUFFOLK Pennant 55
Kent class heavy cruiser May 1941

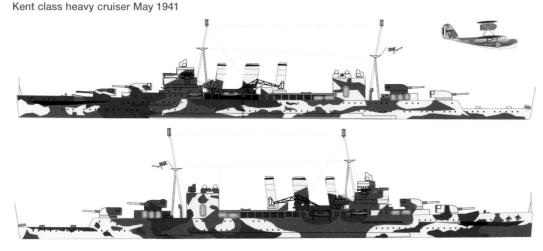

Suffolk adopted an Admiralty-designed disruptive scheme when she emerged from a repairs in 1941. On a base colour of 507c, there were irregular patches and panels of 507b and MS2. The decks were dark to medium grey. This type of scheme was designed to present the viewer with a confusion of colours that conflicted. The intention was not to hide the ship, but to make it difficult for the viewer to tell what it was, as well as the details of its course and distance. Type 279 radar aerials were at both mastheads and Type 285 radar was fitted to the HACS each side of the bridge. Four 20mm AA guns were added and the quad 0.5in MG mounts were retained. Two of the single 4in AA guns were removed and replaced by twin 4in AA guns, but the forward singles remained. The aircraft facilities were retained. On her return to service, *Suffolk* served with the Home Fleet and was involved in hunting down the German battleship *Bismarck*, as well as protecting convoys to Russia.

HMS SUFFOLK Pennant 55
Kent class heavy cruiser 1942–3

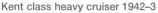

The scheme adopted in 1941 was modified by 1942. When the ship was sent to join the Eastern Fleet, the same basic style was retained, but the boundaries were changed, and in some cases the colour too. The funnel tops were painted white, with a heavy black line to give the impression of shorter funnels. The actual intention behind this remains unclear, despite much speculation. The shades used were still 507c, 507b and MS2 or MS3. The decks remained medium grey. It is possible two to four extra 20mm guns were added, as opportunities arose.

HMS SUFFOLK Pennant 55
Kent class heavy cruiser 1944

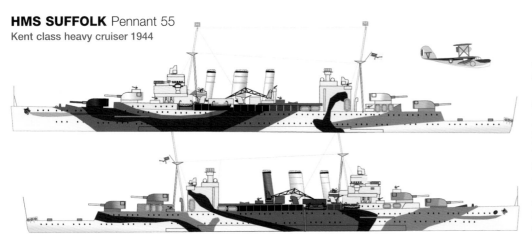

Suffolk returned from refit in April 1943 with a new style of Admiralty disruptive scheme, which had some elements of a light scheme, but with some dark areas added. The main colour was 507c, with a large area of 507b and sections of B15 blue black. The decks remained mid- to dark grey. Aircraft facilities were retained as the ship proceeded to the Indian Ocean as part of the Eastern Fleet, where she served various fleet and patrol duties. By this time, the ship had landed the Type 279 radar and was fitted with Type 281 instead. However, this set still required two aerials and thus were mounted at both mast tops. The AA armament was officially increased to nine single 20mm guns, although some may have been fitted earlier. A typical lantern for Type 273 radar was fitted on top of the hangar. Her catapult and aircraft were removed in 1943, but the hangar was retained because of its usefulness for other purposes. Like many ships, the hangar became a cinema in part, but also provided extra accommodation and workshops.

HMS SUFFOLK Pennant 55
Kent class heavy cruiser 1945

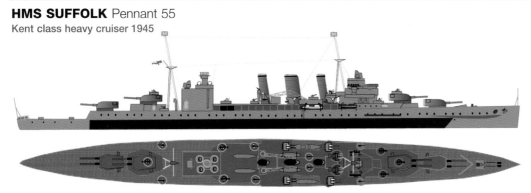

Suffolk was showing her age as the war was coming to its conclusion, and she received no further modifications. Her final service was mostly on patrol in the Indian Ocean, although raiders and enemy shipping were almost totally absent. She also covered carrier raids on Japanese bases and provided protection for convoys. She is shown here wearing the MS3 overall, with a panel of MS1 to provide a shortening effect. The ship remained with the Eastern Fleet until the end of World War II.

HMAS CANBERRA Pennant 133
Kent class cruiser 1928

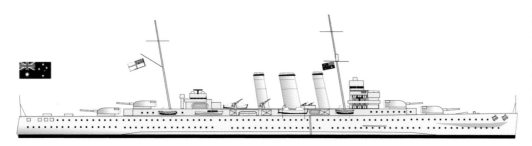

Having had its funding for the new cruisers reduced, the Admiralty was pleased when Australia ordered two of the class and fund them entirely. *Canberra* was delivered with an area for aircraft set aside but not fitted. She was built with slightly taller funnels. Superstructure was carried slightly further aft, and there was no gap between 'X' gun mount and the deckhouse. Delivered in a time of financial crisis, the ship was not refitted or updated often. She is shown here in her delivery state, painted in 507c overall. The White Ensign was flown by Australian ships, but the Australian national flag itself was flown as well. In port it was flown from the bow instead of the Union Jack, as shown here. The arrangement was that these ships would be available for the defence of Australia and to operate mostly in Pacific and Indian Ocean waters. But in war they would come under the orders of the British Admiralty, which could allocate them based on need and perceived threats.

HMAS CANBERRA Pennant I33
Kent class cruiser 1936

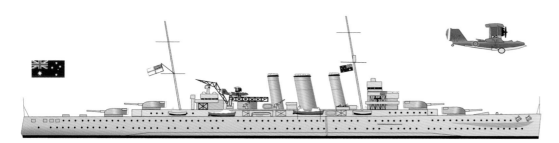

There was no funding available to upgrade *Canberra* until 1936, when she finally received a catapult. But she had to make do with the old Seagull III aircraft left over from the seaplane tender *Albatross* for a time. Before the installation of the catapult, she carried a Seagull III on deck and handled it with the crane that was installed on her starboard side. In this illustration, she has adopted MS4a as her basic colour and the black boot topping has been reduced in size. The wooden decks were unchanged, but the horizontal metal surfaces probably followed the rest of the ship in MS4a. *Canberra* had light grey turret tops to distinguish her from *Australia*, which had dark grey. The letters 'CA' were painted on top of 'A' turret in black. Note that even at this time she still carried single 2pdr AA guns opposite the forward funnel and the 4in AA guns had not been increased in number. Unlike many of the Royal Navy ships, she retained her torpedo tubes. An HACS was installed on top of the after control position between the searchlights. The ship went to war in this state, with the only other additions being quad 0.5in MG mounts port and starboard, and the aircraft replaced by a Walrus.

HMAS CANBERRA Pennant D33
Kent class cruiser early 1942

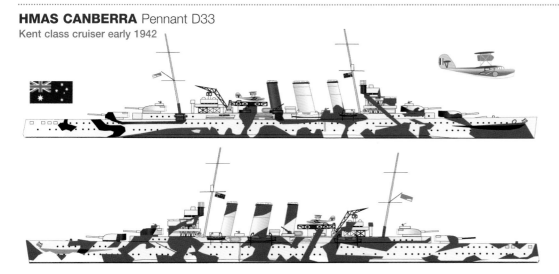

Canberra appeared in a relatively complicated camouflage pattern for a few months. Like so many others at this time, it was based around easily available paint. The ship had a base colour of 507c with areas of 507a, and some areas near the waterline in white for a false bow wave effect. The 4in AA guns remained singles. The actual number is unclear, but at least six single 20mm AA guns were added and the quad 0.5in MG mounts were retained. The turret tops were still painted light grey, but the letters 'CA' were removed. Note that a lantern for Type 271 radar has been added to the rear of the bridge top. No other radars were fitted.

HMAS CANBERRA Pennant D33
Kent class cruiser 1942

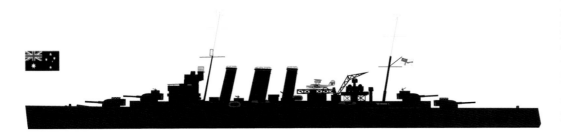

Prior to her loss at the Battle of Savo Island in August 1942, *Canberra* had been given an overall camouflage of what was known as 'Chicago blue'. This was very similar to the dark blue used by the US Navy, but was mixed in Australia and was slightly lighter. It is not known if the decks were painted grey blue, as were those of the US ships she was operating with, and there are no records of it. However, it does seem quite possible. The shade was mixed for US ships visiting Australian ports at the same time as *Canberra* received her coat. Note that the mast tops were white. The 20mm positions on 'B' and 'X' turrets now held two single 20mm guns each, in a side by side orientation. But there is no record of others being added. This ship never had her single 4in guns replaced by twins. Similarly, some sources say she had received Type 286 radar at the mastheads and others that she had not. Photographs taken just before and on the morning after her final battle are not of high quality, but the masts do seem to show some sort of aerials on her tops. If these are Type 286, then they would have had to be on both mastheads. However, I remain unconvinced.

HMAS AUSTRALIA Pennant I84
Kent class cruiser 1928

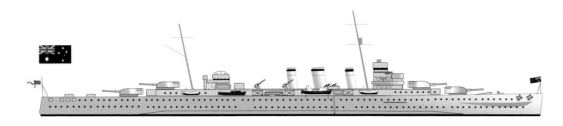

Australia was completed, as designed, with short funnels. However, it was quickly found that smoke interfered with the bridge in a following wind, and with the aft control tower at other times. The Australian government requested the funnels be raised by 18ft to counter the problem. British ships of this type had their funnels raised by only 15ft. Although space had been allocated for an aircraft catapult and supporting facilities, none were actually fitted at this time and, unlike others, did not originally complete with even the base for a catapult. Her main armament comprised eight 8in guns. There were four single 4in AA guns as secondaries and four single 2pdr AA guns. After her funnels were raised and further trials completed, she worked up off the UK and then proceeded to Australia. Her paint scheme during this early period was a grey similar to MS4a. The wood decks were made of fir, rather than oak, to save weight and cost.

HMAS AUSTRALIA Pennant I84
Kent class cruiser 1935

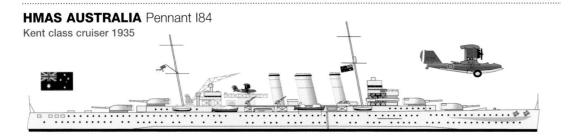

Australia is shown here with a catapult and crane fitted, but otherwise not yet much altered. This was the form in which she served much of her peacetime period with the RAN. The ship is painted in overall 507c, but the turret tops and all horizontal metal surfaces were 507a. This made her immediately distinguishable from her sister ship *Canberra* when seen from the air. The letters 'AU' were painted on 'A' turret top in white. Wood decks were unpainted, scrubbed wood. A Seagull III aircraft was initially carried, but it was replaced by the Seagull V. The armament has remained the same, except for quad 0.5in MG mounts on each side of the bridge.

HMAS AUSTRALIA Pennant D84
Kent class cruiser late 1940

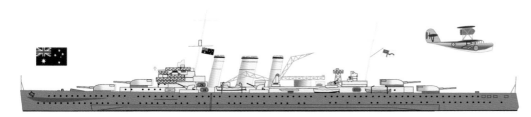

Australia adopted a dark grey hull and lighter upper works while serving with the Royal Navy in the Atlantic. This appears to have been 507c with 507b. The mast tops were pale grey or white and the wood decks, as yet, unpainted. The ship shows some of the alterations carried out in a refit that ended just as World War II broke out. The single 4in AA guns have been replaced by twin mounts on the main deck and widely dispersed. She was the only County type to have her 4in mounts in this configuration. Multiple 2pdr mounts have been added aft of the catapult. The quad 0.5in MG mounts were moved to the aft deckhouse to avoid blast interference from the forward 4in mounts. There are numerous splinter mats fitted to the bridge as protection from strafing. The ship may have appeared like this at the time of the Dakar operation, where she sank a Vichy French destroyer and damaged another. She was, in turn, hit by three shells from a French light cruiser.

HMAS AUSTRALIA Pennant D84
Kent class cruiser 1941

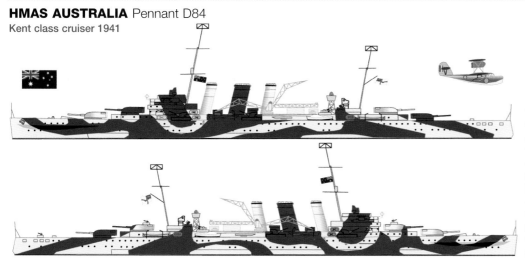

The above illustrations show *Australia* after her December 1940 refit, during which she was given a camouflage scheme based on 507a and 507c. The shade of 507a seems to be somewhat dark. Sweeping areas of dark on light were common in this period and the scheme could have been an Admiralty one, designed on the ship, or by the dockyard. Official schemes were mostly still being developed. Turret tops were still dark grey, but the letters 'AU' had been painted out. Other horizontal metal surfaces were 507a, but the wood deck areas are believed to have still been unpainted. In the port side illustration, she is depicted without the addition of extra light AA. The starboard shows her with 20mm mounts on the turret tops, the bridge wings and the quarterdeck. Type 286 radar is carried at both mastheads to provide a sending and a receiving aerial. The HACS was fitted with Type 285 radar.

HMAS AUSTRALIA Pennant D84
Kent class cruiser 1942

The US Navy requested that this, and other Royal Australian Navy ships serving with their fleet, be painted in dark blue to avoid them being mistaken for Japanese ships. The mix was carried out in Australia, as no official USN paint was available. The resulting shade was referred to as 'Chicago blue'. Decks may have been painted in a shade similar to that of US warships, as this paint was available at the dockyard where the work was done. The 20mm AA tubs on 'A' and 'X' turrets were enlarged to accommodate two weapons in each. Two single 20mm guns were added at the front of the forward deckhouse and two more in the bridge wings. The quad 0.5in MG mounts were not removed until late 1943, and were therefore still part of the light AA armament. Air attacks were so intensive during the Solomons campaign that it was probably considered wise to retain these until something better was available. To avoid US gunners, who tended to shoot at any aircraft with a red dot, the insignia of the Walrus (Seagull V) became blue and white. The aircraft also adopted US Navy-style paintwork.

HMAS AUSTRALIA Pennant D84
Kent class cruiser 1943

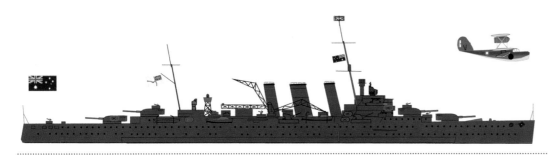

Australia is shown here in an extremely dark camouflage while serving with Task Force 44. This was at the request of the TF commander and worn for a short time only. The tone seems to match G5 soot black. All decks were painted, with the horizontal metal areas in G5, but the wood deck colour is not known. It may have been the same blue-grey as US warships. Note that a radar lantern for a Type 273 radar has been added on the bridge and the main gun director has been fitted with Type 284 gunnery radar. A US SC radar is carried at the foremast top. An additional 20mm gun position has been added by the catapult, just behind the aft funnel, giving a total of eleven such weapons. This would have been considered a very small number compared to the US ships she was operating with. However, at around this time seven twin 20mm mounts were added and some singles removed. This could not have been a total swap, as suggested in some books, because during the Leyte Gulf operations in 1944, the 20mm guns on the top of 'B' turret were definitely still singles, as photographs clearly show. The Walrus aircraft adopted a scheme more suited to the island-to-island operations this ship was primarily engaged in at this time.

HMAS AUSTRALIA Pennant D84
Kent class cruiser mid-1944

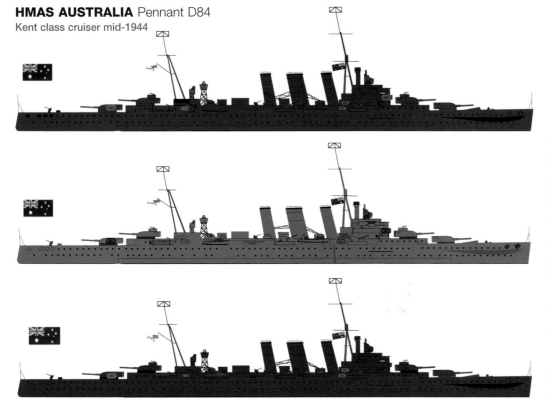

There is some confusion and debate as to the actual colour of *Australia* at the time of the Leyte Gulf battle. The official version is unclear and G10 is suggested, but G5, as she wore previously, is also possible. But in numerous photographs taken at the time, she appears lighter, even taking into account the poor quality of some World War II film. As she was operating with the US fleet, it seems more probable that she wore very dark US Navy blue, as did many of the US ships present. In addition, the G10 suggested does not seem right for tone. I have therefore shown her in three alternative schemes of G10, G5 and US Navy blue. I asked an officer who served on her which was the correct shade. He said the ship had been repainted so many times he could not recall her Leyte colour. The aircraft catapult was removed and only one crane carried to save weight. *Australia* was considered a very lucky ship, having seen much action, but seldom been damaged. However, at Leyte Gulf she was attacked by five kamikaze aircraft and severely damaged. There were many casualties, including her commanding officer. After assistance from US repair ships, she limped home to Sydney for repairs, which did not complete in time for her to return to the front line. Note that eight single 40mm Bofors guns had been added to her armament at this time, some of which replaced 20mm mounts. Type 281 radar is now at the mastheads and the HACS has Type 285 radar mounted.

HMAS AUSTRALIA Pennant D84
Kent class cruiser 1945

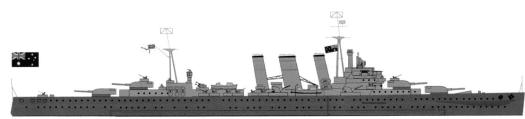

Australia was repaired in the dockyard at Sydney, but had to proceed to the UK for the completion of some work. The colour scheme is a typical Admiralty standard with MS3 upper works and MS2 hull. In August 1945 she was ready for service again, but the war ended before she could join the fleet now operating off the coast of Japan. 40mm Bofors AA guns were added in some numbers, as can be seen. Singles on 'B' and 'X' turrets, singles abreast the bridge, six singles on each side amidships, where the aircraft facilities had been, as well as retaining the single on her quarter-deck. There are also twin 20mm mounts each side of the bridge front and four more on the aft deckhouse. This gave her a total of seventeen 40mm, sixteen 2pdr and twelve 20mm barrels – quite a strong, light AA fit for a cruiser of her type. The torpedo tubes were removed. An extra HACS was added aft and the searchlight tower removed. The Carley floats were also more organised. A US Navy SC radar is carried just below the Type 281 radar on the foremast.

HMAS AUSTRALIA Pennant D84
Kent class cruiser mid-1947

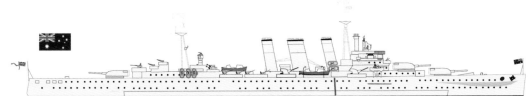

Australia was rebuilt in the UK and returned home in 1947, minus her 'X' turret, but with her AA enhanced. US-type quad 40mm mounts were installed each side of the bridge, and a twin mount replaced the 'X' turret. She carried four singe 40mm guns per side amidships and had twin 20mm mounts each side of the bridge front. The octuple 2pdr mounts were retained at this time. This gave her a total of eighteen 40mm, sixteen 2pdr and four 20mm barrels. There was provision for the twin mount to be replaced by a quad 40mm mount if required, and this could be done for the 2pdr mounts as well. The twin 4in mounts were also retained. The ship is shown here in 507c pale grey and the turret tops were the same colour. Wood decks were apparently restored to plain wood after the removal of all paint. However, in photographs the ship also appears to be wearing the Royal Navy standard MS3 and MS2, which she may have retained for some time before reverting to peacetime 507c. Note the 2pdr directors behind the aft twin 40mm mounting and a 40mm director above that. There is also a 40mm director on each side of the bridge.

HMAS AUSTRALIA Pennant D84
Kent class cruiser 1950

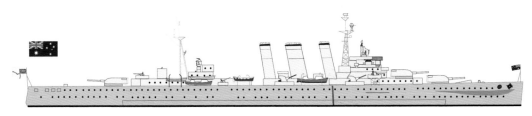

By 1950 *Australia* had been relegated to training duties and, being in good general condition, continued in service until 1955, when she was sold for scrap. The ship seems to have worn 507c for much of the time, but there are periods in which the hull seems to have been painted in 507b. It is not known why this was done. In photographs, the turret tops seem to be 507b, regardless of the overall scheme. The foremast was replaced by a lattice mast to carry the additional weight of new electronics. The lantern for the Type 273 radar was removed and replaced by a Type 277 on the lattice, with a Type 293 at the foretop. She still retains Type 285 radar on the HACS directors. At various times, trials were made of US radar types, along with various Royal Navy developments. It is therefore not possible to give a clear coverage of all radar types and other electronics fitted. The remaining aircraft crane was removed and the aft twin 40mm mount was not always carried. Although the 8in mounts were going out of service with this ship, the other armament was important for training purposes, as these weapons were mounted on other ships of the RAN. The same applied to radar equipment.

LONDON CLASS CRUISERS

HMS SUSSEX Pennant 96
London class cruiser 1930

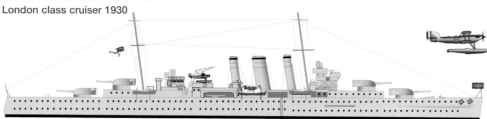

No catapult was fitted to *Sussex* as completed, but she still carried a Fairey IID aircraft. The large crane was used to place the aircraft on the water for take-off and retrieving it later. She is shown here while serving in UK waters and is painted in overall MS4a Home Fleet grey. Metal decks were painted slightly darker grey and wood decks were, of course, holystoned. There were only four single 4in AA guns and four single 2pdr AA guns for the AA battery. She had a quite uncluttered look compared to later years.

HMS SUSSEX Pennant 96
London class cruiser 1936

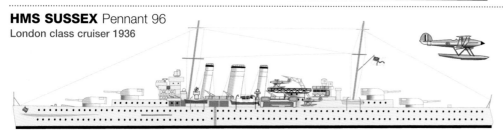

Sussex was sent to operate with the Australian squadron from 1934 to 1936. For that service she adopted a colour of 507c, the standard colour for Australian warships before World War II. Metal deck colours were unknown, but possibly 507c. Wood decks were unpainted. The ship had been fitted with a heavy catapult prior to leaving the UK, along with the then-standard quad 0.5in MG mounts. The catapult was capable of launching heavier aircraft that were not yet available. During this time, *Sussex* embarked two Osprey fighter-reconnaissance aircraft. One was usually stowed on the catapult, whilst the other was on deck. The crane was on the starboard side of the ship.

HMS SUSSEX Pennant 96
London class cruiser 1939

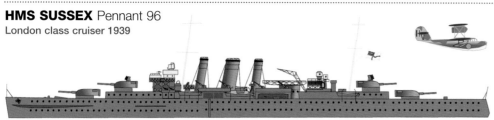

At the outbreak of World War II, *Sussex* was engaged in many of the same roles as her sister ships, including searching for raiders in the South Atlantic and duty with the Home Fleet. She adopted an overall 507b colour at some point during this period, but with the wood decks remaining unpainted. The masts were white or pale grey, as was the upper section of the bridge and directors. Anti-splinter protection was applied in the form of mats around some of the bridge areas and the quad 0.5in machine gun positions. The distinctly useless UP (Unrotated Projectile) rocket AA weapon was fitted on 'B' and 'X' turrets. No other light AA was added at this time.

HMS SUSSEX Pennant 96
London class cruiser 1940

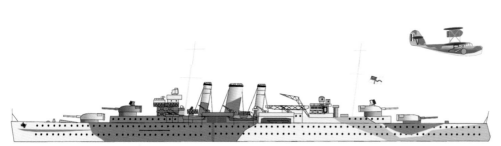

In September 1940 *Sussex* was hit by German bombs during an air raid on Glasgow. She was in dry dock for some hurried machinery repairs, but had not de-ammunitioned before entering, as it was expected to be a very short stay and the ship was urgently required elsewhere. She was critically damaged during an air raid on the night of 17/18 September, set on fire and almost lost due to consecutive explosions before the dock was flooded. She was sunk to the bottom of the dock to prevent further fires and explosions. Heavy casualties were suffered and the Glasgow Fire Brigade had to be called in to fight the fires. The damage meant she did not return to service until August 1942. At the time she was wearing camouflage, but the details are vague and hard to come by. It is also not known when it was applied, but during and after the Norwegian campaign many ships hurriedly adopted camouflage, mostly unofficial schemes. Camouflage of the funnels was quite common in 1940. The illustration here is only an approximation of how she looked and cannot be taken as definitive. Nothing is known of the starboard side, but it was usual for ships to have the same pattern on both sides in 1940. It would seem that the 507b previously worn was given some coats of 507c and MS4a or a specially mixed shade of mid-grey. The decks presumably remained as before.

HMS SUSSEX Pennant 96
London class cruiser August 1942

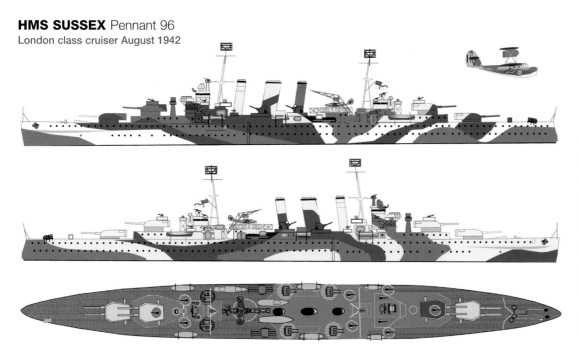

After prolonged repairs, *Sussex* emerged with a new Admiralty disruptive camouflage scheme using an overall colour of 507c, with areas of 507a and B5. The wood decks remained unpainted as shown, but the other horizontal surfaces were painted in a mid-grey, possibly 507b. The turret tops were MS4a, except for 'B' turret, which was possibly 507a. The single 4in AA guns were removed and replaced by twin mounts. Octuple 2pdr mounts were added on the port and starboard sides of the aft control position. Ten single 20mm AA guns were also added and the UP mounts removed. She still retained her aircraft and catapult at this time. Type 281 radar was fitted to the mast top, and Type 284 and 285 were added for gunnery control. Rather strangely, a Type 273 radar was fitted on a platform between 'B' turret and the front of the bridge. This would have given a good sweep forward and for a few degrees aft, but would have been completely blocked by the bridge and other structures for use directly aft.

HMS SUSSEX Pennant 96
London class cruiser October 1942

In October 1942 *Sussex* was repainted in another Admiralty scheme that retained 507c as the base colour, but altered the layout of the areas of 507a, and added MS3 instead of B5. Why this was done after such a short period in the previous scheme is unknown. In the early part of World War II, shades of green paint were in short supply, with the army and air force having priority for their use. Despite the change of scheme, the armament remained the same as did the electronics fit. During this time, *Sussex* was serving in the Atlantic Fleet and intercepted the German blockade-runner *Hohenfriedberg* off Cape Finisterre. She also had a close call with the U-boat *U-264*, which fired a salvo of four torpedoes, but failed to score a hit.

HMS SUSSEX Pennant 96
London class cruiser May 1943

By May 1943, *Sussex* had adopted another Admiralty disruptive scheme. That was applied on the base colour MS4a, with some patches of B6 and rather larger areas of MS2. It is presumed the decks remained the same at this time. Note that the Type 273 radar was moved from its very cramped position forward to the back of the aft control station. This location would have produced better results, but coverage directly forward would have been limited. This type of radar seems to have been placed in non-all-around cover positions on many ships, accepting the limitations on some bearings for the excellent reception it gave on all others. The Type 281 radar required two rather large aerials, as shown, and many vessels changed over to the single aerial Type 281B when it became available. However, *Sussex* moved to the Eastern Fleet and any upgrade was delayed.

HMS SUSSEX Pennant 96
London class cruiser 1945

Sussex underwent major alterations in June 1944 and did not re-enter service until June 1945. During this work, the 'X' turret was removed and replaced by two quad 2pdr mounts, along with their directors. Two more quad 2pdr mounts were added each side of the fore funnel, thus giving her four quads, plus her original two octuple mounts for a total of thirty-two barrels. Two single 20mm guns were added on 'B' turret, plus two more at the front of the bridge. Six twin 20mm mounts were also added and the remaining single 20mm guns removed, except for two aft above the 2pdrs. Four single 40mm AA guns were added while in the Far East. Type 281B radar with Type 244 IFF was added to the top of the mainmast, and Type 293 radar was added on the top of the foremast. Directors for the 2pdrs were all fitted with Type 282 radar. The previous Type 285 and Type 284 radar were retained. Note that many lower portholes have been closed over to assist in damage control.

HMS SUSSEX Pennant 96
London class cruiser 1949

Having been so recently refitted and modernised, *Sussex* continued in post-war service, but was finally paid off in 1949, to be scrapped the following year. She is shown here in peacetime 507c. The wood decks were scrubbed once again to a pre-war brightness. It was common for many of the ship's boats and launches to be painted blue, as shown. Note that all single and twin 20mm guns were removed after the war and the quad 2pdr tubs on each side of the fore funnel were empty. The other octuple and quad 2pdr mounts were deactivated, although the tubs remained. The directors and their Type 282 radar were also removed. Four single 40mm Bofors guns can be seen as the sole active light AA. The number of Carley floats was reduced considerably, as well.

HMS DEVONSHIRE Pennant 39
London class cruiser 1932

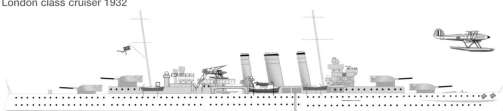

Devonshire spent most of her peacetime cruising with the Mediterranean Fleet, but went out to the China Station for two years. During that time, she wore a typical buff upper works and white hull paint scheme, with primrose funnels. The barrels of her 8in guns were painted black. Only four single 4in AA guns were carried at the time, along with four single 2pdr guns, which were mounted abreast the bridge, port and starboard. The wood decks were scrubbed and the horizontal metal surfaces were buff. Turret tops also appear to be buff. Her quad 0.5in MG mounts had not been fitted at this time. The ship carried Hawker Osprey aircraft, which were not only expected to perform scouting duties, but also able to act as fighters. One is shown on the catapult and the other was usually stowed on the port side main deck.

HMS DEVONSHIRE Pennant 39
London class cruiser 1939–40

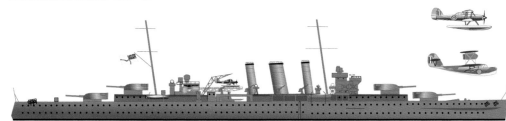

Devonshire joined the Home Fleet on the outbreak of war and is shown dressed overall in 507b. In 1940 the decks are reported as being painted dark grey, but it is unclear when this occurred. It is more likely that they were still unpainted wood. Note that four additional single 4in AA guns had been added, as well as quad 0.5in MG mounts on each side between the bridge and fore funnel. These heavy MG mounts were efficient weapons, but did not live up to expectations, because newer aircraft of the time proved tougher and needed something heavier to knock them down. Apart from a change in the location of some of her boats, because of the added 4in guns, and a heavier catapult, there seem to be few other changes to the ship. She carried two Fairey Seafox aircraft as a temporary measure until a Walrus could be provided. Type 132 Asdic was carried by this ship.

HMS DEVONSHIRE Pennant 39
London class cruiser late 1940

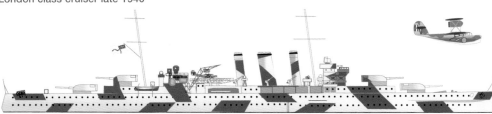

The admiral on station and the commanding officer conferred on this camouflage pattern. It comprised 507c with 507a areas. It was considered very effective and was worn from mid-1940 right through to May 1943, but as following illustrations show, it gradually varied in detail. The pattern was the same on both sides. It would have been easy to design this scheme from paints held in most naval dockyards. At this time the decks were painted dark grey, which would probably be 507a, as it was the most likely to be available. The tops of 'A', 'X' and 'Y' turrets were 507a, but until late in 1941 the top of 'B' turret was 507c. The letters 'DV' were painted on it in 507a. At the time of the top illustration, *Devonshire* had no additions to the light AA armament, but had been provided with a Walrus aircraft.

HMS DEVONSHIRE Pennant 39
London class cruiser late 1941

The lower illustration depicts *Devonshire* in 1941. It is a good example of how a camouflage can appear to be the same, but has actually varied from the original. The basic pattern had been followed, but there were changes during times when the ship was repainted. The dark grey at the bow has extended all the way forward. There is now grey on 'A' turret, the middle funnel has changed, there is grey on the back of 'Y' turret, and some of the areas on the hull have changed in shape or size. All turret tops were 507a and the letters on top of 'B' turret were painted over. The ship had Type 281 radar added at the mastheads, and the masts were turned into tripods to take the extra weight. There are now octuple 2pdr mounts on each side of the aft control position and single 20mm guns on 'B' and 'X' turrets. The diamond-shaped object on the starfish of the mainmast is an aerial for HF/DF.

HMS DEVONSHIRE Pennant 39
London class cruiser 1942

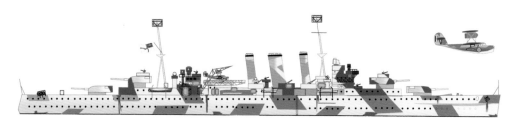

The same camouflage scheme as before is carried, but the paint had badly faded while serving in the Indian Ocean. It is still intended to be 507c as the base, but the areas of 507a have faded so much that it appeared to be three shades, varying from 507b to a lighter grey. This was particularly noticeable on the funnels. It could even be possible that some of the areas were patched up with 507b, or shades mixed onboard from available paint. There is an area of grey on the hull below 'A' turret that was not there previously, and one near the stern is gone. Yet to the casual viewer, photographs of the ship would seem to indicate she is in the same scheme as originally applied. We can presume that hard service has left little time for the ship to be repainted, and I have included some rust streaks that seem prominent in photographs. Except for the funnels, most areas, other than the hull, appear to have been better kept up, which would, of course, have been easier to do, even when at sea. Note that a Type 273 radar is in a lantern on the bridge. Surprisingly, there has been no Type 284 or Type 285 gunnery radars fitted. Six single 20mm AA guns were added for a total of eight.

HMS DEVONSHIRE Pennant 39
London class cruiser 1943

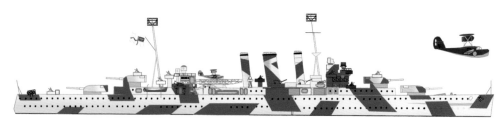

Once again, the same scheme continued to be used until May 1943, when *Devonshire* went in for updates. Even so, there are changes, with those at the bow being the most prominent. The panels amidships have changed in size, and one is now much deeper. The aft control area is now mostly 507c. Note that the ship has gained octuple 2pdr mounts on each side of the mainmast. All the single 20mm guns have been removed, and replaced by twelve twin 20mm mounts. The aircraft is still retained. In all cases, the port side was supposed to be identical to that of the starboard side shown, but photographs show the same variations. I believe this ship is a great example of the TLAR (That Looks About Right) principle and the difficulty of maintaining a camouflage while a ship is engaged in heavy use.

HMS DEVONSHIRE Pennant 39
London class cruiser 1943–4

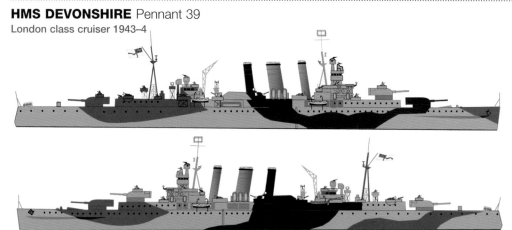

Devonshire received a major refit in mid-1943, emerging with an Admiralty four-colour camouflage scheme. It used G45 overall, with an area of G10 forward, B15 amidships and B30 aft. The wood decks were previously painted dark grey and probably remained that colour. The refit saw the removal of 'X' turret. 'Y' turret top was painted G45, while 'A' and 'B' tops were G45 or MS3. But the lighter shade could have been obtained by simply mixing some white with G45. All aircraft facilities were removed, but the crane remained, as it was very useful for other purposes. The 4in twin mounts were slightly repositioned and a crew shelter built between them. *Devonshire* now mounted a formidable six octuple 2pdr mounts and eleven twin 20mm mounts. Type 284 and Type 285 radars were fitted and the original Type 281 was replaced by a Type 281B, which only required a single aerial. Directors for the 2pdr mounts were also installed and equipped with Type 282 radar. A lantern with Type 273 radar was added amidships where the catapult had been. Type 244 and Type 253 IFF were installed, along with a Type 650 missile jammer. While the ship was now minus one twin 8in turret, the AA capability was quite powerful.

HMS **DEVONSHIRE** Pennant 39
London class cruiser 1945

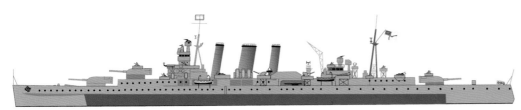

By 1945, *Devonshire* had adopted the Admiralty standard scheme and was dressed overall in G45 with a B30 hull. At around this time the wood deck was restored to scrubbed wood, with all dark grey paint removed. Horizontal metal surfaces remained dark grey. Turret tops were in G45. Other equipment remained the same as before, with no apparent changes to electronics or weaponry. Reports say eight single 20mm guns were added, but the location of these is unclear. The ASW rack held six depth charges, which was standard for cruisers, as they were considered something to scare submarines off with, rather than offensively attack them. Type 132 Asdic was carried, which was capable of picking up a torpedo moving through the water and giving warning of an attack.

HMS **DEVONSHIRE** Pennant 39
London class cruiser 1947

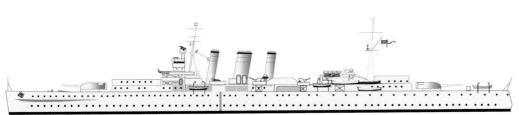

The major upgrade of this ship shortly before World War II ended left the Admiralty with a ship in very good condition and with some years of service life left. The decision was made to turn her into a training ship. She is shown here in that role, wearing 507c overall. Note the thick black boot topping at the waterline has returned in the post-war era, when general smartness was again important. A cadet classroom was fitted forward and 'B' turret removed to allow this. The AA batteries that replaced 'X' turret were also removed for classroom space. Almost all the rest of the light AA was removed over a period of time, some having been retained for training, then taken off, and occasionally replaced as per training requirements. The torpedo tubes were removed permanently. A multitude of ship's boats were clustered around the aft control position and the crane was retained to help move them.

HMS **LONDON** Pennant 69
London class cruiser 1932

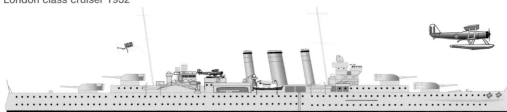

London completed in much the same form as *Devonshire* and was assigned to the 1st Cruiser Squadron for much of her early service. During 1932 she carried a Ripon reconnaissance aircraft on what was intended to be the catapult base. Due to the lack of a catapult, the aircraft had to be put over the side in order to take off. She is shown here operating in UK waters wearing MS4a Home Fleet grey. There is a heavy black boot topping along the waterline. Wood decks were scrubbed and horizontal metal surfaces painted to the same as the rest of the ship. Turret tops were believed to be painted MS4a. Only four 4in AA guns were carried at this time.

HMS **LONDON** Pennant 69
London class cruiser 1936

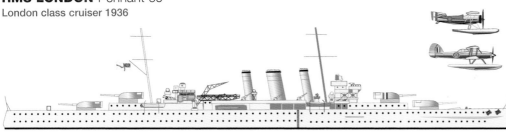

London is shown here in the pale grey of 507c and carries national identification stripes on 'B' turret, owing to the then-raging Spanish Civil War. This ship received a major refit in 1935–6, during which she had an additional four single 4in guns, quad 0.5in MG mounts and octuple 2pdr mounts added. Her engines were overhauled and other repairs carried out. A heavy catapult was fitted to enable her to carry the Supermarine Walrus aircraft, which was soon to enter service. Until the Walrus was available, *London* would carry a variety of aircraft, including the little Fairey Flycatcher shipborne floatplane fighter. In 1939 *London* was chosen to receive a rebuild that would change her entire appearance. This was somewhat surprising, since the ship had recently been through a major refit, and war with Germany was looming.

HMS LONDON Pennant 69
London class cruiser March 1941

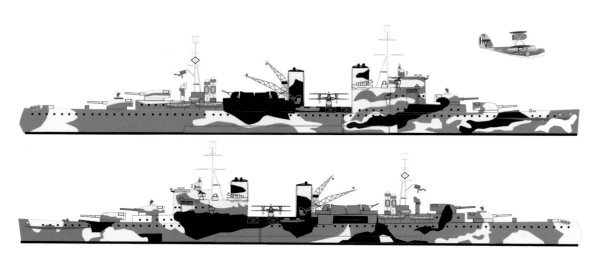

London emerged from her rebuild with a profile rather like the new cruisers of the Colony class then entering service. A different arrangement of colours had been intended for her camouflage scheme, but as not all the paint required was actually available, the scheme was altered to a 507c base, with 507b, B5 and MS1. The heavy contrast of black-green, provided by MS1 against 507c and the intermediary colours, was effective in breaking up the silhouette of the ship. All decks were reported as dark grey, most probably 507a. The ship had an athwartships catapult and a hangar for two Walrus aircraft. The main armament remained the same, but octuple 2pdr AA mounts were placed on top of the hangar, either side of the fore funnel. 'Y' turret had a dark grey top, but the other three were painted with 507c tops. This contrast against the dark deck may have been an attempt at camouflage. Twin 4in AA mounts were added aft of the second funnel and the third funnel was removed. Aircraft cranes were placed opposite the aft funnel, with a coverage of the catapult area and the boat nest between the aft funnel and the aft control station. Additional AA included the quad 0.5in MG mounts on 'B' and 'Y' turrets. Mounting such a weapon on 'Y' instead of 'X' turret could have been due to top weight considerations.

HMS LONDON Pennant 69
London class cruiser May 1941

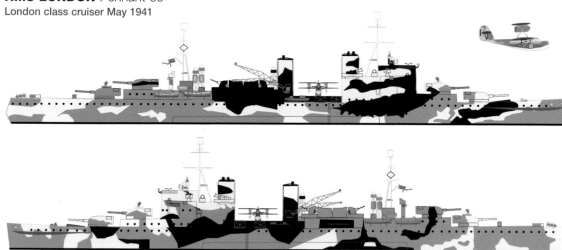

Within two months of the rebuild, London dropped the B5 colour from her camouflage scheme and switched to B6 instead of 507b. The pattern basically followed that of the original, except that some areas changed shape or were deleted. The lighter shade of B6 gave even more contrast against the dark MS1 and blended well with 507c. This camouflage was considered most effective in areas of dull light and misty conditions, but similarly useful in haze. After initial sea trials, it was realised that the reconstruction had added too much weight, which strained the hull and caused many other defects. As shown here and as first rebuilt, she carried the less common Type 279 radar at the mastheads and an aerial for HF/DF on the mainmast. She still carried two anchors on the starboard side at this time, but would eventually have one removed to save weight. Type 132 Asdic was carried, along with the usual six depth charges for ships of this size.

HMS LONDON Pennant 69
London class cruiser early 1942

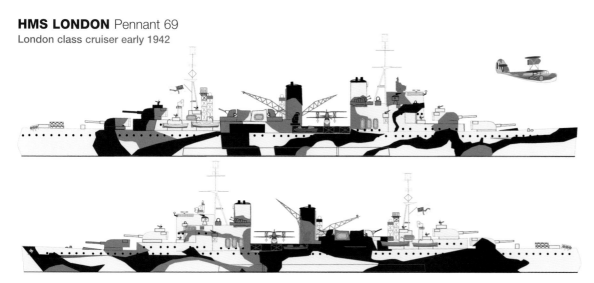

London went in for another of her many repairs and refits in late 1941, and returned to service in early 1942 with another camouflage pattern. MS1, B5 and 507c now made up the scheme, which, as with the previous pattern, was intended to break up the silhouette of the ship through the use of the dark areas provided by MS1. The deck remained dark grey as before. Type 273 radar was placed on a lattice mast just forward of the mainmast tripod and Type 282 on the 2pdr directors. Type 285 radar was placed on the HACS directors. The quad 0.5in MG mounts were removed and replaced by eight single 20mm guns. Overweight problems and insufficient structural strength continued to plague the ship ever since she had been rebuilt. At this time many defects had been corrected, but it would require more yet before these difficulties were overcome.

HMS LONDON Pennant 69
London class cruiser August 1942

Around August 1942, *London* had her scheme simplified and changed to 507c and 507b for easier crew maintenance. Note that the pattern of the 507b is similar to the areas of MS1 previously carried, with B5 eliminated. There were a few changes to the shape of the patterns, but they generally followed the same lines. The decks remained grey. The number of light AA guns had not changed, but those by the front of the bridge were raised up higher for better coverage. Electronics were the same as before, even though better radar types were available. This was the last scheme the ship carried before going into the dockyard in December 1942 for some major changes to her hull and internal structure to finally overcome the overweight stresses caused by her rebuild.

HMS LONDON Pennant 69
London class cruiser early 1943

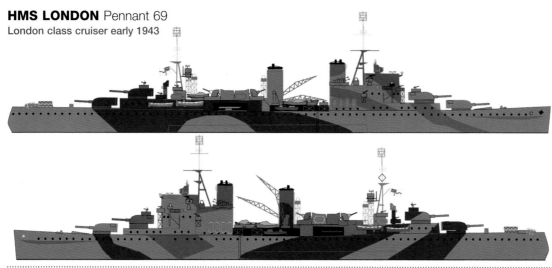

London returned to service after her faults had been corrected and wore an Admiralty design that used G45 light olive overall, with areas of G10 grey and B30 olive. The decks remained 507b grey. The radar lantern was upgraded to Type 273Q. Some countermeasures were also added, including Type 244 IFF on top of the radar lantern. At the mast tops, the Type 279 was replaced by Type 281 radar. Aircraft facilities were removed, but the cranes were retained. The 20mm AA guns were increased to twelve singles, with some on the former catapult deck where some ship's boats were now also stored.

HMS LONDON Pennant 69
London class cruiser 1945

London adopted an Admiralty standard scheme for the last part of World War II, using the familiar MS3 or G45 overall, with a B30 hull-shortening panel. The decks remained dark grey, probably 507b. The AA armament was strengthened as follows. The eight single 20mm guns were retained and eight twin 20mm mounts added. Additionally, she carried four single 40mm Bofors guns. Two of these were normal mounts, but two appear to be Boffins, where a 40mm was placed on a former 20mm powered twin mount. It was intended to replace the two aerials for the Type 281 radar with a single aerial for Type 281B, but this was never carried out. No depth charges can be seen in photographs and it is presumed they were no longer carried or the rack and charges were stowed away.

HMS LONDON Pennant 69
London class cruiser 1949

Cruisers were preferred as flagships on foreign stations and so much had been spent on *London* during her rebuild that she was retained in service and is shown here with overall peacetime 507c. Wood decks were restored. Type 277 radar was added to the foremast. Type 273 was carried for some time and may have been deactivated or used for training. Light AA was reduced. For a time, she carried four single 40mm guns and four twin 20mm guns in addition to the octuple 2pdr mounts, eventually changed to six single 40mm guns plus the octuple 2pdrs. As *London* was not fully air-conditioned, portholes welded over during conversion were reopened to allow ventilation in hot areas. She became flagship on the China Station. At the time of the Yangtze Incident she was hit twenty-three times by Communist Chinese gun batteries, sustaining external damage and fires, while trying to assist the sloop HMS *Amethyst*. On return to the UK it was decided she was not worth the expense of repair, was sold the following year, and scrapped.

HMS SHROPSHIRE Pennant 73
London class cruiser 1930

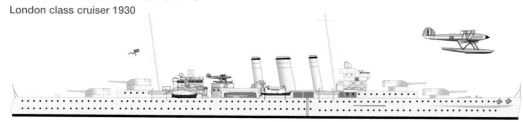

On completion, *Shropshire* went to the Mediterranean Fleet. No catapult was initially installed, but she carried a single Osprey on the intended base. The aircraft was handled by crane only. The ship is shown in overall 507c. This style was for ships in the Mediterranean and, being mostly engaged in showing the flag at various ports, would have been kept in immaculate condition. The wood decks were scrubbed daily to a yellowish-white shade. Just after her trials, she was fitted with an early HACS aft to control her four single 4in AA guns. There was a director on the bridge for the 8in guns, and an emergency rangefinder on the aft control structure as well.

HMS SHROPSHIRE Pennant 73
London class cruiser 1936

During 1936 *Shropshire* was on station off Spain during that country's civil war. She is shown here in MS4a Home Fleet grey with red, white and blue neutrality stripes on 'B' turret. The wood decks remained holystoned, and horizontal metal surfaces were almost certainly in the same colour as the rest of the ship. By this time, her 4in AA armament had been increased to eight singles. Quad 0.5in MG mounts were added on either side of the foremast. Between August and September, she played a major part in operations that evacuated many civilian refugees from Barcelona. During the previous year, *Shropshire* stood by off Ethiopia during the Italian invasion, which almost brought on war between Italy and Great Britain. By 1936 she had received the heavy RIIH catapult and the then-new Seagull V aircraft, which would later be better known as the Walrus.

HMS SHROPSHIRE Pennant 73
London class cruiser August 1941

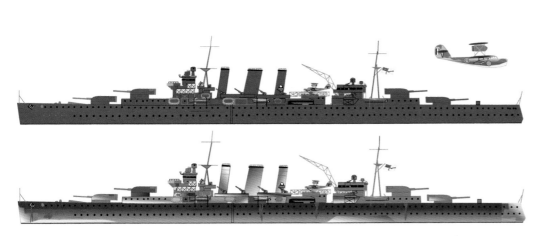

These illustrations show the intended camouflage view and what the ship really looked like after heavy sea service in the Atlantic. At top, *Shropshire* is painted as intended in 507a, which was applied over a previous coat of 507c from 1938. But heavy demands on ships for patrol, fleet work and intercepting blockade-runners left little time to touch up the paintwork and keep it fresh. In the lower illustration she is shown much as she appeared at Scapa Flow in late 1941, after some considerable steaming in all kinds of weather. Not only were there the problems of rust, but the 507a was starting to fade, and areas had peeled off to show the previous coats of 507c and MS4a underneath. Maintenance was a continuing problem for a ship's crew who struggled with corrosive salt effects. Also, if painted and the paint was not given sufficient time to actually set, it become prone to flaking off to show the underneath coats. In some cases, it could flake or corrode right down to the red lead undercoat if not dealt with quickly enough. Swinging on a platform up on the funnels was not practicable at sea, and in wet weather the paint would not take. Ships such as *Shropshire* would eventually have the problem solved by a quick dockyard visit, but the crew often had to chip away the old paint and rusting areas they could reach to get ready. At this time the ship is still armed as in 1936 and had neither radar nor additional light AA added. For a major warship such as this to be unaltered at this date is an indication of how much call there was on them for sea duty.

HMS SHROPSHIRE Pennant 73
London class cruiser 1942

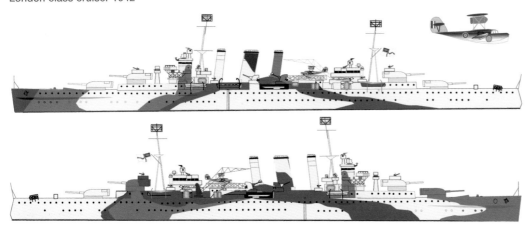

Shropshire underwent a badly needed refit at Chatham from October 1941 until February 1942. The colours 507c, 507a and B5 were applied in an Admiralty disruptive pattern. It is interesting that standard hues were still being used in camouflage patterns, no doubt because they were still available in quantity from reserve stocks, or the pigments required were not in short supply, as with other colours. At this time, the wood decks were still unpainted, but had probably faded to a greyish colour. Radar was added during the latest refit. At the mastheads were aerials for Type 281 radar, and a lantern for Type 273 radar was placed between the bridge and 'A' turret. Type 285 and Type 282 radars for the AA control were added as well. The single 4in AA guns were replaced by four twin mounts. Two single 20mm guns were placed on 'B' turret, a single on 'Y' turret and four others were added as well. Three more single 20mm guns were added later. The quad 0.5in MG mounts were still carried. The aircraft facilities and the Walrus were remained.

HMAS SHROPSHIRE Pennant 73
London class cruiser June 1943

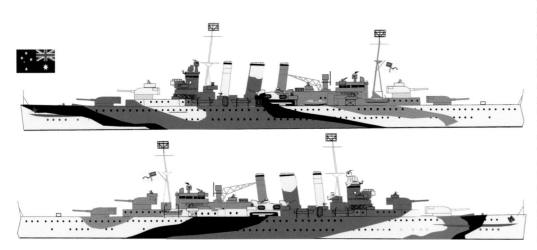

Shropshire underwent another refit starting in November 1942, whilst the Admiralty negotiated handing the ship over to the Royal Australian Navy as a replacement for HMAS *Canberra*, which had been lost in 1942 at the Battle of Savo Island. The Royal Navy had several new cruisers entering service, and manpower problems were starting to be felt, especially for experienced men. Once the decision was made, all aircraft facilities, except the crane, were removed. The quad 0.5in MG mounts and four single 20mm guns were removed, but these were replaced by seven twin 20mm mounts, in addition to the six single 20mm guns still aboard. This would prove insufficient for operations in Pacific waters and was strengthened by the RAN. The torpedo tubes were still in place and would remain until 1945. The radar fit remained the same as previously carried. Due to the need to train her crew, work up, and then proceed to Australian waters, it was October 1943 before the ship could join Task Force 74 ready for action. The Admiralty had given the Australian government and the RAN the opportunity to rename the ship, as *Shropshire* was a county of England and its name had little relationship to the new owners. However, the RAN decided that it was 'bad luck' to rename a ship. This had been done with the three *Apollo* class cruisers, two of which, *Sydney* and *Perth*, had been lost by then. Therefore, the name *Shropshire* was retained, although in Australian service she was usually referred to as 'The Shroppy'.

HMAS SHROPSHIRE Pennant 73
London class cruiser late 1943

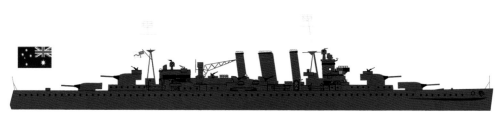

Under Australian control, *Shropshire* was painted overall in an Australian mixed shade known as Chicago blue, an attempt to produce a local paint as close as possible to that used on US warships (US Navy blue 5/N). It had been found that when operating with US ships it was wise to look as much like them as possible in order to avoid friendly fire. Decks and horizontal surfaces were painted blue-grey in US style, but the paint was mixed in Australia for US ships repainting there, and for RAN use as well. The mast tops were white. The 20mm AA guns were recognised as lacking sufficient punch to knock down determined Japanese aircraft, therefore 40mm Bofors guns replaced the previous twin 20mm mounts on 'B' and 'X' turrets. Gradually, more 20mm guns were replaced by single 40mm guns, or they were simply added in addition to the existing AA armament.

HMAS SHROPSHIRE Pennant 73
London class cruiser Leyte Gulf 1944

The US Navy adopted a darker blue for ships in plain camouflage, and Australian warships engaged in operations to liberate the Philippines did the same. It has been claimed that Japanese kamikaze pilots seemed to be drawn to vessels in vivid camouflage schemes, hence many US ships changed to a very plain dark blue overall, so as not to stand out. The claim may or may not have been true, but Australian ships engaged in the invasion seemed to suffer more than their share of suicide attacks, anyway. The addition of single 40mm Bofors guns was increased, owing to the difficulty of knocking down a determined suicide attacker. Eventually, all the twin 20mm mounts were replaced with single Bofors guns, as they took up the same amount of space and the 40mm not only had better hitting power, but also longer range. The torpedo tubes were still carried at this time.

HMAS SHROPSHIRE Pennant 73
London class cruiser mid-1945

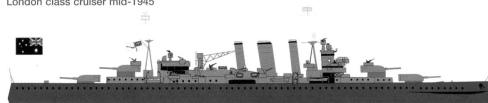

Shropshire adopted the Admiralty standard scheme in mid-1945 with prospects of serving with the British Pacific Fleet (BPF) looming. The previous US Navy-type schemes were dropped in favour of something more compatible with the current Royal Navy standards. In this instance, *Shropshire* wore MS2 on the hull and G45 on the superstructure. The octuple 2pdr mounts were retained, but all twin 20mm mounts were replaced with single 40mm Bofors guns, for a total of eleven such weapons. The ship supported Australian landings at Balikpapan in June 1945, and was sent to Japan to represent Australia at the surrender in August. She then helped repatriate POWs and return combat troops home to Australia.

HMAS SHROPSHIRE Pennant 73
London class cruiser 1947

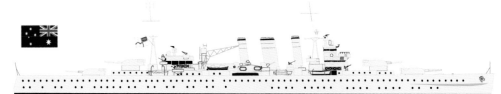

Shropshire remained with the Royal Australian Navy post-war, seeing service first in securing ex-Japanese bases and then trooping duties. The AA mounts were removed from turret tops. The multiple 2pdr mounts were retained, along with six single 40mm AA guns. Some sections of the ship were deactivated while acting as a training ship, and she is shown here in that role. A peacetime scheme of overall 507c was applied and the wood decks restored through the removal of wartime paint. Some plated-over portholes were also restored to help with conditions in hot climates. The US radar was removed. Although paid off in 1949, the ship was retained in reserve while the situation in China and Korea was under observation. By 1954 she had fallen into a sorry state of repair and was considered a very ugly, rust-streaked site in Sydney harbour. In 1955 *Shropshire* was towed away for scrapping, being one of the last of her type to be removed from the naval lists.

NORFOLK CLASS CRUISERS

HMS DORSETSHIRE Pennant 40

Norfolk class cruiser 1935

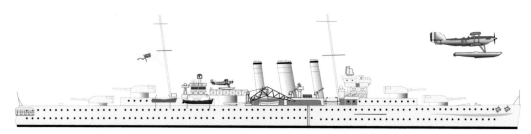

This class received a few improvements, owing to experience with the earlier groups; one of these was the lowering of the bridge. *Dorsetshire* is shown here in 507c overall while serving on the African Station from 1933 to 1935. Ships employed on overseas stations were vital to showing the flag and the power of Great Britain. The wooden decks would have been scrubbed almost white and the paintwork continually attended to, in order to make a good impression on colonial representatives and the people of each colony. In this illustration, quad 0.5in MG mounts have been placed on either side before the second funnel. Most other County class had them in front of the fore funnel. There are still single 4in guns fitted and single 2pdr AA guns each side of the bridge at boat-deck level. The crane was placed aft of the third funnel, rather than by the aft control tower, and when not in use was usually swung forward. A short EIIIH catapult was fitted, and a Fairey III three-seat reconnaissance aircraft was carried. An admiral's stern walk was included, on the presumption that these ships would be cruiser flagships.

HMS DORSETSHIRE Pennant 40

Norfolk class cruiser 1940

By the time of the failed Dakar operation, this ship had been painted overall 507b. The wood decks remained unpainted, and horizontal metal surfaces were most probably the same 507b as the rest of the ship. The previous heavy black topping at the waterline had been painted out. Just prior to World War II, her single 4in AA guns had been replaced by twin mounts that were spread further apart. Octuple 2pdr mounts were added each side of the aft control area and she now carried two HACS, but as yet without radar. The bridge was also slightly enlarged. The light catapult was replaced by a heavier one that could deploy the new Walrus amphibian.

HMS DORSETSHIRE Pennant 40

Norfolk class cruiser
27 May 1941

This was an unofficial scheme adopted in 1941. The intent was to give a false impression of the ship in both size and type by disguising the length of the hull and the number of funnels. The turret tops were painted in the same colour as their sides. To take advantage of available paint colours, 507c and 507b were used. This was an easy way to provide a camouflage over the base of the 1940 507b scheme. Wood decks remained unpainted. The 4in mounts were protected by splinter shields. No radar was fitted at this time. This was her appearance when she torpedoed and finished off the German battleship *Bismarck*, which had been crippled by HMS *Rodney* and HMS *King George V*.

HMS DORSETSHIRE Pennant 40

Norfolk class cruiser 1942

Dorsetshire is shown here in her final appearance when sunk by Japanese aircraft in 1942. Prior to departure for the Far East, she received nine single 20mm AA guns. The single 2pdrs were removed, but the quad 0.5in MG mounts were retained. The camouflage remained almost exactly the same, except for the usual minor alterations during repainting. The scheme was also well worn and fading by the time of her sinking and I have shown her with rust and areas of fading paint. The decks remained as before, and the turret tops still matched the sides. Type 279 radar was fitted at both mast-heads in early 1942. Note that, as with many other ships, the lower ports were welded over due to damage-control requirements.

HMS **NORFOLK** Pennant 78
Norfolk class cruiser 1933

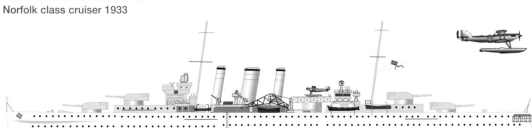

Norfolk served with the Atlantic Fleet, later known as the Home Fleet, for the first two years of her career and then went to the West Indies. She is shown here wearing an overall scheme of MS4a Home Fleet grey, but with a white hull. Decks were, of course, scrubbed wood, except for metal surfaces. She was fitted as a flagship like her sister ship *Dorsetshire*. Although originally completed without a catapult, one had been fitted, along with the new quad 0.5in MG mounts, prior to her deployment. A Fairey III aircraft was carried and another could be stowed on deck, if required. However, usually only one was carried. Only four single 4in AA guns were mounted, and 2pdr AA guns were limited to two each side of the bridge at the 'B' turret level. The HACS aft was carried from completion.

HMS **NORFOLK** Pennant 78
Norfolk class cruiser 1937

By the time *Norfolk* was deployed to the China Station she had been modified, having octuple 2pdr mounts added and her single 4in AA guns replaced by twin mounts. A heavier catapult enabled her to deploy the new Walrus amphibian during her assignment to that station. In 1935 she transferred to the East Indies Station and then returned home. At some point, the buff funnels were painted dark grey, but the ship remained white until war broke out in Europe, after which she was repainted in 507c overall, and the national markings on 'B' turret were painted out. The turret tops appear to have been the same colour as the sides.

HMS **NORFOLK** Pennant 78
Norfolk class cruiser 1939

Having been called home for a refit, *Norfolk* was still in dockyard hands when war was declared, and was painted in overall 507b. This also applied to all horizontal metal surfaces, but the wood decks remained unpainted. No other changes were made, and the ship proceeded to join the 8th Cruiser Squadron patrolling the Denmark Strait for German warships trying to break out, and for merchant ships trying to reach German ports. She later became flagship of the 1st Cruiser Squadron operating out of Scapa Flow with the Home Fleet, but was damaged by a German air attack and forced to go into the Clyde for repairs.

HMS **NORFOLK** Pennant 78
Norfolk class cruiser mid-1940

By mid-1940, the Admiralty had issued instructions that all ships were to apply camouflage utilising paint available. However, there were no instructions on what sort of schemes were to be applied, which left it up to the ships' officers to design an appropriate scheme. The one worn by *Norfolk* was extremely distinctive. The application of 507a on the hull shows the general outline of a merchant ship, possibly a tanker, but is deliberately shorter than the actual length of the ship. The pattern used Royal Navy black, 507c, 507a, and a shade a little lighter than 507b, which was probably mixed for the purpose. This scheme was worn on both sides of the ship. During her bomb repairs, the rather useless UP (Unrotated Projectile) rocket AA weapon was placed on both 'A' and 'X' turrets. Protection was placed around the 4in twin mounts, but no other alterations were made to the armament.

HMS NORFOLK Pennant 78
Norfolk class cruiser May 1941

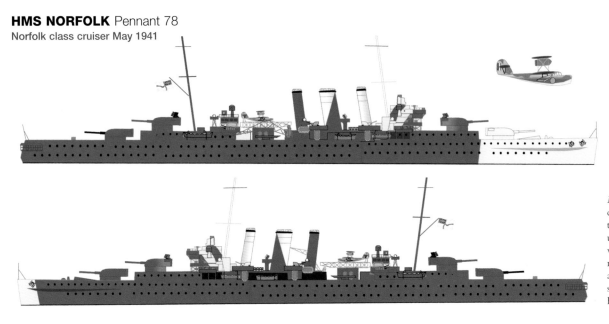

Norfolk had the most complicated part of her previous camouflage painted out by 1941, and only remnants of the hull-shortening scheme still remained. The colours used were 507a and 507c. At this time the wood decks were painted in a dark blue shade, and all horizontal metal surfaces in 507a. The foremast was painted white and the mainmast 507a. This was the appearance of the ship at the time of the *Bismarck* action. The armament had not changed and radar was not yet fitted.

HMS NORFOLK Pennant 78
Norfolk class cruiser September 1941

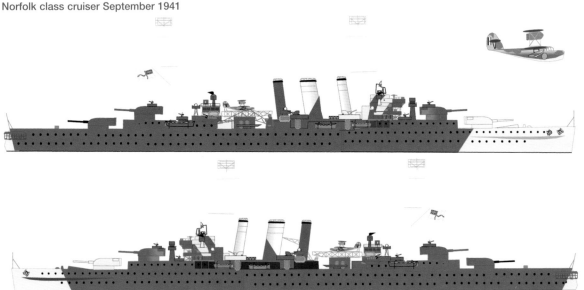

Norfolk was in refit from July to September 1941, and had a few subtle changes to the general layout of her camouflage scheme, but still within the concept of making the ship look shorter. All masts were now white and the decks remained dark blue. Horizontal metal surfaces were possibly 507b. The quad 0.5in MG mounts were removed and six single 20mm AA guns added. The 20mm guns were placed with one on top of 'B' turret, one on top of 'X' turret, one on each side of bridge and on each side aft of the rear control position. The UP mounts were removed altogether, along with the original single 2pdr guns. Type 281 radar was fitted to the mast tops and Type 273 before the bridge, in a position that was found to be very restricted in its coverage. The main director received Type 274 radar and the HACS were fitted with Type 285 radar. There was no provision for Type 282 radar on the 2pdr directors during this refit. Note that the admiral's stern walk was retained.

HMS NORFOLK Pennant 78
Norfolk class cruiser June 1943

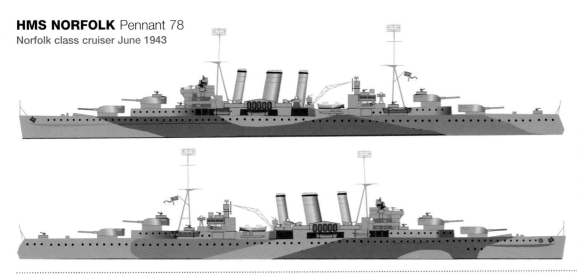

In 1943 *Norfolk* received a refit and returned to service in an Admiralty-designed scheme that utilised B55 as the base, with MS3 and B30. However, the scheme was on the hull only and did not carry up onto the superstructure. The decks remained painted, but it is unclear if they were dark grey, or the shade of blue previously used. The Type 273 radar was moved from the very restricted position in front of the bridge to the top of the aft control position, where it replaced the older HACS. As there were HACS with Type 285 radar on either side of the bridge, coverage was obviously considered to be adequate. Directors for the 2pdr AA guns were fitted with Type 282 radar and placed behind the aft funnel. The number of 20mm guns was increased to twelve singles, two of which were carried side by side on 'B' turret.

HMS NORFOLK Pennant 78
Norfolk class cruiser December 1943

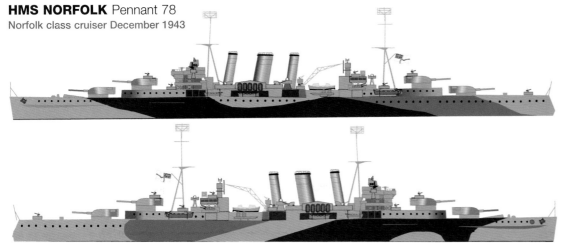

These images show the appearance of *Norfolk* when she engaged the German battleship *Scharnhorst* at the Battle of the North Cape. The overall shade remained B55, but 507a replaced MS3, and B15 replaced B30. The scheme was otherwise the same in layout, with only minor changes, as previously shown. All aircraft facilities, except the crane, were removed, with the area taken up by ship's boats. Between the twin 4in AA mounts, she carried five upright Carley floats in a single row. This is a strong recognition point when examining old photographs, because she was the only cruiser of the County class to carry such a cluster of rafts. Most of her service at this time was in northern waters and, in particular, covering convoys to Russia. The number of 20mm AA guns remained at twelve singles.

HMS NORFOLK Pennant 78
Norfolk class cruiser November 1944

Norfolk was damaged in the Battle of North Cape, during which the German battle-ship *Scharnhorst* was sunk. During repairs she was upgraded and was out of service from January–November 1944. On re-entering service, she adopted an Admiralty standard camouflage pattern of MS3 overall with a panel of MS2 on the hull. During the rebuild, 'X' turret was removed and replaced by two quad 2pdr mounts. The octuple 2pdr mounts were also replaced by quads, while two more quad 2pdr mounts were added between the first and second funnels. Two single 20mm were removed, leaving ten singles, but eleven twin 20mm mounts were added, giving a light AA armament of thirty-two 20mm barrels and twenty-four 2pdr barrels. Type 281 radar was replaced by Type 281B, which only needed an aerial on one mast. Type 293 radar was added on the forward starfish, Type 277 on the aft control position and Type 274, for barrage and blind fire, on the bridge front. Type 273 radar was removed. Type 650 missile-jamming equipment was also fitted. After the rebuild, *Norfolk* resumed duties in northern waters.

HMS NORFOLK Pennant 78
Norfolk class cruiser
December 1945

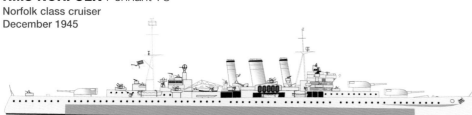

Norfolk remained in service after the end of World War II, cruising in the Mediterranean, where she visited various hot spots left over from the war. She dressed in overall 507c, and for a time carried a light blue panel. However, the panel was removed after 1945, leaving her in peacetime 507c. The previously painted wood decks were restored back to plain wood. In December 1945 all the single 20mm AA guns were removed and replaced by single 40mm Bofors guns. The Royal Navy had been keen to keep the most recently upgraded heavy cruisers in service for as long as possible, but post-war economic measures meant that most were placed in reserve and scrapped soon after the war. *Norfolk* lasted in active service a little longer than most, but she was finally sold for scrapping in 1950.

YORK CLASS CRUISER

HMS YORK Pennant 90
York class cruiser
1931

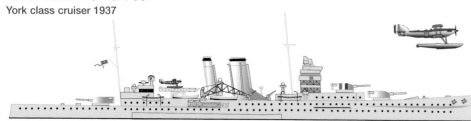

York spent most of her early years on overseas stations, where she wore the usual white hull with buff funnels. However, on occasion she appears to have worn a dark grey upper works and funnels. As built, the after deck was open to the front of the forward funnel. No catapult was fitted, but provisions were made for one, and it was to be fitted later. Unlike the County class, *York* was built with only three twin 8in turrets, as a cost-saving measure, but mounted the usual four single 4in AA guns. Single 2pdr guns were fitted each side of the bridge at shelter-deck level, making the initial AA armament very weak indeed. Triple torpedo tubes were carried, again to save weight, but the protection level for vital areas was actually superior to most of the County class ships.

HMS YORK Pennant 90
York class cruiser 1937

During the Abyssinia Crisis, *York* adopted an MS4a Home Fleet grey colour and wore nationality stripes on 'B' turret. By this time, the forecastle plating was extended aft to the torpedo tubes to provide more accommodation and keep the aft areas drier. The single 2pdr AA guns had been removed, and quad 0.5in MG mounts fitted on either side of the bridge at shelter deck level. A catapult was installed, and she initially carried a Fairey III aircraft. The ship remained in this state at the start of World War II. *York* was assigned to the America and West Indies Station and was immediately engaged in convoy duties. The neutrality markings were painted out at some point, and she might have adopted 507b or 507a overall, but the wood decks remained unpainted. A Walrus aircraft replaced the Fairey III as soon as one was available.

HMS YORK Pennant 90
York class cruiser October 1939

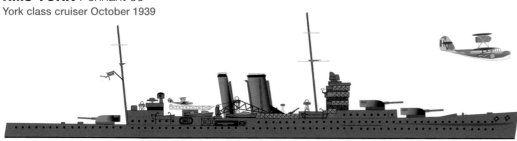

York adopted a very dark shade of grey at the start of World War II, when she was sent to patrol the North Atlantic for enemy shipping. The colour was most likely 507a, which would have been readily available. The wood decks remained unpainted, but horizontal metal surfaces were almost certainly 507a. Note that splinter mats were applied in various places to protect vital areas of the bridge, but also to the quad 0.5in machine gun positions and the single 4in AA mounts. No extra AA had been added. By this time the ship had been equipped with a Walrus amphibian aircraft.

HMS YORK Pennant 90
York class cruiser 1940

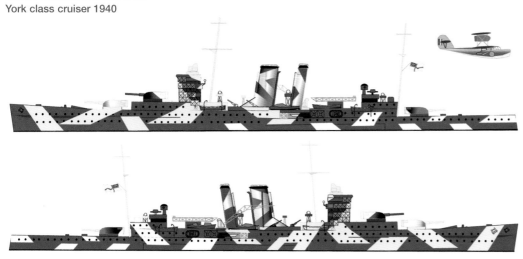

In 1940 the Admiralty issued orders for ships to adopt camouflage utilising the paint available to them, but gave no instructions on how this was to be done. That left the decision with the ship's officers and, in this case, the simplest decision was to use a scheme similar to that of *Devonshire*. Irregular areas of 507c were applied over the existing 507a. The decks, however, remained as plain wood, or if metal, painted 507a. Although at first glance it might seem that the resulting scheme was the same on both sides, this is not correct and it did vary. It must be remembered that someone had to plan the scheme, along with measurements, and then it would have to be chalked onto the side of the ship, so the crew could fill in the areas of 507c. In the lower illustration I have shown *York* based on photographs of her at Suda Bay, just before she was sunk. Once again the pattern is generally the same, but there are variations to the size, shape and positioning of some of the light areas. The masts were pale grey. Turret tops were very dark, probably 507a, but possibly even black. Note the 4in gun positions were given protective plating. Just prior to her loss, two 20mm AA guns were added. The mount on top of 'B' turret had no protection, but the mount on the quarterdeck had an octagonal protective zareba. There also appears to be a MG mount at the front of the bridge top. This was probably an unofficial addition. Note the external degaussing cable as protection against magnetic mines. I have been unable to find any reliable photographs of the port side immediately prior to the ship's loss to Italian explosive motor boats. Attempts made to save her proved impossible. The ship was stripped of important equipment and scuttled with explosive charges that left her a total loss and not worth raising when the wreck fell into enemy hands.

HMS YORK Pennant 90
York class cruiser 1941

EXETER CLASS CRUISERS

HMS EXETER Pennant 68

Exeter class cruiser
November 1932

Exeter is shown on the West Indies Station in the traditional white and buff. There were patches of wood deck around each of the 4in guns, but the metal decks around the catapult area were a mid-grey. Unlike her half-sister *York*, her funnels were upright, and the older style bridge was replaced by a modern aerodynamic bridge, inspired by that of the battleship *Nelson*. The new bridge had a bulletproof roof over the compass platform. The catapult arrangement was unique. Two EHII catapults were angled out into a 'V' shape and joined at the rear. This enabled the ship to launch aircraft to port or starboard. Two aircraft were carried. As with *York*, this ship was an attempt to produce a less expensive 8in gun cruiser, and savings in various areas did allow for a higher standard of armour protection than the County class ships. Six 8in guns in twin turrets provided the main armament and the AA provisions were the same as the larger eight-gun ships, with four single 4in guns and four single 2pdr guns.

HMS EXETER Pennant 68

Exeter class cruiser
November 1937

The Abyssinia Crisis resulted in *Exeter* being transferred to the Mediterranean and then to patrols off East Africa. She is shown here in MS4a overall; the decks, both wood and metal, remained as previously noted. However, her turrets all had the letters 'EX' painted on them for aerial identification. Armament remained the same, except for the single 2pdr guns being replaced by quad 0.5in MG mounts abreast the bridge. By this time, a Walrus aircraft was assigned. The twin catapult arrangement was retained, along with the single crane, which also doubled for handling some of the larger ship's boats.

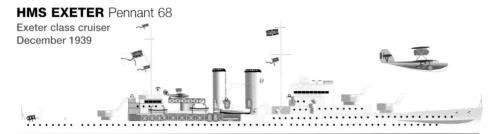

HMS EXETER Pennant 68

Exeter class cruiser
December 1939

Exeter played a major role in the Battle of the River Plate in December 1939, when with *Ajax* and *Achilles*, she fought *Admiral Graf Spee*, armed with 11in guns, as well as 5.9in and 4.1in guns. *Exeter* used her 8in guns to great effect, but was severely damaged. She is shown here in 507c, which all British ships in the action wore. In battle, she flew several ensigns, including a Union Jack, in World War I custom, to avoid confusion with the similar German ensign. One was a huge silk flag sewn for her by the women of Exeter. Badly battered, *Exeter* was forced to break off action and head to the Falkland Islands for emergency repairs. She later returned to the UK for all damage to be rectified. The three turret tops had the letters 'EX' in black for aerial recognition.

HMS EXETER Pennant 68

Exeter class cruiser November 1941–2

Exeter underwent extensive repairs and did not re-enter service until March 1941. At this time, she appeared in a mid-grey that was probably 507b. Metal decks seem to be the same shade, but the wood decks were unpainted. The single 4in AA guns were replaced with twin mounts that were widely spaced. The torpedo tubes were moved forward, so as not to obstruct the ammunition lifts for the aft twin 4in mounts. Lower ports were plated over to help with damage control and numerous Carley floats fitted. Type 279 radar was fitted. An additional HACS was placed on the rear of the bridge, which necessitated it being slightly lengthened. Tripod masts were fitted to carry the weight of the radar. Octuple 2pdr AA mounts were added by the forward end of the aft control area and positions for two single 20mm guns fitted, one on 'B' turret and one on 'Y' turret. However, these were not available and she carried twin machine guns, probably Lewis guns, instead. The 20mm weapons were not fitted prior to her loss. Tubs for two others were fitted abreast the mainmast, but remained empty. *Exeter* was sunk after the Battle of the Java Sea when, already damaged and limping for safety, she was attacked by a superior Japanese surface force.

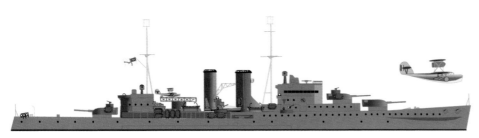

CONTENTS

LEANDER CLASS CRUISERS

HMS LEANDER Pennant 75
Leander class cruiser 1934

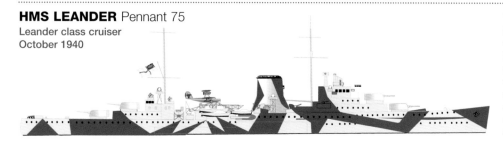

HMS LEANDER Pennant 75
Leander class cruiser 1937–9

HMS LEANDER Pennant 75
Leander class cruiser
October 1940

HMNZS LEANDER Pennant 75
Leander class cruiser
June 1941

When completed in 1933, *Leander* lacked some equipment, but by 1934 this had been made good. She was serving in the Home Fleet at the time and is shown dressed overall in MS4a. Wood decks were scrubbed, while the deck forward of the anchor winches was grey metal. This class introduced enclosed twin 6in turrets for all main armament. The heavy AA armament was the standard four single 4in guns, as carried by most Royal Navy cruisers built after World War I. The light AA armament was considered quite strong for the period, with three quad 0.5in MG mounts, and there were plans to fit two quad 2pdr mounts as well. Two quad 21in torpedo tube mounts were also carried. It was intended that the ship would carry the Fairey IIIF floatplane, but the much lighter Osprey floatplane was issued instead. Two aircraft could be carried, with one stowed on the catapult and one athwartships on the aft superstructure. However, they actually only carried a single aircraft.

In 1937 *Leander* was loaned to New Zealand, but retained her HMS prefix, as New Zealand had not yet established its own navy. She is shown here in overall 507c, as worn by all other ships on the New Zealand and Australian stations. Prior to transfer, the single 4in guns were removed and twin 4in mounts installed, with splinter-proof protection. During the refit, the quad 0.5in MG mounts previously carried opposite the bridge were moved to the aft deckhouse. This was a concentration of weapons, which could be knocked out by a single hit. The catapult was strengthened to carry the new Seagull V aircraft, later known as the Walrus; the crane was repositioned on the centreline, and the ship's boats had to be rearranged. *Leander* was in this condition when World War II commenced, when she was engaged in covering troop movements across the Indian Ocean and patrols against enemy shipping and raiders.

While visiting Alexandria, *Leander* received a camouflage scheme with a base of 507c, and irregular patterns of 507a over it. Both sides were painted the same. This was known as the Mediterranean style. The decks, wood and metal, appear to have been painted with 507a at this time. There were no armament changes in 1940, although there appear to be MG mounts on each side of the bridge. When ships were busy, it was common to fit new equipment over more than one port call. Thus gun tubs, and even weapon stands, could be added one time, with the weapons added later when they became available. Hence in this illustration the gun tub aft is empty, and those opposite the bridge only mount machine guns. No radar was fitted at this time.

Other alterations took place at Alexandria in June 1941. The catapult was removed and a quad 2pdr mount placed on the centreline in its place. No 20mm guns were available, although gun tubs were ready for them. The camouflage pattern was starting to show signs of fading. The exact lines of the scheme varied, as the ship was painted and repainted. The area at the bow was the most different. Strikingly different is that 'A' turret was now painted in 507a. The decks remained 507a, but were showing signs of wear. After serving in the Red Sea and Indian Ocean, *Leander* transferred to the Mediterranean. She then proceeded to New Zealand for service in the Pacific. While in the Indian Ocean, she sank the Italian raider *Ramb 1* off Bombay. These ships carried a depth-charge rack aft, along with a small number of charges – usually six but this was increased to fifteen in 1940. These were for defensive purposes only, even though the very efficient Type 132 Asdic was carried.

HMNZS LEANDER Pennant 75
Leander class cruiser October 1942

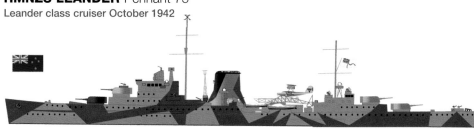

On return to New Zealand, the catapult and air facilities were reinstalled and the quad 2pdr mount on the catapult stand removed. Five single 20mm AA guns were added, one on 'B' turret, one each side of the bridge, and two on the quarterdeck. Only the centreline 0.5in machine gun remained. The 507c was replaced by 507b; decks were 507a. Turret tops were painted as follows, 'A': 507b, 'B': 507a, 'X': 507b and 'Y': 507a. A New Zealand-built air-warning radar, Type SW, was fitted between the bridge and funnel on a tall lattice. Gunnery radar on the director was a New Zealand-designated SWG type. British Type 291 radar was on the foremast.

HMNZS LEANDER Pennant 75
Leander class cruiser early 1943

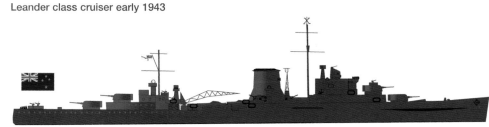

A dark blue scheme was adopted in early 1943 and the decks remained dark grey, but this paint scheme had a tendency to fade badly. Type 273 radar was fitted off-centre aft of the crane. Aircraft facilities were permanently removed and occupied by ship's boats, which were handled by the crane. All quad 0.5in MG mounts were removed and nine single 20mm guns fitted. The tubs intended for 2pdrs only contained single 20mm. The poor AA armament is surprising. The ship was engaged in a fierce action during the Battle of Kolombangara and hit by a Japanese 24in torpedo. She proceeded to the USA where final repairs and reconstruction took until August 1945.

HMS LEANDER Pennant 75
Leander class cruiser November 1945

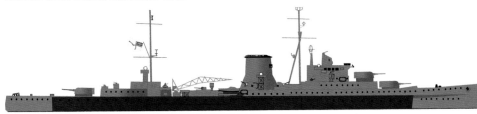

Repairs were finally completed in August 1945. A modernisation similar to other British cruisers took place. Turrets were reduced to three. 'X' turret was replaced with a power-operated twin 20mm mount and two single 20mm guns. Two more power-operated 20mm mounts were added on the front of the aft deckhouse. Amidships US quad 40mm mounts were added and two single 20mm forward. HACS directors with Type 285 were added each side of the bridge. Radar Type 277 radar replaced the HACS director on the bridge. Type 273 radar was removed plus SW radar and its lattice mast. Type 293Q radar was added. Other electronics were fitted. The overall colour was G45, with a hull panel of B15.

HMS LEANDER Pennant 75
Leander class cruiser 1946

Leander continued in service immediately post-war in MS4a Home Fleet grey. Deck colours are not known, but probably reverted to plain wood. A typical peacetime black boot topping was painted at the waterline. All 20mm guns were removed. The previous 'X' turret position now contained three single 40mm Mk III Bofors guns and others were mounted on each side of the bridge. The quad 40mm mounts were removed and replaced by twin 40mm Mk V mounts. The electronic suite remained the same. *Leander* was finally sold for scrap in 1949.

HMS NEPTUNE Pennant 20
Leander class cruiser 1932

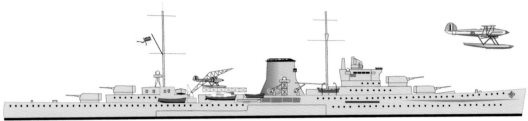

Neptune was completed without her HACS or quad 0.5in MG mounts, although provision had been made for them. Her only AA armament was the four 4in single guns under local control. However, she almost certainly carried Lewis guns, as did most Royal Navy ships. She is shown here wearing MS4a for her first commission with the Home Fleet. The foredeck around the anchor chains and winches was painted grey, probably the same shade. The wood decks were scrubbed wood. There were areas of wood around the 4in AA guns. An Osprey floatplane was carried.

HMS NEPTUNE Pennant 20
Leander class cruiser 1937–9

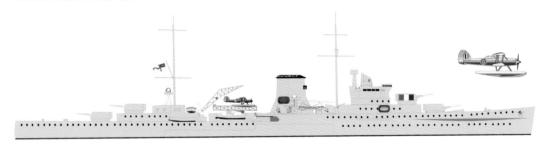

Neptune is shown here wearing MS4a overall. The foredeck around the anchor chains and winches was still painted grey. The wood decks were as before. She wore national identity colours on 'B' turret at this time, but they were removed when war broke out. The size of the black boot topping was reduced. The ship had her HACS placed on the bridge. Surprisingly, no quad 0.5in MG mounts were shipped. As part of the 6th Cruiser Squadron in the South Atlantic, she intercepted two German ships, *Inn* and *Adolph Woermann*, and took part in the hunt for the *Admiral Graf Spee*. She went to the Western Mediterranean, bombarding Bardia, and was at the Battle of Punto Silo. *Neptune* sank an enemy tanker when sent to the Eastern Mediterranean. She was then recalled to the Atlantic to search for the German cruiser *Admiral Scheer*.

HMS NEPTUNE Pennant 20
Leander class cruiser May 1941

Having seen considerable service, *Neptune* was recalled to the UK for a refit and emerged in a four-colour Admiralty light disruptive scheme. Shades used were MS4a as the base with B5 and B6 plus MS2 to provide a light but mottled effect. Schemes such as this were fine in theory, but took little account of how much time they would take for a busy crew to maintain. During her refit, she received three quad 0.5in MG mounts; one was on top of 'B' turret and the other two on the aft deckhouse. Three single 2pdr guns were also installed, one each side of the bridge at deck level and one at the rear of the aft deck-house. There was a large, but empty, gun tub on each side of the bridge, which was possibly intended to receive a quad 2pdr mount, but this was never fitted. The single 4in guns were removed and replaced with twin mounts, as well as some of the plating being carried further aft from the forecastle. At the mast tops she received Type 281 radar. For gunnery control, she added Type 285 radar on the HACS and Type 284 radar on the main gun director. On resuming service, she helped in the hunt for enemy supply ships intended for the German battleship *Bismarck*, during which she torpedoed and sank *Gonzenheim*.

HMS NEPTUNE Pennant 20
Leander class cruiser July 1941

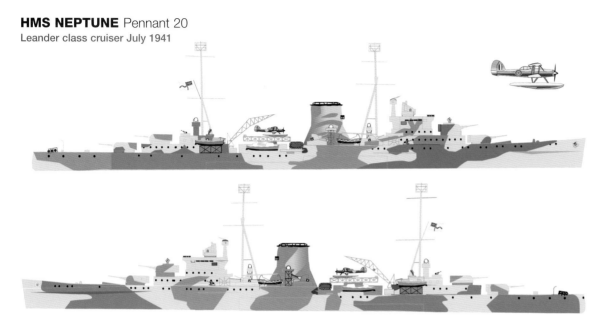

The previous camouflage scheme proved too difficult to maintain and was reduced to a simpler three-colour pattern using MS4a, B5 and B6. At this time she was serving in the Mediterranean, where the last two colours were difficult to find. So it could be that the crew was using up paint supplied during the May refit. The usual schemes for ships in the Eastern Mediterranean were 507c and 507a, which were in plentiful supply at Alexandria. According to records, no changes were made to the armament or electronics of this ship after her UK refit. Although some sources state that the three quad 0.5in MG mounts were removed and replaced by 2pdr guns, that is apparently an error. The ship had neither before the early 1941 refit at Chatham.

HMS NEPTUNE Pennant 20
Leander class cruiser December 1941

In late 1941, traces of the old schemes still remained, but now there were only two colours: 507a and MS4a. But it is possible that the MS4a had been replaced by 507c. The decks appear to have been painted grey. There are no records, and photographs are few and not very clear. Once again the ship was extremely active and was transferred to join the famous Force K at Malta. These ships comprised cruisers and destroyers that harassed Axis supply lines across the Mediterranean, usually in night actions and with great daring. However, on 19 December 1941 *Neptune* ran onto a mine-field, detonating one mine, and eventually three more as she drifted out of control. Realising the great peril for any rescuers, the ship sent a signal for all ships to stand clear, as the minefield was obviously an extensive one. *Neptune* eventually sank and only one man survived the loss of this ship.

HMS ORION Pennant 85
Leander class cruiser 1937

Orion was on the Americas Station in 1937, wearing an overall scheme of 507c, with natural wood decks and mid-grey horizontal metal surfaces, except for the turret tops, which were 507c. As completed, she had four single 4in AA guns, but under the programme to have these changed for twins, only two were available, so for some time she only carried one set of twin 4in mounts per side. Note that at this time 4in mounts were not provided with splinter protection. The quad 0.5in MG mounts were available and she received one on top of the aft control position, as well as two on the forward edge of the aft deckhouse. The aircraft carried by this ship was intended to be either a Fairey Seal or an Osprey, but by 1937 she was equipped with the new Fairey Seafox. She remained on this station until the outbreak of war, when she was transferred to the Mediterranean Fleet.

HMS ORION Pennant 85
Leander class cruiser 1940

By late 1940 *Orion* was still with the Mediterranean Fleet and wore a camouflage scheme applied in Alexandria. The shades available in quantity on that station were 507a and 507c, from which a rather wavy pattern was produced. Ships based in this war zone often designed their own camouflage schemes and used whatever was available at the dockyard. Decks were in a dark shade, which was probably 507b, or a mix to something similar. At this time, she not only had all her 4in AA guns, but they also had splinter protection. The light AA remained the same as before in theory, but many ships of this fleet made use of captured Italian Breda heavy machine guns or 20mm weapons. There would probably have been one or two of these weapons on board. Because of the heavy air threat, it was also common to utilise the Lewis guns in the ship's armoury for additional AA defence. As *Orion* had not received a heavy catapult, the aircraft carried remained a Fairey Seafox. Type 132 Asdic was carried. *Orion* was at the Battle of Matapan and took part in many actions.

HMS ORION Pennant 85
Leander class cruiser 1942

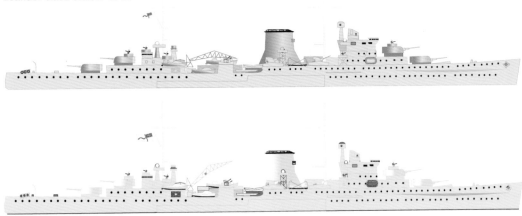

Orion suffered extremely serious damage in the Mediterranean during the evacuation of Crete, even losing one forward turret. The ship was made safe to travel to Simonstown, South Africa, where further seaworthiness repairs were made to enable the ship to steam to the United States for repairs. It could be that during the Simonstown work, or in the US, that the previous camouflage was painted out. But by the completion of repairs, she proceeded to the UK in a mid-tone that could be a shade of grey or of light Mountbatten pink. It is possible this was MS4a or a temporary application of a US shade of grey, but the actual tone would suit either the pink or grey scheme. The above two illustrations are theoretical only, and allow the reader to see how the ship looked in tone, but with two different possibilities. During the repairs in the US, the AA armament was increased and the old quad MG mounts removed. But radar was not installed, although provision was made for where it would go. She then proceeded to the UK to finish the work.

HMS ORION Pennant 85
Leander class cruiser April 1942

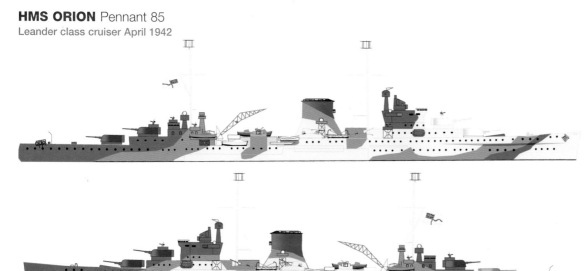

After completing the major repair work at Mare Island in the US, *Orion* returned to the UK for the outfitting of electronics and other equipment at Devonport. *Orion* also received a new three-tone camouflage scheme using a base of 507c, with areas of 507a and MS3. The decks remained 507a. There was still a black waterline, but it was very narrow so as not to affect the camouflage. The masts were either white or very light grey. Other changes included the removal of all quad 0.5in MG mounts and the addition of quad 2pdr mounts, as well as seven single 20mm AA guns. The catapult was removed, along with the aircraft and other aircraft facilities, but the crane was retained to handle the boats and loading of stores. Type 284 and Type 285 gunnery radars were added, along with Type 279 radar with the aerials on the mastheads. At the time of fitting, Type 279 radar was already being replaced by better sets, such as Type 281, but it may be that none of the improved sets were available. After the refit was completed in April 1942, the ship returned to the Mediterranean.

HMS ORION Pennant 85
Leander class cruiser late 1942

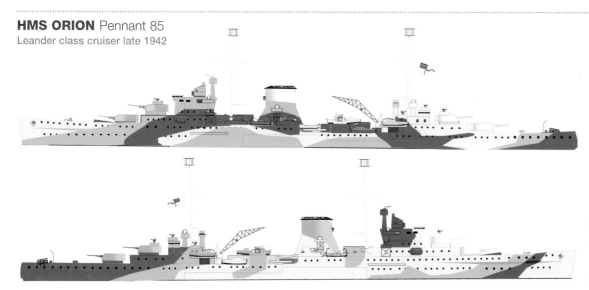

Like so many ships, the camouflage scheme applied to *Orion* changed during repainting. MS3 paint was most likely not available in quantity in the Mediterranean, so instead the scheme used MS4a with 507a and the usual 507c base colour. These diagrams were prepared from photographs of the ship taken just prior to changing to a two-colour pattern. Note that one can see many of the remnant areas of the original scheme applied in the UK, even if they have been painted over into another shade. The colour of the decks appears to be the same as before. All armament and electronics remained the same. *Orion* took part in the invasion of Sicily, Calabria, Anzio and Salerno, and was then ordered home to provide support for the Normandy invasion.

HMS ORION Pennant 85
Leander class cruiser 1944

Orion is shown here wearing her D-Day scheme, with a MS3 upper works and a hull in MS2. Having been at many of the Mediterranean landings to provide support, she was brought back to UK waters for the landings on the coast of Normandy. She appears off Gold Beach in several photographs, firing her guns at shore targets. There had been no changes in her armament at all since her post-damage refit, but IFF and missile jammers were added to most ships used in Operation Neptune, and *Orion* was probably no exception. Her stay in those waters was relatively brief, and she soon returned to the Mediterranean for the landings in the south of France.

HMS ORION Pennant 85
Leander class cruiser 1945

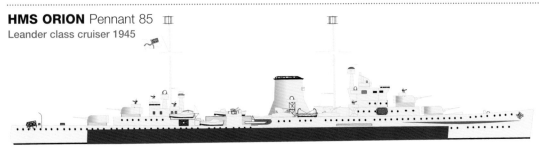

Orion changed over to a new scheme in late 1945. It comprised 507c for the upper works and hull, with a B20 hull panel. The deck apparently remained grey throughout the rest of the war. Mediterranean operations included the reoccupation of Athens, bombardments in the Aegean, and then the Ligurian coast, before the war ended. Because of severe damage suffered during the war, she was not selected for the post-war fleet and instead, in 1946, was allocated to experiments to determine the effect of explosives on modern vessels. At the conclusion of these tests she was sold for scrap and broken up during 1949–50.

HMS ACHILLES Pennant 70
Leander class cruiser 1939

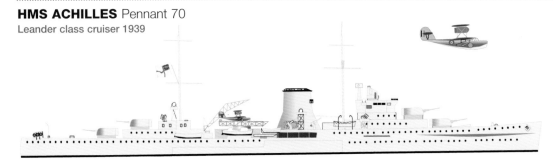

Achilles completed trials in 1931, then proceeded to New Zealand to become part of the NZ squadron. The prefix HMS remained, as the Royal New Zealand Navy was not yet founded. There is an overall paint scheme of 507c, and an almost peacetime look with her black boot topping. Her decks remained plain wood. Three quad 0.5in MG mounts were carried, but only single 4in AA guns. *Achilles* carried a heavier catapult in order to operate a Walrus aircraft. She was present at the Battle of the River Plate where, along with her sister *Ajax* and the heavy cruiser *Exeter*, she engaged the German raider *Admiral Graf Spee*. *Achilles* received only light damage during the battle.

HMS ACHILLES Pennant 70
Leander class cruiser 1940–mid-1941

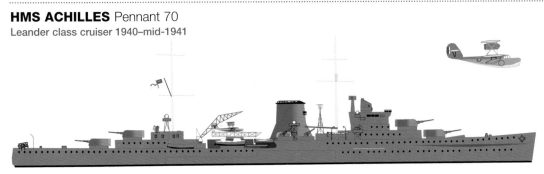

Achilles remained in New Zealand and Australian waters during 1940 and into 1941, protecting trade, hunting suspected raiders and escorting troop convoys into the Indian Ocean. She adopted a much darker style paint scheme, which seems to have been 507b overall. Her wood decks remained unpainted. New Zealand authorities were concerned about her lack of radar and, having developed their own, fitted her with Type SW radar in early 1941. This was a surface search set with similar performance to Type 286 radar, then being fitted to ships in UK waters. The single 4in AA guns remained, but preparations were made for twin mounts to be fitted when that was possible. Splinter protection tubs were placed around the single 4in guns, but that was the only change in armament.

HMNZS ACHILLES Pennant 70
Leander class cruiser mid-1941

Achilles was painted in an Admiralty disruptive scheme in mid-1941. It was comprised of four colours: MS4a, B5, B6 and MS2. This type of camouflage was intended to disrupt the viewer from working out the dimensions and the type of ship they were viewing. Having colours fade into each other made distinguishing various recognition features quite difficult, while the higher contrasts hindered this even further. The problem was, as always, that while a four-colour scheme might have seemed effective to the shore-based designer, it was hell for a busy wartime crew to maintain it in good order. Without it being in good order, it gradually lost its effectiveness. Nonetheless, it was retained until the middle of 1942. Note that single 20mm AA guns were added on each turret top. The Royal New Zealand Navy was established by royal decree in July 1941. All ships that were part of the New Zealand force adopted the prefix HMNZS from then on.

HMNZS ACHILLES Pennant 70
Leander class cruiser mid-1942

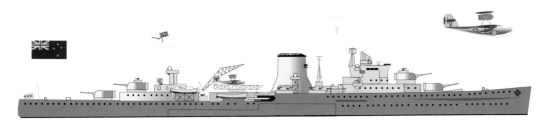

Achilles had her Admiralty disruptive scheme painted out in mid-1942. It was replaced with a dark hull/light uppers scheme, which seems to have used 507b and MS4a. The colour of the wood decks is not known for certain, but it was probably grey. The single 4in guns were removed and each was replaced by a pair of single 20mm guns. It was probably done in the expectation that the twin mounts were about to be fitted, but the ship was still required for service. This gave a total of ten single 20mm guns and the three quad 0.5in MG mounts for AA defence. The masts were converted to tripods, which was also most likely in expectation of imminent fitting of more radar. On 5 January 1943 a bomb hit wrecked 'X' turret off New Georgia. The damage was so severe that *Achilles* had to be sent to the UK for repairs.

HMNZS ACHILLES Pennant 70
Leander class cruiser May 1944

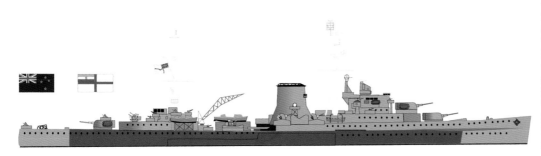

'X' turret was removed during repairs and replaced by two quad 2pdr mounts. Two more were added amidships. The catapult was removed. Twin 4in mounts were fitted, with a crew shelter between them. Five twin 20mm mounts and six single guns were added. The torpedo tubes were retained. The HACS was removed from the bridge; instead HACS with Type 285 radar were sided. A Type 277 radar on a tall stand was on the bridge. Type 282 radar was provided for the 2pdr directors. Type 282B radar with the associated IFF was on the mainmast. Type 293 radar was carried on the foremast with various missile jammers and IFF sets. She was painted in an Admiralty standard scheme using MS3 with an MS2 hull panel. Wooden decks were stained grey. She was present when Japan surrendered in August 1945. The ship returned to Royal Navy control in September 1946, after operations to repatriate New Zealand POWs. She was temporarily decommissioned and then sold to India as INS *Delhi* in 1947.

HMS AJAX Pennant 22
Leander class cruiser 1935

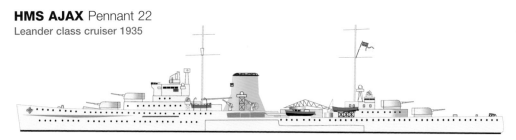

Ajax completed without a catapult, although the base was aboard, pending the availability of one. On completion, she was sent to the West Indies Station and is shown here in a scheme that comprises 507c with her funnel in primrose. The wood decks were scrubbed, and most peacetime spit and polish was present in order to make a good impression during 'showing the flag' visits. These ships had a powerful look for the time, with their large funnel and four twin 6in gun mounts. The heavy AA comprised four single 4in. Her light AA was three quad 0.5in MG mounts, one on the top of the aft control position and one each side of the bridge at the level of 'B' gun deck.

HMS AJAX Pennant 22
Leander class cruiser
late 1939

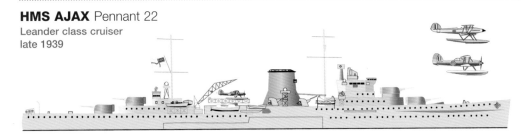

Prior to the start of World War II Ajax received twin 4in AA mounts and a catapult. The initial aircraft was the Osprey, but it was replaced by a Seafox before hostilities commenced. Forecastle plating was carried further aft to the torpedo tubes, because of wetness experienced in heavy seas. She went to the South American Squadron at the outbreak of war and wore a darker grey than previously. Although not recorded, this was probably MS4a. It is unlikely that the wood decks were painted. This ship took part in the Battle of the River Plate. She was hit seven times by the Admiral Graf Spee and seriously damaged. After the enemy ship had scuttled, Ajax returned to the UK for repairs.

HMS AJAX Pennant 22
Leander class cruiser July 1940

Ajax joined the 7th Cruiser Squadron of the Mediterranean Fleet and adopted light Mountbatten pink overall. The wood decks remained unpainted, but all horizontal metal areas were mid grey. Masts were very pale grey or white above the level of the funnel and Mountbatten pink below that. Mountbatten pink was at its most effective in bright sunlight, but at dawn or dusk its red tones made it look darker than the equivalent shades of grey, and at night it was much darker than ships painted in grey of the same tone. This scheme was retained until around October 1940. During repairs, the light catapult had been removed and replaced with a heavier one for the Walrus. Radar Type 279 was installed during her repair. To carry these, and anticipated future radars, the masts were given tripod legs. An improved HACS was fitted. No armament changes were effected at this time.

HMS AJAX Pennant 22
Leander class cruiser October 1940

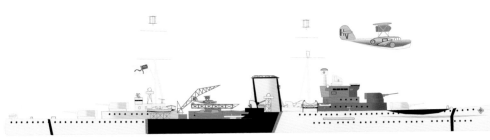

Ajax wore this unofficial scheme from October until December the same year. It comprised 507c overall with areas of black and 507b. The central area of black was outlined with 507b. Outlining seems to have been a common practice with camouflages applied at Alexandria late in 1940 to early 1941. The black on the funnels was obviously an attempt to disguise the very prominent and easy to recognise uptakes of the Leander class, while the other areas were almost certainly intended to make the ship look much shorter than she was. Both sides were the same. This was one of the most unusual camouflage schemes worn by any British warship in World War II. Wood and steel decks were a uniform 507b. Like many ships in the region, captured enemy weapons were used and two to four Italian 20mm Breda were carried. Such weapons were always unofficial.

HMS AJAX Pennant 22
Leander class cruiser
early 1941

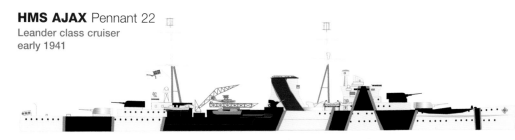

At the end of December 1940, *Ajax* had some elements of her previous scheme expanded on to produce this unusual look. Around this time, the dockyard at Alexandria produced camouflage schemes for several ships where a lighter colour was used to outline a darker one. As with the previous scheme, the pattern for this was the same on both sides, and used paint that was available in quantity at that yard. The turret tops were painted in 507b. All decks, including wood, were also painted in 507b. The tops of the 4in gun mounts were the same as the sides. Once again, despite the very hostile air environment, *Ajax* had not had her light AA armament officially increased.

HMS AJAX Pennant 22
Leander class cruiser
June 1941

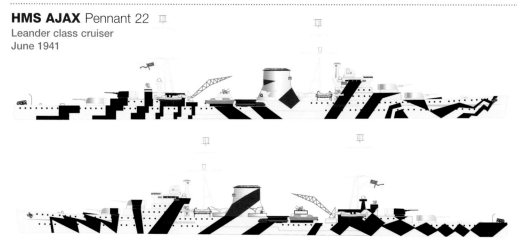

This scheme was applied to *Ajax* at Alexandria in the middle of 1941. It was only two colours: 507c overall with a black disruptive dazzle pattern. This was quite unique, and legend has it that when *Ajax* first took a buoy near the flagship, Admiral Cunningham sent her a private signal saying to move to another buoy as she was hurting his eyes! True or not, *Ajax* certainly was easy to distinguish from other ships in her squadron. She had been damaged by bombs during an attack by German Stukas on 21 May and this pattern was possibly painted on when she was undergoing repairs. She was back in action in June off Syria, before transferring to Malta. While undergoing repairs, the catapult was removed and replaced by a quad 2pdr AA mount. This was her only official light AA armament upgrade, but her armament was still poor compared to other ships in the Mediterranean. However, six single 20mm guns were fitted by the end of the year. The dockyard at Alexandria was under considerable pressure to repair damaged ships and it would seem, based on the camouflage schemes they applied, that the range of paints available must have been very limited.

HMS AJAX Pennant 22
Leander class cruiser October 1942

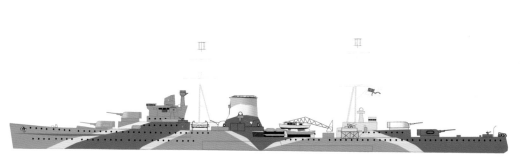

After a period of repair at Chatham, *Ajax* emerged in an Admiralty-style pattern. The shades used were MS4a, B6 and MS2. The deck, which had previously been medium grey, would probably have remained that way. The starboard side pattern was probably similar to the October 1943 starboard side pattern. It is noticeable that from this period onward early-war shortages of paint pigments were obviously being overcome and more colourful schemes were possible. The centreline quad 2pdr mount was removed. Two quad 2pdr mounts were added, one on either side forward of the aft deckhouse where the ship's boats had previously been carried. Surprisingly for this late in the war, only three single 20mm guns were added to replace the three quad 0.5in MG mounts. One was on the quarterdeck and the others were placed on each side of the bridge, where two of the quad MG mounts had previously been. The HACS on the bridge was removed and replaced by one on each side of the bridge and these were equipped with Type 285 gunnery radar. The vacant position on the bridge rear had a Type 272 radar with its lantern mounted on a high stand to clear the gun director. The director itself was fitted with Type 284 radar and the Type 279 radar at the mastheads was retained, despite newer and better sets becoming available. Aircraft were no longer carried and all facilities, except the crane, had been removed. The area was now taken up by ship's boats.

HMS AJAX Pennant 22
Leander class cruiser
October 1943

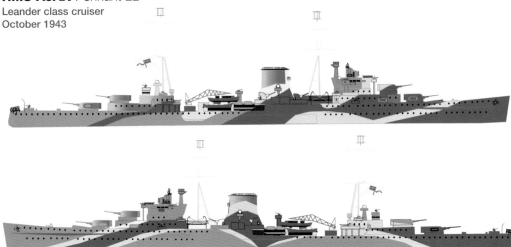

Ajax had some additional work done in the US, and in October 1943 emerged with a camouflage pattern similar to the previous one, but with a few changes to border lines. The shades in use remained the same: MS4a, B6 and MS2. The decks were still mid-grey. This was how she appeared during the Normandy landings off Gold Beach, where she provided fire support. Her electronic fit remained the same, apart from the addition of a barrage director in front of the bridge. There were changes to the light AA armament. The quad 2pdr mounts were replaced by quad 40mm mounts of US naval pattern. Note the typical USN director tubs above the mounts. There were two single 20mm, side by side, on the quarterdeck and one on top of the aft control position, plus another on the former catapult deck. There were two twin 20mm mounts on the aft deckhouse, two more at 'B' turret level on each side of the bridge, and two more in the forecastle deck level on each side of the bridge. Sources vary on the total number of 20mm guns carried and I relied on a USN drawing of *Ajax* for my illustration.

HMS AJAX Pennant 22
Leander class cruiser 1945

Ajax was sent to the Mediterranean after D-Day and, after covering the landing in the south of France, went to the eastern end for the reoccupation of Greece and other Aegean Sea operations. During this period she adopted the late-war Admiralty standard pattern, using MS3 overall with a central panel of B15. Note that the instructions were that central panels were always supposed to have a slight rake at the bow, although this was not always done. The panel was to start just in front of the forward turret and end just aft of the aft turret. The scheme was intended to provide a shortening effect for the hull, giving an illusion of being further away when viewed through a periscope. Owing to her various wartime repairs, *Ajax* was not considered for the post-war fleet and went straight into reserve at the end of hostilities. She was sold for scrap in 1949.

IMPROVED LEANDER CLASS CRUISERS

HMS APOLLO Pennant I63
Improved Leander class cruiser 1936–7

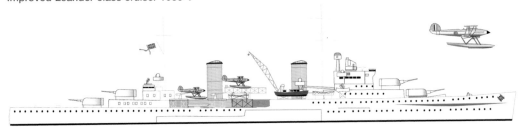

Apollo was the first of the improved design, and was sent to the West Indies for her first deployment. She is shown here in a typical white and buff scheme for colonial service. The wood decks were scrubbed. Deck forward of the anchor winches was painted in 507b. A light catapult was fitted. The 4in guns were singles. Three quad 0.5in MG mounts were carried. Internally, the ships were very cramped. The ship entered service with crew accommodation inferior to ships built during World War I, and on her first cruise was found to be almost unbearable below decks in hot climates. When the Australian government enquired about new light cruisers, the Admiralty immediately offered this ship, and her sisters already under construction. The RN was no doubt pleased to be rid of them, and for the Australian Navy it was a case of 'buyer beware'.

HMAS HOBART Pennant I63
Improved Leander class cruiser early 1940

In September 1938 Australia took over *Apollo*, renaming her *Hobart*. However, she remained in European waters during the Munich crisis. She was rearmed with twin 4in AA guns. The RAN insisted on a heavier aircraft for reconnaissance, and although the Royal Navy had considered a larger catapult not possible, they soon found room to meet the buyer's requirement. At the outbreak of war, *Hobart* was in overall 507c and operated in her home waters, seeking out German merchant shipping trying to make it back to Germany. The state of the ship was more or less as in peacetime, with neat paintwork and scrubbed decks. She was to remain like this while escorting convoys of troops across the Indian Ocean and the East Indies. *Hobart* was at Aden when Italy entered World War II and she took part in the Red Sea and East African campaigns. A shelter for the 4in gun crews was added between the mounts during 1940. Two single 20mm Breda guns are shown mounted on the quarterdeck.

HMAS HOBART Pennant I63
Improved Leander class cruiser December 1940

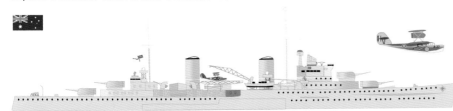

In 1968, while on an invited visit to the Cockatoo Island Dockyard in Sydney, Australia, I met a man who had been a foreman painter there during World War II. He told a funny story about the cruiser *Hobart* arriving home in pink. He thought it was because they were short of paint and mixed undercoat with grey to provide enough. He was unaware of the use of 'Mountbatten pink' where *Hobart* had recently been serving. Although unable to find official confirmation, Australian War Memorial photo PD5292.002 of *Hobart*, just before her return home after a refit at Colombo, shows a tone that could be Mountbatten pink. According to the foreman painter she was repainted in plain grey after arrival in Sydney, which would be consistent with the ship's operational area in the following months. My thanks to Wes Olson for his help in finalising this bit of research that had plagued me for almost fifty years.

HMAS HOBART Pennant D63
Improved Leander class cruiser early 1941

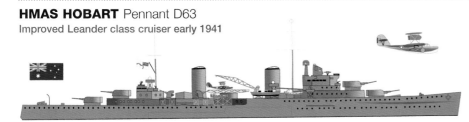

Hobart spent time in Australian and South Pacific waters on escort duties during early 1941. During this time she was painted a solid grey, which appears to be 507a. It is believed her decks were painted in the same grey, but with the amidships wood decks unpainted. All armament and equipment remained the same, except some reports say she was fitted with four single .303 Vickers machine guns arranged two at the front of the bridge and two on the aft deckhouse. No radar was fitted at this time and the aircraft was still carried. Like most of the later Royal Navy cruisers, she carried Type 132 Asdic and eight depth charges.

HMAS HOBART Pennant D63
Improved Leander class cruiser July 1941

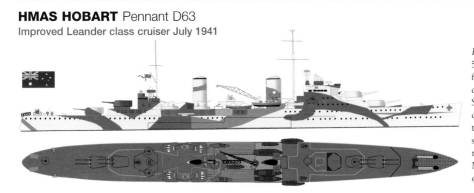

Hobart is shown here with a scheme using typical Mediterranean shades of 507a, 507b and 507c, which was essentially the same on both sides. The decks were almost solid grey, except for an area amidships where the wood was unpainted. On arrival in the Mediterranean, she cross-decked AA with *Perth*: that ship was returning home and light AA was in short supply. She received one quad 2pdr mount on the former catapult base and another on the quarterdeck. There were single Italian 20mm Breda each side forward of the aft funnel. It is possible that there were two others aboard, as well. All quad 0.5in MG mounts were retained. Four single tubs, intended to have 20mm mounted, carried single .303 machine guns as a temporary measure. The torpedo tubes were still carried. Because of the submarine threat in the Mediterranean, additional depth charges were installed, along with two throwers, for a total of eighteen depth charges.

HMAS HOBART Pennant D63
Improved Leander class cruiser December 1941–May 1942

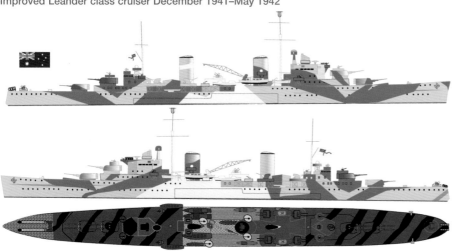

In December 1941 *Hobart* was ordered home when Japan entered the war. While escorting troop convoys, she came under intense air attack. At Singapore, she was ordered to land a quad 2pdr mount so it could be returned to the UK. The captain disobeyed and sailed with it still aboard. She came under further intense air attacks near Tandjong Priok, which prevented her being part of the fatal Java Sea sortie. A refit in Australia took place: the main camouflage was altered by the elimination of areas of 507b, leaving the ship in 507c and 507a, plus a mid-grey that was probably specially mixed. The decks were painted olive green and black, but some wood areas were left unpainted. An additional quad 2pdr mount was added aft on the quarterdeck alongside the existing one, but slightly offset to improve arcs of fire, giving her three quad 2pdr mounts. Each single .303 machine gun was replaced by a single 20mm gun. Two other 20mm AA were added on the aft deckhouse area. Note that the 20mm tubs in front of the bridge were raised higher. All quad 0.5in MG mounts were still carried. Her armament comprised eight 6in guns, eight 4in AA guns, three quad 2pdr mounts, six single 20mm guns, and three quad 0.5in machine mounts. There were two unidentified weapons, possibly 20mm Breda guns brought from the Mediterranean. A New Zealand Type SW radar set was added at the foremast, but its performance was little better than a navigational set. These illustrations depict *Hobart* at the time of the Battle of the Coral Sea. The overhead scheme is interesting. Having the amidships area in lighter shades may have been intended to make the ship look like two smaller vessels rather than a medium-sized one. The reason is not recorded and will probably never be known.

HMAS HOBART Pennant D63
Improved Leander class cruiser December 1942

The ship was repaired in New Zealand and then went to Sydney after collision damage in 1942. She emerged from this in an overall coat of what appears to be similar to US Navy measure 11. The ship was the same on both sides. The previous olive and black deck areas were painted in the Australian mixed version of US deck blue. The silhouette was altered with a Type 273 radar tower amidships. US SC search radar was placed on the foremast and a US Mk3 gunnery radar was placed on her main gun director. All quad 0.5in machine guns were replaced by single 20mm AA guns. There were two single 20mm guns on 'B' turret and the same on 'X' turret. Two more singles were placed in front of the bridge and abreast it, and one more single on top of the aft control position, for a total of nine single 20mm AA guns. There were two unidentified guns abreast the mainmast on the aft deckhouse, which were probably the Italian 20mm guns. *Hobart* almost sank when torpedoed by Japanese submarine *I-11* off New Georgia.

HMAS HOBART Pennant D63
Improved Leander class cruiser early 1945

During repair many other changes were carried out and finally *Hobart* was painted in a US-style dark blue scheme similar to US Navy measure 21, using USN dark blue 5/N. Masts were converted to tripods to take the weight of new electronic equipment. Lower parts were dark blue and upper areas pale grey or white; decks were probably dark blue. The 4in twin mounts were spread out so that one hit couldn't knock out both mounts. Single 40mm Bofors guns were added. Hazemeyer twin 40mm mounts with radar were added either side of the bridge and on the quarterdeck, and single 20mm guns on each side on the bridge. The quad 2pdr mounts were replaced by later models with radar. The new electronic fit was extensive. At the top of the mainmast was a British Type 281B radar with IFF on top; below were radar detectors and jammers. At the head of the foremast was a USN SG radar with a British Type 276 radar just under it, below that an IFF interrogator with British Type 277 radar. The main gun director had US Mk 3 radar. The previous HACS was replaced by directors with Type 285 radar each side of the bridge. There were barrage directors and 2pdr directors carrying Type 282 radar.

HMAS HOBART Pennant D63
Improved Leander class cruiser December 1947

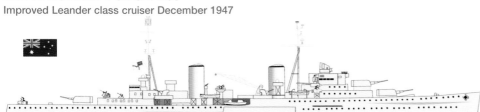

Hobart was to be sent into reserve at the end of the war. Before that was done, it was decided to give her a refit. 'X' turret was removed and she received a twin 40mm power-operated STAAG mount and two twin power-operated 20mm mounts. All the single 40mm guns were removed, along with the single 20mm guns. This left her with four twin 40mm Bofors mounts, two quadruple 2pdr mounts and two twin 20mm mounts. There were some changes to electronics. *Hobart* went into reserve in 1947 and never returned to service. In 1952 it was decided to convert her to a training ship, but after some work, which included a lattice foremast, the project was suspended.

HMS AMPHION Pennant I29
Improved Leander class cruiser 1937

Amphion was commissioned in 1936 and sent to the South Africa Station as flagship. She is shown here with a white hull and grey upper works that approximate 507b. Ships on foreign or colonial stations usually adopted schemes that were specific to that location. At this time she was not fitted with a catapult, but carried two aircraft which could be lowered overboard. The ship was completed with twin 4in gun mounts and three quad 0.5in MG mounts as AA armament. The 6in mounts were able to engage aircraft at longer ranges with barrage fire. She was equipped with a HF/DF at the head of the foremast, as was then standard for all new cruisers.

HMAS PERTH Pennant I29
Improved Leander class cruiser 1939–40

Amphion paid off for refit in 1938 in order to be sold to Australia. She recommissioned on 29 June 1939 as *Perth* and sailed to New York for the World's Fair, representing Australia. War was declared during her visit to US ports and she was sent to patrol the East Indies. *Perth* sailed for Australia in March 1940, still in a peacetime appearance of 507c overall. Wooden decks were scrubbed but other horizontal surfaces were 507c, except for the area around the anchor winches, where she was painted 507a, as were the turret tops. She had a short refit in Sydney, then took part in escorting convoys and patrolling for German raiders. *Perth* did not have a catapult at this time and did not carry aircraft.

HMAS PERTH Pennant D29
Improved Leander class cruiser February 1941

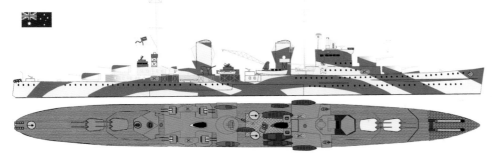

Perth was painted in a camouflage scheme at Alexandria in December 1940. Typical of Eastern Mediterranean schemes, it comprised two highly contrasting shades: 507c overall, with 507a forming a pattern of swirls. It was identical on both sides. In Australia she had been fitted with baffles on each funnel to distort enemy rangefinders. Although this had been common in World War I, it was not often used in World War II and made *Perth* very distinctive. She cross-decked light AA with *Sydney*, which was returning home, receiving three single 20mm Breda AA guns, with two placed between the funnels and one on the quarterdeck. Captured weapons were popular and shore parties scrounged for ammunition when visiting captured ports. A quad 2pdr mount from the cruiser *Liverpool* was fitted on what was intended as the base for the catapult, which had not been fitted. Type 286 radar was fitted at the head of the mainmast.

HMAS PERTH Pennant D29
Improved Leander class cruiser July 1941

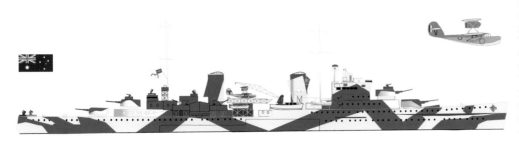

Perth was given a new camouflage scheme at Alexandria in May 1941, and still carried the quad 2pdr mount amidships until a catapult from the cruiser *Ajax* was fitted during a minor refit at Port Said in July. However, a Walrus aircraft was not available until after another refit from August to October, when she had returned to Australia. The original baffles were somewhat altered, but remained part of the new camouflage scheme. As usual for Alexandria schemes, the two shades used were 507c as the base, with 507a forming a pattern over it. Wood decks remained unpainted, but horizontal steel decks were 507a. Turret tops complied with the camouflage on their upper sides. When the quad 2pdr mount was landed, two quad 0.5in MG mounts were placed well aft on the quarterdeck, and those previously on each side of the bridge moved behind the aft funnel. The mount on top of the aft control tower remained in place, giving a total of five mounts. Single 20mm guns were placed on each side of the bridge and one each on top of 'B' and 'X' turrets. The Italian 20mm guns were cross-decked to *Hobart* when *Perth* was relieved to return to Australia.

HMAS PERTH Pennant D29
Improved Leander class cruiser March 1942

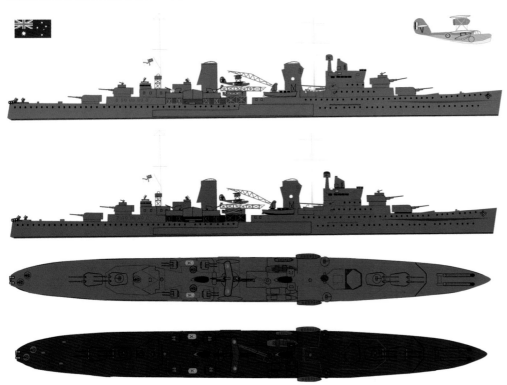

The final appearance of *Perth* has been much debated. Photographs taken before leaving harbour on her last sortie show a very dull and worn paint scheme, which some claim indicates a camouflage pattern of some kind. However, I am of the opinion that what it shows is that due to wear and tear, wave action, and lack of time to paint ship, some of the previous camouflage was starting to show through. It was very common for paint to wear off after hard steaming for lengthy periods. In the top illustration, I have shown the ship in 507a, which seems to be what she would have been painted during her last dockyard visit. In the one below, I have shown her in 5/0 US Navy ocean grey overall, which is claimed by some sources. There are claims of the ship having been painted in a shade of blue while operating with US ships that were part of the ABDA Force. I have shown what would be the effect, both in a side view and from overhead. In the last view, I have shown her with much darker blue decks, as some claim. It is also possible that if the ship was dressed in 507a, then that may well have been the deck colour as well. My opinion is that she was painted in 507a overall, because at the time of that last visit to Sydney, the US had not yet entered the war. If it was done it would have been during the hectic days of the Japanese invasion of Southeast Asia and the time span seems against that. She sailed to join ABDA Force on 14 February and, with the American cruiser USS *Houston*, survived the Battle of the Java Sea later that month. She was sunk on 1 March in an unequal battle. It seems unlikely there would have been time to paint ship. Furthermore, the battered condition of her paintwork prior to sailing on her last mission would seem to indicate she had not been fully painted since Sydney. The armament had not been altered prior to her loss. Type 286 radar was carried.

HMAS SYDNEY Pennant I48
Improved Leander class cruiser 1935

Laid down as HMS *Phaeton*, she was sold to Australia in 1934 before completion and renamed HMAS *Sydney*. As delivered, she had single 4in AA guns and departed from the UK to Australia before they could be replaced. *Sydney* lacked a catapult as none suitable for the Seagull V was available. Her armament was standard, with eight 6in guns in four twin turrets. Light AA was limited to three quad 0.5in MG mounts. The light guns on the aft deckhouse were only saluting guns. She was completed in 507c overall, with wood decks in a peacetime well-scrubbed state. The boats were painted blue, as was often done in peacetime. At the head of the foremast she carried a HF/DF aerial, which was becoming standard for the Royal Navy. A catapult was eventually fitted and a Seagull V (Walrus) aircraft issued to the ship. She was the only one fitted with a roof for the compass platform.

HMAS SYDNEY Pennant I48
Improved Leander class cruiser July 1940

Sydney went to the aid of British destroyers that were engaged by two Italian cruisers north of Crete on 19 July 1940. During the action she crippled *Bartolomeo Colleoni* and damaged *Giovanni delle Bande Nere*. Each of these ships was, on paper, equal to her. *Sydney* continued in pursuit, but although hits were scored, *Bande Nere* was able to outrun her. *Sydney* entered the harbour at Alexandria to a huge welcome. Her own damage was minor. More Carley floats were added and some areas of wood were painted over. Her main scheme was still 507c on vertical surfaces, but many horizontal areas were painted in dark grey or black as shown. Turret tops remained in 507c. Splinter protection was added around the 4in guns and the quad 0.5in MG mounts. A large catapult was fitted just before war broke out. Her aircraft was lost before the Cape Spada action and she did not receive a replacement for some time. The illustration shows her with the battle ensigns and national flag, as she would have appeared during the battle with Italian cruisers. On 28 June she sank the Italian destroyer *Espero* with gunfire and was under air attack many times. *Sydney* had picked up captured Italian single 20mm guns, but it is not recorded where they were fitted.

HMAS SYDNEY Pennant D48
Improved Leander class cruiser end of August 1940

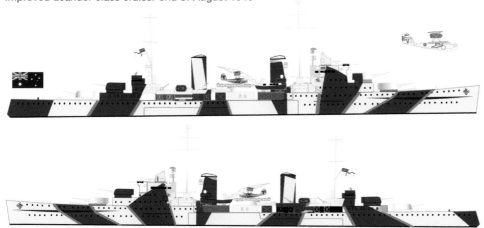

Sydney took on a fairly typical Mediterranean camouflage scheme at Alexandria, while undergoing repair to the hole in her funnel sustained during the Battle of Cape Spada. This took on the usual form for that dockyard at the time, using the existing 507c and overpainting that with areas of 507a. It is said in Australian records that she only ever wore one camouflage scheme. However, there can be no doubt at all that in close-up photographs while embarking troops for Crete, and then later while unloading them at Suda Bay, the camouflage is mostly outlined in a shade that would appear to be 507b. At this time, the decks of the ship were stained blue for concealment from the air. This type of camouflage was intended to hide the identity of a ship by creating confusion in the eye of a viewer as to angles of a ship, such as funnels, or the location of bow and stern. *Sydney* wore this camouflage throughout the Crete campaign. Although no extra AA guns can be seen, there are conflicting reports of up to four 20mm guns being added. These could have been captured Italian weapons. No radar was fitted at this time.

HMAS SYDNEY Pennant D48
Improved Leander class cruiser January 1941

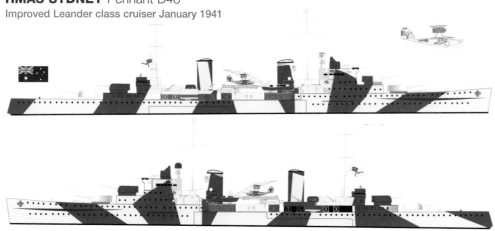

This was the appearance of the ship upon her return to Australia after Crete. The boundaries of some dark areas had changed, while others had not. The 507b outlines had been removed, but in general the camouflage remained the same. The ship was given an enormous welcome in her namesake city and the crew invited to a state dinner in their honour. Many thousands flocked to Sydney harbour to see the ship and welcome the crew home during a triumphal march through the city. War with Japan was still months away, and no secret was made of her return. There seem to be no changes of armament in the many photographs of the ship at this time. If she did carry captured 20mm Breda guns while in the Mediterranean, she had probably left them behind for her replacement.

HMAS SYDNEY Pennant D48
Improved Leander class cruiser March 1941

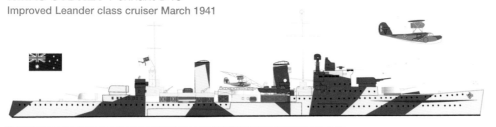

On her departure for Fremantle, *Sydney* seems to have been wearing much the same scheme, but with minor differences to the angles and dimensions of some patches of 507a. Forward, the 'B' turret was not entirely 507a. The area on the bridge now covered more and extended to the HACS, as well as to the rear of the bridge. The area under the fore funnel ended in a sharp point as it reached the waterline. The area under the aft funnel was a slightly different shape. Aft, the 'X' turret was no longer in 507a, and the shape of that patch of camouflage had changed. Further aft, the area of 507a was smaller, with the base reaching the waterline at the stern. Both sides were supposed to be the same, but I suspect had similar variations. Again no armament changes were made.

HMAS SYDNEY Pennant D48
Improved Leander class cruiser September 1941

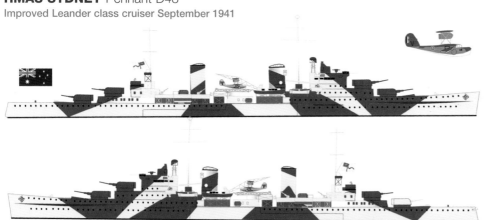

The scheme was again altered in September 1941. This was the last variation, as the ship was lost with all hands in a fight to the death with the German raider *Kormoran* off the coast of Western Australia. Against all orders to the contrary, and with known near-misses experienced by other ships, *Sydney* closed to within a mile of the enemy, which was masquerading as the Dutch *Straat Malacca*. Although at action stations, the Germans managed to fire before *Sydney*, scoring immediate hits on the bridge and gunnery control, and probably disrupting command control on the warship. *Sydney* did eventually fire back, scoring fatal hits on her attacker. At a range of one mile, *Kormoran*'s guns could easily penetrate the cruiser's armour, making the gunfight against the unarmoured German ship more equal than it should have been. Had *Sydney* stood off while identifying the suspicious merchant ship, she would have been at a greater advantage. Although many of the survivors of *Kormoran* were taken prisoner by other ships and on shore, there were no survivors of the Australian ship. She remained missing for sixty-six years, during which many theories were published and a conspiracy by the German survivors alleged. After the wreck was located, the story, as given by the German survivors, was shown to be basically correct when the location of damage to the cruiser was examined.

ARETHUSA CLASS CRUISERS

HMS **ARETHUSA** Pennant 26
Arethusa class cruiser
1935

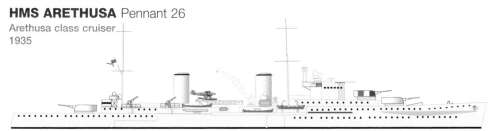

This was the appearance of *Arethusa* as completed. Note there is one less 6in turret than on the preceding classes. The single 4in AA guns were unshielded, and had no protective splinter protection. Her only light AA comprised a quad 0.5in MG mount on each side forward of the fore funnel. Compared to later in World War II, she has a very spartan look. Her first deployment was to the Mediterranean and she is shown wearing the expected 507c for that station. Wood decks were unpainted, and horizontal metal decks were probably 507b, with the area forward of the anchor winches 507a. She was a member of the 3rd Cruiser Squadron.

HMS **ARETHUSA** Pennant 26
Arethusa class cruiser
1940

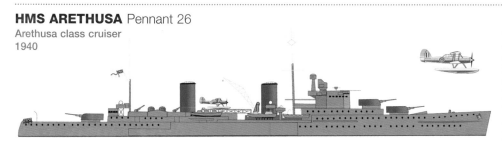

In early 1940, *Arethusa* was urgently recalled to home waters and, with her sisters, formed the 2nd Cruiser Squadron. She was painted overall in 507b. Wood decks remained unpainted and horizontal metal areas were 507b. Note she has a HF/DF at the foremast, but no other changes. The inadequacy of the light AA on most British ships was about to be discovered, when she and her squadron took part in the Norwegian campaign. In May, she raced to English Channel waters to assist and help evacuate British troops from Calais and other ports. After that she went to Gibraltar as part of the new Force H, operating both in the Atlantic and the Western Mediterranean. The aircraft carried was the Fairey Seafox, which was a disappointing performer that was in some cases replaced by its predecessor, the Osprey, if available.

HMS **ARETHUSA** Pennant 26
Arethusa class cruiser mid-1940

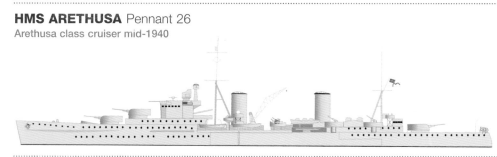

Arethusa is shown in a Mediterranean favourite camouflage of Mountbatten pink, which she wore from around the middle of 1940 until her refit in April 1941. The catapult and aircraft were removed and replaced with two quad 2pdr AA mounts, port and starboard. At this time she still had single 4in AA guns. Deck colours are not known, but were probably as before. Type 286 radar was fitted at the top of both masts to provide a sending and a receiving aerial. Depth-charge capacity was increased from eight to twelve about this time. Type 132 Asdic had been carried since construction. Early operations had shown the smaller type scout planes were of limited use and a programme to replace them with extra AA guns was considered urgent. However, this could only be done as extra guns became available. Hence some ships lost theirs early, as did *Arethusa*, and others much later.

HMS **ARETHUSA** Pennant 26
Arethusa class cruiser July 1941

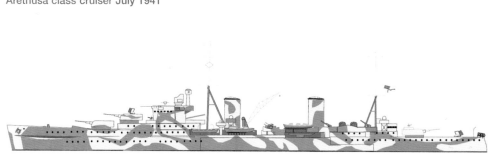

During April 1941 the Mountbatten pink camouflage was abandoned, because *Arethusa* spent a lot of her time in the Atlantic, even as far north as Iceland. It was a scheme intended for areas of bright sunlight and was therefore totally unsuited in dull areas. For the new, and quite unofficial, pattern, the ship was painted in 507c, and then given a scheme of overlays that appear to be 507b, although it could have been 507a and faded. It can be notoriously difficult to interpret black and white photography of the period due to fading, light conditions, and poor quality film. In July the ship was given additional AA weapons. Unrotated projectile (UP) mounts were added on the quarterdeck and the top of 'B' turret. Four single 20mm AA guns were also added; two on the shelter deck at the front of the bridge and two on top of the aft turret. The wood decks were painted a medium grey, which was most likely 507b. Horizontal metal surfaces would also have been 507b or a similar grey, depending on what was available. This was not only a year of serious ship losses, but the height of the convoy battles, making paint and other materials in very short supply.

HMS ARETHUSA Pennant 26
Arethusa class cruiser December 1941

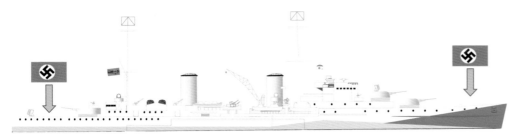

In December 1941 *Arethusa* was given a special low visibility camouflage scheme for the Lofoten Islands raid to enable her to approach unseen in the mists and fogs of that region. Posing as a German warship, she flew a large enemy battle ensign aft, and had a typical Kriegsmarine swastika recognition flag painted on her foredeck. The scheme appears to have been white mostly, with MS4a Home Fleet grey, and B5. The decks presumably remained unchanged. During the commando operation she was badly damaged by near-misses, and had to return to the UK for repairs. Because of the lessons learned during the Norway campaign, her light AA had been strengthened, but not sufficiently, as this operation soon showed. Her 4in AA guns, for example, were still singles. The swastika markings were painted out as the operation ended, and on return to the UK she went back to overall 507b, as she had worn in early 1940.

HMS ARETHUSA Pennant 26
Arethusa class cruiser April 1942

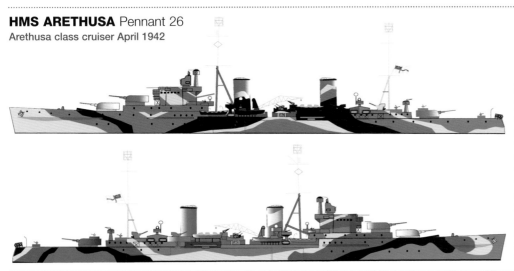

After returning from her clandestine operation, *Arethusa* had many changes. The most visible was a new four-colour camouflage, using MS4a, B5, MS4 and B15. The metal decks were 507a, and the wood areas had been stained to a dark blue-grey. The stain was not on the Admiralty colour chart, but was probably similar to PB10. The single 4in AA guns were removed and replaced by twin mounts. Extra 20mm guns were added, for a total of eight. The UP mounts and quad 0.5in MG mounts were also removed. The aft searchlight was moved to between the 4in guns and in its place a second HACS, fitted with Type 285 radar, was added. The gunnery radar was also fitted on the original HACS. The main gun director received Type 284 radar and at the mastheads were aerials for Type 281 radar. There was a lantern with Type 273 radar on the front of the bridge, in a rather cramped position with only coverage forward and 90 degrees each side. Type 282 radar was provided for the quad 2pdr director amidships. Three more 20mm guns were added later in various positions.

HMS ARETHUSA Pennant 26
Arethusa class cruiser December 1943

The four-colour scheme applied in 1942 proved too difficult to maintain and a simpler style was adopted, using G20 and B55 which gave total contrast, the ship appearing like a single-funnel vessel so it was difficult to pick the real silhouette from a distance. The decks remained dark blue-grey. When torpedoed and badly damaged during a Malta convoy run, the ship underwent temporary repairs and then went to the United States for complete repairs. The quad 2pdr mounts were removed and replaced with two of the far more powerful US quad 40mm Bofors mounts. Officially, the light AA armament was changed to four twin 20mm mounts, one each on 'B' and 'Y' turrets, and two more abreast the fore funnel in the old quad 0.5in MG mount position. However, photographs show that she still carried two single 20mm guns on each side aft of the bridge after these repairs. The awkwardly placed Type 273 radar was removed from the front of the bridge and she carried Type 272 radar on the foremast. Type 283 barrage directors were added on the front of the bridge and aft.

HMS ARETHUSA Pennant 26
Arethusa class cruiser Normandy landings 1944

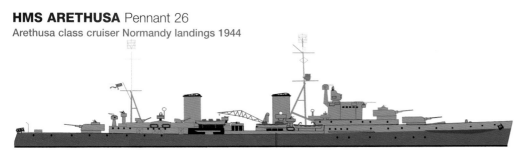

By the time of the D-Day landings, the heavy green and light grey previous scheme had been replaced with a standard Admiralty type. The lower hull was MS2, while the upper hull and superstructure was MS3. It is believed the decks and other horizontal surfaces remained grey as previously. Repairing the major torpedo damage took from February until December 1943, and even then she had to return to the UK for some final work to be done. After working up and trials, it was the end of June before she was again ready for action. *Arethusa* joined Force D and provided fire support off Sword Beach during the Normandy landings, remaining off the coast until no longer required, when she was sent to the Mediterranean. There are no known changes of armament during this period.

HMS ARETHUSA Pennant 26
Arethusa class cruiser
Mediterranean 1945

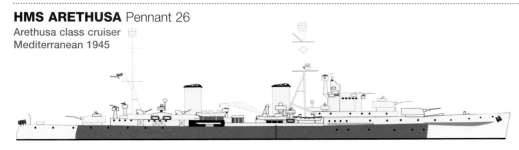

As World War II in Europe drew to an end, there was still a lot of mopping up to do, especially in the Mediterranean. *Arethusa* changed her scheme to one of overall 507c, with a 507a panel on the hull. The decks remained dark grey. Weight problems and the reduced threat of air attack saw the removal of the two quad 40mm mounts, which were apparently shipped to the UK for use on one of the cruisers earmarked for post-war service. As a result, she completed the war with four twin 20mm mounts and two singles as her light AA. Not required for further use, she was quickly placed in reserve, then for trials and experiments. In 1949 she was sold, and scrapped during 1950.

HMS AURORA Pennant 12
Arethusa class cruiser May 1935

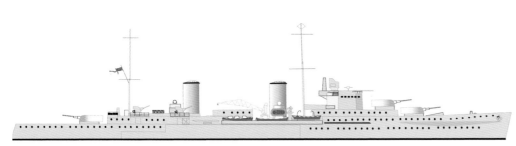

Many of the previous cruisers used for the role of flagship for Rear Admiral of Destroyers were getting old and due for replacement. So the Royal Navy decided that it would complete one of the *Arethusa* class to serve in this role. The catapult was to be dispensed with, and replaced with extra accommodations and offices for such a role. As a side bet, they nonetheless retained the other basic equipment, should there ever be a requirement to make her into a catapult-equipped ship. As first completed, she had fittings for a HACS forward and aft, but they were not actually fitted for some time. Twin 4in AA mounts were provided from completion, along with two quad 0.5in MG mounts. The six 6in guns in three twin turrets had some AA ability at long ranges, but could not train or load fast enough for close work. The ship first appeared in MS4a Home Fleet grey. The decks were scrubbed wood and horizontal metal surfaces in the same colour as the vertical surfaces, except at the bow, where the area forward of the anchor winches was 507a.

HMS AURORA Pennant 12
Arethusa class cruiser
May 1939–40

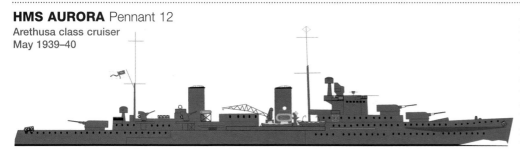

At the outbreak of World War II, *Aurora* was serving with the Home Fleet as flagship of Rear Admiral (D). Like many others, a winter scheme was adopted with the ship in overall 507a, except for the wood decks which remained unpainted. Horizontal metal surfaces were 507a. The false bow wave is based on a verbal description given to me and may, or may not, be correct. The same source stated there were some white patches on the funnels, but the description was too vague to include in this illustration. Other ships, however, did have some white funnel marks at that time. Both HACS directors had been installed, but the ship was basically unchanged from her peacetime appearance. She took part early convoys to Scandinavia and in the Norwegian campaign while wearing this scheme.

HMS AURORA Pennant 12
Arethusa class cruiser
1940–41

Aurora adopted Mountbatten pink (medium) in 1940, but the mix must have been poor, or it was not allowed to set correctly, because she weathered badly. Photographs show patches of her previous grey showing through. The effect occurred all over the ship, but the worst affected areas were the stern and the front of 'A' and 'B' turrets. Type 290 radar was at the head of both masts for sending/receiving and Type 284 radar was placed on the main gun director. The light AA weapons varied, but by the end of the period covered there had been quad 2pdr mounts added port and starboard amidships. There were quad 0.5in MG mounts on each side of the bridge and six 20mm AA guns, with one each on top of 'B' and 'X' turrets, one each side of the aft deckhouse and two more on top of the amidships flag officer accommodation and offices. An Unrotated Projectile (UP) weapon was mounted on the quarterdeck.

HMS AURORA Pennant 12
Arethusa class cruiser
June 1942

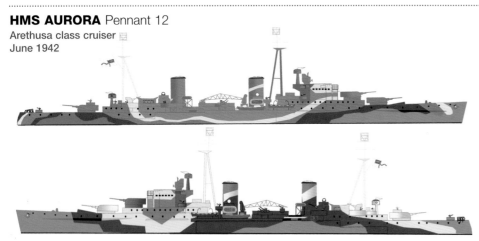

Aurora was mined off Tripoli in December 1941 and was out of action until the following June. During her repair, an Admiralty disruptive-pattern camouflage was designed for her, and she returned to service in that scheme. The scheme consisted of four colours: 507a, B5, MS4a and MS4. The wood deck was stained grey, but the exact shade is not known. Other horizontal metal surfaces were a mid- to dark grey. The grey of her turret tops appears to be 507b, and the area forward around the anchors and winches was probably 507a, as it appears darker than the turret tops. This form of camouflage was an attempt to disrupt the view of an observer in such a way as to disguise the identity of the ship, its course, and so forth. As part of her refit, new equipment was installed. Type 281 radar replaced Type 290, and Type 285 was added to the bridge and aft HACS. A Type 273 radar was crammed in between 'B' turret and the bridge front. This was an unsatisfactory location, as it was blocked from any search aft of about 75 degrees. Directors for the quad 2pdr mounts were fitted with Type 282 radar. The aft control station was removed to save weight.

HMS AURORA Pennant 12
Arethusa class cruiser
June 1943

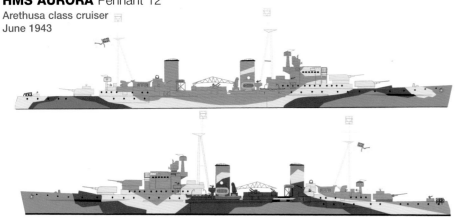

These images show *Aurora* a year later. The boundaries of some areas have changed and there are some changes in colour. But, in general, the same camouflage scheme can be seen still following the original design. No other changes have been made. Note that because of the position of the Type 273 radar, it was not possible to place a light AA weapon on top of 'B' turret.

HMS AURORA Pennant 12
Arethusa class cruiser 1944

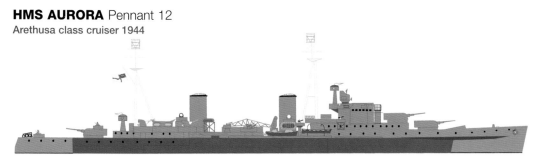

Aurora was painted in an Admiralty standard pattern while undergoing repairs at Taranto, adopting the version intended for the Mediterranean. The overall colour was MS3, with a dark hull panel of MS2. The deck colours remained the same and the masts were white. There was a small alteration to her light AA armament. Only four single 20mm guns were retained, but two twin 20mm mounts were added. The singles were on each side of the fore funnel and each side of the bridge. The twin mounts were placed with one mount on the quarterdeck and one on the aft turret. *Aurora* was under repair from November 1943 until April 1944, as a result of bomb damage while serving in the Aegean. Electronic equipment remained the same. The Carley floats stacked on the 4in gun shelter were removed and two placed each side instead.

HMS AURORA Pennant 12
Arethusa class cruiser 1945

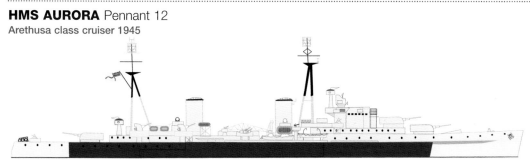

Aurora was refitted at Malta from June to October 1945. Various counter-measures and IFF were added, and she emerged in a scheme of 507c with a hull panel of B20. The wood decks were no longer painted and, having been subjected to wear, had started to appear as a shade of dull wood. Lower masts were pale grey and the area above the funnels was black. She continued to serve during the general mopping-up period in the Mediterranean region and for a short time post-war. Note that the arrangement of 20mm AA guns changed again. The singles each side of the bridge were removed and replaced by twin mounts. The singles each side of the fore funnel remained. The twin mount on the aft turret was removed. This gave a total of three twin 20mm mounts and two single 20mm AA guns, as well as the quad 2pdr mounts.

CHUNG KING May 1948
TCHOUNG KING March 1949
HSUANG HO 1951
PEI CHING 1951
KUANG CHOU 1952
Arethusa class cruiser

Aurora was partly sold to the Nationalist Chinese Navy, which accepted her in May 1948. She was painted MS4c. Wood decks were restored. Metal decks were B5 and the turret tops B6. Extra support was added to the fore-mast tripod and a heavier strut to the mainmast tripod. Single 20mm guns were placed on each side of the bridge at the forecastle deck level. Twin 20mm mounts were on each side of the front of the fore funnel. Another twin 20mm mount was placed on top of 'Y' turret. Quad 2pdr mounts were still carried, but directors for these, along with their Type 282 radar, were removed. More Carley floats were added as well. The lantern Type 273 radar was removed, but the other radars were still carried. A depth-charge rack was retained on the quarterdeck. A crew was eventually gathered, but among these were Communist agitators. The new crew required a lot of training, as no vessel of this size and type had previously been part of the NCN, and it was nearly a year before she could sail. The Communists persuaded crewmen to support their cause. On arrival in China, much was made of her size and strength as the flagship of the NCN and she was declared the pride of the navy. However she secretly slipped out of a Nationalist port and changed sides, wearing a white flag with a red star on it. The defection was a huge propaganda triumph for the Communists, and the Nationalists set out to destroy their former flagship. An air raid scored hits, causing her to capsize. It was beyond the capacity of the Communists to raise, repair and re-equip such a sophisticated Western warship and she never re-entered service.

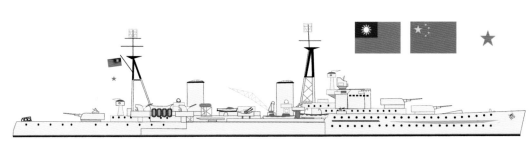

HMS PENELOPE Pennant 97
Arethusa class cruiser 1937–9

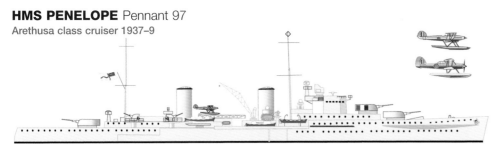

Painted in an overall scheme of 507c, Penelope joined the Mediterranean Fleet in 1937. The wood decks were scrubbed; horizontal metal surfaces were 507c, except for the area around the anchor winches forward of the ship, painted in 507a. 'B' turret carried British neutrality colours due to the Spanish Civil War. These were painted on the sides and across the top of the turret. She was completed with twin 4in AA mounts and a second HACS aft in place of the originally planned searchlight and control station. Two searchlights were placed aft of the rear funnel. The usual quad 0.5in MG mounts were carried on each side. There was a square radio direction-finder on the front of the bridge, which seems to be unique to *Penelope*, and she carried a HF/DF on the foremast. The original aircraft was the much-liked Osprey, unlike the more temperamental Fairey Seafox which replaced it by 1939.

HMS PENELOPE Pennant 97
Arethusa class cruiser 1940

Penelope was painted in a scheme that was temporarily favoured for ships operating with the Home Fleet out of Scapa Flow. The dark brown and contrasting white was supposedly good concealment while ships were at anchor there. The patches of green were not as extensive as on other units, but again intended to match in with the background. Obviously this was best when viewed at waterline or periscope level and, perhaps, reflects a certain fear of another sinking like the *Royal Oak* incident. The colours used on horizontal surfaces are not known, but the camouflage may have been carried across them. The colours used were white, 1940 brown and 1940 green. The ship was recalled from the Mediterranean and served with the Home Fleet during the Norway campaign, where she was badly damaged due to grounding off Vestfjord.

HMS PENELOPE Pennant 97
Arethusa class cruiser July 1941

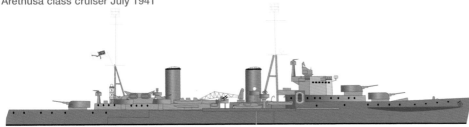

During the extensive repairs required after her grounding, *Penelope* received tripod masts along with Type 281 radar at the mastheads. Type 285 radar was fitted to both HACS, and Type 284 radar to the main director. The catapult was removed, and two quad 2pdr mounts replaced it. No other light AA changes were made. Splinter protection tubs were placed around the 4in and the quad 0.5in mounts. Note that a distinction at this time was the way the side plating was extended up to just above the forward shelter deck. This was intended to eventually become an AA platform, but it also helped deflect seas washing up onto the forecastle deck and continuing all the way amidships. The paint scheme appears to be a 507b hull, while the grey used for the superstructure was a few tones lighter, possibly a special mix of a lightened 507b. The scheme was only worn for a short time and has proven difficult to confirm.

HMS PENELOPE Pennant 97
Arethusa class cruiser December 1941

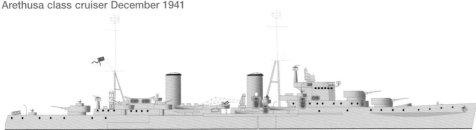

Penelope was sent to the Mediterranean in October 1941 to join Force K out of Malta, where the then-popular Mountbatten pink was applied. The decks were mid-grey, probably 507b, but exact details are not known. In December, four single 20mm AA guns were added: one on each side of the bridge on the platform previously prepared, one on the aft turret and one on the quarterdeck. *Penelope* was severely damaged by mines when the cruiser *Neptune* was lost. While under repair at Malta she came under concentrated attack. It was thought she would have to be scuttled to save further loss of life and injury, but the crew refused to give up. They were allowed to take her to sea and try to reach safety, but she was in such poor condition that they were not given much hope. They did make it to safety and the ship was patched up enough to make it to the New York Navy Yard, arriving in May 1942 for full repairs.

HMS PENELOPE Pennant 97
Arethusa class cruiser November 1942

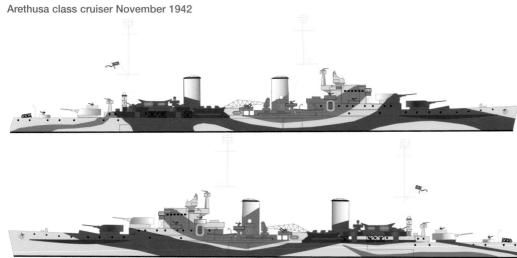

After major repairs in the United States, *Penelope* returned to the UK, where an Admiralty standard camouflage scheme was applied. The colours were MS4a, with B5 and MS2 disruptive areas. The decks and all horizontal surfaces were dark grey, probably G10. A major change to her profile was the placement of a Type 273 radar lantern in front of the bridge. This was not the best position for such a set, as it could only give coverage ahead and 90 degrees each side with all aft arcs being blocked by the bridge. However, it was probably considered the only place available at the time. Four additional 20mm guns were added at this time and the quad 0.5in MG mounts were removed. After this work, the ship returned to the Mediterranean and again saw extensive service.

HMS PENELOPE Pennant 97
Arethusa class cruiser February 1944

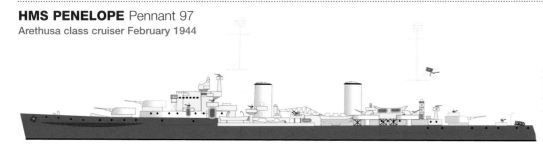

In 1944 *Penelope* adopted a scheme based on a dark hull, using 507a, with a lighter upper works of 507c. Her decks and horizontal surfaces were dark grey, as previously. The armament and electronics remained the same. She was very busy during the allied amphibious actions in the Mediterranean, where she escorted invasion vessels and took part in bombardment of enemy positions. It was while returning from the Anzio landings that she was torpedoed and sunk by the German U-boat *U-410*.

HMS GALATEA Pennant 71
Arethusa class cruiser 1940

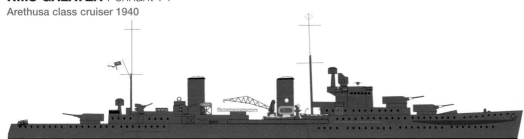

On completion, *Galatea* was sent to the Mediterranean as the flagship, Rear Admiral (D). At that time she wore the usual 507c overall, with peacetime polished wood decks. However, in 1939 she was recalled to the UK, where she was repainted and appeared in a sombre scheme of 507a overall. There were no armament changes or radar added at this time. She engaged in hunting enemy blockade-runners, and when the Norway campaign got under way was part of the British fleet which took part in that desperate struggle.

HMS GALATEA Pennant 71
Arethusa class cruiser July 1941

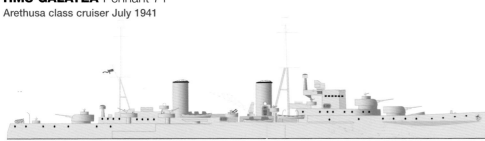

Mediterranean based ships were still using Mountbatten pink at this time and *Galatea* adopted it. During a refit, the catapult had been removed and replaced with quad 2pdr AA mounts. The quad 0.5in machine guns were replaced by single 20mm. Two more 20mm guns were placed on top of 'B' turret and two on each side of the bridge; another was placed on the aft turret and one on the quarterdeck. Type 279 radar was placed on both mastheads. This radar was an improved version of the Type 79, one of the first sets to go to sea. Although not perfect, it gave around 70 per cent serviceability, better than the original version that had a serviceability rate of only 40 per cent. In November, *Galatea* was stationed at Malta with Force K. Force K was tasked with intercepting Axis convoys to North Africa, a task they achieved with considerable success.

HMS GALATEA Pennant 71
Arethusa class cruiser December 1941

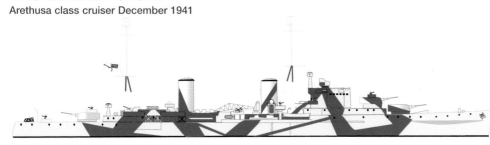

During service with the Mediterranean Fleet, *Galatea* adopted a typical 507c with 507a camouflage scheme of an unofficial type, but typical of ships in that fleet. The two shades were arranged in a pattern unique to each ship. At this time, it is believed her decks were still natural for the wood and 507b for horizontal metal surfaces. There had been no changes to her armament or electronics since her last refit in the UK. However, as with other ships serving in the region, it is possible that captured Italian Breda guns were unofficially added to her armament. This ship was torpedoed and sunk off Alexandria on 14 December 1941 by the U-boat *U-557*.

TOWN CLASS CRUISERS
HMS SOUTHAMPTON Pennant 83
Town class (Southampton) cruiser 1938

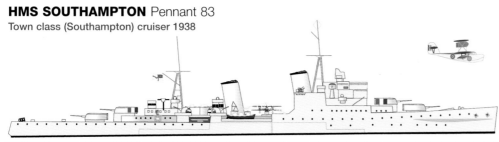

The ships in this class were powerful cruisers, with twelve 6in guns in four triple turrets and four twin 4in AA. *Southampton*, the lead ship, is shown above in 1938, serving with the Home Fleet. She is painted overall in MS4a Home Fleet grey. The wood decks were scrubbed to a pale, fresh wood colour. The areas around each 4in AA mount were also wood. The horizontal metal decks appear to have also been MS4a, but the area around the anchors was a darker shade, probably 507a. The compass platform had timber slats laid on it for the comfort of crew standing watch. Note the lack of a third HACS aft, as some of her later sisters, and a control station instead of a second main gun director.

HMS SOUTHAMPTON Pennant 83
Town class (Southampton) cruiser May 1940

In this illustration, *Southampton* is shown in overall 507b, adopted at the outbreak of World War II when she was serving as flagship of the 2nd Cruiser Squadron. Only a few weeks after the war broke out she was hit by a German bomb, but suffered little damage. This scheme was worn during the Norwegian campaign. In May 1940 she was fitted with Type 279 radar. The HF/DF was moved to the starfish on the forward mast. The hangars could accommodate one Walrus aircraft each. The original plan was to carry three Swordfish: one on the catapult and two stowed in the hangars. Torpedoes were provided so that they could launch an air strike against enemy ships.

HMS SOUTHAMPTON Pennant 83
Town class (Southampton) cruiser
June 1940

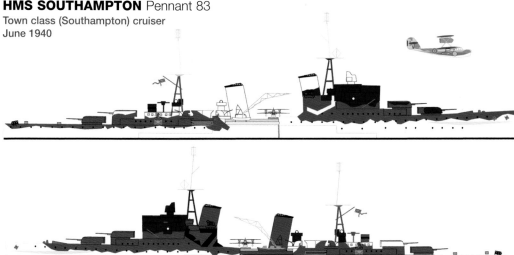

Owing to German air raids on the British Home Fleet base at Scapa Flow, the ships stationed there tried various camouflage schemes to make themselves less visible when at anchor and at sea. This was generally known as the Flotta system, but it was nonetheless a semi-unofficial style. The colours used were white, black, 1940 brown and an unknown green, that might have been a lighter mix of 1940 green. The turret tops were the same green. Wood decks were unpainted and horizontal metal surfaces seem to have been painted in MS4a. The scheme was only popular for a few months in mid- to late 1940. The AA armament of *Southampton* remained as designed, with quad 2pdrs on each side of the fore funnel and quad 0.5in MG mounts on each side of the aft control position.

HMS SOUTHAMPTON Pennant 83
Town class (Southampton) cruiser January 1941

Southampton moved to the Mediterranean and Indian Ocean areas in late 1940, where the Flotta scheme was impracticable. 507b was adopted and she wore this colour during East African and Mediterranean operations, including the Battle of Cape Spartivento, during which she also wore a prominent false bow wave. Note the black boot topping at the waterline has been considerably reduced in height to prevent it providing an estimate of length for an attacking U-boat. Most camouflage schemes called for the complete removal of black boot topping, but it was rarely done away with altogether on large warships. Southampton was hit by a stick of bombs off Sicily in January 1941 and completely disabled. Uncontrollable fires broke out and the ship had to be abandoned and sunk by torpedoes from *Orion* and *Gloucester*.

HMS NEWCASTLE Pennant 76
Town class (Southampton) cruiser January 1937

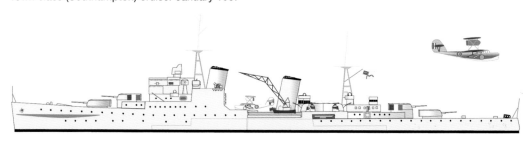

The first two *Southampton* class cruisers were easily identified from their sisters when first built by the lack of a third HACS aft. The last three of the class also had another main gun director aft. Although shown here in pale grey, so they can be seen, the mast tops above the tripod level were plain white. Masts below that were the same as the rest of the ship. As completed, *Newcastle* was painted in overall MS4a Home Fleet grey. The wood decks were scrubbed and the horizontal metal surfaces were MS4a, except for the area forward around the anchors, which was 507b or 507a. Ship's boats were in peacetime colours and the Walrus was very pale grey. Note that the neutrality markings were carried on both 'B' and 'X' turrets. Note the complete lack of splinter protection around the 4in AA guns, the 2pdr mounts and the quad 0.5in MG mounts.

HMS NEWCASTLE Pennant 76
Town class (Southampton) cruiser May 1940

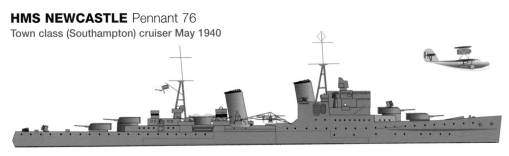

When World War II commenced, *Newcastle* was in dock and emerged painted in overall 507b except for the wood decks. The ship was engaged in trade protection patrols with the Northern Fleet, against German shipping trying to make it home and raiders trying to get out. In November 1939 she briefly sighted the German battleships *Scharnhorst* and *Gneisenau*, but was unable to maintain contact. She underwent a refit and emerged in May 1940 with two Unrotated Projectile (UP) mounts, one on 'B' turret and one on the quarterdeck. Her overall paint colour remained the same, but the top of 'B' turret appears to be painted a darker grey, probably because of the blast from the UP launcher. Note that some of the Carley floats previously hung on the rear of the hangar were moved to the sides.

HMS NEWCASTLE Pennant 76
Town class (Southampton) cruiser 1941

Newcastle was part of Force H from late 1940 to mid-1941, operating in both the Mediterranean and the Atlantic so seems to have adopted a scheme reasonable for both areas. She is illustrated in overall MS4a, but with white tripods and mast tops. The wooden decks remained unpainted, but horizontal metal surfaces seem to have been the same as the rest of the ship, except the area around the anchors and the top of 'B' turret, which were 507a. More Carley floats were moved to the side of the hangar and one aft. Type 286 radar was fitted at the mastheads while the ship was visiting Simonstown, South Africa, in April. No other changes had been made to the light AA by that time. Much of her service during this period was in the South Atlantic, but she was present with Force H for the Battle of Cape Spartivento in the Mediterranean. In August 1941 she was sent to Boston, USA, for a refit.

HMS NEWCASTLE Pennant 76
Town class (Southampton) cruiser January 1942

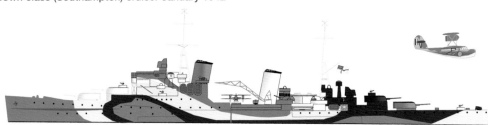

Upon completion of her US refit, *Newcastle* went to Plymouth in the UK on 29 December 1941. An Admiralty-designed camouflage scheme was applied, as in the top illustration. The colours were B5, with 507c and B15. This scheme was intended to confuse the viewer at a distance and was apparently the same on both sides. Type 291 radar was fitted at the mastheads and Type 273 radar in front of the bridge. Quad 0.5in mounts and UP launchers were removed, and a total of nine 20mm guns were added. *Newcastle* then joined the Eastern Fleet, with detachment to the Eastern Mediterranean as required. While on detachment, she was hit by a torpedo from the German E-boat *S56* and severely damaged. Patched at Bombay, she arrived in the United States on 10 October 1942. However, as with her previously, she had to return to the UK before all issues were rectified. The camouflage in the lower illustration shows that the areas of 507c were eliminated, and there were changes in shapes and areas covered. The decks were painted dark grey. Aircraft facilities were removed by the time of the second illustration. Type 291 radar had been replaced with Type 281 radar. Type 285 radar was fitted to the HACS and Type 284 radar to the main gun directors. The 2pdr directors received Type 282 radar. Six medium Carley floats were placed each side of the hangar. 20mm guns were increased to nineteen with the addition of another ten singles. They were arranged two on 'B' turret, two on each side of the bridge at the shelter deck level, five on each side of the former catapult deck, one on each side of the aft deckhouse, one on 'X' turret and two on the quarterdeck. Both cranes were retained.

HMS NEWCASTLE Pennant 76
Town class (Southampton) cruiser
March 1943

HMS NEWCASTLE Pennant 76
Town class (Southampton) cruiser
September 1943

Newcastle moved to the Eastern Fleet, and by 1944 had adopted a scheme typical of that region. The overall shade was 507c, with a washed-out mid-blue panel on the hull. The deck and upper surfaces were 507a. By this time, there were some changes to the light AA. Six single 20mm guns were removed and replaced with four twin 20mm mounts. These were arranged one on top of 'B' turret, one on each side of the bridge, and one on the quarterdeck. The ship served in the Eastern Fleet until early 1945, when she returned to the UK.

HMS NEWCASTLE Pennant 76
Town class (Southampton) cruiser September 1952

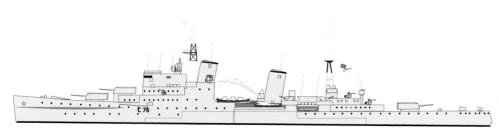

This post-war image shows *Newcastle* in duck egg blue. The Royal Navy never officially adopted this colour, but nonetheless it was a shade some ships were painted for a time. The decks were reinstated to peacetime unpainted timber. Horizontal surfaces appear to have been 507b. 'X' turret was removed, plus the HACS previously on the aft deckhouse. Four twin 40mm Bofors were placed there. A more advanced twin 40mm is shown on each side of the bridge. Self-inflating rafts enclosed in boxes replaced Carley floats on each side of the bridge and between the 4in mounts. Although empty, the depth-charge racks on the stern were retained until the end of the ship's service. Note the modernised electronics with lots of whip aerials and only one crane on the centreline. The HACS was removed and new directors placed on each side of the fore funnel. It was common to paint the area of masts most exposed to fumes from the funnels black, but the areas above and below in lighter shades. As per international agreement, her pennant was displayed on the side.

HMS BIRMINGHAM Pennant 19
Town class (Southampton) cruiser China Station 1938–9

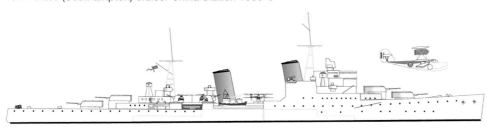

On completion, *Birmingham* was sent to join 5th Cruiser Squadron on the China Station and was an impressive advance on the older cruisers sent prior to World War II. She was given the usual overall coat of white, except for the funnels which were painted 507b instead of the previous buff. Wood decks were scrubbed daily. Horizontal metal surfaces were white, except for the area around the anchor chains and winches which was a shade approximating 507b. Larger boats were blue with a white lower hull and masts were white. Unlike the two previous ships, *Birmingham* had a third HACS aft. She was closely monitored by the Japanese in these waters and on the outbreak of war, stopped several foreign vessels suspected of transporting German reservists to Europe, causing some tension with Japan. She did not have the usual knuckle at the bow, which had become common to British-built cruisers. Instead, she had a flared bow to see if that was advantageous.

HMS BIRMINGHAM Pennant 19
Town class (Southampton) cruiser China Station 1940

During a refit in December 1940, *Birmingham* adopted an unofficial and fairly simple camouflage scheme, similar to schemes adopted by other ships at this time. Some areas were painted 507c to break up the silhouette when seen at sea level. The wood decks were left natural, but no longer scrubbed. The rest of the ship and all other horizontal metal surfaces were painted in 507b. After experience during the Norway and France campaigns, she was fitted with a UP launcher, but no other light AA was available, so she retained her original fit. She took part in the hunt for the German battleship *Bismarck* in 1941, and was frequently employed to escort valuable, high-speed convoys of troops and material around the Cape to the Middle East. The UP mount was removed in July 1941.

HMS BIRMINGHAM Pennant 19
Town class (Southampton) cruiser April 1942

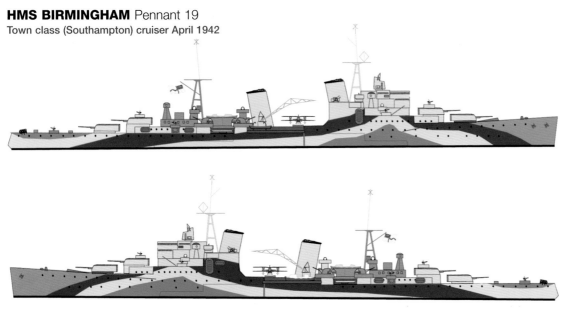

Birmingham was refitted at Simonstown and emerged in April 1942 with a four-colour Admiralty standard light scheme. The main shade was MS4a, with dark areas of G10 and sections of B5 and B6. The deck colours are not known, but at this time of the war most ships had their decks painted in dark grey, or even dark green. The catapult deck was, however, definitely dark grey, probably 507a. During the refit, Type 291 general warning radar was fitted at the mastheads. Type 294 radar was fit to the main gun director. The quad 0.5in MG mounts were removed and seven single 20mm guns added. These were placed as follows: one on top of 'B' turret and one on 'X' turret, one on each side of the bridge, one each in the old machine gun positions and one on the quarterdeck.

HMS BIRMINGHAM Pennant 19
Town class (Southampton) cruiser August 1943

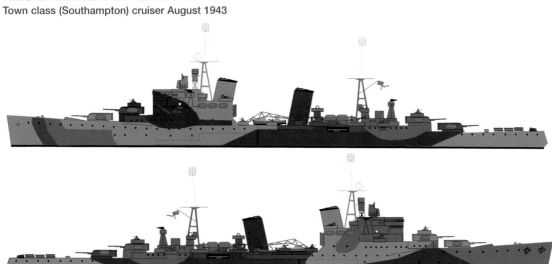

Birmingham was in refit in the UK from April to August 1943, during which a completely new camouflage was added. It took the form of darker colours. The base was G45, with areas of G10 and B30. The decks seem to have been dark grey in all areas. The lower portions of the tripod masts were the same as the colour below them, while the upper portions were white. The Type 291 radar was replaced by the superior Type 281 radar. Type 273 radar was fitted on top of the bridge, a far better position than on her sister *Newcastle*. The three HACS received Type 285 radar. All but two of the single 20mm guns were removed and replaced by eight twin 20mm mounts. Aircraft facilities were removed, but the cranes were retained for use with ship's boats. Because so many ships had sunk rapidly, especially due to the new German radio-controlled bombs, extra Carley floats were added to give crews the maximum chance of getting to one. Larger versions were carried on the rear of the former hangars. The hangars themselves were converted into badly needed extra accommodation, a cinema and offices. Although the accommodation was initially better than previous ships, the growth of wartime equipment meant that ships of this class quickly became crowded. The conversion of the redundant hangars, plus aircraft fuel and weapon storage spaces, considerably improved the situation.

HMS **BIRMINGHAM** Pennant 19
Town class (Southampton) cruiser November 1944

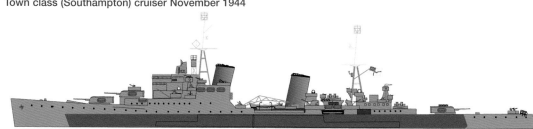

From July to November 1944, *Birmingham* was given a considerable AA upgrade. The 'X' turret was removed and replaced by two US-style quad 40mm mounts and directors. Two more were placed higher up between the 4in AA mounts. The 20mm guns were changed as well, giving her a total of ten twin mounts and seven single guns. *Birmingham* was then attached to the Home Fleet, where she served out the war in Europe, carrying out offensive sweeps along the coast of Norway and escorting carrier strikes against German targets. For these purposes, she adopted the new standard fleet scheme, painted in MS3 with a panel of G10 on the hull. All horizontal surfaces were dark grey, probably G10. The electronic fit was unaltered, apart from the addition of IFF and missile-jamming equipment.

HMS **BIRMINGHAM** Pennant C19
Town class (Southampton) cruiser Korean War

Service during the Korean War saw few external changes to *Birmingham*, although all 20mm AA guns had been removed. While shown here in MS4a overall, the ship did change to a darker grey during the winter. The decks had returned to unpainted wood, but the horizontal surfaces remained dark grey. A peacetime black boot topping was applied to the waterline. Like many ships post-war, the area of the masts where funnel fumes caused staining were painted black. The pennant was displayed on the hull on each side of the bridge, in keeping with international and NATO agreements. *Birmingham* received other upgrades during her long service until paid off in December 1959, the longest serving of her class. She was towed away for scrapping on 7 September 1960.

HMS **GLASGOW** Pennant 21
Town class (Southampton) cruiser July 1940

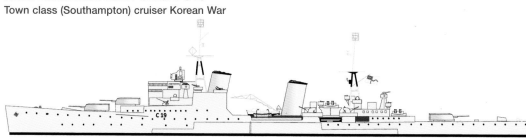

Glasgow had originally been painted in MS4a, but on the outbreak of war adopted 507a. The wood decks remained natural wood and horizontal metal surfaces seem to be a lighter grey, possibly remaining MS4a. After the Norway campaign, she was fitted with two sets of Un-rotated Projectile (UP) launchers, one on 'B' turret and one on 'X' turret. No other changes to the AA armament were made at this time. Type 286 radar was fitted, making her an early recipient. However, this set was not as good as those that followed. It was fixed at the top of the foremast and only gave bearings directly ahead and somewhat to each beam.

HMS **GLASGOW** Pennant 21
Town class (Southampton) cruiser
August 1941

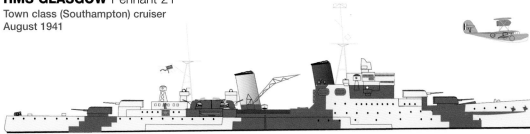

During 1941 a proposal was put forward for a camouflage described as a contrast type. The objective was to use two totally opposite shades to break up the outline of the ship and confuse a distant viewer. A similar style was used on the battlecruiser *Repulse*. The shades used were 507a on 507c. The wood decks remained unpainted, and horizontal metal surfaces appear to have been the same as the shade used on the side of that area, except for the turret tops, which were dark grey. As yet there were no changes to the light AA armament or radar fit. This scheme was applied at Singapore while the ship was undergoing damage repairs from when she was torpedoed during operations off Crete. It was worn until September 1942.

HMS GLASGOW Pennant 21
Town class (Southampton) cruiser
1949

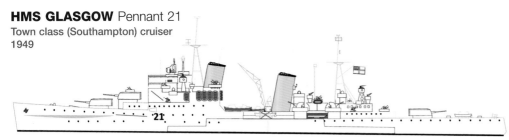

Post-war, some ships on station at the remaining colonies adopted pre-war paint styles: in this case, a white overall with buff funnels. Steel decks were mid-grey, but the turret tops were white. The wooden decks were cleared of wartime paint and, once again, buffed to a light yellow wood shade. The pennant number was painted on the side in black. The arrangement of her Carley floats remained for most of her service life and very few other changes were made, except for a profusion of whip aerials. The ship transferred to the Mediterranean and remained there from 1951–5, then returned to the UK for a brief period as flagship for Flag Officer (D). Paid off in 1956, *Glasgow* remained in reserve until 1958 and was then sold for scrapping.

HMS SHEFFIELD Pennant 24
Town class (Southampton) cruiser October 1938

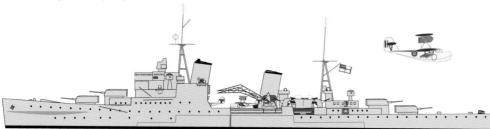

Sheffield joined 18th Cruiser Squadron of the Home Fleet and is shown here in MS4a overall. Her wood decks were unpainted. Other horizontal surfaces were grey, quite probably MS4a, like the rest of the ship, but the metal deck area around the anchors and winches was darker, probably 507a. Large ship's boats appear to have been brown. She was the first British cruiser to be fitted with radar, a Type 79y radar set placed at the mastheads. The installation was so secret that only specific officers, along with the team working the set, were permitted to know what it was, and visiting officers could not visit the radar room without specific Admiralty permission. Cover stories explained away the unusual aerials. It was a surprisingly effective set, but being new technology, its reliability was only about 40 per cent because of malfunction and inexperience. As operators became used to the set, performance improved. It led to the development of Type 279 radar.

HMS SHEFFIELD Pennant 24
Town class (Southampton) cruiser
1939

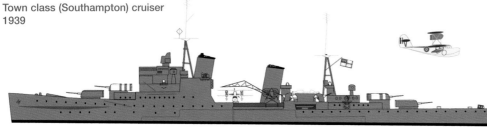

Sheffield had an unusual arrangement of white bands on the 'B' and 'X' turrets in 1939. It is possible they were for a fleet exercise to designate which side the ship was on. They were carried up over the top of each turret. The top of 'Y' turret was painted very dark grey, possibly 507a, as was the area around the anchor winches at the bow. The anchor chains were painted white. The colour for the rest of the ship was 507b, including the other turret tops. The wood decks were unpainted and appear very light, suggesting this was the appearance prior to war being declared. Boats and the aircraft also appear to be white, and masts above the tripod were also painted white. There were no armament changes since completion.

HMS SHEFFIELD Pennant 24
Town class (Southampton) cruiser
early 1941

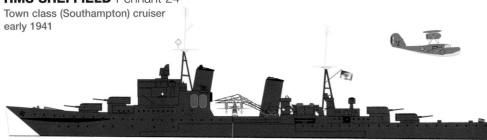

Relying on the description of an ex-rating who served on the ship, the previous scheme was painted over with a grey he called almost black. I presume that would have been 507a. He stated there was a white triangle at the bow and this general scheme was retained during the winter of 1940–1. However, when the ship went to join Force H, it was repainted in a much lighter tone and the white bow area painted over. I have no information of what the lighter tone was, but as Force H operated in both the Mediterranean and the Atlantic, it was most likely 507b. She was apparently wearing the lighter tone during the hunt for the German battleship *Bismarck*. Interestingly, the same ex-crew member was aboard when the Flotta scheme of dark brown and green was used, but he could not recall enough detail for me to illustrate this elusive scheme.

HMS SHEFFIELD Pennant 24
Town class (Southampton) cruiser
September 1941

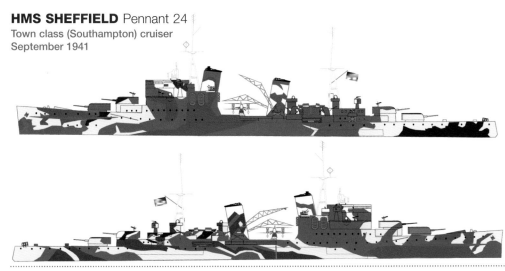

Sheffield was painted up in an Admiralty-designed, and very complicated, disruptive scheme in 1941 while undergoing repairs in the UK. The colours used were white, 507c, 507a, MS1, MS2, and B5. While it may have indeed been disruptive to the viewer, one can only think how hard it must have been to maintain, and how often the person who designed it must have been roundly cursed by the men who had to keep painting it. The scheme was carried up over the decks and adjacent superstructure, which would have increased the amount of work considerably. Most of the Admiralty schemes were designed using models, which were viewed against a variety of backdrops in rooms with varied lighting. The designers did not, however, go to sea often, and rarely had the opportunity to view the results of their work. No doubt they also rarely had the chance to speak to those responsible for keeping up such complicated schemes. At the time of this dockyard visit, the ship also received six single 20mm AA guns and the quad 0.5in MG mounts were landed. Protective splinter shields were placed around each of the twin 4in mounts. Some of the 20mm were installed without protective splinter tubs.

HMS SHEFFIELD Pennant 24
Town class (Southampton) cruiser
July 1943

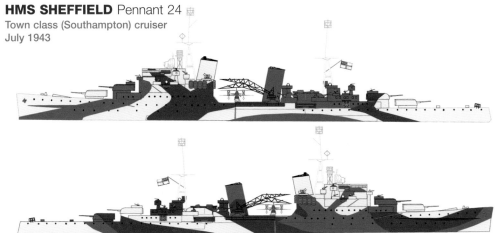

Sheffield was repainted to an Admiralty-designed intermediate disruptive scheme in 1942. This reduced the number of colours to 507c, 507a and B5. The decks were dark grey. This would have made maintenance of the scheme far more practicable, and reduced the number of paint shades needed to be carried. During this time the original radar was removed, and Type 281 radar was fitted at both mastheads. Type 273 radar was placed on the bridge between the main director and the foremast. Type 283 radar was added just in front of the bridge for barrage fire. The 2pdr directors received Type 282 radar. The light AA was increased with the addition of several more 20mm guns, raising the total to nine or ten. Protective splinter shields were placed around all the light AA guns.

HMS SHEFFIELD Pennant 24
Town class (Southampton) cruiser
October 1943

Sheffield was painted in a new scheme of G10 for the lower hull and B55 for the upper works in October. The decks were also G10, as well as the tops of the main turrets and the 4in gun mounts. Aircraft facilities were removed during 1943. Extra 20mm single AA guns were added and by February 1944 the total number had risen to twenty-two. There were several extra Carley floats added aft, as well. Overcrowding had become a problem, due to all the new light AA weapons, and the availability of the hangars for other use helped ease that. She was present during the sinking of the German battleship *Scharnhorst*. After covering carrier raids on the German battleship *Tirpitz*, she went to the United States for a major refit.

HMS SHEFFIELD Pennant 24
Town class (Southampton) cruiser May 1945

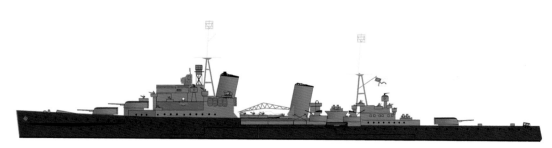

After her US refit, *Sheffield* returned to the UK in an Admiralty standard scheme, using G45 for the upper works and B20 for the hull. All decks were B20, as were the main turret tops. Considerable changes to the profile had taken place. Most prominent was the removal of the 'X' turret, which enabled the fitting of four US Navy quad 40mm AA mounts. Ten twin 20mm mounts were placed aboard and seven single 20mm guns were also carried. Extra barrage directors were fitted, and accommodation in the now empty hangars improved. The electronic fit remained the same on her return, but individual director tubs for the quad 40mm mounts were added. However, the Admiralty decided that as the war in the Pacific appeared likely to continue for some time, the ship should go into a British dockyard for further alterations, particularly for new and improved Royal Navy radar and electronics. Since the war in Europe had ended by the time of her return, *Sheffield* did not see war service in this scheme.

HMS SHEFFIELD Pennant 24
Town class (Southampton) cruiser June 1946

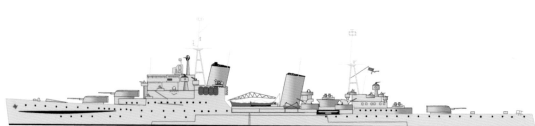

Although it had been intended to finish the UK part of her refit and send the ship to join the British Pacific Fleet, *Sheffield* was still undergoing alterations when the Japanese surrendered. As a result, work did not proceed with the same urgency as before. So it was actually June 1946 when the refit was completed, and the ship was again ready for service. She is shown here in MS4a Home Fleet grey, prior to her departure for service on the West Indies Station. The metal decks were still G20 and some Cemtex had been applied here and there. The wood decks were restored to their pre-war appearance. Type 293 radar, a target acquisition set, replaced the Type 273 radar on top of the bridge. The Type 281 radar was removed from both mastheads. Type 293 radar was placed on the foretop and Type 960 on the top of the mainmast. Type 275 radar replaced the original Type 284 on the main gun director. One crane was removed and the remaining one relocated on the centreline. More alterations were carried out during the post-war service of this ship, but those are outside the scope of this book.

HMS MANCHESTER Pennant 15
Town class (Gloucester) cruiser 1938

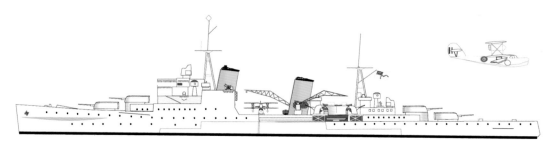

Manchester went to the East Indies Station upon completion and wore a peacetime colonial garb. The funnels were buff and superstructure white. Wood decks were, of course, scrubbed wood, and horizontal metal surfaces appear to have been white, except for the area at the bow around the anchor winches and chains. This was pretty much a last gasp for such fancy dress, as war was fast approaching. She did not wear any of the usual international red, white and blue stripes on her turrets on departure from the UK, but they would almost certainly have been added on arrival. At some point in 1939, the funnels were painted in 507b. On the outbreak of war, the ship seems to have adopted 507c as the main colour, including the funnels. Note that this ship had an extra main armament director aft and the quad 0.5in MG mounts were located higher.

HMS MANCHESTER Pennant 15
Town class (Gloucester) cruiser
December 1939

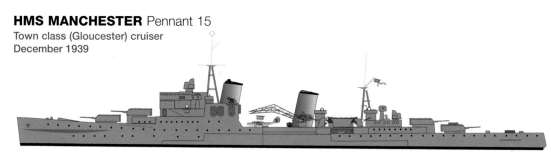

Manchester was recalled to the UK, joined the Home Fleet in November 1939, and was repainted to 507b overall, except for the wood decks which remained unpainted. A heavy peacetime boot topping seems to have been retained for some time. At some point in 1940, a Flotta scheme was adopted; there are no records of the pattern used, but the colours were almost certainly brown and green on grey. At this time, the only warlike measures seem to have been the addition of Carley floats on the quarterdeck, on top of 'Y' turret, at various places along the side of the hangar, and on the bridge at shelter deck level. Note that Carley floats came in several sizes. There were no changes to the AA armament or electronics.

HMS MANCHESTER Pennant 15
Town class (Gloucester) cruiser
September–November 1940

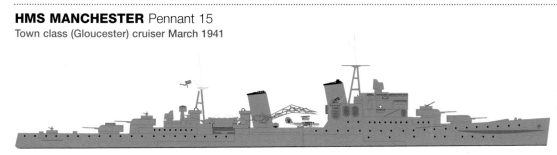

After the Norway campaign and the fall of France, Manchester was sent to the Mediterranean Fleet operating out of Gibraltar, where she adopted a Mountbatten pink camouflage at the height of its popularity. The pinkish grey had a tendency to shade toward a red hue in dull light and shade, or at dawn and dusk. It was always at its most effective in bright sunlight. The wood decks remained unpainted, while the horizontal metal surfaces were painted in 507b. Type 286 radar was fitted at the head of the foremast in November 1940. This was a fixed aerial giving ahead bearings, with some coverage to each beam. The ship needed to be turned to sweep aft bearings with it. The light AA armament remained the same at this time.

HMS MANCHESTER Pennant 15
Town class (Gloucester) cruiser March 1941

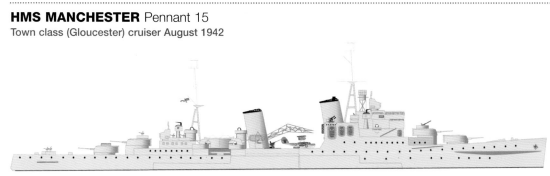

Manchester underwent a refit on the Tyne from January to March 1941. The quad 0.5in MG mounts were removed. A single MkIII 40mm Bofors gun was placed on 'B' turret and five 20mm AA guns were added. The ship is shown here in 507b, which was worn during the hunt for the German battleship Bismarck, when Manchester patrolled the Denmark Strait. Decks are believed to have been painted grey and were most likely also 507b. The mast tops were white. By July she was sent back to the Mediterranean. Some sources state that the ship remained in Mountbatten pink during this period, but it seems unlikely she would have patrolled the Denmark Strait in Mountbatten pink, which was designed for bright sunny regions.

HMS MANCHESTER Pennant 15
Town class (Gloucester) cruiser August 1942

Manchester is shown here just prior to her loss, in Mountbatten pink which has been carried thoroughly even onto the Carley floats. The deck colour was probably 507b. In July 1941 she was torpedoed and, after temporary repairs, was sent to the United States. Type 286 radar was replaced by Type 279 radar at both mastheads. The gunnery directors received Type 284 radar and the 2pdr directors Type 282 radar. All three HACS received Type 285 radar and a Type 273 radar in a typical lantern, between the director and the foremast. Three more 20mm AA guns were added. During Operation Pedestal two army-type single 40mm guns were added on the aft end of the catapult deck, as shown. The ship was hit by a torpedo from an Italian motor torpedo boat and crippled. It proved impossible to get the ship underway again and she had to be scuttled.

HMS LIVERPOOL Pennant 11
Town class (Gloucester) cruiser
1938–9

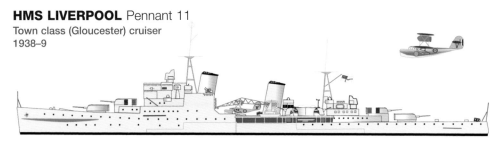

Liverpool was sent to the West Indies on entering service, but joined the 5th Cruiser Squadron in the South China Sea in 1939. There she wore 507c overall, but with prominent nationality markings on 'A' and 'X' turrets, as Japan and China were at war. Note that the waist was very open at this time, which turned out to be disadvantageous in high seas, as she tended to ship water that swept from the flight deck to the stern. Quad 0.5in MG mounts had not been fitted. The only light AA for the ships was provided by the quad 2pdr mounts. These were considered very powerful ships with good range and protection. The design, with the hangars each side of the fore funnel, was at first viewed with trepidation by the seagoing officers of the fleet. But the class soon proved their many good points and became popular ships.

HMS LIVERPOOL Pennant 11
Town class (Gloucester) cruiser 1940

Liverpool joined the Eastern Mediterranean Fleet in May 1940. Like so many ships, she adopted a camouflage based on available paint, in this case 507a on 507c, the same on both sides. Wood decks were natural. Metal surfaces were apparently painted dark grey, probably 507a. By now, quad 0.5in MG mounts were fitted and rifle-calibre machine guns also used. She assisted in sinking the Italian destroyer *Espero* only eight days after arriving, but was hit by a 4.7in shell in the action. *Liverpool* was struck by a dud bomb causing minor damage in July 1940 and critically damaged by an aerial torpedo off Leros on 14 October, causing an explosion of aviation fuel, damaging the bow and blowing the roof off 'A' turret. Eventually the bow broke off, assisting her salvage as it made towing difficult. By April 1941 she was seaworthy enough to go to the United States for permanent repairs, completed that December.

HMS LIVERPOOL Pennant 11
Town class (Gloucester) cruiser 1942

After repair, *Liverpool* returned to the UK. The camouflage scheme used 507c as the base with 507a and B5. The deck was dark grey forward; quarterdeck colour is unknown. The quad 2pdr and quad 0.5in MG mounts had been removed during repair. Nine 20mm guns were fitted for the homeward voyage. In the UK, the 2pdrs were restored. Radar Type 284 was put on the main director forward, another HACS aft, and all three fitted with Type 285 radar. Type 273 radar was added, the lantern aft of the main director; Type 282 was provided for the 2pdr directors, with Type 281 radar soon after. She covered Russian convoys, and went to the Mediterranean in June 1942 (Operation Harpoon), and was hit by another aerial torpedo, abreast the aft engine room, totally disabled and thought to be lost. She was towed to Gibraltar and patched enough to get to the UK. Almost declared a total loss, repairs kept her out of service until May 1944. She was assigned to care and maintenance and took no further active role in the war.

HMS LIVERPOOL Pennant 11
Town class (Gloucester) cruiser
October 1945

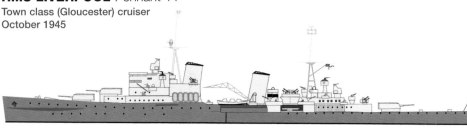

In care and maintenance since 1944, *Liverpool* was recommissioned just after the war for the Mediterranean Fleet, where for seven years she was flagship of 1st and 15th Cruiser Squadrons. However, her wartime damages caused trouble and she was paid off, lingering in reserve for six years until scrapped in 1958. She is shown here in her 1945 scheme of 507c upper works and 507b hull. The wood decks were no longer painted, but all other horizontal surfaces were 507a. The electronics were updated, with the original air-warning radar replaced by Type 281B. There was Type 293Q radar at the foremast top, and the main gun directors now had Type 274. The light AA had been altered to five quad 2pdr mounts, two of which replaced 'X' turret, and with two on the centreline between the 4in guns. Four late-model, powered, single 2pdrs were fitted, as well as six powered twin 20mm mounts.

HMS GLOUCESTER Pennant 62
Town class (Gloucester) cruiser 1939

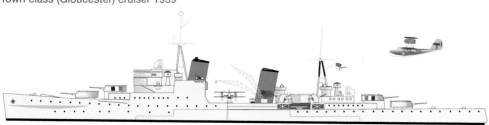

After completion, but before the outbreak of World War II, *Gloucester* served as flagship of the 4th Cruiser Squadron in the East Indies. As a concession to more troubled times, particularly with China and Japan at war, she dispensed with the usual buff funnels and overall white for a more warlike 507c overall. The funnels were 507b for a short time, and then also painted 507c when hostilities commenced. The wood decks were unpainted. The horizontal metal surfaces were initially 507c, but photographs from the time show them to be somewhat darker when the ship was operating in search of German raiders and blockade-runners in the Indian Ocean. The black sections at the top of the aft tripod mast seem to have only been present up to the start of the war, after which they were painted white, as were the upper masts and yards.

HMS GLOUCESTER Pennant 62
Town class (Gloucester) cruiser 1940–1

While with the 7th Cruiser Squadron in the Mediterranean, *Gloucester* adopted a typical East Mediterranean camouflage scheme using 507c as a base, with 507a providing a dark contrast. There was a plentiful supply of these paints at Alexandria. Steel decks were painted dark grey, probably 507b, but the wood decks may have been stained grey with oil rather than painted. All turret tops, except 'B', were painted 507a, while 'B' turret top was white. This may have been a squadron recognition feature. *Gloucester* was at the Battle of Cape Matapan. On one occasion she was hit by a dud bomb, and on another by one which caused only minor damage. On 22 May 1941 she was attacked by German Stuka dive-bombers and hit four times, along with three near-misses. *Gloucester* was abandoned and sank.

MODIFIED TOWN CLASS CRUISERS
HMS EDINBURGH Pennant 16
Modified Town class cruiser 1939

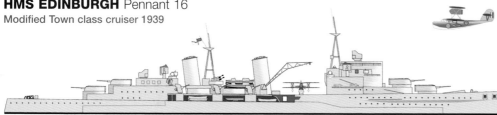

Edinburgh was the first of a two-ship class to complete five months before World War II and is shown here in a 1939–40 MS4a Home Fleet scheme, with unpainted wood deck, but the fore deck around the anchors was darker grey, possibly 507b. All other horizontal metal surfaces seem to match the overall scheme of MS4a. The black waterline was of peacetime size. The funnels were set back further than the Town class. 'Y' turret was carried a deck higher, instead of on the quarterdeck, in order to allow enough room for the magazine shell-handling system. There were six twin 4in AA mounts and two octuple 2pdr mounts, which were carried port and starboard at the amidships position. These were roomier vessels and the largest Royal Navy cruisers built since the County class 8in gun cruisers.

HMS EDINBURGH Pennant 16
Modified Town class cruiser late 1941

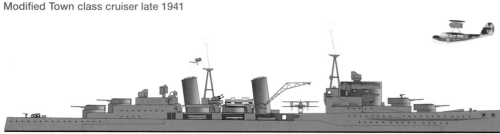

Edinburgh is illustrated in a drab 507b scheme, worn from October 1940. Wood decks were unpainted, but the foredeck around the anchors was darker grey, possibly 507a. All other horizontal metal surfaces seem to match the overall scheme of 507b, but photographs do suggest the catapult deck area may also have been 507a. The black boot topping at the waterline was reduced in height. At this time there were apparently quite a few twin .303in Lewis gun mounts added as a temporary measure, with the number possibly as high as ten mounts. They would presumably have been distributed around the ship on the super-structure. At each masthead are aerials for Type 279 radar, which was a produc-tion, and slightly improved version, of the Type 79Y radar tested on Sheffield. In late 1941, six 20mm AA guns were added, two on 'B' turret, one on each side of the bridge and two on the quarterdeck. None had protective gun tubs.

HMS EDINBURGH Pennant 16
Modified Town class cruiser March 1942

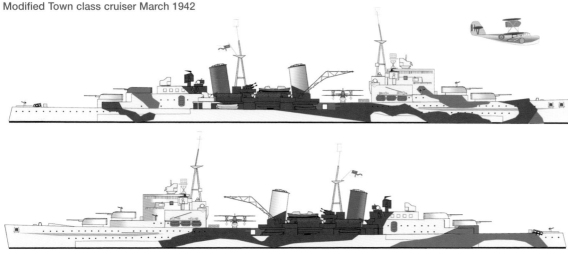

Edinburgh adopted an Admiralty-designed three-colour scheme during March 1942, only three months before her loss. The shades used were 507c as the base, with areas of 507a and B5. The wood decks of the quarterdeck were unpainted, but all other decks were a medium grey, possibly 507b. Type 284 radar was fitted to the forward main gun director and Type 285 radar to the three HACS. A platform was built on the bridge to allow Type 273 radar, with its distinctive cheese aerial, to be placed aft of the main director. No extra AA guns were added, but it is possible that the 20mm mounts on 'B' turret did receive a splinter-protective zareba prior to her sinking. On 30 April *Edinburgh* was hit by two torpedoes from the German U-boat *U-456* while escorting a convoy. She was able to get underway again but on 2 May, while she was limping home, she was attacked by German destroyers. Despite her previous damage, *Edinburgh* sank the German destroyer *Hermann Schoemann*, but was in turn hit by a torpedo. Without power and unable to control flooding, she was ordered to be scuttled and finished off by the destroyer *Foresight*.

HMS BELFAST Pennant 35
Modified Town class cruiser August 1939

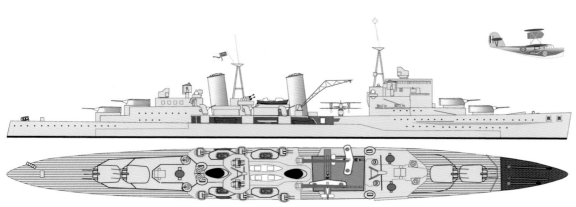

Belfast completed in MS4a Home Fleet grey a month before World War II started. Wood decks were scrubbed spotless and the horizontal metal decks were in MS4a, except for the area forward of the breakwater, which was probably 507b. Her size allowed for extra heavy AA guns, giving the class a total of six twin 4in AA mounts. The 2pdr mounts were octuple. However, it was not considered necessary to provide extra light weapons, as those fitted were expected to be capable of dealing with air threats as seen pre-war. With this ship and her sister, the Admiralty disregarded treaty weight limitations because war was obviously looming. These ships were much better protected than the *Southamptons*. Upon the outbreak of war, *Belfast* was painted a darker grey, probably 507b, and joined the 18th Cruiser Squadron. Her service was short as she ran afoul a mine laid in the Firth of Forth by the German U-boat *U-21*. The detonation broke her back and inflicted massive damage. *Belfast* was so new it was decided to repair her, despite the massive damage. Actually, this took as long and cost as much as it would to have built a new cruiser, but an advantage gained from the rebuild was more stability, due to added bulges. This provided the ability to absorb additional weight in AA weapons, radars and all the associated extra crew that went with them. The ship that emerged was stronger than as originally completed.

HMS BELFAST Pennant 35
Modified Town class cruiser December 1942

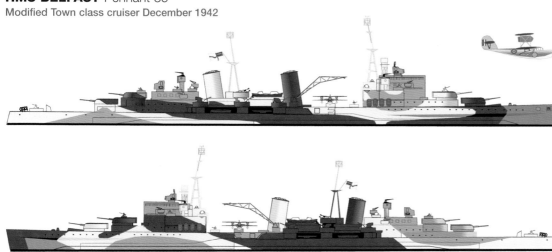

After her long repair time, *Belfast* returned to service in an Admiralty four-colour camouflage scheme. The decks and turret tops were all painted in 507a. The scheme carried on the sides used 507a, 507c, B5 and B6. Although B5 is given as the shade, it appears to have been several tones lighter and may actually have been the washed-out 1941 blue. The intent of the layout was apparently to concentrate the eye of an observer on the central dark area, and cause confusion when trying to identify the ship and details needed to estimate course and speed. This general pattern would be retained for two years, with only various details being altered and some rearrangement of colours. Aircraft were still carried at this time. The quad 0.5in MG mounts were removed. Five twin and four single 20mm AA guns were added. The twin 20mm mounts on 'B' turret initially had no protective splinter tub and the shield seems to have been incomplete. During the rebuild it was possible to provide for new radar developments. Type 281 radar was fitted to both masts, with Type 244 IFF on top of the forward aerial. Type 273 radar was fitted on the bridge aft of the main director and the forward director received Type 284 radar. All three of the HACS received Type 285 radar, and the 2pdr directors were fitted with Type 282 radar.

HMS BELFAST Pennant 35
Modified Town class cruiser December 1943

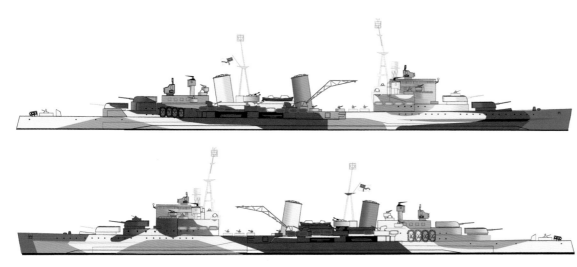

Belfast no longer carried aircraft by the Battle of North Cape, but the catapult remained for a time, in case it was again needed. The scheme was overall similar to the previous one, but the areas changed somewhat and the position of colours, as well. Decks remained 507a, as did all other horizontal metal surfaces. B6 seems to have been replaced by B5. The admiral's barge was still blue at this time. Type 283 barrage directors were now fitted for co-ordinated combined AA fire. With the flight deck now available, eight single 20mm gins were fitted, four port and four starboard. Since her repair from mining, *Belfast* had seen much heavy steaming, being involved with fleet operations in support of convoys to Russia mostly. Her service in the Arctic led to her presence when the German battleship *Scharnhorst* sortied to attack convoy shipping. In the gloom of an Arctic darkness, the battle fought out was confusing at times, but *Belfast* and the other ships succeeded in keeping the German vessel illuminated with starshell for much of the time it took the battleship *Duke of York* to sink it. She was docked briefly prior to the Normandy landings, when one twin 20mm AA mount was removed. *Belfast* then went on to carry out bombardment and HQ ship duties for the D-Day landings in the eastern section of the task force, remaining on station until July 1944. The ship was earmarked for the Pacific theatre and taken in hand for conversion in August.

HMS BELFAST Pennant 35
Modified Town class cruiser
June 1944

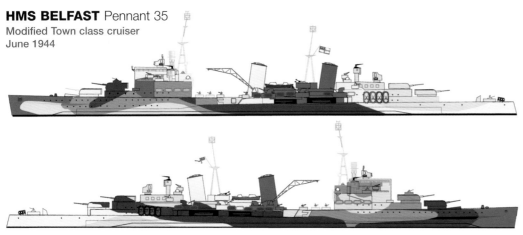

These two illustrations are based on the way the ship is now painted in her status as a museum ship. Although the colours and angles do not entirely match with photographic evidence, this is nonetheless claimed to be her appearance at some time in her career. The closest match to this is after December 1942. The colours would seem to be 507c, 507a, B5, B6 and duck egg blue. The physical appearance at present does not, of course, entirely match that era, as there were many alterations later. But the general sense is visible to the eye. It was interesting to compare the photographs I took of this ship with those online, and note that many of the colours seem to change depending on the angle of light and the angle from which a photo is taken.

HMS BELFAST Pennant 35
Modified Town class cruiser August 1945

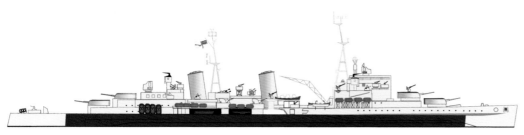

Belfast received a major refit for warfare in the Pacific. She was painted in 507c with a central panel of B15 on each side. In Sydney the armament was improved again. Changes to the ship from both refits were as follows. Type 281B replaced Type 281; Type 283 radar topped the foremast; on the bridge the Type 273 radar was replaced by Type 283 radar using the same platform; the main director received Type 274 radar and Type 268 was also installed. All guns, except the single 20mm, had some sort of fire control. Two quad 2pdr mounts were added on each side of the aft DCS and two more just behind the fore funnel. 'A' turret carried a single 40mm Bofors gun, there were two more abreast aft of the bridge and two others on each side of the aft funnel. Four power-operated single 2pdr guns were also included in Boffin mounts on each side of the bridge and each side of the aft funnel. Four single 20mm guns were carried, two on each side of the front of the bridge and two on the boat deck. One crane was removed and the other repositioned centrally. The ship remained in the Far East and provided support during the Korean War.

HMS BELFAST Pennant C35
Modified Town class cruiser 1959

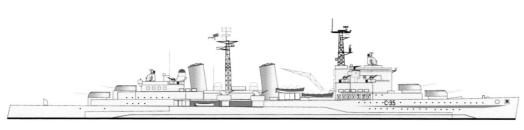

Having been rebuilt during the war, *Belfast* was considered to be well worth modernising to extend her service. A large refit was undertaken, which was expected to extend her useful life by another ten years. She returned to service with lattice masts and all modern radars. The light AA was reduced to six twin 40mm radar-controlled mounts. The heavy AA remained at four 4in twin mounts. All the weaponry could be controlled from the main directors if required, although additional radars were provided. During this period, the quarterdeck was returned to natural wood, but all other horizontal surfaces were Brunswick green. Although expected to serve for a much longer period, she was instead reduced to reserve due to financial cutbacks and then paid off in 1963. However, instead of the scrapyard, she was chosen to become a museum ship on the Thames in London, where she remains today as a memorial to the men and ships that served in World War II.

CONTENTS

DIDO CLASS CRUISERS

HMS NAIAD Pennant 93
Dido class cruiser June 1940

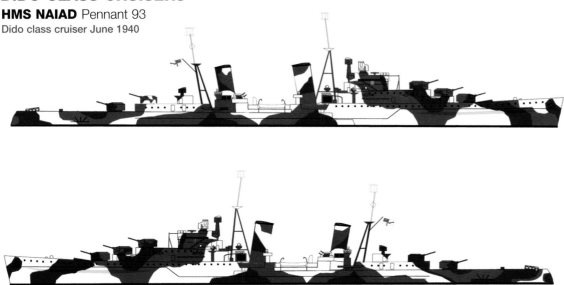

The camouflage style known as 'Flotta' was briefly popular with the Home Fleet in 1940, especially for ships based on Scapa Flow. The colours were 1940 green, 1940 brown and, in this case, white. The wood decks were unpainted and allowed to fade as a reaction to seawater. Horizontal surfaces were probably same as the overhead view of *Bonaventure*. *Naiad* had Type 279 radar from just after completion, because new cruisers, especially those of the *Dido* class, had a priority for radar. The armament of this ship was as designed, with five twin 5.25in turrets, two quad 2pdr mounts and two quad 0.5in MG mounts. This class proved to be less effective against aircraft than the 4in gun armed AA cruisers, but that was accepted in order to give a good mix of surface and AA capability. Note that depth charges were carried from completion.

HMS NAIAD Pennant 93
Dido class cruiser 1941

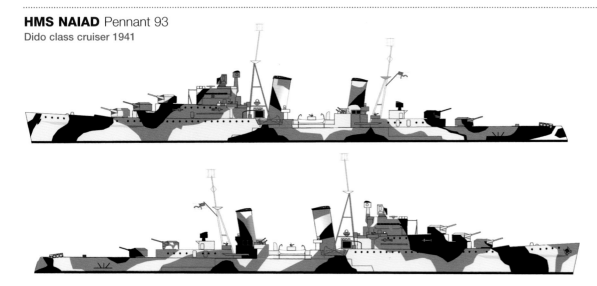

The Flotta-style camouflage fell out of popularity very quickly and was replaced with a scheme that used paint that was more readily available and considered more effective. The camouflage on *Naiad* basically followed the pattern of the previous scheme, but changed by using the colours black, 507b and 507c. The quad 0.5in MG mounts were removed and she received five single 20mm Oerlikon guns. No other changes were made, and claims in some sources that she received Type 285 radar do not seem to be backed up by records or photographs. After Home Fleet duties, *Naiad* took part in escorting convoys to Freetown and then joined Force H, becoming flagship of the 15th Cruiser Squadron. She went on to take part in the evacuation of Crete and various operations associated with containing the Vichy French.

HMS NAIAD Pennant 93
Dido class cruiser March 1942

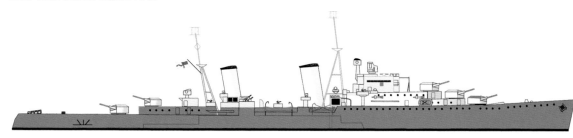

Prior to her loss, *Naiad* was given a dark lower hull/light upper works scheme using 507b and 507c. Her wood and metal decks were painted in mid-grey, probably 507b. The ship was engaged on duties in the Mediterranean and runs to Malta where the Royal Navy was still hard-pressed. No official changes were made to the armament, but it is possible that, like other ships serving in the region, there may have been some captured Italian light AA weapons added. Machine-gun calibre weapons were also often added. After a very busy service, this ship sortied to investigate a report of a disabled Italian cruiser. The report turned out to be false, but while returning to harbour on 11 March 1942, *Naiad* was torpedoed and sunk by the German U-boat *U-565*.

HMS PHOEBE Pennant 43
Dido class cruiser 1940

Phoebe was completed with a form of Flotta camouflage but, apart from a false bow wave, it was entirely comprised of 1940 brown and 1940 green. The wood decks were natural. The colour of the horizontal metal surfaces was not known, but tops of turrets were the same colour as camouflage on their sides. This ship completed without the 'Q' turret, in this case aft of the 'B' turret, owing to a shortage of mounts. Instead, a 4in gun for firing star-shell took that position. The light AA armament comprised two quad 2pdr mounts and two quad 0.5in MG mounts. The ship was fitted with Type 279 radar at the top of both masts, prior to joining the Home Fleet. Two banks of triple torpedo tubes were also carried in the waist.

HMS PHOEBE Pennant 43
Dido class cruiser 1941–2

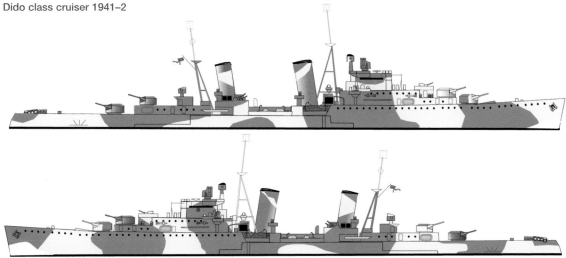

Phoebe changed over to a simple camouflage style in late 1940 and wore it until early 1942. The pattern used a base of 507c, with areas of 507b as contrast. At this time, all decks and turret tops were painted 507b. The masts were white from the starfish upward. Type 279 radar was still the only type carried, and the light AA had not been upgraded. During late 1940, *Phoebe* operated in the North Atlantic, protecting trade and providing cover for convoys. In April 1941 she was sent to the Eastern Mediterranean, where the ship took part in the evacuation of Crete and then engaged in operations against Vichy-held Syria, during which she was narrowly missed by torpedoes from a submarine. *Phoebe*'s luck ran out on 27 August when she was hit by a torpedo dropped from an Italian aircraft off Tobruk. She made it back to Alexandria, where temporary repairs were carried out to enable the ship to make her way to the United States for full repairs. Note that smoke floats were carried by the depth-charge racks and also below the 4in gun mount.

HMS PHOEBE Pennant 43
Dido class cruiser April 1942

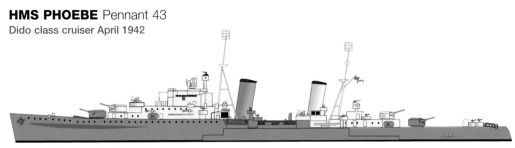

Phoebe was hit by an aerial torpedo off Tobruk, and temporarily repaired at Alexandria, after which she made her way to the United States for full repair. The ship was repainted with a dark hull/light upper works style. But in this case it was also a disruptive pattern, as 'A' and 'Y' turrets, along with the fore funnel, were painted the same colour as the hull. The colours used were 507b and 507c. All deck areas were 507b. The star-shell gun was replaced by a quad 2pdr AA mount. Additionally, eleven single 20mm guns were added and the quad 0.5in MG mounts removed. Type 281 radar was fitted at both mast-heads. Type 285 radar was fitted on both HACS and Type 284 radar on the main gunnery director. Several other items were dealt with at Devonport before she returned to service in May 1941.

HMS PHOEBE Pennant 43
Dido class cruiser June 1943

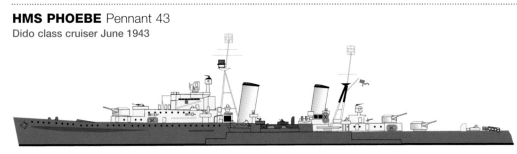

Phoebe was torpedoed again on 23 October 1942 off French Equatorial Africa. During temporary repairs, 'A' turret had to be landed and the ship proceeded to the United States again for repairs, with a 60ft by 30ft hole in her hull. She emerged in a very plain scheme of dark hull/light upper works. Decks and horizontal surfaces were 507a, the hull was 507a and the upper works 507c. The tripod mainmast was painted black halfway up because of funnel discharge. All three quad 2pdrs were replaced with US Navy quad 40mm mounts. Seven single 20mm guns were removed, but six twin 20mm mounts were fitted. Type 273 radar was installed on the foremast. The original 'A' turret was still in Africa. Therefore, repairs were completed with only three turrets.

HMS PHOEBE Pennant 43
Dido class cruiser July 1943

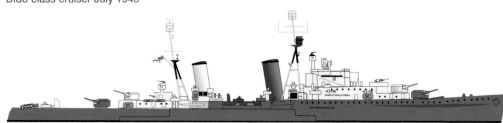

Phoebe returned to the UK after the major repair in the United States. 'A' turret was eventually restored and various other modifications completed. Type 244 IFF was added on top of the Type 281 radar aerial. IFF Type 253 was fitted, plus Type 242 and a Type 650 jammer. A Headache radio intercept was installed and the HF/DF removed. Note that the aerials for Headache were added above the Type 273 radar. The foremast also had the top section of the tripod painted black, because of problems with fumes from the fore funnel in a following wind, and the Type 273 radar was also painted in a darker shade, possibly 507a. The general scheme returned to her 1942 style, but with the lower hull area 507a and upper works in 507c. The decks were reported as being 507a. *Phoebe* supported the landings at Anzio and other operations in the Mediterranean before being sent to the Far East.

HMS PHOEBE Pennant 43
Dido class cruiser April 1945

Phoebe joined the British Eastern Fleet in late 1944, where she adopted a typical scheme of that region. The overall colour was 507c with a panel of mid blue (washed-out 1941 blue). Decks remained 507a and turret tops were painted the same. *Phoebe* never received the third forward turret of her design. Even so, her AA armament made her a valuable asset when covering landings in Burma and raids on other locations, where she operated as a fighter direction ship. To facilitate this, a light mast with an aircraft homing beacon on it was added between the aft funnel and the mainmast. She was relieved by the cruiser *Royalist* in April 1945. *Phoebe* continued in service, the only external change being the removal of the blue panel. She went into reserve in 1951 and was sold for breaking up in 1956.

HMS **DIDO** Pennant 37
Dido class cruiser December 1940

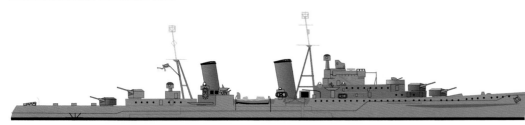

Dido was the first to take the new Type 281 radar to sea, shown here at the top of both masts. No other radar was fitted. The ship is painted in overall 507b, which apparently included all horizontal metal surfaces. The wood decks, however, were unpainted. A prominent degaussing cable can be seen running along the outside of the ship as protection against magnetic mines. Paravanes for minesweeping can also be seen on the forward superstructure, so the ship could have some measure of self-protection. Due to a shortage of 5.25in mounts, she was completed without 'Q' turret and had a 4in star-shell gun added in its place. The quad 0.5in MG mounts did not have splinter protection and the crews were completely exposed. The large ship's boats carried amidships were later removed to save weight when AA updates were added.

HMS **DIDO** Pennant 37
Dido class cruiser
December 1941–2

Dido, like so many other British warships, was badly damaged off Crete. Temporary repairs were carried out and the ship proceeded to the United States for repairs. During this time, the 'Q' turret was shipped to the yard and installed. Five single 20mm AA guns were also added. The ship was painted overall in MS4a Home Fleet grey. The wood decks remained unpainted and all other horizontal decks were 507b. The ship returned home to the UK in this form to have other items fixed. The electronics remained the same, but by early 1943 the HF/DF carried on the mainmast was removed.

HMS **DIDO** Pennant 37
Dido class cruiser June 1943

Between this camouflage and the one shown above, *Dido* apparently wore two other schemes, one of three colours and one of four. However, there are no records, nor photographic evidence. I have therefore chosen only to mention it. This scheme followed a style similar to other *Dido* class cruisers with a dark lower hull, in 507b, and a lighter superstructure, in 507c. Turrets 'A' and 'Y', as well as the funnel, were painted in 507b. The hull colour of 507b extended up and slightly onto the sides from the hull in a low band. Turret tops appear to have been 507c and wood decks remained unpainted. Light AA was altered, with the addition of four twin 20mm and the removal of four singles. Type 285 radar was fitted to both HACS and Type 284 radar to the main director. Type 282 radar was provided for the 2pdr directors and a typical lantern with Type 272 radar was installed at the top of the tripod on the foremast. *Dido* was very active in the Mediterranean, taking part in many major operations and achieving a battle history matched by few other ships.

HMS **DIDO** Pennant 37
Dido class cruiser 1945

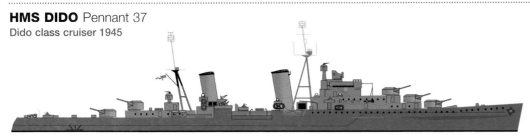

Dido was sent to join naval forces protecting convoys to northern Russia in late 1944. She adopted a scheme based on the new Admiralty standard, with G45 green for the upper works and MS2 for the hull. The wood decks seem to have still been unpainted and the horizontal metal surfaces probably adopted G45; turret tops were also G45. Two single 20mm were removed, leaving the ship with four twin 20mm mounts. *Dido* remained on the Russian convoy routes, and operations off the Norway coast until the end of World War II. Post-war, *Dido* was painted in a general 507c scheme, but having seen very extensive war service she was paid off in 1947 and sold for scrap in 1957.

HMS EURYALUS Pennant 42
Dido class cruiser June 1941

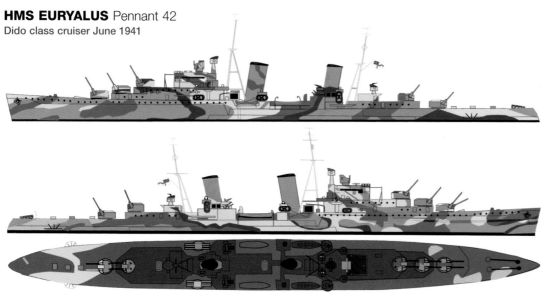

Euryalus was completed in an Admiralty five-colour design that used B5, B55, MS3, MS4a, and 507a. It is possible that 507c was used instead of MS4a. With the dangers of air attack now well understood, the deck was also camouflaged with 507b and patches of 507c, while the metal deck areas were 507a. It was a complicated pattern, and one that required a lot of maintenance. Consequently, she only wore it for a short time, and was repainted prior to being sent to the Mediterranean. Like many ships of the time, war shortages meant she was completed with what was available. Consequently, *Euryalus* only had Type 285 radar installed on the aft HACS. The main director had Type 284 gunnery radar and the 2pdr directors had an early, and rather prone to difficulties, version of Type 282 radar. Some sources state that the ship had no surface or air search radars at this time, but did carry the brackets ready to fit Type 279 radar. Others say that the radar was fitted before the ship left the UK. A photograph of the ship on transit of the Suez Canal seems to only show the brackets, and I have therefore illustrated the ship accordingly. But she definitely had Type 279 radar shortly after her arrival, and it may have been added at Alexandria.

HMS EURYALUS Pennant 42
Dido class cruiser September 1941

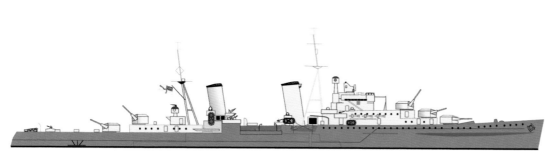

The Admiralty five-colour scheme was painted out by September and replaced with a two-colour scheme with dark hull and light upper works. The colours used were 507c and 507b. Unlike some of her sisters, the 'A' and 'Y' turrets were not painted the same colour as the hull. The decks may have remained the same colour as above, but were probably painted all dark grey. On being sent to the Mediterranean, this ship still lacked anything other than gunnery radar, as mentioned above. However, she was fitted with Type 279 radar shortly after arrival at Alexandria. Before her departure, the quad 0.5in MG mounts were removed, and the ship was fitted with five single 20mm Oerlikon guns. This was an obvious recognition of the threat of air power and, of course, that region was particularly dangerous. It was quite common for the *Dido* class cruisers to have their guns at different elevations and the turrets on different bearings in high-risk areas, in order to deal with sudden air attacks, and I have illustrated the guns at different angles. Although the history of the class was not good as aircraft-killers, ships with 4in guns quite often outclassed them; their long-range heavy AA drove off many aircraft before they could complete attacks. This made them successful AA ships, even if they did not actually score as many kills as was hoped.

HMS **EURYALUS** Pennant 42
Dido class cruiser 1942

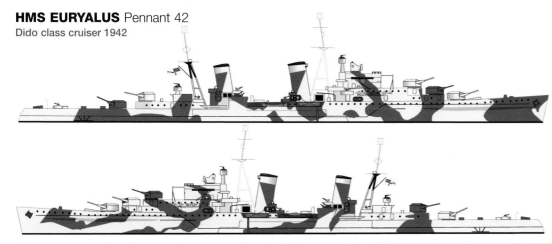

Euryalus adopted an Alexandria-type camouflage while serving in the Mediterranean Fleet. It was typically two shades, with the bulk of the ship in 507c, while the camouflage contrast was provided by 507a. The deck colours are unknown, but were probably painted a dark grey. The turrets that were painted 507a also had that colour carried over onto their roofs. The others were 507c. She now carried seven single 20mm guns. Type 285 radar was finally installed on the forward HACS. While in the Mediterranean, *Euryalus* took part in major operations to support the 8th Army, support amphibious operations, cover carrier groups, convoys to Malta, and many other duties.

HMS **EURYALUS** Pennant 42
Dido class cruiser March 1942–October 1943

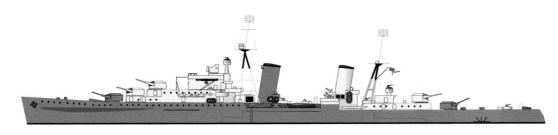

The Alexandria scheme was painted out and replaced by a fairly standard scheme for the class. Colours were 507b and 507c. Note how the hull colour was carried part way up the 2pdr location and funnel. The decks were dark grey at this time. This type of camouflage was applied to the smaller Royal Navy cruisers, and was apparently intended to make them look like single-funnel destroyers at a distance, perhaps in the hope of enemy submarines avoiding them. Five of the seven 20mm guns previously carried were removed, and four twin 20mm mounts added. Type 281 radar was added at both mastheads in place of the previous Type 279 radar. A Type 273 radar was fitted on the starfish at the head of the foremast tripod. Aerials for Headache radio intercept were placed at the top of the forward tripod. *Euryalus* returned to the UK after the Salerno landings for a large refit.

HMS **EURYALUS** Pennant 42
Dido class cruiser July 1944

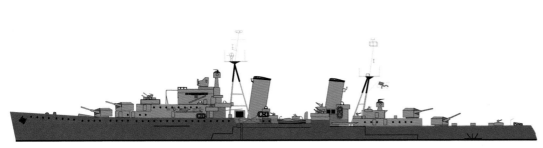

From October 1943 to July 1944, *Euryalus* underwent a major refit, which involved the replacement of the 'Q' turret with a quad 2pdr mount. The number of twin 20mm mounts was raised to six, and she still retained five single 20mm guns as well. Her electronics were considerably upgraded. The Type 281 radar, which needed aerials on both masts, was replaced by Type 281B, which only required a single aerial on the mainmast. The Type 273 radar was replaced by Type 277 radar, and Type 293 was placed at the top of the foremast. Type 285 radar was retained for both HACS, but was upgraded to an improved standard, as was the Type 284 radar on the main director. Various types of IFF were fitted and more Headache aerials were added, as well as Type 650 missile jammers. The camouflage adopted was similar to the standard type then being introduced into the British fleet. The hull was B30 olive and the superstructure was MS3 or G45. The decks were 507a. In this form, the ship joined the Home Fleet and covered carrier raids on German positions in Norway until November 1944. She then proceeded to the Pacific to join the British Pacific Fleet.

HMS EURYALUS Pennant 42
Dido class cruiser 1945

Euryalus was sent to Australia to join the British Pacific Fleet, which had its main base on Sydney. She adopted the typical scheme of that fleet with a 507c hull and a B15 hull panel. Officially, the front of the panel was supposed to angle forward like a ship bow, but many disregarded this and went for a single block-type panel from just forward of 'A' turret to just aft of 'Y'. The decks were dark grey, almost certainly 507a. The AA was not increased prior to leaving the UK, but I have seen a reference that she may have shipped a couple of single 40mm Bofors guns on a temporary basis due to the kamikaze threat. She was involved in operations off Okinawa, and then directly against the Japanese mainland. *Euryalus* was present for the Japanese surrender of Hong Kong.

HMS EURYALUS Pennant 42
Dido class cruiser 1948

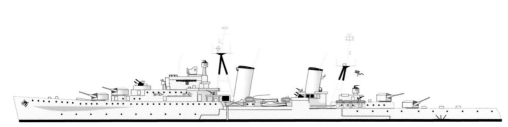

Euryalus remained overseas until 1946, and then went into reserve during February of that year. However, it was decided to recommission her for further service, and from August 1947 until January 1948 she was in refit. As illustrated, the overall scheme became 507c. The turret sides and sloped edges were the same, but the tops were a mid-grey, as were all the horizontal metal surfaces. The wood decks were restored to natural colour, but the area forward around the anchors was a dark colour, very possibly Brunswick green. The anchor cables seem to have been white and the ship's boats were white. The three quad 2pdr mounts remained, but all 20mm guns were removed. Four single 40mm Bofors were carried instead. Some Carley floats were removed, and a new rack of four per side was established on the aft deckhouse. Aerials for communications were added, but most other electronics remained the same. The ship took up station with the Mediterranean Fleet in February 1948, serving with the 1st Cruiser Squadron. In 1952 she went to the 6th Cruiser Squadron in the South Atlantic, where she remained until 1954. She was paid off into reserve in September the same year. *Euryalus* was sold for scrap in 1959.

HMS HERMIONE Pennant 74
Dido class cruiser March 1941

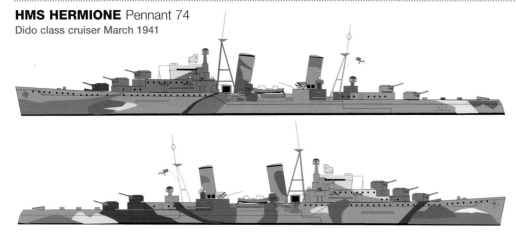

Hermione saw only fifteen months of service before her loss. She was completed in a scheme similar to her sister *Euryalus* in March 1941. The accuracy of this illustration is as best as could be produced from very limited sources. The colours were B55, B5, MS3, MS4a, 507c and 507a. However, it is possible that 507c was used in place of MS4a. The rear turrets were painted dark on the starboard side and lighter on the port, the area of light meeting the dark a quarter of the way across the turret. The wood decks were natural. Steel decks were painted a medium shade, which was possibly B5. The extra boats and handling davits were removed not long after entering service, and the camouflage scheme was also altered. This ship carried white bands on both HACS, like her sister *Bonaventure*.

HMS HERMIONE Pennant 74
Dido class cruiser May 1941

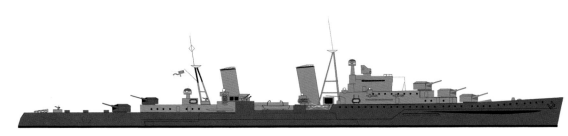

Hermione was repainted in a dark hull/light upper works style, but rather darker than most of her sisters. The hull was 507a and the superstructure 507b. The decks were dark grey, almost certainly 507a, the same as the hull. The ship had white bands on both HACS. The aft turrets on the starboard side were painted 507a, but only on that side. On the port side, they were 507b. This is a curious arrangement I have not seen on any other *Dido* class cruiser that had darker turrets. It could be that they were left that way after the removal of her initial camouflage scheme, where they had the same arrangement. The ship carries brackets at both mastheads for Type 279 radar, but it was apparently never installed. This ship was with the 2nd Cruiser Squadron while hunting the German battleship *Bismarck*, and then went to Force H in June.

HMS HERMIONE Pennant 74
Dido class cruiser November 1941

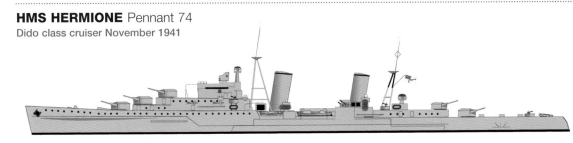

Hermione participated in escorting convoys to Malta, following her transfer to Force H. She rammed and sank the Italian submarine *Tembien* in the Strait of Sicily on 2 August 1941, and went to Gibraltar for repairs. The quad 0.5in MG mounts were removed in November 1941 and five single 20mm guns were installed: one each in place of the MG mounts, one on the quarterdeck and one on each side of the mainmast. After repairs, she went to the Eastern Mediterranean, where it is believed she adopted Mountbatten pink (medium). On 16 June, *Hermione* was torpedoed and sunk by the German U-boat *U-205* south of Crete.

HMS SIRIUS Pennant 82
Dido class cruiser May 1942

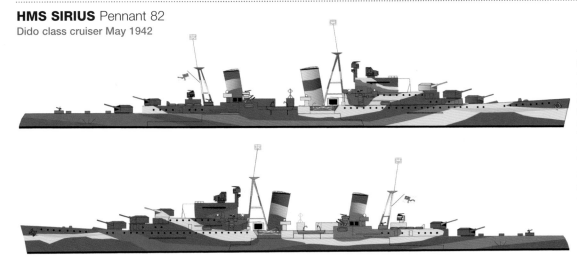

Sirius entered service in an Admiralty disruptive scheme with dark grey decks. The colours used were B5, MS4, MS4a, MS2, and the deck colour was probably 507a, as it was being widely used at the time. Schemes such as this were quite effective, but they required a lot of touch-up paint to be carried, and the amount of work required for the crew to keep such a camouflage fresh was considerable. Unlike her earlier sisters, she had a full set of radar fitted. Type 281 radar was at the head of both masts. The main gun director had Type 284 radar and both HACS had Type 285 radar. The directors for the 2pdr mounts had Type 282 radar. The HF/DF was moved from the mast to a position between the funnels. As built, she mounted ten 5.25in guns in five twin turrets, two quad 2pdr AA mounts and five single 20mm AA guns. This ship was completed late due to bombing of her shipyard by the Germans. After work-up, she joined the Home Fleet for several months, before being sent to the Mediterranean for Operation Pedestal.

HMS SIRIUS Pennant 82
Dido class cruiser late 1942

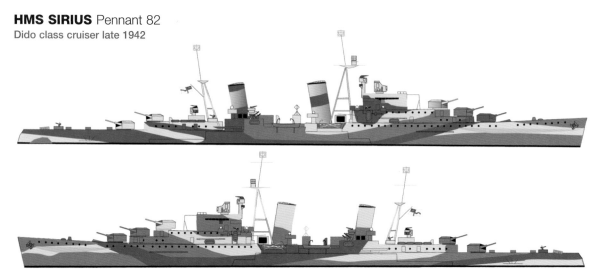

Sirius had her scheme modified to three colours late in 1942, presumably to make it easier to maintain. The colour B5 was removed, but the overall layout was much the same with the three colours MS4a, MS4 and MS2. The decks were all 507a, while the tops of the turrets were MS4a, regardless of the colour on the turret sides. More care was given to make the masts lighter, as they were, of course, the first thing seen over the horizon, and it was important that enemy vessels should not be forewarned of the ship's approach. By this time, Type 273 radar was added on the top of the forward tripod. Two extra 20mm guns were added shortly after, for a total of seven guns. *Sirius* was very active in the Mediterranean during 1942–3 and was present at most major actions and landings.

HMS SIRIUS Pennant 82
Dido class cruiser February 1944

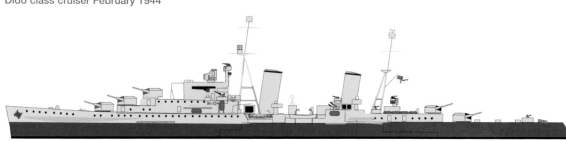

A dark lower hull and lighter grey upper works became the third camouflage pattern this ship wore. Other British cruisers adopted a full grey hull, but the style shown here seems to have been more popular in the Mediterranean. The dark grey decks were continued and the turret tops were now the same colour as the turret sides, as MS4a became the dominant light grey of the scheme. 507a seems to have been used for the hull. The ship was damaged by air attack off Scarpanto in November 1943, and went to Massawa for repairs. This took until February 1944, by which time the new paint scheme shown had been applied. She had two 20mm guns removed, but had two 40mm guns fitted on each side of the bridge in their place.

HMS SIRIUS Pennant 82
Dido class cruiser 1945

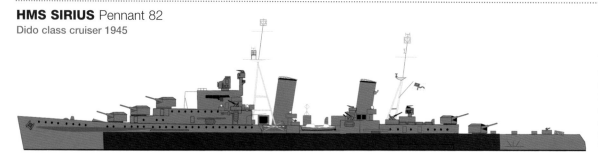

The scheme changed in 1945 to that of an Admiralty standard pattern. She is shown here in B20 and MS2. The decks remained as before. Her masts and fittings were white. The 20mm guns each side of the tripod mainmast were removed and replaced with single 40mm mountings. In all other respects, she remained as he had been in 1944, except for the addition of IFF 242 and 253 on the mainmast, and a Type 650 missile jammer on the rear of the aft funnel.

HMS **SIRIUS** Pennant 82
Dido class cruiser late 1947

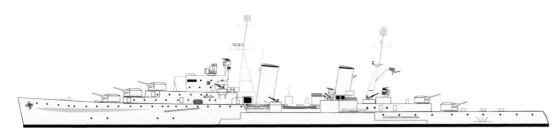

Sirius remained in the Mediterranean as part of the 15th Cruiser Squadron until 1946, when she returned home for refit. She is shown here in peacetime 507c. The wood decks were restored, except for the area forward of the wave break, which was Brunswick green, and the metal decks were mid-grey, probably 507b. The turret tops were MS4a. Note that the black boot topping had greater depth than when worn with wartime camouflages. There were some alterations to the bridge. Type 273 radar was replaced with Type 293Q radar. Most other electronics remained the same, except for the provision of some whip aerials. All 20mm AA guns were removed, and six single 40mm Bofors guns were carried, as well as the original quad 2pdr mounts. She went to the Home Fleet for two years after the refit, but was then paid off into reserve. The ship did not return to active service and was sold for scrap in 1956.

HMS **CLEOPATRA** Pennant 33
Dido class cruiser December 1941

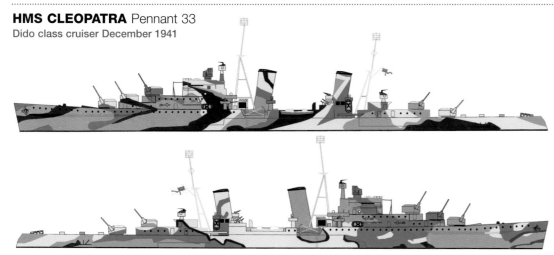

Cleopatra was completed in another of the complicated schemes that the Admiralty produced in 1941. This four-colour scheme was comprised of MS1, B5, B6, and MS4a. The deck colours are unknown, but it is probable that the wood areas were left unpainted and allowed to fade with the effect of salt water. Horizontal metal surfaces were apparently MS4a, but I have heard of statements that some of the camouflage was carried up and over on these. As first commissioned, Type 281 radar was at both mastheads. Type 285 radar was added shortly after, along with Type 284 radar for gunnery. The 2pdr directors appear to have had Type 282 radar from early in her service, possibly on completion. The usual pair of quad 0.5in MG mounts were not fitted, and in their place were single 2pdr guns. This would remain her light AA armament for some time, although it is possible that it was supplemented with captured Italian weapons while serving in the Mediterranean. She was wearing this scheme when she took part in the Battle of Sirte in March 1942.

HMS **CLEOPATRA** Pennant 33
Dido class cruiser December 1942

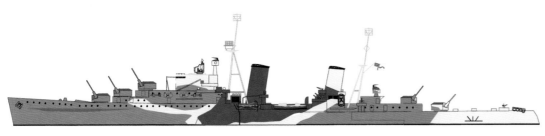

Cleopatra adopted a simpler style in mid-1942, and wore it until mid-1943. The colours used were MS3, 507a and 507c. It is probable that the wooden decks were still unpainted and metal decks were grey, but no other information is available. The turret tops and the sloping edges were 507a. Type 284 radar is prominent on the main gunnery director. Type 272 radar was mounted on the forward tripod. The single 2pdrs were removed not long after she entered service, and five 20mm guns were installed. A sixth was added later. *Cleopatra* was active as a part of Force K, raiding Axis communications and then covering the landings in Sicily. She was torpedoed by the Italian submarine *Dandolo* on 16 July 1943, and the damage was so severe that it took until October before she was seaworthy enough to sail to the United States for permanent repairs.

HMS CLEOPATRA Pennant 33
Dido class cruiser November 1944

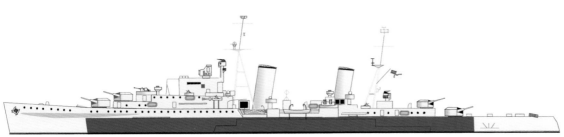

Repairs to *Cleopatra* were completed in November 1944, when she appeared in 507c with a hull panel of 1941 blue, or similar; decks were 507a. In photographs, the blue hull panel always appears worn: perhaps not applied correctly, or the paint was faulty. Both quad 2pdr mounts were removed, along with 'Y' turret. In their place, three US Navy-type quad 40mm AA mounts were added. All single 20mm guns were removed and six twin 20mm mounts were fitted. The ship was sent to the British Far Eastern Fleet and served in various operations, including the reoccupation of Singapore. She returned to the UK in early 1946 with the hull panel still intact. At that time the hull panel was removed and she reverted to peacetime standard, with unpainted wood decks. Around 1949 the twin 20mm mounts were replaced by single 40mm Bofors guns. She continued to serve with the Home Fleet and then the Mediterranean Fleet until 1953 with little further alteration. The ship was put into reserve in February 1953 and sold for scrap in 1958.

HMS ARGONAUT Pennant 61
Dido class cruiser August 1942

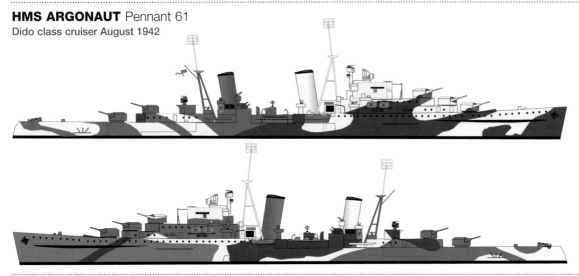

Argonaut was completed as a five-turret *Dido* class cruiser. Technically, she was of the second group, but completed to the same plan as the first group. She was painted up in an Admiralty-designed disruptive scheme using three colours, 507a, B5 and 507c. All decks were painted 507a, and the very top of each turret was 507a. Having been completed later, this ship never mounted the obsolete quad 0.5in MG mounts, but instead had four single 20mm guns, as well as a full set of radar. There was a Type 284 radar for the main gun director, Type 285 for HACS directors, Type 282 for the 2pdr directors, and at both mastheads were aerials for Type 281 radar. The HF/DF aerial was moved to a deckhouse between the funnels. She was the last of the original *Dido* group to be completed and went to the Home Fleet at first, with which she took part in operations covering convoys to Russia.

HMS ARGONAUT Pennant 61
Dido class cruiser late 1942

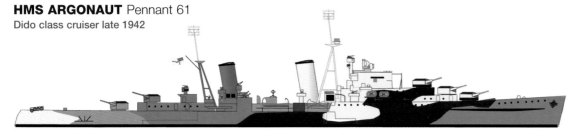

For details, see opposite page.

HMS ARGONAUT Pennant 61
Dido class cruiser late 1942

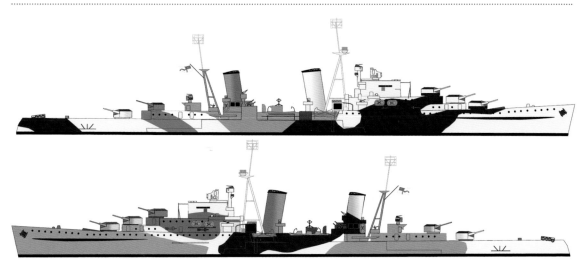

There are several sources for the colours worn by *Argonaut* in late 1942, up to the time she was torpedoed, but they do not all agree, therefore I have shown a couple of options. The colours used were 507c, B5, B6, and MS1. Some sources show B20 instead of MS1. The ship was badly damaged in this period, having both her bow and stern blown off. It is possible that a loss of records due to damage could be the cause of the confusion. The turret tops are consistently described as very dark and I believe that corresponds with 507a, as first commissioned, but others say MS1. We do have a consistent description of the decks as being a medium grey, which was the deck colour as completed. In addition to the colour confusion, the four single 20mm AA guns are reported to have been exchanged for twin mounts, but again sources differ. Regardless of the scheme, we do know that in November, while operating out of Bone against Axis shipping to and from North Africa, she was torpedoed by aircraft. There was a hit forward and one aft, blowing off her bow and stern respectively. Although most ships might have been expected to sink from the massive damage suffered, the crew contained the flooding and managed to get the two outer propeller shafts working. She made it back for temporary repairs and then proceeded across the North Atlantic to the US naval dockyard at Philadelphia, where whole new sections were built. It took almost eleven months for this ship to return to service and while under repair she was given a thorough AA modernisation as well.

HMS ARGONAUT Pennant 61
Dido class cruiser November–December 1943

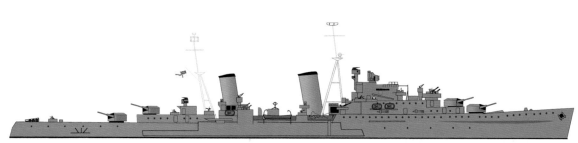

Out of Philadelphia, *Argonaut* appeared in grey that would appear to have been 507b, or a locally provided US paint shade. This was possibly just a temporary thing, because it was not long before she could be seen in a two-tone, light and dark style. The masts were white, decks mid-grey, but the timbered areas had been removed and replaced with Cemtex. 'Q' turret was removed during the repairs and replaced by a quad 2pdr mount. Single 40mm Bofors guns were added on each side of the bridge rear. Five twin 20mm mounts were added and, on arrival in the UK, six single 20mm guns were also added. During repairs, her previous four single 20mm guns had been removed, possibly due to damage. Type 281B radar, with its single aerial, with Type 244 IFF, was placed at the top of the mainmast. Type 293 radar was fitted at the top of the foremast, and Type 277 radar on the starfish at the head of the forward tripod.

HMS ARGONAUT Pennant 61
Dido class cruiser June 1944

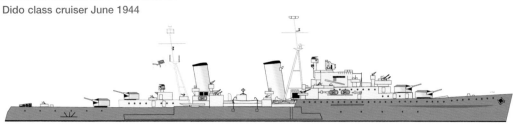

On her return to service with the Home Fleet, *Argonaut* adopted the dark hull/light upper works style using 507c and 507b. The Cemtex decks were grey. The masts were white and turret tops 507b. Armament and electronics remained the same, except for the addition of various IFF and countermeasures. She was part of Force K off the Normandy beachheads during the allied invasion of France in June 1944. She also took part in Operation Dragoon in the Mediterranean and, for a time, was part of the naval force engaged in operations in the Aegean, where German and Italian Fascist forces were attempting to run supplies down the coast of Italy to the battlefront there.

HMS ARGONAUT Pennant 61
Dido class cruiser late 1944

Being so recently rebuilt and refitted, *Argonaut* was considered up-to-date enough to go to the Pacific, where she adopted an overall scheme of 507c with a panel of B5. Decks were medium grey Cemtex. The areas around the anchor winches forward of the wave break were much darker. A section of the aft tripod mast was painted black because of funnel fumes. Single 20mm on each side of the fore funnel were replaced by single 40mm Bofors, for a total of four such weapons. The 20mm gun count was five twin and four singles. The turret tops and sloped edges seem to have been the same tone as the hull panel. Barrage directors were installed either side of the bridge forward. *Argonaut* took part in operations against Japanese bases in Sumatra and Arakan, before being transferred to the British Pacific Fleet.

HMS ARGONAUT Pennant 61
Dido class cruiser mid-1945

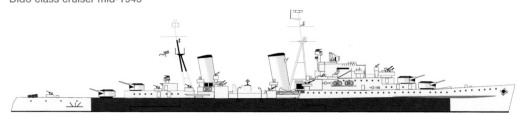

Argonaut adopted the dark blue B15 hull panel on 507c of many ships that were part of the British Pacific Fleet. For her role in the Pacific, *Argonaut* added five more 40mm in mounts known as Boffins. These were powered twin 20mm mounts, but with a single 40mm gun instead. One was placed on the quarterdeck and four on the aft superstructure, replacing 20mm weapons previously in those places. This gave her a light AA armament of three quad 2pdr mounts, nine single 40mm guns, two twin 20mm mounts and two single 20mm guns. The singles were mounted on each side of the bridge front and the twin 20mm power mounts on each side of the bridge aft, where they had been since her US repair and refit. She took part in various operations off Okinawa and then against the Japanese mainland.

HMS ARGONAUT Pennant 61
Dido class cruiser July 1946

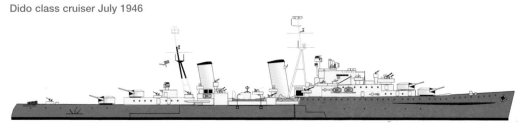

Argonaut returned home in 1946 in a dark grey hull, light superstructure style. The hull appears to have been 507a and the upper works 507c, but also possibly MS4a. The starboard launch was in peacetime blue. Decks were presumably as before, but the turret tops were now the same colour as the superstructure. An additional single 40mm was mounted on the centreline between the funnels. *Argonaut* was present for the reoccupation of Shanghai. As soon as she could be freed, the ship journeyed home to the UK, carrying returning servicemen and repatriating ex-prisoners. She was put straight into reserve, because the serious damage and shock effects she had suffered required constant attention to machinery defects. *Argonaut* never recommissioned and was sold for scrap in November 1955.

HMS SCYLLA Pennant 98
Dido class cruiser June 1944

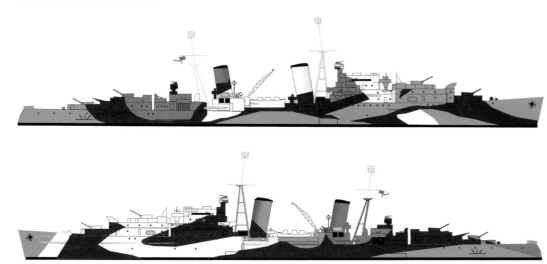

Scylla was painted in an Admiralty intermediate scheme when completed in June 1942. The hues were B5, white, MS3 and MS1. Wood deck areas were pale grey. Horizontal metal areas are believed to have been 507b. The roofs of 'A' and 'B' shields were painted white. The tops of 'X' and 'Y' shields were MS3. Difficulty manufacturing 5.25in turrets delayed completion, so a decision was taken to arm her with 4.5in AA mounts, similar to those used on *Ark Royal*. The weight of broadside was less for surface action, but the higher rate of fire made them better AA vessels. Without turrets, there was spare top weight, so they were altered to provide additional accommodation spaces and offices. The gun director was never installed, giving more room on the bridge. Light AA armament was two quad 2pdr mounts and six 20mm guns. *Scylla* carried the latest Asdic, and depth-charge rails were placed to drop directly over the stern. It was inevitable that her duties would be as escort for convoys and high-value ships. Runs to Russia were frequent, but also in the Mediterranean and anti-submarine operations in the Bay of Biscay. She detonated a mine off Normandy in 1944 and was towed home. It was found that the bottom of the hull was severely corrugated and many internal fittings had broken loose from their mountings; she was declared a constructive total loss. *Scylla* was used for some trials, then scrapped in 1950 wearing the same camouflage scheme.

HMS CHARYBDIS Pennant 88
Dido class cruiser December 1941

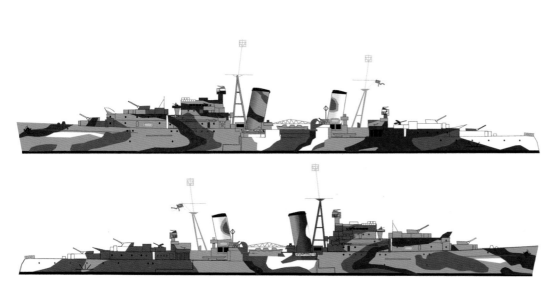

Like her sister ship *Scylla*, *Charybdis* was completed without her designed armament owing to a shortage in the production of 5.25in gun turrets. The scheme she commissioned with comprised 1940 green, MS1, MS3 and white. The decks were unpainted wood, and metal areas medium grey, probably 507b. This was a complicated scheme, typical of some designed by non-seagoing staff in the Admiralty, many of whom were recruited from artists. They painted models, which were examined against differing sky backgrounds under various light conditions. The results were usually quite effective, but they did not take into account the difficulty of keeping these up at sea and on a ship under wartime pressure. Nor, of course, did they allow for various inaccuracies during repainting or the availability of colours. Green was in particularly short supply at this point in World War II. Pigments and dyes went to the army and air force as first priority. The more common schemes were based around the three greys: 507a, 507b and 507c, which were sure to be available at overseas bases as well. This scheme was worn until April 1942, while serving with the Home Fleet and taking part in covering convoys to Russia. As with her sister, she was completed with a full radar array and Asdic. In addition to the eight 4.5in guns, she had two single 2pdr guns in front of the bridge and four single 20mm guns, plus the quad 2pdr mount amidships. There was a 4in star-shell gun just aft of the rear HACS, but it had a very limited arc of fire. With spare top weight available, *Charybdis* carried a centreline crane to handle ship's boats.

HMS CHARYBDIS Pennant 88
Dido class cruiser 1942–3

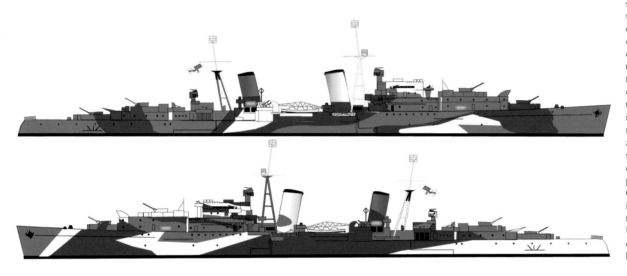

Before her loss, *Charybdis* had been repainted in different colours, but some traces of the old scheme, such as on the port side of the bridge, could still be seen. The colours used were 507a, B5 and white. The decks were all 507a. This scheme was much less complicated, and only B5 would have been less common on overseas stations. Note that sections of the mainmast tripod were painted black because of funnel discharge, but the area was much smaller than on other *Dido* class ships. Type 272 radar was fitted to the tripod head of the foremast. The single 2pdr guns in front of the bridge were replaced by twin 20mm mounts. Two more single 20mm guns were also added and the star-shell gun was removed. This scheme was applied immediately before the ship deployed to the Mediterranean, where she was present for several major convoy battles, and Operations Pedestal and Harpoon. She also took part in operations to cover various amphibious landings for Torch and later Salerno. After returning to the UK, she was torpedoed and sunk in a night action off Brittany. Her assailants were the German torpedo boats *T23* and *T27*.

HMS BONAVENTURE Pennant 31
Dido class cruiser June 1940

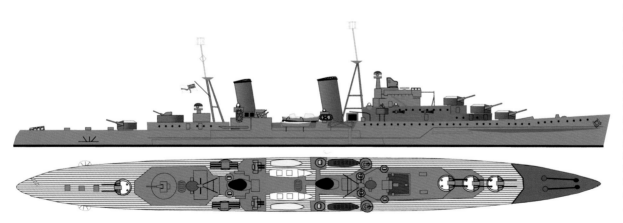

Bonaventure was the first of the *Dido* class to be completed. With World War II already underway, her first paint scheme was an overall 507b. The tops of the turrets were painted pale grey, most likely 507c. The wood decks on the forecastle deck and the quarterdeck were left natural wood and allowed to fade to a pale grey wood shade. All horizontal decks were 507b. The HACS directors had white bands around them and 507a tops. Ship's boats were grey, but with pale grey canvas. Due to a shortage of turrets, the 'X' turret was not fitted. Instead, a single 4in star-shell gun with a very high splinter shield was placed in that position. As the 5.25in guns were already intended for AA work, it was felt that two quad 2pdr mounts and two quad 0.5in MG mounts would be sufficient for light AA. Type 279 radar was fitted with aerials at both mastheads. A HF/DF was fitted on the mainmast. This ship had a very short, but eventful, service. She was initially sent to the Home Fleet and, while escorting a convoy, exchanged fire with the German cruiser *Admiral Hipper* without scoring, or receiving hits in return.

HMS BONAVENTURE Pennant 31
Dido class cruiser January 1941

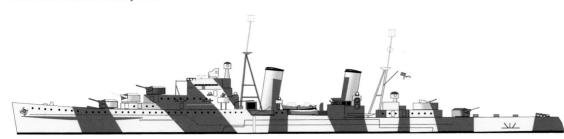

Bonaventure was given an early-style camouflage scheme in January 1941. It was comprised of 507c overall, with areas of 507a. The wood decks were not painted. It is possible that the camouflage was carried across horizontal metal areas. The forward turret tops remained 507c, but 'Y' turret top was 507a. This scheme was carried on both sides. There were no alterations to armament or electronics, but note the very visible degaussing cable on the outside of the hull. *Bonaventure* was sent to the Mediterranean and during Operation Excess she sank the Italian torpedo boat *Vega*, and drove off the torpedo boat *Circe*. She was damaged by near-misses during an air raid while at Malta on 22 March. Repairs were carried out at Malta and she was quickly made ready for sea again.

HMS BONAVENTURE Pennant 31
Dido class cruiser late March 1941

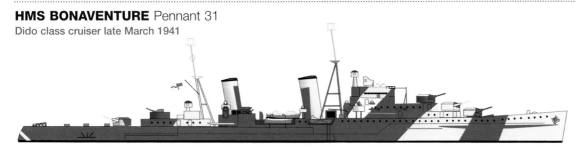

While undergoing repairs, some changes were made to the camouflage scheme. Some areas remained the same, but much of the hull was repainted in 507a. This could have been deliberate, or simply because the most readily available paint during her hasty repair was 507a. The wood decks remained unpainted and turret tops were as before. The front of the bridge was 507a, and it is possible that side colours were carried up over the horizontal metal decks. The anchor-handling area forward of the breakwater was still 507a. The ship sailed in this condition, but while escorting a convoy near Crete on 31 March, she was torpedoed and sunk by the Italian submarine *Ambra*.

MODIFIED DIDO CLASS CRUISERS

HMS SPARTAN Pennant 95
Modified Dido class cruiser August 1943

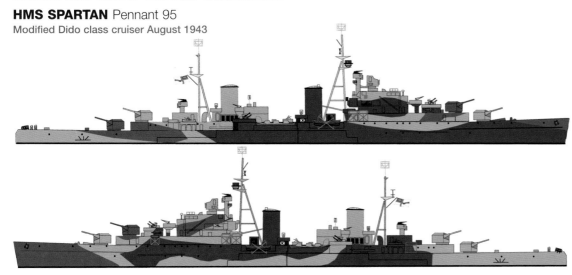

Spartan only wore one camouflage pattern, that being an Admiralty disruptive style. The colours were B30 and B55, with dark areas of B10. The decks and horizontal surfaces were B10. This class adopted a four-turret design, which enabled the bridge to be lower and improve stability. More accommodation was included midships and these were generally better than on the five-turret group. The funnels were upright, and these ships were finished with a full range of radar. *Spartan* is shown here with the standardised armament of four twin 5.25in turrets and three quad 2pdr mounts. There was room for the forward quad 2pdr mount to have its own director, mounted behind it along with Type 282 radar. There were also six twin powered 20mm mounts. Type 281 radar was carried at the mastheads and Type 285 radar on the HACS directors. The main gun director was fitted with Type 284 radar, and there was a Type 272 radar on the forward tripod mast. IFF sets were carried, but no missile jammers. That was unfortunate, because after a rather short service life, *Spartan* was sunk by a German Hs293 glide bomb while off the beachhead at Anzio. The damage from the large missile was fatal, despite the efforts of her crew to save the ship. She sank an hour after being hit on 29 January 1944, after only six months' service.

HMS BELLONA Pennant 633
Modified Dido class cruiser October 1943

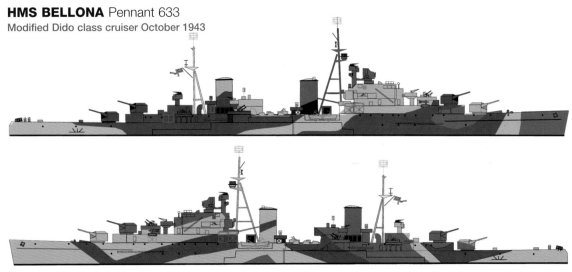

Bellona is shown here in the Admiralty disruptive scheme she wore on completion. The colours are B55, B30 and G10. No wooden decks were fitted. All horizontal surfaces were G10, but the turrets seem to have had B55 tops. Most of her initial service was in the English Channel and home waters. She received four single 20mm guns during this time. Later, she covered carrier raids on the German battleship *Tirpitz*, and escorted, or was involved in, covering vital convoys to Russia, before moving to home waters in preparation for the Normandy landings. She had Type 281 radar at the mastheads and Type 272 at the head of the forward tripod mast, along with the various gunnery radars, as well.

HMS BELLONA Pennant 633
Modified Dido class cruiser mid-1944

Bellona is shown here in the Admiralty standard scheme she wore at D-Day and after. The colours are MS3 and G10. All horizontal surfaces were G10, as were the turret tops. She was engaged in the support of allied landings on the beaches of Normandy, but then returned to her previous duty of escorting and covering convoys to North Russian ports. She was present for the allied entry into Denmark and at the German surrender. By that time, she had twelve single 20mm guns and eight twin 20mm mounts as part of her light AA armament. Electronics were as before, except for the addition of Type 650 missile jammers and aerials for Headache. After the surrender of Germany, *Bellona* remained in European waters and joined the Home Fleet, before being offered on loan to New Zealand in 1946.

HMNZS BELLONA Pennant 633
Modified Dido class cruiser 1950

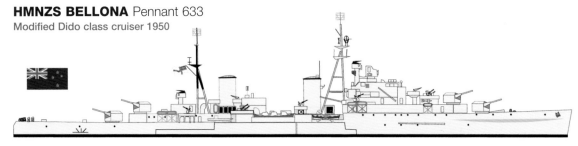

Bellona is shown here post-war, when was she was loaned to New Zealand. The colour used during this peacetime service was a pale grey, probably 507c. The decks remained dark grey. Turret tops were 507c. The upper section of the mainmast tripod was painted black because of funnel gases. The quad 2pdr mounts were retained, but all single 20mm guns were eventually removed and replaced by six single 40mm Bofors guns. The older Type 272 radar was replaced with Type 277 radar. *Bellona* was returned to the Royal Navy in 1956, when her place was taken by the cruiser *Royalist*. She was sold for scrap in 1958.

HMS BLACK PRINCE Pennant 81
Modified Dido class cruiser November 1943

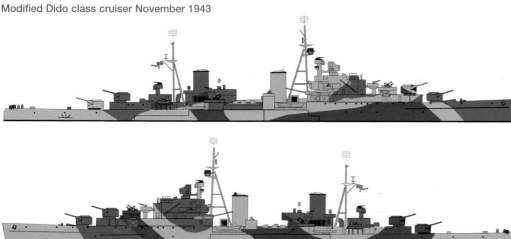

Black Prince entered service in an Admiralty disruptive scheme, as shown here, which was very similar to that of her sister ships. The colours used were B55, B30 and G10. The decks were very dark, probably G10. The radar fit had become standard for the class, as were the light AA weapons as completed. By June 1944, *Black Prince* had received another eight single 20mm guns and two twin mounts. The initial service of this ship was with convoys to North Russia, after which she carried out offensive sweeps against German shipping off Brittany and the Bay of Biscay ports. During this time she fought a surface action, accompanied by destroyers, in which the German torpedo boat *T29* was sunk, and its sisters *T24* and *T27* damaged. *Black Prince* served off the beaches of Normandy in June 1944 as part of the gunnery support for Utah Beach. After that she sailed for the Mediterranean, where she was present for the invasion of southern France, then off for operations in the Aegean.

HMS BLACK PRINCE Pennant 81
Modified Dido class cruiser October 1944

Black Prince adopted this scheme in late 1944, but the date is uncertain. She may have had this scheme during the invasion of southern France. The hull was B30 and the upper works MS4a. The decks were dark grey, as before, as were the turret tops. Although she had carried eight twin 20mm powered mounts, two were removed and replaced by single 40mm Bofors guns on each side. The electronics remained the same. She was sent to the British Eastern Fleet, where she covered raids on Japanese positions in Sumatra and Malaya. The ship was then ordered to the British Pacific Fleet, during which her hull appears to be much darker in photographs and was probably dark blue, in the form of a central panel. Apart from that, her appearance was unaltered. After covering operations off Okinawa and the Japanese surrender, *Black Prince* was present at the reoccupation of Hong Kong.

HMNZS BLACK PRINCE Pennant 81
Modified Dido class cruiser 1959

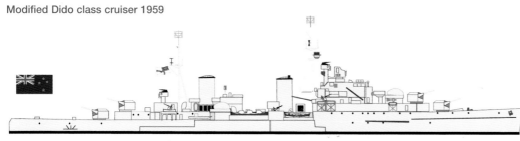

Black Prince was not modernised while in New Zealand service, where her duties mostly involved acting as a training ship. She was painted in 507c overall, except the decks, which remained dark grey. Most of the 20mm AA guns were gradually removed, but their gun tubs remained. The 2pdr mounts remained aboard, but were deactivated at some point. The Type 272 radar was also eventually deactivated. Six single 40mm guns were carried in her final state. The ship reverted to the Royal Navy in 1961, and was immediately sold for scrap without returning to the UK. She was towed to Japan and scrapped there in 1962.

HMS DIADEM Pennant 84
Modified Dido class cruiser 1944

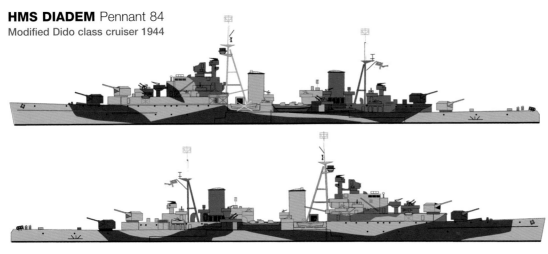

Diadem was completed in January 1944 and spent most of her wartime service in the Admiralty camouflage scheme shown. The colours are B55, G30 and G10, applied in a manner very similar to her sister ships. The decks were Cemtex and appear mid-grey, but there are sources that say the Cemtex had a greenish tint. The turret tops appear to have been G30, or a grey of similar tone. The tripod mainmast was in G30, while the foremast was in B55. The areas at the very top of both masts were white. The light AA was increased, with another two twin 20mm mounts and eight single guns added. Her duties in 1944 included covering Arctic convoys and providing AA support during carrier raids on the German battleship *Tirpitz*. She was part of Force E, which covered Juno Beach during the invasion of France on D-Day. *Diadem* went on to take part in offensive sweeps against German shipping along the coast of Brittany and then returned to Arctic convoy work.

HMS DIADEM Pennant 84
Modified Dido class cruiser 1945

Diadem adopted the new Admiralty standard scheme in mid-1945, near the end of the war in Europe. The upper works and hull were G45, with a B20 hull panel. Admiralty instructions were for the panel to have a slight lean at the forward end to represent the bow of the ship, thereby assisting the shortening effect of the hull panel. Mast tops were white and the decks were G10. The ship remained on her Arctic work until the end of hostilities. She had sunk a German auxiliary minesweeper and engaged German destroyers during her wartime service. Like most of her class, the addition of so many extra light AA guns meant the crew spaces were very overcrowded and adaptation for Arctic conditions was barely adequate, making her an uncomfortable ship. Nonetheless, she was much better than ships built pre-war on the same duty. She continued with the peacetime fleet until 1950 and then went into reserve.

PNS BABUR Pennant 84
Modified Dido class cruiser 1957

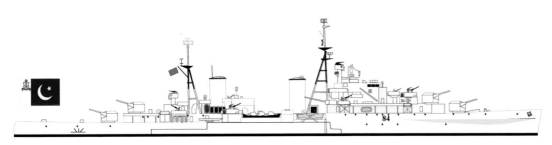

Pakistan sought British help with the purchase of a cruiser in the mid-1950s. *Diadem* was selected and, after agreement, was refitted with a modernised light AA armament and other equipment. But there were some limitations due to cost, most of which was paid for out of funds provided by the United States. On completion, the ship was taken over by Pakistan and renamed *Babur*. She is shown here in her new style with an overall paint scheme of pale grey, so pale as to be virtually white. There was a heavy black boot topping of Royal Navy style. The decks were mid-grey. She retained the pennant 84 and, in post-war agreed style, it was displayed on the hull just before the front of the bridge. She became a cadet training ship in 1961 and was renamed *Jahangir*. But in 1965 she participated in the war with India, leading a task force to bombard the Indian port of Dwaka. After that the ship became a static training ship, and was finally broken up for scrap in 1985.

HMS ROYALIST Pennant 89
Modified Dido class cruiser September 1943–45

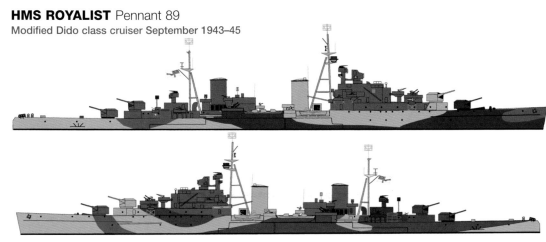

Royalist was completed as an escort carrier squadron flagship, with all the extra offices and accommodation required. This made her somewhat cramped and uncomfortable. She is shown wearing a scheme very similar to her sister ships and using the same colours B55, B30 and G10. This ship had two extra twin 20mm mounts and four single 20mm AA guns. The decks were G10 and her turret tops were the same. She covered convoys to Russia and carrier raids on the German battleship *Tirpitz*, as well as a diversionary operation before D-Day, during which she and other ships sailed high into Arctic waters to fool the Germans into thinking there was a major convoy operation underway with supplies to Russia, to draw away U-boats that might have been deployed against the Normandy landings. *Royalist* then went to the Mediterranean, where she was with Escort Carrier Squadron TF88.1 for the landings in southern France. She sank two German naval transports off Cape Spada, then operated in the Aegean during 1944. Later, *Royalist* was deployed to the British Eastern Fleet as flagship of the 21st Escort Carrier Squadron wearing the same camouflage.

HMS ROYALIST Pennant 89
Modified Dido class cruiser 1945

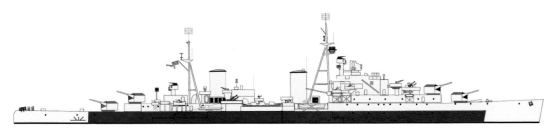

Royalist was still with the British Eastern Fleet when World War II ended. The original camouflage was replaced with a simple 507c overall, with a dark hull patch of B20. Her cramped conditions were made worse by an air-conditioning system that could not cope with the hot climate. The ship was the flagship of the 21st Escort Carrier Squadron when it took part in the Rangoon operations. Her squadron was involved in attacks against Japanese warships and other shipping evacuating the Andaman Islands, then in carrier raids against bases in Sumatra and other Japanese-held areas. She was present for the surrender of Singapore, and took part in various mopping-up operations in the Southeast Asia region. As soon as possible, she sailed home to the UK, taking with her as many liberated naval personnel as possible. *Royalist* was immediately decommissioned and placed in reserve.

HMNZS ROYALIST Pennant 89
Modified Dido class cruiser September 1956

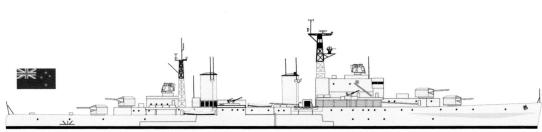

Royalist was the only modified *Dido* class cruiser to be modernised when taken out of reserve in 1954 for transfer to the NZ Navy in 1956. New directors that could perform both surface and AA direction replaced the old. All 2pdr mounts were removed. Light AA was two twin radar-guided 40mm mounts and two single 40mm guns. Self-inflating floats replaced Carley ones. The bridge was enlarged, accommodation and internal improvements made, and ineffective air-conditioning replaced. Lattice masts that could carry more weight replaced tripod masts. Whip aerials for various purposes were also evident. The ship was painted 507c overall. Decks were mid-grey, probably 507b, and the very tops of each turret the same. The area around the anchors was painted a darker colour, possibly Brunswick green. Various in-service changes were made to the ship, including adding its pennant, as per NATO agreement. She spent much of her time on training duties, as a cadet training ship, and static harbour training duty. Reverting to the RN in 1967, she was sold to Japan for scrapping.

COLONY CLASS CRUISERS
HMS FIJI Pennant 58
Colony class cruiser June 1940

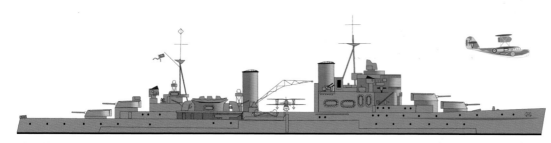

Fiji is shown as completed in 507b. The wooden decks were in natural wood, while the steel decks appear to be in 507b, as were the turret tops. The area forward of the breakwater was painted 507a. There were not as many Carley floats as this class would later carry. Armament was the standard design, with four triple 6in turrets and four twin 4in mounts. Light AA comprised two quad 2pdr and two quad 0.5in machine guns on the aft deckhouse. There was HF/DF at the head of the mainmast. Type 132 Asdic was fitted and a single rack of depth charges carried aft. She could carry two Walrus aircraft, but only one was issued due to shortages. The HACS arrangement was one on each side of the bridge and another just forward of the 'X' turret. There was only one main gun director, but 'X' turret had a large rangefinder on top, in the event the main director was knocked out or split fire was required. *Fiji* joined the Home Fleet on completion and was present at the attack on Dakar: she was damaged by a torpedo and was in repair until March 1941.

HMS FIJI Pennant 58
Colony class cruiser March 1941

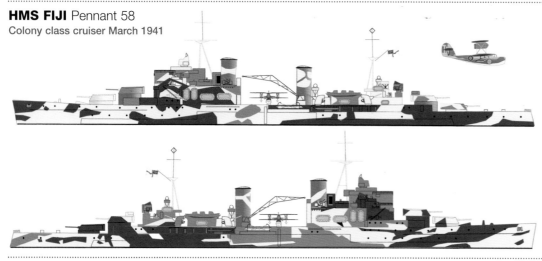

After repairs in March 1941, *Fiji* adopted a rather strange camouflage using 507a, 507b and 507c. The irregular shapes were dissimilar to most other camouflages of that year, and the use of those particular shades suggest some element of Eastern Mediterranean style, with an application of three main shades rather than two. The decks are believed to have been natural wood, and all horizontal metal surfaces were 507b. During repairs, additional quad 0.5in MG mounts were added on each side of the bridge, in lieu of the navigational rangefinders. Type 284 radar had been fitted to the main gunnery director, but she still did not carry any search radars. *Fiji* took part in escorting convoys through to Malta, and then in the campaign for Greece. During the Crete campaign, she was under heavy and continuous air attack for so long that she ran out of AA ammunition, and resorted to firing practice rounds at attacking enemy aircraft in an attempt to persuade them she still had AA capability. However, she was eventually overwhelmed by Axis aircraft and sunk. *Fiji*'s loss led to the realisation that the amount of AA ammunition a ship could carry determined how long it could remain in a combat area. *Fiji* was the first of her class to be completed and the first to be sunk.

HMS NIGERIA Pennant 60
Colony class cruiser late 1940

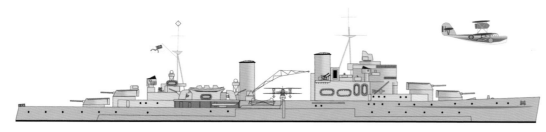

Nigeria was completed in mid-grey, probably 507b, but within a very short time was repainted into Mountbatten pink, using the recommended style of a light version for the superstructure and a medium version for the hull. The wood decks were unpainted, while the turret tops and horizontal metal surfaces were in mid-grey, similar to 507b. The use of this camouflage style was unusual, as the ship was serving with the Home Fleet covering Atlantic convoys, and even took part in the Lofoten raid, Operation Claymore. Her northern operations included capturing the German weather ship *Lauenberg* off Jan Mayen Island, which yielded valuable codes. Her armament was standard as completed. Later, additional quad 0.5in MG mounts were added on the sides of the bridge, but owing to ship stability issues, this required the removal of the manual rangefinders used for navigation.

HMS NIGERIA Pennant 60
Colony class cruiser mid-1941

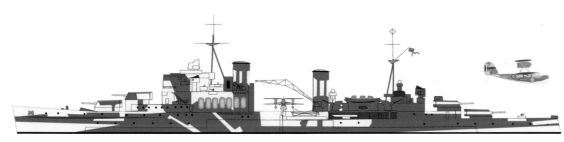

Nigeria is shown in the middle of 1941 wearing an extremely unusual camouflage scheme that was most likely an experiment. It is even more unusual in the large amount of MS2 required, as green was in very short supply at the time. Such a scheme could have been thought up locally while the ship was in a dock, but it was certainly very different from anything one would expect. By that time, four single 20mm guns had been added to the armament, but no radar was yet fitted. The wood decks were probably still unpainted. The tone of the turret tops suggests that they may have been MS2, or a grey of similar hue, such as 507b. I cannot locate any photographs of the starboard side of the ship in this scheme, and we can only surmise that it was similar. On 6 September, in company with the cruiser *Aurora*, she sank the German minelayer *Bremse*.

HMS NIGERIA Pennant 60
Colony class cruiser August 1941

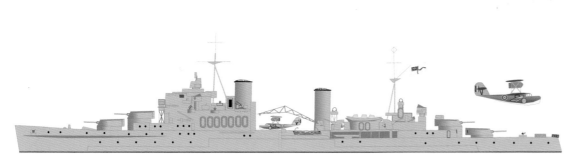

Nigeria returned to Mountbatten pink within a short time of the above camouflage scheme, but this time it appears to have been a solid medium style rather than a light upper works/dark hull type previously worn. The arrangement of Carley rafts into a grouped, recognisable recognition point was now becoming common for Colony class ships. It was also common for the camouflage of a ship to be carried over the Carley rafts, rather than allow them to spoil the overall effect. There were also more efforts to cut down on distinctive areas and highlights standing out from the rest of the ship. The black boot topping at the waterline was also considerably reduced. Radar Type 284 was added to the main gun director and a radar Type 273 placed in front of the bridge, in what was a very unpopular location. It was not only wooded for coverage aft, but obstructed the view from the wheelhouse and for other bridge personnel.

HMS NIGERIA Pennant 60
Colony class cruiser December 1941

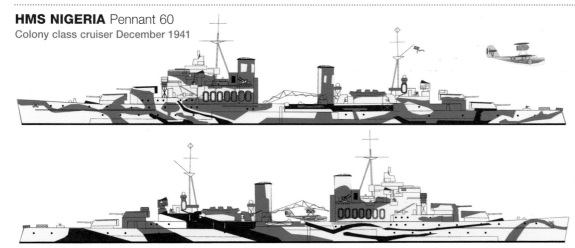

Nigeria wore another scheme for a short time from the middle of December 1941 until February 1942. The camouflage appears to have been carried up across the ship, including wood decks and turret tops. Tones used were 507c overall, with areas of B5 and MS1. There were no changes to armament or to the electronic fit at this time, leaving radar Type 284 and radar Type 273 as the only sets carried. Note that the 4in AA guns had no zareba tubs to provide protection against splinters. *Nigeria* was mostly engaged in covering convoys to Russian Arctic ports, as the Allies attempted to get war material through to the embattled Soviet armies struggling against the German invasion. These were long and difficult operations, with danger from enemy surface forces, U-boats and aircraft.

HMS NIGERIA Pennant 60
Colony class cruiser
February–August 1942

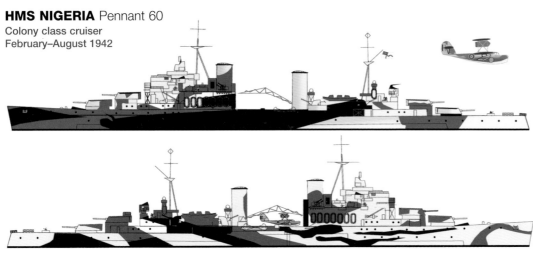

The scheme worn by *Nigeria* was altered in various ways on the star-board side, but the port side was substantially changed during this period. The colours were still 507c, B5 and MS1. Files say the radar had not been upgraded, yet in photographs, Type 285 radar is clearly visible on the aft HACS, although it does not seem to be present on those each side of the bridge. Surprisingly, she still carried four quad 0.5in MG mounts and only four 20mm AA guns. The aircraft crane on the port side was landed to save weight. During this period, her service mostly involved covering convoys to Russia and other operations in Arctic waters, including sweeps against German shipping along the coast of Norway. *Nigeria* was sent to join Operation Pedestal in late 1942, and was apparently still wearing this camouflage scheme. During that operation, she was torpedoed by the Italian submarine *Axum* and, after some temporary patching up, was sent to the United States for full repairs.

HMS NIGERIA Pennant 60
Colony class cruiser June 1943

After repairs, the camouflage pattern had changed, although it appears similar in many ways and the colours were still 507c, B5 and MS1. The port side was the same as before. The quad 0.5in mounts and single 20mm guns were replaced by eight twin 20mm mounts. This class lacked sufficient stability to take on too much top weight without sacrificing something else. Even the rangefinder on 'X' turret was removed to save weight. This is probably why the light AA armament was not increased compared to other cruisers. The 2pdr directors received Type 282 radar. Type 273 radar was landed, clearing the front of the bridge, and with some of the weight saved, a Type 272 radar could be placed on top of the foremast starfish. Although the ship had surface search radar, records state it still lacked any air-warning radar. However, photographs taken after this repair show she clearly had Type 281 radar. *Nigeria* returned to service on convoys to Russia. No aircraft were carried, though facilities had not been removed, and the ship's boats were stored on the catapult deck.

HMS NIGERIA Pennant 60
Colony class cruiser late 1943

Near the end of 1943, *Nigeria* appears to have adopted a pattern with 507b for the hull and B55 for the superstructure. The deck colours are not known for certain, but probably followed the standard style of the time in mid-grey. There had been few changes, other than in the electronics, where IFF types were added, along with Type 650 missile jammers. This sort of equipment had been rapidly produced after the success of German glider bombs used against shipping. The ship was apparently only in this form for a very short time, before painting to Eastern Fleet colours. Note that at about this time it was usual for the depth-charge rack at the stern to have some sort of a cover over it, possibly because the charges were rarely used and needed to be protected to stop them becoming useless due to the effect of salt water.

HMS NIGERIA Pennant 60
Colony class cruiser January 1944

After further work, *Nigeria* was sent to join the British Far Eastern Fleet and is shown in a simple scheme of 507c, with a hull panel of B5. The deck appears as medium grey in photographs. Aircraft facilities were removed and ship's boats were moved to the original catapult deck, which was lower and so helped with stability. Type 281b radar was placed at the top of the mainmast and four single 40mm Bofors were added. A barrage director was fitted to the front of the bridge. The ship took part in many Indian Ocean operations, covering carrier air strikes against Japanese positions in Sumatra, Java, Borneo and Arakan. She was present for the Japanese surrender of Malaya before going to the South Atlantic as flagship. In 1950 she returned to the UK to be put in reserve.

INS MYSORE Pennant C60
Colony class cruiser 1970

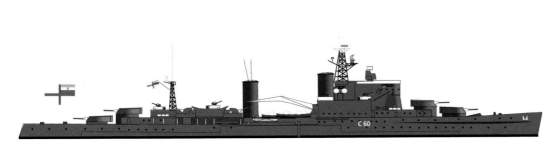

Nigeria was sold to India and, after a major refit, sailed as *Mysore* in 1957. Her crest came from Gandaberunda, a mythological double-headed eagle on the coat of arms for the former state of Mysore. She wore a very dark grey, popular for Indian warships, approximating 507a. Many items were picked out in white on the deck, others in Brunswick green. The author visited an Indian warship in this scheme and found it smart, if rather garish. *Mysore* had a long, sometimes dramatic, career. In 1957 she collided with the British destroyer *Hogue*, causing serious damage. In 1969 she collided with the Indian destroyer *Rana*, which had to be scrapped. In 1972 she collided with the Indian frigate *Beas*. It was suggested by a high-ranking officer that she should be fitted with bumper bars. *Mysore* led the Indian Navy attack against the Pakistani port of Karachi in 1971. This was a ship on which many Indian naval officers learned the art of command. In 1975 she became a training ship for naval cadets and lasted until 1985, when she was sold for scrap.

HMS KENYA Pennant 14
Colony class cruiser 1940–1

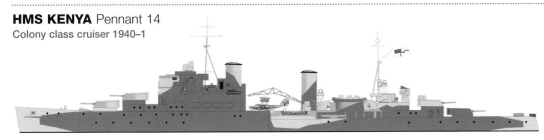

Kenya entered service in a two-tone camouflage based on light and dark Mountbatten pink. The deck colour is unknown, but in photographs it appears to be a tone similar to 507b. The turret tops seem to match the side, including 'Y' turret, which appears darker than the other three. The starboard side was apparently the same as the port side. The ship joined the Home Fleet, and took part in the search for the German battleship *Bismarck* in 1941. There was no radar fitted at this time. She was in collision with the destroyer *Brighton* in June, and did not return to service until August. Two extra quad 0.5in MG mounts and two single 20mm guns were added during her repairs.

HMS KENYA Pennant 14
Colony class cruiser
Operation Halberd 1941

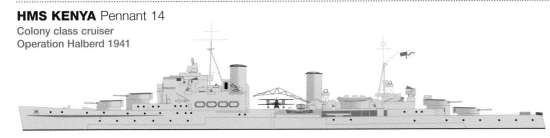

In September 1941 *Kenya* was dressed in light Mountbatten pink overall. Decks and turret tops appear to have been mid-grey. She remained in this scheme until May 1942. In December 1941 Type 284 radar was added on the main gunnery director and Type 273 radar placed in front of the bridge in a wooded aft position. This was mostly due to the need to keep weight down low because of the ship's low stability. She was detached to take part in Operation Halberd and it is possible that some army light AA guns were added for this operation only. In late 1941 she covered the Vaagso raid, Operation Archery, and remained with the Home Fleet until 1942.

HMS KENYA Pennant 14
Colony class cruiser May 1942

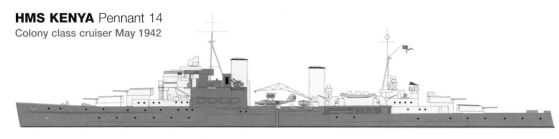

The 'Pink Lady', as this ship was now being called, changed her scheme yet again and in May 1942 had adopted a dark Mountbatten pink hull, with extensions up onto the bridge and superstructure, and 507c for the rest of her upper works. Again, the decks appear to be mid-grey from photographs. For some reason, 'A' turret was painted white during this period. The light AA and radars remained the same. She went to the Mediterranean again, this time for Operation Harpoon and Operation Vigorous.

HMS KENYA Pennant 14
Colony class cruiser June 1942

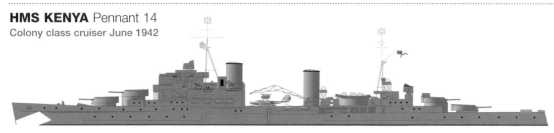

Kenya switched to overall dark Mountbatten pink in mid-1942, and continued to support operations in the Mediterranean. During Operation Pedestal, she was torpedoed by the Italian submarine *Alagi* and returned to the UK for repairs.

HMS KENYA Pennant 14
Colony class cruiser December 1942

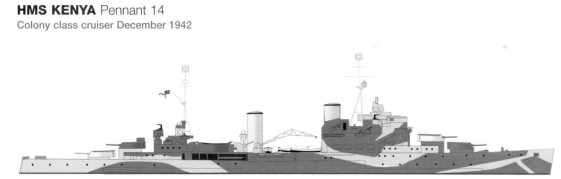

Kenya emerged from repairs with a completely new look. The two shades used were MS4a and MS4. The decks were very dark grey, probably 507a. The tops of 'A' turret and 'X' turret were also 507a, but the others were a lighter shade, possibly 507b. The aircraft facilities were not yet removed, but were no longer in use. This enabled the ship's boats to be placed on the catapult deck. The quad 0.5in MG mounts were finally removed, along with the single 20mm guns. In their place, six twin 20mm mounts were added. The Type 273 radar in front of the bridge was removed and replaced by a Type 272 radar on the forward tripod mast. Type 285 radar was installed on all three HACS. Type 282 radar was fitted to the 2pdr directors, and a Type 283 barrage director was added. She continued operation in northern waters with the Home Fleet throughout 1943 in this scheme, before being sent to join the Eastern Fleet.

HMS KENYA Pennant 14
Colony class cruiser January 1944

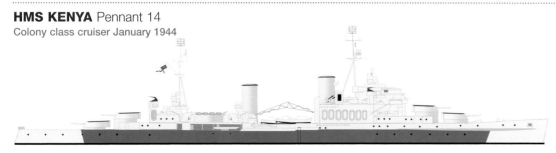

Kenya joined the Eastern Fleet in January 1944 and adopted the scheme used in that region. She was painted 507c overall with a B5 blue hull panel that, as per regulation, had a forward slope near the bow. The decks were 507a, as were the turret tops. Two more twin 20mm mounts were fitted for a total of sixteen barrels, but no 40mm guns. She retained her previous radars, and added an extra Type 283 barrage director. The usual IFF and countermeasures were added, as well as aerials for Headache. No aircraft were carried, but the facilities were not yet removed. She provided cover for raids by British aircraft carriers against Japanese targets in the Indian Ocean, strikes on Malaysia and the amphibious landings at Arakan.

HMS KENYA Pennant 14
Colony class cruiser 1947

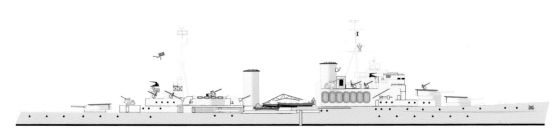

Kenya underwent a major refit after her Eastern Fleet service. 'X' turret was removed to save weight, enabling the light AA to be enhanced, two twin 40mm replacing the turret and two more the quad 2pdrs forward, with another located on the centreline over the old boat stowage area. Two single 40mm guns were mounted each side of the aft deckhouse. All aircraft facilities and the port crane were landed. The starboard crane was placed on the centreline facing aft. *Kenya* went to the Far East as part of 5th Cruiser Squadron, serving in the Korean War. As shown, the ship has her upper works in 507c, the hull in MS4a. By 1948 she was wearing 507c overall. Metal decks were grey and the wood decks scrubbed to natural colour. Boats took on their peacetime appearance. Type 293Q radar was carried at the head of the foremast with Type 277 radar on the starfish at the head of the forward tripod. Type 281B radar was at the head of the mainmast. The 40mm on 'B' turret was removed by 1948; some others were removed later.

HMS KENYA Pennant C14
Colony class cruiser September 1958

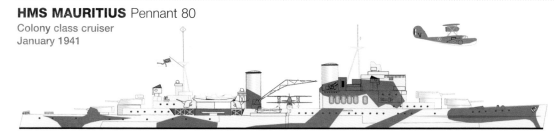

Kenya is shown here at the end of her service in overall 507c. The wood decks were natural, and metal decks mid-grey, approximately 507b. The lower masts were painted black. Single 40mm guns had been removed, but five twin 40mm mounts remained. All Carley floats had been replaced by self-inflating rafts, which took up far less space. There were a multitude of whip aerials for various purposes. The HACS directors were covered and presumably deactivated by the time she paid off. By international agreement, her identity is shown by the C14 carried on her side. She was in reserve four years before being scrapped in 1962.

HMS MAURITIUS Pennant 80
Colony class cruiser
January 1941

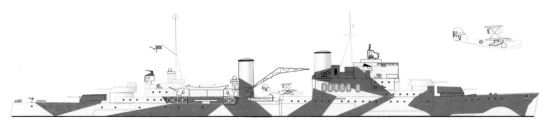

Mauritius was completed to the original design, with no added radars or extra light AA. Within weeks of completion in 507c, she had areas of 507a added to form a camouflage scheme. The same scheme was repeated on the port side. The decks seem to have been natural wood, or mid-grey for steel decks. In this form she joined the Home Fleet, and was engaged in Atlantic patrols searching for enemy raiders and blockade-runners. In late 1941 she was sent to reinforce the Eastern Fleet, as war with Japan loomed. In that region she continued with anti-raider and blockade-runner patrols in the Indian Ocean and South China Sea.

HMS MAURITIUS Pennant 80
Colony class cruiser December 1941–February 1942

Mauritius wore a variation of her original scheme at Singapore in December 1941, and when she returned to the UK in February. This remained 507a and 507c, plenty of which was stocked at Singapore. Turret tops, wood decks and steel decks all remained the same; the pattern was worn on both sides. Two single 20mm were added side by side on the quarterdeck, but this was inadequate for the intensity of the Japanese air war. The Walrus aircraft was painted in very pale grey, probably 507c. Although this ship was to refit at Singapore, it proved too dangerous due to incessant Japanese air raids and she was recalled to the UK for refit at Devonport. It is possible that the aft HACS had Type 285 radar fitted before the Singapore refit was interrupted, and that other equipment was carried home to be installed in the UK.

HMS MAURITIUS Pennant 80
Colony class cruiser April 1942

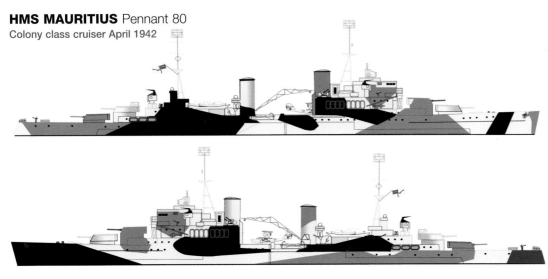

Mauritius completed her refit and rejoined the fleet in a style using colours readily available wherever she would be posted: black, 507b and 507c. The deck area forward of the breakwater was 507b, while the deck from there aft to the superstructure was very dark, either black or 507a. The 'B' turret deck level was 507c. The hangar top was 507c, but all decks from there aft appear to be very dark grey. The quarterdeck was unpainted wood. The top of 'A' turret was 507c, the top of 'B' turret was 507b, the top of 'X' turret was 507b and the top of 'Y' turret was 507b. Two more single 20mm guns were added, one on each side of the bridge. The ship's boats, carried high on the centre of the ship between the 4in gun mounts, were heavy, and the Admiralty sought to reduce the number and size. However, complaints from commanding officers of various ships of this class pointed out that when moored off various ports the number of boats was already insufficient when transferring liberty men ashore and then back, the whole process sometimes taking up as much time as had been allocated for shore leave. Although sources do not credit this ship with Type 281 radar, photographs clearly show aerials at both mastheads.

HMS MAURITIUS Pennant 80
Colony class cruiser June 1943

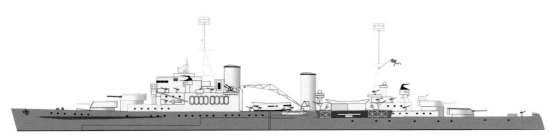

Mauritius joined the Eastern Fleet in 1942, and the Mediterranean Fleet in April 1943. She was damaged by grounding and was repaired in Suez, where aircraft facilities were removed and boats moved to the old catapult deck. Quad 0.5in machine guns were removed and twenty single 20mm guns added, for a total of twenty-four such weapons, an amazing number for a Colony class cruiser. After repairs, she had a dark hull/light upper works scheme based on 507b and 507c. Decks appear to have been uniformly mid-grey, probably 507b. She took part in landings on Sicily, Operation Husky, and at Salerno, then patrolled the Bay of Biscay for German blockade-runners. She returned to the Mediterranean for the Anzio landings, then home for D-Day and sweeps along the coast of Brittany. She supported carrier raids off Norway, and was involved in surface actions in August 1944 and January 1945. She went to the UK for a major refit in February 1945.

HMS MAURITIUS Pennant 80
Colony class cruiser January 1947

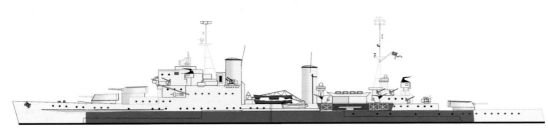

Mauritius was in refit until March 1946, then went to the Mediterranean, where she had a B5 blue panel on a 507c overall hull. From photographs, the deck appears to be dark grey, rather than unpainted wood, and medium on horizontal metal areas; turret tops appear 507b. Removal of 'X' turret enabled the fitting of two quad 2pdr mounts instead. All 20mm were replaced by eight single 40mm Bofors, but the number of 40mm varied across the rest of her service; the 2pdr mounts were finally deactivated. The port crane was removed and the other placed on the centreline facing aft. December 1951 saw final decommissioning and she was in reserve until 1965 before being sold for scrap. During her peacetime service, the hull panel was removed and she was eventually painted 507c overall, with the identification C80 painted on each side on the hull below the bridge.

HMS **TRINIDAD** Pennant 46
Colony class cruiser October 1941

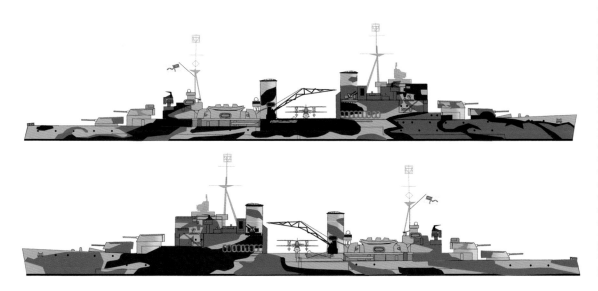

Trinidad was delayed by air raids on her building yard and only saw seven months' active service between completion and loss. An Admiralty four-colour camouflage scheme of B5, MS1, B30 and B55 was applied. Decks were natural wood and steel decks 507b. Sources are confusing in relation to the radar carried, so I have relied on photographs. These clearly show that *Trinidad* had Type 281 radar at both mastheads, Type 285 radar on each of the HACS and Type 284 radar on the main gun director when she joined the fleet. Quad 0.5in mounts were on each side of the bridge, and shortly after completion two single 20mm were added on the aft deck-house. With the Home Fleet there were runs to Russia covering convoys against German warships. She engaged the German destroyer *Z26* while covering PQ-13, forcing it to flee. However, during the action one of *Trinidad*'s own torpedoes circled back after launch and struck her. It is probable that icy conditions caused the torpedo rudder to stick. She made it to the port of Murmansk, where repairs were carried out for her to take passage back to the UK. However, on the way she was attacked by the Luftwaffe and hit by bombs that left her crippled. There was no choice but to scuttle her. There are no known changes to her paint scheme during her brief service.

HMS **GAMBIA** Pennant 48
Colony class cruiser early 1942

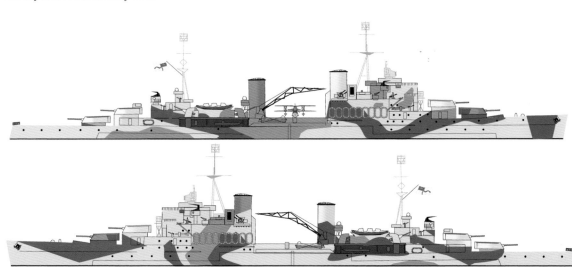

Gambia was completed with a scheme using MS2, MS3 and MS4a. The quarterdeck was left natural wood, while the decks forward were medium grey. A turret top was MS4, 'B' turret was MS3, while the aft turret tops were MS2. The catapult deck appears to have been MS2, or a grey of similar tone. The use of MS4a with the other shades was somewhat unusual. Camouflage was considered so important that it was carried up and over the Carley floats, so as not to break up a design. Because this ship entered service two years after the war started, she was fully fitted out with radar. At the mastheads she had Type 281 radar, Type 284 radar on the main armament director, Type 285 radar on all three HACS, and Type 282 radar on the 2pdr directors. This ship was not fitted with the quad 0.5in MG mounts, because by the time she was completed, it was realised the weapon was ineffective against most modern aircraft. Instead, single 2pdr guns were fitted on each side of the bridge forward of the directors for the quad 2pdr mounts. Six single 20mm guns were also provided. *Gambia* was part of the force sent to occupy Madagascar in September 1942. She then patrolled the Indian Ocean in search of enemy raiders and blockade-runners, and covered the movement of convoys.

HMNZS GAMBIA Pennant 48
Colony class cruiser September 1943

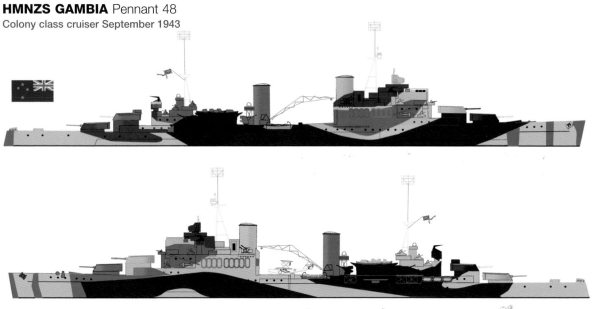

Gambia went into refit in mid-1943. The ship had been manned by many New Zealanders for some time, and in September 1943 was transferred to the RNZN. Her new scheme used the colours G10, B15, B30 and B55. The single 2pdrs and single 20mm guns were all removed, and ten twin 20mm mounts added instead. The Type 273 radar, which had been in front of the bridge, was landed, and a Type 272 radar was added at the top of the forward tripod. The Type 281 radar remained at the head of both masts. Type 283 barrage directors were fitted in front of the bridge. The original HF/DF aerial was removed. The decks appear to have been 507b forward, but the quarter-deck remained unpainted wood. The turret tops were also 507b. All aircraft facilities were removed, and only a single crane, relocated on the centreline facing aft, remained. After the refit, she went on patrols of the Bay of Biscay and covered other operations in European waters.

HMNZS GAMBIA Pennant 48
Colony class cruiser early 1944

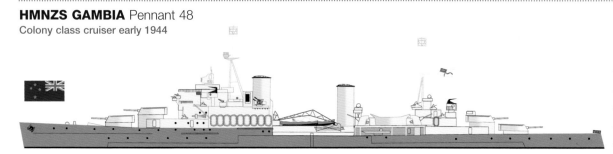

Gambia was sent out to join the Eastern Fleet in early 1944. She patrolled in the area of the Cocos Islands for suspected blockade-runners, and then covered fleet operations against Japanese-held areas of Java and Sumatra. The camouflage scheme was changed to a two-shade style, with a dark lower hull and light upper works. The colours used were 507b and 507c. The decks remained as before. Another set of Type 283 barrage directors were added in front of the bridge.

HMNZS GAMBIA Pennant 48
Colony class cruiser September 1944

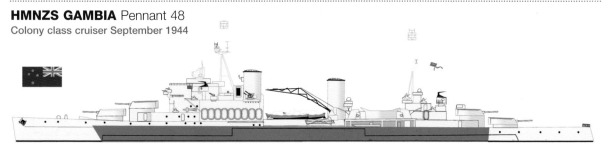

Gambia received a new camouflage scheme in mid-1944, with a blue hull panel using B5, while the rest of the ship was painted in 507c. The quarterdeck seems to have remained unpainted wood, but all other horizontal surfaces, including turret tops, were 507b or similar. During this period the HF/DF aerial was removed from the mainmast, Headache was installed, and IFF and other countermeasures were added.

HMNZS GAMBIA Pennant 48
Colony class cruiser 1945

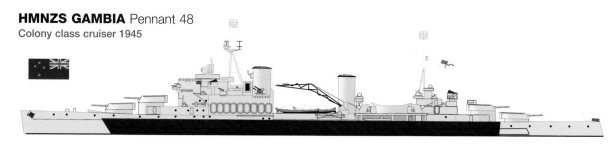

In 1945 *Gambia* transferred to the British Pacific Fleet and adopted a scheme using overall MS4a, with a dark panel of B15 blue-black. There were no other changes of armament or electronics. The ship was present for operations off Okinawa, Formosa, and then the Japanese mainland. At the end of the war, it was decided that the crew requirements of this vessel were too excessive for New Zealand's fledgling navy. As a result, she sailed for the UK, and was formally handed back to the Royal Navy on 27 March 1946.

HMS GAMBIA Pennant 48
Colony class cruiser 1950

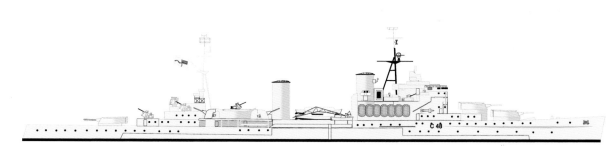

Gambia continued to serve post-war and received several refits. She was posted to many regions of the shrinking British Empire until December 1960, when she paid off into reserve. She sat in the reserve fleet for eight years, before finally being sold for scrap in 1968. She is shown here in about 1950, prior to further upgrades, which involved lattice masts and the removal of the distinctive row of Carley floats. New directors were fitted in place of the earlier HACS and seven twin 40mm AA mounts were added. All the 20mm guns and the quad 2pdr mounts were removed. Her electronics were modified at various times. The colour scheme is peacetime 507c, with a heavy black boot topping at the waterline. The wood decks were scrubbed back to natural colour, and all horizontal metal surfaces were a shade approximating 507b. However, at some point, the area forward of the breakwater was painted, at least partially, in Brunswick green.

HMS JAMAICA Pennant 44
Colony class cruiser 1942

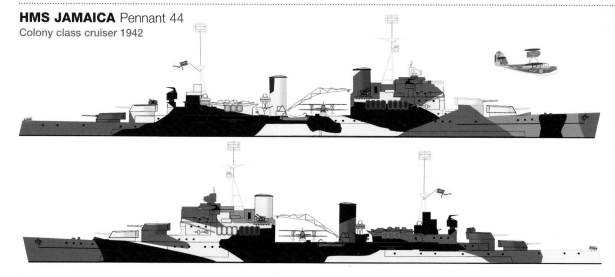

Jamaica completed in mid-1942, at a time when Royal Navy casualties had been heavy. She wore a four-colour Admiralty disruptive scheme using 507c, B5, B6 and MS1. The forward deck areas appear to have been dark grey, but the wood quarterdeck was unpainted. 'A' and 'B' turret tops were 507c, 'X' turret was possibly MS1 and 'Y' turret was B6. Unlike earlier ships, she had radar and 20mm AA guns from the start and never quad 0.5in MG mounts. The radar fit was the now standard Type 281, Type 282, Type 284, Type 285 and Type 273. The latter was placed at the head of the forward tripod instead of the unpopular position at the front of the bridge. *Jamaica* had twelve 6in guns in triple mounts, eight 4in guns in twin turrets, two quad 2pdr AA mounts and eight single 20mm guns. Two of the single 20mm were placed on either side of the rangefinder on 'X' turret. This ship served on convoys to Russia, escorting carrier raids off Norway, and anti-shipping patrols in those waters. She was present at the sinking of the German battleship *Scharnhorst*.

HMS JAMAICA Pennant 44
Colony class cruiser 1943

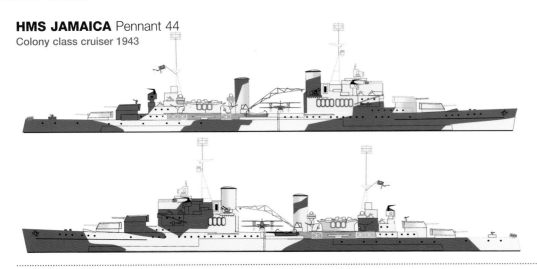

This scheme is reported in *Warship Perspectives, Camouflage Four, Royal Navy: Supplemental*, by Alan Raven (see bibliography). It is a totally non-standard camouflage pattern, reportedly applied to *Jamaica* some time in 1943. Although the base colour is 507c, the contrasting colour was based on the *Book of Color* by Munsell, published in 1929. This book classifies all colours of the spectrum and their variations between dark and light across hundreds of choices. The resulting colour was a blue-green which, when combined with the pale of 507c, would probably have been very well-suited to the Arctic region where this ship spent so much of its time. The paint would have had to be mixed especially for *Jamaica*, which would be very unusual. It is therefore possible that this was one of the other Royal Navy colours of a similar hue. The rangefinders on 'X' turret were removed, and the two single 20mm guns previously located there remained in place. Two others were relocated to the quarterdeck. Eight twin 20mm mounts were also added, two on each side of the bridge and two on each side on the aft superstructure.

HMS JAMAICA Pennant 44
Colony class cruiser 1945

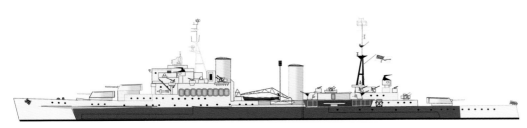

As the war drew to a close, *Jamaica* was taken in for modernisation and major AA upgrade, as was done for most of her surviving sisters. The war had ended by the time she was ready to return to service. As usual, the 'X' turret was removed and replaced by two quad 2pdr AA mounts. Another was added on the centreline amidships which, along with those originally carried, gave her five quad 2pdr mounts. Single 40mm guns were added on each side of the bridge, and two more on each side of the aft superstructure. All but two 20mm guns were removed, with the remaining guns placed on each side of the tripod mainmast. All the usual advanced radars and other electronics were installed, including an air beacon for communication with aircraft and fighter direction. As she was sent to the Far East on completion, she was given an overall coat of 507c, and the standard blue panel running from just forward of 'A' turret to just aft of 'Y' turret.

HMS JAMAICA Pennant C44
Colony class cruiser 1954

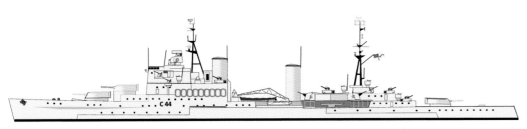

Jamaica went into reserve for a time in 1951, but was refitted 1953–4 for further service with the Home Fleet and in the Mediterranean. All the 2pdr mounts were removed and replaced by six twin 40mm mounts. There were two in place of the 'X' turret, one on the deckhouse above, another on the centreline between the aft funnel and the mainmast, and one on each side of the fore funnel. Two single 40mm guns were also carried on each side of the bridge, and two more on the aft superstructure. The aircraft beacon was removed, and a new main gun director was installed. The twin 40mm all had directors in tubs, but the singles did not. By this time, the masts were black and the overall colour was 507c, with a heavy black boot topping at the waterline. Wood decks were natural wood, and horizontal metal surfaces were mid-grey. The area around the anchors forward of the breakwater was painted Brunswick green. The anchor cables were white, and the runs where the anchor chains ran across the deck were deep red. This commission was a short one, as *Jamaica* was laid up again in 1957, and sold for scrap in December 1960.

HMS BERMUDA Pennant 52
Colony class cruiser August 1942

An Admiralty light disruption scheme was applied to *Bermuda* on completion. The colours were MS4a, MS2 and MS3. The decks were not planked and were mid-grey. The 'X' and 'Y' turrets had tops of MS2, while 'A' and 'B' turrets tops were MS4a. The deck forward of the breakwater in front of 'A' turret was much darker, and probably something like 507a. This ship was the last of this group, and carried a full range of radar on completion. This included a Type 273 radar in the awkward position in front of the bridge, which blocked it for all aft detection. There were ten single 20mm AA guns, and the quad 0.5in machine guns mounts were never fitted. She took part in Operation Torch with the 10th Cruiser Squadron, during which she came under heavy air attack, and then the landing at Bougie, where she again was subject to heavy air attack. Unlike the earlier 'new' cruisers, she had a adequate amount of AA ammunition and was able to fight off the intensive attacks. *Bermuda* then served in the Bay of Biscay, where the Germans were desperate to get blockade-runners through, and supported that effort with destroyers and torpedo boats.

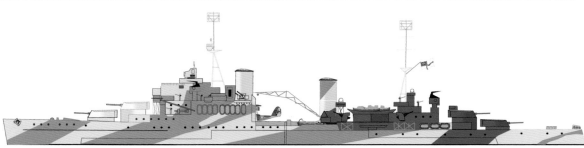

HMS BERMUDA Pennant 52
Colony class cruiser 1943

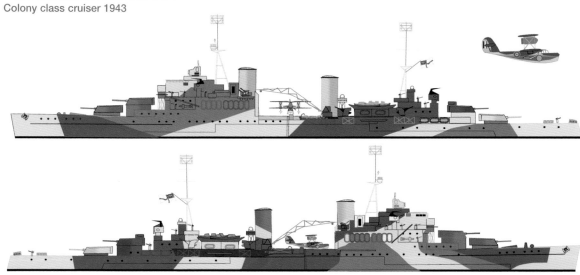

MS4, MS4a and MS2 formed the colours for the camouflage applied to *Bermuda* in September 1943. The decks apparently remained the same. The light AA was increased to sixteen single 20mm AA guns. The aircraft facilities were still in place, but aircraft were rarely carried at this time. The ship remained in European waters and was engaged in a variety of tasks, including transporting men and supplies to Spitzbergen, covering vital convoys to Russia, and hunting German merchant shipping carrying ore and nickel, which were vital to enemy war manufacturing, along the Norwegian coast. The aircraft facilities were finally removed in November 1943.

HMS BERMUDA Pennant 52
Colony class cruiser early 1944

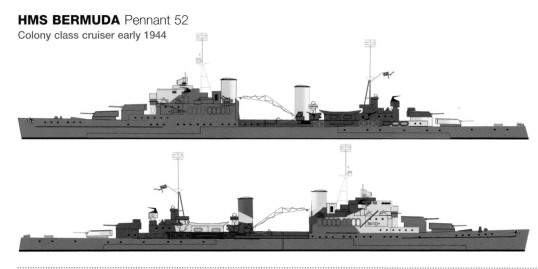

As a result of a short refit on the Tyne, *Bermuda* had the previous camouflage on the hull painted out, but retained the pattern, with a few modifications to the lines, on the upper works. Colours remained MS4, MS4a and
MS2. All but four of the single 20mm guns were removed, and eight
power-operated twin 20mm mounts added. These were much better suited
to Arctic operations, as the gunners had shelter, and even some heating was
supplied. Radar remained the same, since the ship was slated for a major
refit. Her duties continued to be the protection of Arctic convoys.

HMS BERMUDA Pennant 52
Colony class cruiser April 1944

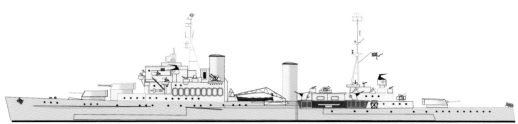

Bermuda underwent much the same major refit as many other British
cruisers, losing 'X' turret, but gaining two quad 2pdr mounts in that position. Another was fitted on the centreline, where the ship's boats had previously been. Two single 2pdr guns of the latest type were added on each
side of the bridge. Four twin 20mm and four single 20mm guns were
retained. Her scheme seems to have been a plain 507c on the upper works,
with an MS4a hull. Presumably decks remained the same as before. The
turret tops appear to have been 507c. The radar fit was substantially altered
with Type 281b radar on the mainmast, along with its IFF aerial. The Type
273 radar, which had been in front of the bridge, was replaced by Type 283
barrage directors. Type 277 radar was fitted on a platform on the foremast
tripod, along with Type 293Q radar. All the usual IFF and missile countermeasures were installed, which brought the ship up to the highest standard
of RN cruisers at the time.

HMS BERMUDA Pennant 52
Colony class cruiser August 1945

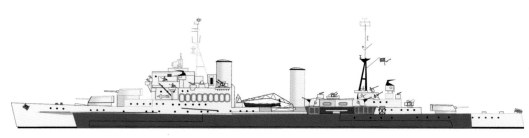

Bermuda went to Sydney in June 1944 in the scheme above, then adopted a
B5 blue panel on the hull, with the rest of the ship in 507c. The decks
remained 507b. The armament was revised. Two single and two twin 20mm
were removed. Two single 40mm Bofors were added on the aft deckhouse
and two single 40mm Boffins one deck below. Although the war ended
before *Bermuda* left Sydney, she still saw some action. While proceeding to
Shanghai via the Philippines to aid prisoners of war, she was attacked by
Japanese aircraft on 6 September. These may have refused to accept the
surrender or simply had not heard about it. The CinC British Pacific Fleet
had already instructed that if they were attacked by 'ex-enemy aircraft' after
the surrender, ships were to 'shoot them down in a friendly manner'. She
remained in the Far East until 1947 and then returned to the UK, to be
refitted, then placed into reserve until 1950.

HMS BERMUDA Pennant C52
Colony class cruiser 1957

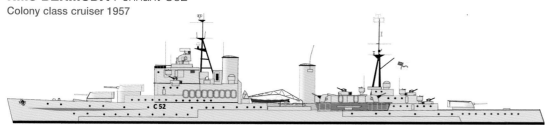

In 1956 Bermuda was taken out of reserve and rebuilt on similar lines to her sister ship *Gambia*, with an enclosed bridge and improved directors, including a US Mk 63 director for the 4in guns. All 2pdrs were removed, while six twin 40mm mounts were retained with their own original director control. The deck colours are unknown, but probably mid-grey. She is shown here in overall MS4a Home Fleet grey in the winter of 1957, but she was probably painted in 507c when in the Mediterranean. Her peacetime duties included humanitarian assistance to Cyprus. She worked with the NATO fleets for some time, and was not taken out of service until 1964, then finally scrapped in 1965.

MODIFIED COLONY CLASS CRUISERS

HMS UGANDA Pennant 66
Modified Colony class cruiser
January 1943

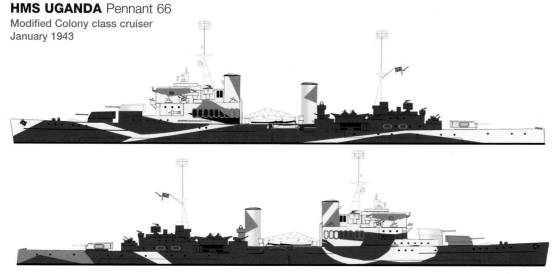

Uganda did not wear camouflage for long, but her initial scheme was comprised of 507a, 507b and 507c. The decks were Cemtex of a mid-grey colour. No wood decks had been fitted, to speed completion and save weight. The 'X' turret was omitted from the design of the previous group, and the space taken up by a quad 2pdr mount, although the original intention had been to place an additional twin 4in mount in that position. There were ten twin 20mm mounts. The quad 2pdr mount was moved further forward than on the Colony class, and the HACS on each side of the bridge moved further aft. This gave a better forward arc of fire for the 2pdr mount, without affecting the coverage of the HACS. *Uganda* was equipped with a full range of radar and the Type 272 radar was on the forward tripod, instead of the awkward position in front of the bridge. Aircraft facilities were included, but not used. Initially, only one crane was carried, the port side one having never been fitted. Later, the crane would be moved amidships, on the centreline facing aft, but initially it was placed where originally planned. Upon entering service, she joined the Home Fleet, but later went on to take part in the landings on Sicily and then at Salerno, where she was seriously damaged by a German radio-guided bomb. *Uganda* was sent to the United States for repairs.

HMCS UGANDA Pennant 66
Modified Colony class cruiser January 1944

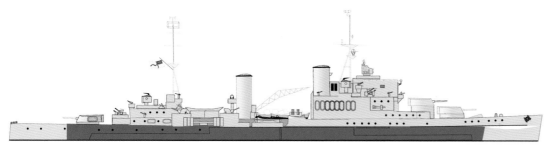

After repairing her damage in the United States, *Uganda* was handed over to the Royal Canadian Navy, but retained the same name for some years. On re-entering service, she adopted a scheme of MS4a overall with a B5 blue panel on the hull. WSB bright white was used to counter the shadow of the bow knuckle. The decks were almost certainly the same mid-grey. All aircraft facilities were removed, having never been used. US Navy quad 40mm AA mounts were placed on each side of the catapult deck; as these were heavy, all but four of the twin power-operated 20mm mounts were removed. Eight single 20mm guns were also added. Type 281B radar was carried at the head of the mainmast, with Type 293Q radar at the head of the foremast, and Type 277 radar at the head of the forward tripod. An improved main gunnery director was also added. The ship proceeded to the Pacific for service with the British Pacific Fleet.

HMCS QUEBEC Pennant C66
Modified Colony class cruiser 1954

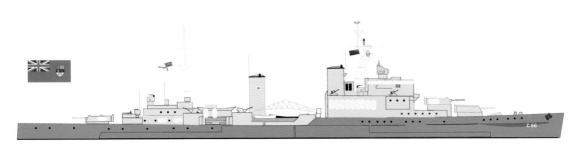

Uganda was renamed *Quebec* in 1952, by which time she was a training ship. Most light AA had been removed. In the position previously occupied by the 'X' turret was a single US-pattern twin 40mm, and on each side of the bridge were single 40mm Boffins. The original Carley floats were retained and a few more added, all of which had white canvas covers. The paint standard was 507b for the hull and MS4a for the superstructure. Decks forward of the 'B' turret were mid-grey. All other decks were possibly 507a. The anchor areas on deck were Brunswick green and the rest mid-grey. Turret tops were 507b and the masts white. The ship's pennant was applied in US Navy style. A Canadian maple leaf was on each side of the aft funnel. Whip aerials do not seem as numerous as they were on many other cruisers at this time. Most of the radar installations were the same as before. She was sold for scrap in 1956.

HMS NEWFOUNDLAND Pennant 59
Modified Colony class cruiser 1943

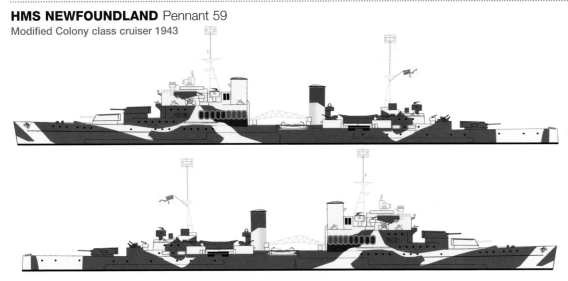

Newfoundland entered service equipped to carry aircraft, because she was already being built that way and the Royal Navy did not want to delay her entry into service. However, they were removed just over a year later. Her first camouflage scheme, as shown here, was a rather stark one of 507a over 507c. The decks were Cemtex, not wood, and mid-grey. Most horizontal metal surfaces were painted 507a, as were the turret tops. There were still four twin 4in mounts, but it had been intended another should be fitted in the 'X' turret position, but for various reasons this could not be done in time for completion. Instead, she had a quad 2pdr mount in that location, along with its director. The quad 2pdr mounts forward were on each side of the centre of the bridge, instead of opposite the forward funnel. Sixteen twin 20mm mounts were fitted for a total of thirty-two barrels, an enormous number considering the very weak light AA of the original Colony class.

HMS NEWFOUNDLAND Pennant 59
Modified Colony class cruiser 1944

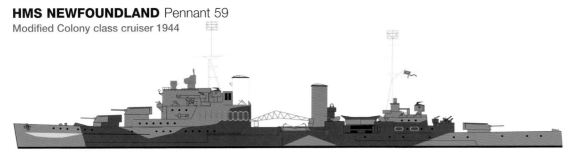

Newfoundland was torpedoed by the Italian submarine *Ascianghi* on 23 July 1943. She went to Malta for temporary repairs and then to the United States for more permanent work. At the completion of the repairs she returned to the UK wearing the temporary camouflage shown. The ship underwent a long refit, which included fitting some of the equipment she had carried home as cargo. The ship only wore this scheme for about two months. The starboard side pattern is not known, but believed to be very similar to the port side. The armament and electronic equipment had not changed, as the repairs did not encompass that.

HMS NEWFOUNDLAND Pennant 59
Modified Colony class cruiser early 1945

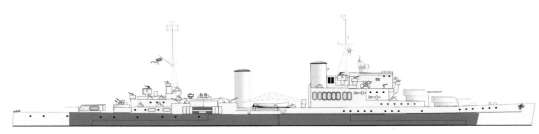

Newfoundland refitted from May–November 1944, then went to the
Eastern Fleet wearing 507c overall with a blue panel of B5 on the hull;
metal decks and turret tops were 507a grey, Cemtex areas were mid-grey.
Under the knuckle of the bow was WSB bright white, to counter the
shadow. Main armament remained nine 6in guns in three triple turrets,
plus four twin 4in mounts. Light AA was strengthened for Japanese
kamikaze attacks. Sources indicate two US-pattern quad 40mm: having
examined photographs, I see only one on the centreline amidships. Nine
twin 20mm and two singles were carried. Type 281B radar was at the head
of the mainmast with its IFF receiver, Type 274 radar on the main director,
Type 285 on the three HACS, and Type 282 for the 2pdrs. There was a
director tub for the 40mm mount amidships, presumably with US radar.
A Type 293Q was at the head of the foremast, and on the forward tripod
Type 277 radar. In front of the bridge were Type 283 barrage directors and
another aft of the mainmast. The ship then went to the Pacific Fleet.

HMS NEWFOUNDLAND Pennant 59
Modified Colony class cruiser
mid-1945

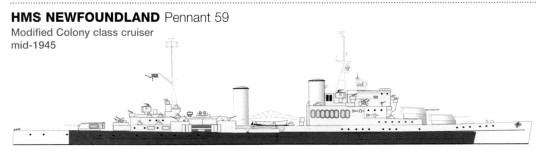

Newfoundland joined Australian units in operations around New Guinea
and various cut-off Japanese garrisons. For these operations, she changed
her hull panel to B20, but retained her general overall 507c. This was, of
course, to ensure the ship had much the same appearance as those she
was operating with. The aircraft facilities had been removed during her
large refit, but they had seldom been used, other than during trials. This
cleared considerable space that became available for accommodation,
recreation and office space for the enlarged crew required to man the
additional light AA weapons. Most ships had not been designed for such
a considerable increase in crew numbers, which in addition to top weight
concerns, also entailed providing mess facilities, stores and berths.

HMS NEWFOUNDLAND Pennant 59
Modified Colony class cruiser
late 1945

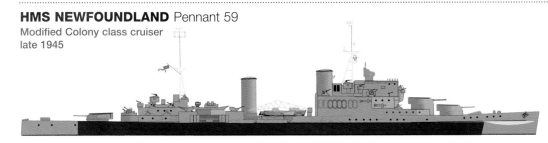

Newfoundland took part in the final operations against Japan, when the
paint scheme was changed to the new Admiralty standard type for all
stations. The hull panel was B15 and the rest of the ship MS3. There was
a WAG or similar section painted onto the overhang of the bow knuckle
in order to counter the depth of shade. The powered twin 20mm on each
side of the fore funnel were changed into 40mm Boffins, as were the two
on each side of the aft deckhouse. There were extra Carley floats heaped
at the stern and on each side of the aft funnel. This was the appearance of
the ship at the time of the Japanese surrender, when she was present in
Tokyo Bay.

HMS NEWFOUNDLAND Pennant 59
Modified Colony class cruiser
1949

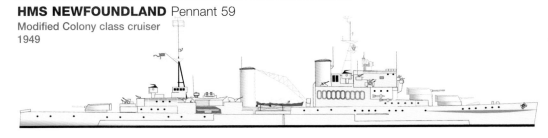

Newfoundland continued to serve post-war, after a short time in reserve.
All 20mm were removed. The light AA became three quad 2pdr, a pair of
40mm Boffins on each side of the fore funnel, and the quad 40mm on
the centreline amidships. The ship was painted in overall 507c without
counter-shading. The decks probably remained mid-grey, but Cemtex
could be painted, and I have had discussions in the past with peacetime
navy people who said that some ships painted whole areas with
Brunswick green. There were ten Carley floats on each side of the
bridge. She served as a training ship during this period.

HMS NEWFOUNDLAND Pennant 59
Modified Colony class cruiser November 1956

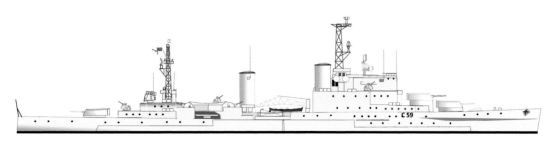

Newfoundland received a modernisation refit that was the most extensive of any of her class or the preceding ships. It included the addition of an integrated fire control system with Type 275 radar and MRS-1 for the 4in and 40mm mounts. The system was prone to occasional failures and was therefore considered too advanced and less reliable than those on her modernised sister ships. *Newfoundland* served mostly in the Far East. She took part in the Suez operation, where she encountered the Egyptian frigate *Domiat*, the ex-British River class *Nith*, patrolling the Red Sea. The Egyptian ship, although hopelessly outgunned, opened fire and inflicted some damage on the cruiser. *Newfoundland*, along with the destroyer *Diana*, then returned fire. *Domiat* was sunk by a combination of gunfire and a torpedo fired by *Diana*. In 1959 *Newfoundland* was paid off for potential sale.

ALMIRANTE GRAU Pennant 81
Modified Colony class cruiser 1961

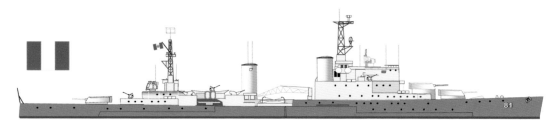

Peru purchased *Newfoundland* in 1960. The ship had a short refit, during which the advanced integrated fire control system was removed. The newer directors remained, but the 40mm were removed and standard US-type twin 40mm mounts with shields were substituted. The hull was painted a bluish-grey colour not used in the Royal Navy and a US-type identification number was placed near the bow. The number was different from the one worn by the ship while in Royal Navy service. Although I show the superstructure here in 507c, the Peruvian shade seems to have been almost white. The decks appear to be a similar colour to the hull and the turret tops pale grey. Although self-opening life rafts were installed, the Peruvian navy reinstated some older World War II type rafts. She was renamed *Capitan Quinones* in 1973, hulked and then scrapped, in 1979.

HMS CEYLON Pennant 30
Modified Colony class cruiser
mid-1943

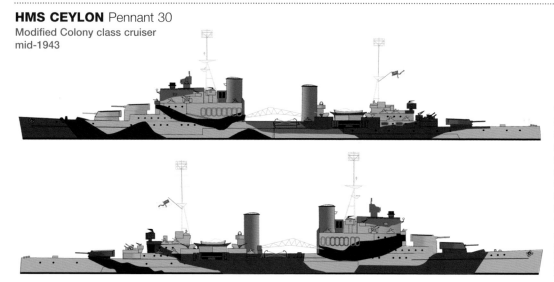

Ceylon is depicted in her first scheme, an Admiralty disruptive comprised of G10, B15, B30 and B55. The decks were not planked and were mostly of mid-grey Cemtex. All other horizontal metal surfaces were B30. The tops of turrets 'A' and 'B' were G10 and the top of turret 'Y' was B55. The light AA comprised three quad 2pdr mounts and sixteen twin 20mm mounts. Type 272 radar was placed on top of the bridge instead of on the forward tripod, which lowered the top weight and still gave good coverage. Type 281 radar aerials were on both mastheads. Type 285 radar was fitted on each of the HACS, and Type 284 radar on the main gunnery director. Only the starboard crane was fitted, to save more weight. The aircraft facilities were present, but not used and soon removed. The ship went to the Home Fleet in this camouflage, but at the end of 1943 was sent to the Eastern Fleet.

HMS CEYLON Pennant 30
Modified Colony class cruiser mid-1944

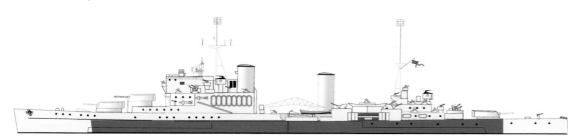

Ceylon was sent to join the Eastern Fleet and adopted the scheme for that region. Note that the blue panel is per instructions, in that it runs between 'A' turret and 'Y' turret fronts, but did not have the full slope forward. The hull and upper works were all in 507c, and the decks were mid-grey Cemtex, or B30 as previously. The radar fit was not altered for this deployment and she still carries the same outfit as previously. Eight single 20mm guns were added, as well as another twin 20mm mount, giving a total of forty-two 20mm barrels. *Ceylon* took part in the carrier raids against Sabang, Surabaya and targets in Sumatra, which also involved gunnery actions against Japanese shore batteries and AA defences. At Sabang, she covered the fleet destroyers when they closed in to destroy enemy batteries.

HMS CEYLON Pennant 30
Modified Colony class cruiser
early 1945

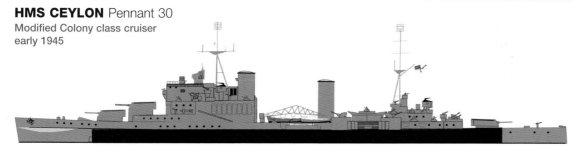

Ceylon joined the British Pacific Fleet, but participated in a carrier raid on Panakalan Bradan during her transfer. The scheme became a B20 dark blue panel and MS3 overall. Deck colour remained the same. Note that, unlike most of the Colony class, she carried eight Carley floats on each side of the bridge, whereas most had nine. After a brief period with the British Pacific Fleet, she rejoined the Eastern Fleet.

HMS CEYLON Pennant 30
Modified Colony class cruiser
September 1945

Ceylon returned to the Eastern Fleet in mid-1945 and adopted an overall 507c again. She seems to have worn a lighter blue panel, which was probably washed-out 1941 blue. The decks remained the same. By the end of the war, her light AA had been altered again. There were now only two single 20mm, fourteen twin 20mm, and four single 40mm Bofors guns had been added on the aft deckhouse. Type 244 IFF was carried on the top of the aft aerial for the Type 281 radar. Type 242 IFF was mounted on the forward tripod mast above the bridge and a Type 650 missile jammer was on the back of the rear funnel. Type 253 IFF was carried below the starfish of the mainmast.

HMS CEYLON Pennant 30
Modified Colony class cruiser 1954

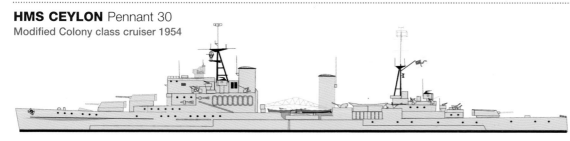

Ceylon is shown here in MS4a Home Fleet grey after peacetime service in the Home Fleet and other stations. The decks were painted and were possibly Brunswick green for at least some time. The area around the anchors may have been dull red. Ships repainted regularly in peacetime and these things could change from one year to another. The masts were painted black, against funnel smoke stains. Note that all the light AA was reduced to the 2pdr mounts and single 40mm guns, but two more 40mm guns added. This was her appearance prior to going in for a major reconstruction in 1955, which lasted well into 1956.

HMS CEYLON Pennant C30
Modified Colony class cruiser 1956

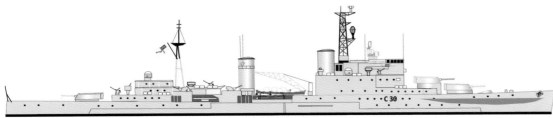

Ceylon had her bridge enclosed during the reconstruction and nuclear fallout sprinklers installed, plus sealed containment areas for the crew. The foremast was converted to a heavy lattice type. The ship appears in most photographs as quite dark and was probably MS4a Home Fleet grey rather than 507c. The black boot topping was very prominent and the decks were mid-grey. The main director was unchanged, except for more modern radar. Simpler directors carried worked better than the integrated system installed on her sister ship *Newfoundland*. Post-war developed radar and electronic systems were added. After her reconstruction, *Ceylon* continued to serve with the RN until December 1959, when she paid off ready for foreign sale.

CORONEL BOLOGNESI Pennant 82
Modified Colony class cruiser
mid-1964

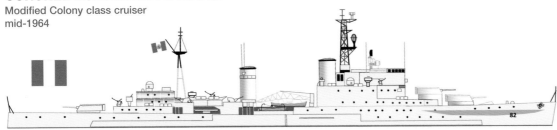

Ceylon was sold to Peru in January 1960 and renamed to *Coronel Bolognesi*. Most of the Royal Navy equipment installed remained the same during her service with Peru. She was not paid off until 1982, when she was sold for scrap and then towed away to Taiwan in 1985.

MINOTAUR CLASS CRUISERS
HMS SWIFTSURE Pennant 08
Minotaur class cruiser 1944

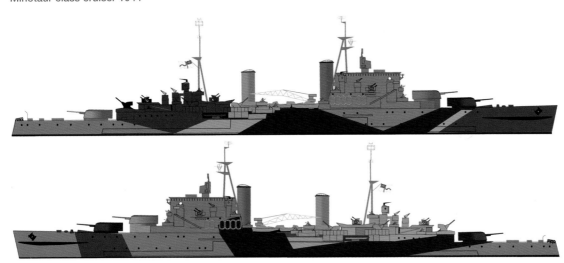

Swiftsure was of a new design. There were no aircraft hangars, which allowed weight to be kept lower and more compact. The camouflage she entered service with comprised G10, B15, G45 and MS3. The deck colour was B5, while the horizontal surfaces were painted to match the shade on the hull directly opposite. The new design allowed for an extra twin 4in AA mount in 'X' turret position. The class carried a greater number of light AA. A quad 2pdr was on the centreline super-firing over the aft 4in mount, another on the centreline between the 4in mounts, and one on each side of the bridge, for a total of four, with three able to bear port or starboard. Sixteen twin 20mm AA were fitted. A crane was on the centreline facing aft to handle the larger ship's boats. Type 281B radar was carried at the top of the mainmast, with a Type 244 IFF on top. Type 293 radar was at the head of the foremast with Type 277 radar on a platform on the tripod. Type 282 radar was on each of the 2pdr directors. Type 284 gunnery radar was fitted on the main director, with Type 285 radar on each of the three HACS. A Type 283 barrage director was at the front of the bridge. She was the ultimate World War II cruiser for the Royal Navy. *Swiftsure* spent the first period of her service with the Home Fleet.

HMS SWIFTSURE Pennant 08
Minotaur class cruiser mid-1944

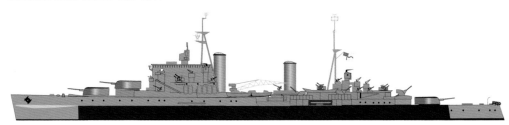

Swiftsure joined the British Pacific Fleet in early 1944, adopting a scheme of MS3 overall with a B15 hull panel. Decks and horizontal surfaces were B5. There was a counter shade of high-gloss WSB, with a touch of MS3 on the bow knuckle. The top of 'B' turret was MS3, while the others were B15. All 20mm weapons were removed. In their place, *Swiftsure* received eight 40mm Boffins and four single 40mm Bofors Mk III. This armament change was because 20mm guns lacked enough hitting power to knock down a determined suicide pilot. She took part in the Okinawa campaign and a major raid on Truk. After the surrender of Japan, she was one of the first ships to enter Hong Kong to liberate prisoners of war. *Swiftsure* could be identified by the single barrage director positioned forward of the bridge, while her sister ship, *Superb*, had two directors.

HMS SWIFTSURE Pennant 08
Minotaur class cruiser 1953

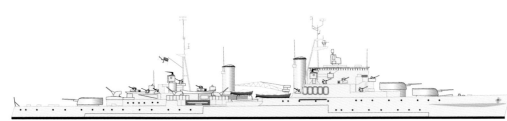

Swiftsure continued in the fleet post-war as one of the most modern cruisers, serving on many stations. Here she is in 507c overall, including turret tops; decks remained dark grey. The black boot topping was much broader in peace-time. She never received the Mk VI secondary directors with Type 275 radar as designed. Type 920 radar was at the top of the mainmast. The number of 4in and 2pdr mounts was the same for some years, but eventually the 2pdrs were replaced by twin 40mm mounts, each with their own director. Four Boffins were retained and nine newer-model single 40mm guns added. She was in collision with the destroyer *Diamond* in 1953 and laid up after repair. She was removed from reserve for a complete modernisation in 1956, but as costs rose, work slowed then stopped in 1959. She was scrapped in 1962 with the reconstruction incomplete.

HMCS ONTARIO Pennant 53
Minotaur class cruiser 1944

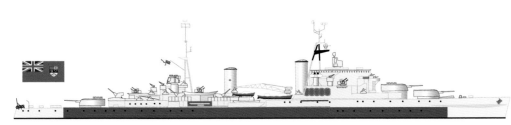

This ship was under construction for the Royal Navy as *Minotaur*, when arrangements were made to hand her over to Canada. This took place before she was completed, and the ship was renamed *Ontario*. The new ship completed after the war in Europe had concluded, so she went to the Pacific for her first deployment, and is shown in 507c, with a blue panel similar to 1941 blue. The decks were 507a and turret tops were 507c. Note that the Carley floats were not painted to match the area around them. She had the new HACS Mk VI directors from completion. Her armament was nine 6in guns in three triple turrets, five twin 4in AA mounts, four quad 2pdr mounts and sixteen twin 20mm mounts. There were new Mk VI directors for the 4in guns. She arrived in the Pacific too late for hostilities, but she took part in the reoccupation of Hong Kong and sailed south to visit Australia before sailing for Canada.

HMCS ONTARIO Pennant 53
Minotaur class cruiser 1952

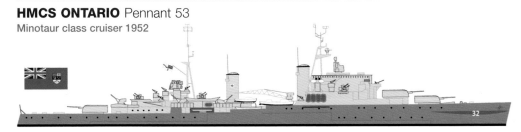

Ontario served in the Royal Canadian Navy during peacetime, first as an active combatant, and later as a training ship. By the time of this illustration, she had adopted a hull of approximately 507b, with the upper works in MS4a. Note that the previous barrage director position was converted to take a single 40mm Bofors AA gun. There were also six 40mm Boffins carried. There were only minor changes to the electronics of this ship during her service, but whip aerials can be seen. The pennant was carried at the bow in US Navy style, but below the hull knuckle.

HMCS ONTARIO Pennant 53
Minotaur class cruiser 1958

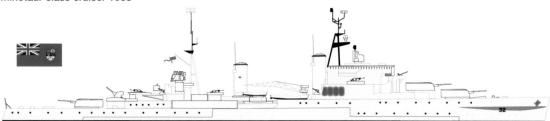

Ontario continued to serve in the post-war fleet. Type 290 radar replaced the earlier set at the head of the mainmast. She had carried Mk VI secondary directors with Type 275 radar since completion, but by this time only the aft one remained. The aft 4in mount was the only one of these mounts left, as the four in the waist were removed. From time to time the armament had varied, with single 40mm guns being part of the weaponry mounted. However, all the quad 2pdr mounts were deleted, and four US Navy-type quad 40mm mounts carried. There were also four Boffin mounts, and at least one single 40mm gun. As shown here, she was painted in a slightly bluish pale grey, before being decommissioned in 1958, and sold for scrap in 1960.

HMS SUPERB Pennant 25
Minotaur class cruiser 1946

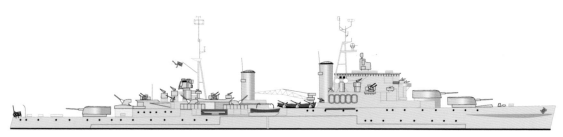

Superb was not completed until January 1946. She was the last of the class completed as planned. Of her five intended sisters, *Blake*, *Lion* and *Tiger* became a completely new type; *Hawke* and *Bellerophon* were cancelled. *Superb* is shown here as she left the yard: MS4a Home Fleet grey overall. The main deck was not planked and its Cemtex was Brunswick green. The horizontal metal decks were 507b. Note the formidable AA armament installed as a result of experience in the Pacific with kamikaze attacks. There were single 20mm guns on each side of the bridge front and quad 2pdrs abreast the bridge with directors, twin 20mm on each side of the fore funnel, and single power-operated 2pdrs lower down. On the boat deck was a row of three single 40mm Bofors guns. Behind the aft funnel was a quad 2pdr with director, at the mainmast twin 20mm guns on each side. There are single 40mm Bofors guns opposite the aft 2pdr directors and another set of quad 2pdr mounts. Most of these weapons had radar control and the five twin 4in had new Mk VI directors with Type 275 radar.

HMS SUPERB Pennant 25
Minotaur class cruiser 1954

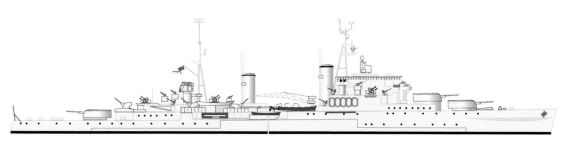

Superb could be distinguished from her sister *Swiftsure* by the double barrage directors in front of the bridge. She is illustrated in her final colour scheme of 507c with a heavy black boot topping. The decks were apparently still Brunswick green. Type 960 radar replaced the Type 281 at the mainmast head. The AA armament underwent some changes. The quad 2pdr remained, but the 20mm guns were removed along with the single 2pdrs. In lieu, she mounted eight single 40mm Bofors. The Bofors on the boat deck were removed by 1950 to make access easier. This ship was earmarked for a major rebuild, which was to see all the quad 2pdr mounts replaced by twin 40mm mounts and the fire control greatly improved with new systems. The bridge was to be covered and many other changes planned. However, once again, the dire shortage of funds caused these plans to be cancelled and she was removed from the programme in 1957. The ship was subsequently sold for scrap in 1960, fourteen years after she had been completed.

CONTENTS

ADVENTURE CLASS MINELAYERS

HMS ADVENTURE Pennant M23
Adventure class minelayer 1926

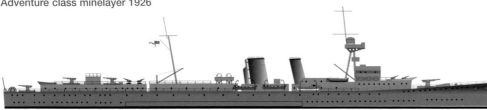

The success of the German minelaying cruisers *Brummer* and *Bremse* led the Admiralty to propose a fast minelaying cruiser for the Royal Navy shortly after World War I. *Adventure* is shown here as completed, painted overall in 507b. There were planked decks forward and around the guns, which at this time remained natural wood. The transom stern caused problems. She was armed with high-angle 4.7in guns of the same type as the battleship *Nelson*. Four single 2pdr AA guns were on the centreline. Around 400 mines could be carried. For the cruising range demanded, she had diesel engines as well as steam turbines. The diesels exhausted through the skinny donkey funnel attached to the central one. The colour scheme also changed, with the ship predominately 507c for some years, but there was also a period when the hull was MS4a and the upper works 507c.

HMS ADVENTURE Pennant M23
Adventure class minelayer 1936

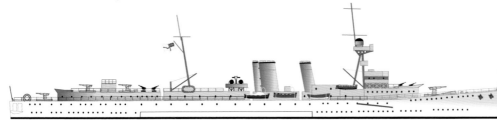

Adventure was deployed overseas on occasion, usually to allow units of the fleet to manoeuvre within the requirements of a minelayer. This would involve escort to a given point, then rendezvous at dawn after a theoretical minefield had been laid. She is dressed in buff and white, with brown masts. The 2pdrs were painted black and the searchlights have black covers. It was also common for the main guns to be covered in black waterproof canvas. Because of the problems with the transom stern mentioned above, the ship was lengthened and given a round stern. The previous diesel exhaust was replaced by a thin funnel attached to the amidships steam funnel. A simple gun director was added to the slightly enlarged and strengthened searchlight platform. The ship was on a high priority list to receive quad 0.5in MG mounts and a quad 2pdr mount, but pre-war shortages prevented this from happening until 1939.

HMS ADVENTURE Pennant M23
Adventure class minelayer 1939

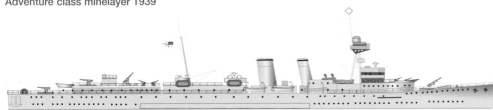

By 1939 *Adventure* wore MS4a Home Fleet grey. Deck colour is unknown. The black boot topping was reduced to a thin line. Two quad 0.5in MG mounts were added ahead of the fore funnel, and twin Lewis guns near the mainmast, but the quad 2pdr mount had not been fitted. Two rangefinders were added, along with an HF/DF on the mainmast. The aft deckhouse was more in shadow, as the deck above was extended out to give more room. The ugly thin funnel was removed and from a distance the ship had the appearance of a 'D' class cruiser. Note that this ship did not have the knuckle at the bow that was characteristic of many between-war British cruiser designs and, unlike the 'C' and 'D' classes, the bow was not flat and had more sheer.

HMS ADVENTURE Pennant M23
Adventure class minelayer October 1941

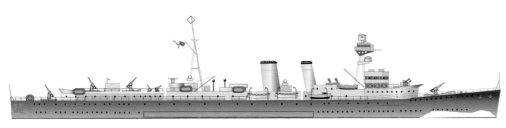

By October 1941 *Adventure* had proven to be a more useful warship than expected and was quite in demand. AA armament was improved by the end of the year, with a quad 2pdr placed in front of the bridge, replacing the two singles. An HACS was placed on the fighting top and the foremast above that removed. The mainmast was converted to a tripod in anticipation of radar soon to be installed, but it had to be moved forward slightly. The single 2pdr guns aft were retained for a short time longer. The HF/DF aerial was moved to the top of the mainmast. The searchlights were spread further apart, with one between the funnels and one on the leg of the mainmast. For a very short time the ship wore a false white bow wave, but for how long is unsure. It may have been for just a single operation. The hull was 507b with 507c upper works. The deck colour is not known, but believed to have been mid-grey, probably 507b.

HMS **ADVENTURE** Pennant M23
Adventure class minelayer 1942–3

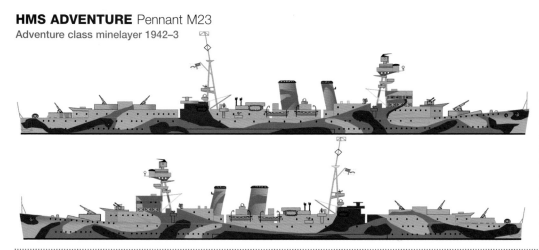

Adventure received an Admiralty disruptive pattern camouflage scheme in 1942. The colours were a base of B55, with areas of B5 and G5. The decks were dark grey, almost black and therefore possibly G5. Type 286PU radar, a rotating set, was at the top of the mainmast and the HACS had Type 285 radar installed. The HF/DF was moved further down the mainmast, and then removed altogether in 1943. Nine 20mm guns were added and the quad 0.5in MG mounts were retained until 1943. The plating of the aft deckhouse was carried out to the sides of the ship to provide more internal space. This was a hard-working ship throughout the war and was used in a variety of tasks, including transporting mines from the UK to locations where they could be picked up by the faster *Abdiel* class, and operating with one or more units of that class to lay minefields.

HMS **ADVENTURE** Pennant M23
Adventure class minelayer 1944

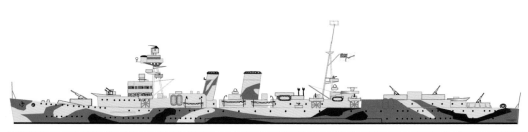

Alterations to the camouflage scheme took place, although the general pattern remained similar. The actual lines of the painted areas could change through various repainting work, while adhering to the general design. In this instance, the colour B5 remained, but the grey has become the lighter MS4a, and the dark areas MS1. The light AA changed, with the quad 0.5in MG mounts being removed, and the 20mm increased to eleven single guns. The mine stowage areas and rear doors in the hull made the ship very versatile, and able to be used for transporting all kinds of stores to front-line areas. Prior to the invasion of France, she laid defensive minefields against the interference of German surface ships and submarines. During the Normandy landings in June 1944, she was able to act as a support ship for landing craft with little alteration, and then resume her normal duties, although these were gradually diminishing as the Axis forces retreated and their territory shrank. It was necessary to remove the Type 286 radar, as it was easily detected by the Germans. Instead, Type 283 radar was placed on the bridge, and Type 281B radar on the mainmast.

HMS **ADVENTURE** Pennant M23
Adventure class minelayer 1945

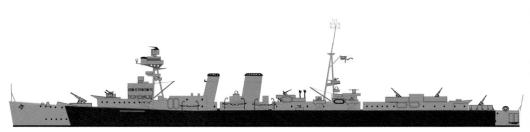

Having seen considerable war service, *Adventure* was worn out by the end of the war, disarmed in October 1945 and placed in reserve. During her last period of service, she appeared in MS3 overall, with a B15 hull panel. The light AA was increased, with the addition of a single 40mm on the centreline amidships and three twin 20mm mounts. Five single 20mm guns were retained. It is possible that the single 40mm gun was a temporary issue. Similarly, the twin 20mm, all or some, may also have been aboard for the D-Day operations. Type 244 IFF was added to the aerial of Type 281B radar. If the value of a ship is to be assessed by how much the user got out of her, this minelaying cruiser, much criticised when built and during her early service, proved a most valuable vessel during her World War II service with the Royal Navy. At the end of her last commission, her top speed was 27 knots and, if pushed, still capable of making 28 knots: quite an achievement by those that built her machinery.

ABDIEL CLASS MINELAYERS

HMS LATONA Pennant M76
Abdiel class minelayer 1941

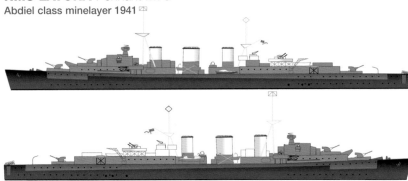

Latona only wore one scheme during her service. It varied only slightly on each side of the ship. The colours were 507a, 507b and white. Wood decks, were painted 507b. Armament was three twin 4in dual-purpose mounts, one quad 2pdr and two quad 0.5in machine guns. Due to her early loss, no light AA weapons were added, but some sources quote up to four 20mm. The need for this ship was so urgent that she did not complete her working-up period before being sent to the Mediterranean via Capetown with desperately needed stores. Eight runs were made to Tobruk, despite heavy air attacks. On her ninth run she was hit and the firefighting system was destroyed. Loaded with ammunition, she was abandoned, the crew being rescued by destroyers.

HMS ABDIEL Pennant M39
Abdiel class minelayer 1943

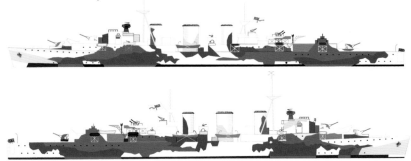

Abdiel is shown here at the time of her loss in a variation of the previous pattern in four-colours of white, sand, G5 and MS2. The style was much the same, but some lines changed while repainted in new shades: note the very unusual waterline. Type 279 radar replaced Type 286. She laid mines in defensive shields against the Japanese, but suffered damage due to grounding. She returned to the UK for repair, then worked with *Adventure* to sow minefields off the French coast, and in the Western Mediterranean. There were also transport runs, with supplies for Malta. She participated in Operations Husky and Avalanche. Her last cruise was carrying troops to Taranto: in port she detonated a mine laid by German E-boats and sank within two minutes with heavy loss of life.

HMS ABDIEL Pennant M39
Abdiel class minelayer 1941

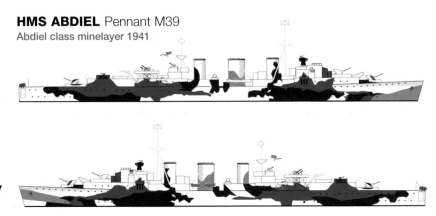

Abdiel was rushed into service part way through her acceptance trials, as the urgency of war was such that the Admiralty needed her immediately. She successfully laid two minefields near Brest, and received a telegram of congratulations for a wonderful effort by the crew of the new ship, who had barely time to familiarise themselves with their ship and its equipment, let alone test it. The four-colour scheme here shows her with a base colour of white, over which there are areas of dark Mountbatten pink, B15 and B20. The wood decks were left natural, but the other horizontal surfaces were painted dark grey. The ship entered service with a fixed Type 286 radar on the foremast. This aerial gave a 45-degree coverage straight ahead, but could not rotate. Type 285 radar was fitted to the director. The light AA was increased, with the inclusion of four 20mm guns initially, but later this would rise to seven such weapons. The small cranes aft were to help with the loading of mines or stores through hatches to the mine deck. These ships all carried Type 132 Asdic and up to fifteen depth charges, as they would often have to act independently, far from the fleet.

HMS MANXMAN Pennant M70
Abdiel class minelayer June 1941

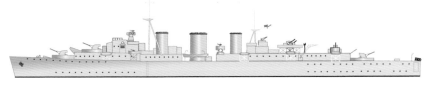

Manxman, unlike her earlier sisters, at least had time to complete trials and working-up before being deployed for action. She is shown here in a very plain scheme of MS4a overall, which she wore for her first few operations. The wood decks were natural, but the metal decks were MS4a. The ship completed two fast runs to Malta, loaded with vital stores and ammunition for the beleaguered garrison. This type of action was so valuable that two modified *Abdiel* class ships were ordered and laid down in April/May, and given priority for weapons, radar and shipyard requirements. *Manxman* returned unharmed to the UK and went to Scapa Flow, with the intention that she would carry out operations with the Home Fleet to lay offensive minefields in German-held waters.

HMS MANXMAN Pennant M70
Abdiel class minelayer August 1941

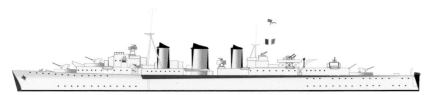

Code name Mincemeat, not to be confused with the later Operation Mincemeat, was conceived and put into effect within days. *Manxman* bore similarities to French destroyers of the *Tigre* class. False caps were fitted to the funnels and an extra rake provided with paint. The hull was altered with areas of black. Mainmast and tops were also raked. She raced to Gibraltar loaded with mines, refuelled at night, passed Spain at a steady speed in daylight, like a French destroyer going to Toulon, then used high speed to lay mines off Livorno. German aircraft near Toulon showed no interest in her, nor did a French warship and another enemy aircraft. After dark, a high speed dash took her to Gibraltar to refuel and return to the UK. For this operation the decks were painted red-brown like French warships. A French flag was worn as a legal *ruse de guerre*, but a White Ensign flown while laying mines. This incredible feat failed because faulty mines floated to the surface, and the field was swept. At the time *Manxman* had five 20mm AA guns.

HMS MANXMAN Pennant M70
Abdiel class minelayer September 1941

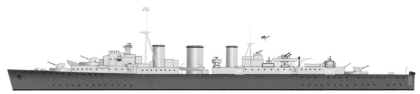

Manxman had her French camouflage painted out, and adopted a dark hull/light upper works style. The hull was 507b, and the upper areas MS4a. The metal decks were also 507b, while the wooden decks were unpainted, but allowed to fade to light grey. In this configuration, she carried out several mining operations, including one in the Bay of Biscay. A supply run to Malta was also part of her busy schedule. She was then transferred to the Far East to replace *Abdiel*, which had been damaged by grounding. There were now seven 20mm guns fitted and the radar fit remained the same, with Type 285 radar on the main director, Type 282 radar for the 2pdr director, and Type 286 radar at the foremast.

HMS MANXMAN Pennant M70
Abdiel class minelayer December 1941–December 1942

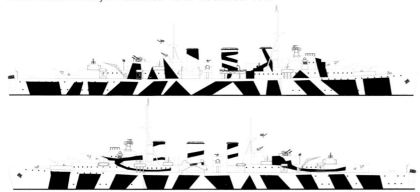

Manxman took on a somewhat dramatic camouflage of black on white for service in the Mediterranean. Wood decks were unpainted, but other vertical surfaces used a grey similar to 507b. Rotating Type 286B radar was at the masthead. The number of 20mm was increased to nine. This ship was involved in numerous operations, including in the Indian Ocean. *Manxman* carried out a supply run to Malta at a time when no other ship had got through for three months. She laid minefields, ran troops and supplies and was rarely not at sea. On 1 December 1942, on her way to Gibraltar, she was torpedoed by *U-375*. The ship was immobilised with her engines and gear room out of action. She was towed to Gibraltar for some patching up, then to the UK for major repair work.

HMS MANXMAN Pennant M70
Abdiel class minelayer May 1945

The repair of this ship took so long and was so costly that, had it not been for the high value put on the class, she would have been declared a constructive total loss. The war in Europe was ending by the time she was restored to service, and she was sent to join the British Pacific Fleet. As seen here, she wears a B5 hull panel on an otherwise 507c ship. The decks were now 507b grey. Type 276 radar was carried at the top of the foremast, with Type 291 radar at the head of the mainmast. She has the usual electronic countermeasures and IFF for late World War II. The light armament comprises two power-operated twin 20mm mounts to port, and two more to starboard. The superstructure aft, along with the single 20mm gun previously there, has been deleted to increase the arc of fire for the quad 2pdr AA mount. The ship proceeded to Melbourne, Australia, after joining *Apollo* at Malta. The ships arrived on 2 August 1945, and were to have proceeded to Sydney to join units of the British Pacific Fleet, but the war ended. *Manxman* assisted with some transport duty and other services, then returned home to the UK in June 1946. Post-war, she was used for many duties, from a flagship to a cadet officer training ship. The armament changed many times, but she generally retained an overall paint scheme of 507c.

HMS WELSHMAN Pennant M84
Abdiel class minelayer August 1941

Welshman is shown here in a four-colour disruptive scheme using white, B5, B6 and B20. The decks were unpainted wood, except for metal decks and horizontal surfaces which were mid-grey, probably 507b. The ship had Type 285 and Type 286 radar at the time of completion. There were three twin 4in AA mounts, like her sister ships, which were controlled by a director on the bridge. The light AA comprised the designed quad 0.5in MG mounts, a centreline 20mm gun between the searchlights, and two 20mm guns on the aft deckhouse. There was a small blast deflector at the aft end of the same deckhouse. The quad 2pdr mount aft had its own director abaft the mainmast. *Welshman* had time to work up and run trials before being sent on combat missions. These were usually carried out from Loch Alsh, which was the base for minelayers. All her first sorties were on minelaying duty, the first of the class to actually be heavily employed on the designed task.

HMS WELSHMAN Pennant M84
Abdiel class minelayer early 1942

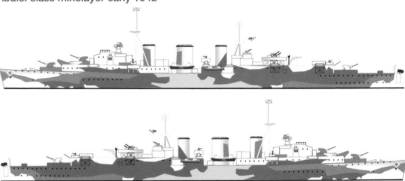

There were a few adjustments to the camouflage above, but it is uncertain when. The colours were MS3, MS4, MS4a and white. In early 1942 she made a fast passage from her base to Gibraltar, then on to Freetown and Takoradi with urgently needed stores, before return to base, and probably wore this variation at the time. All details were as for the previous illustration, with only the lines and areas of colour having changed. The light AA was increased to five, then seven, 20mm singles.

HMS WELSHMAN Pennant M84
Abdiel class minelayer 1942

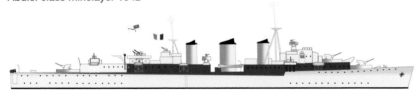

Following on the success of *Manxman* in adopting a French-destroyer disguise, this ship was also sent to the Mediterranean. However, her role was not minelaying, but to run a supply mission to Malta. The disguise was not as elaborate as that used by *Manxman*. False funnel caps were added, and the colours were 507c with black, to give the lines of a French *Tigre* class destroyer. As part of the disguise, there was a fake section of foremast leaning at the approximate angle of the French destroyers she was emulating. She arrived safely on her first run, but was attacked at Malta while unloading, escaping with minor damage. Her second run was also successful and apparently not detected by the enemy. These runs were absolutely vital to enable Malta to hold out against the air and sea blockade, and ships like *Welshman* were ideal for the task. Unfortunately, they could only deliver the bare essentials, but were always morale-raisers for the garrison when they arrived.

HMS WELSHMAN Pennant M84
Abdiel class minelayer January 1943

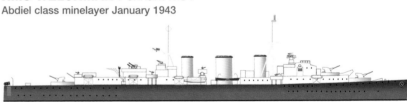

Welshman continued with mining operations during 1942, and then was actively engaged in allied operations against North Africa. Her scheme became the dark hull/light upper works, using 507c on the upper works and 507b on the hull. The armament was not changed, but Type 286B radar replaced the fixed aerial of the previous installation. There were few other alterations and this ship, along with her sisters, was so in demand that it was often difficult to find time for a refit. In between minelaying missions, she was called on to transport troops and supplies to Bone, Algiers, Malta and Gibraltar. In January 1943 she transported 4,300 troops in and out of Cyprus, and then laid two minefields in the Sicilian narrows. However, on 1 February she was torpedoed by the German U-boat *U-617*, forty miles from Tobruk. Although hit aft and all shafts out of action, it was believed she could be towed to safety as she had power, lights and the pumps working. The ship had settled slightly by the stern and was not believed to be in immediate danger, when she suddenly listed to starboard and sank by the stern within three minutes. It was subsequently concluded that there had been hull damage that the damage-control parties were unable to see. Then there had been a sudden rush of water, the mine deck flooded and she sank, taking many of her crew and passengers with her. *Welshman* had run many dangerous missions, and was vital in keeping Malta from having to surrender – her loss was keenly felt.

ABDIEL CLASS MINELAYERS (SECOND GROUP)

HMS ARIADNE Pennant M65
Abdiel class minelayer (second group) September 1943

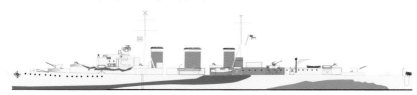

The high value of the first four ships caused the Admiralty to order two more, which, as it turned out, became replacements for the two ships that were lost. *Ariadne* is shown here as completed, with a camouflage of 507c, B5 and B6. Although some unofficial sources give the B6 as Mountbatten pink, that colour was no longer in use. This camouflage scheme only lasted a short time, mostly during trials. The starboard side is believed to have been the same. The decks were uniformly 507b. In this second batch, 'B' mount was replaced by a powered twin 20mm mount. There were another five of these, for a total of six mounts, with twelve 20mm barrels. The 2pdr mount was not included; instead there were twin 40mm Hazemeyer AA mounts with their own radar control on each side, just forward of the cranes. Type 275 radar was on the main director, with Type 273 radar on the starfish of the forward tripod mast. Type 291 general warning radar was at the head of the foremast.

HMS ARIADNE Pennant M65
Abdiel class minelayer (second group) March 1944

Ariadne is shown here with her camouflage yet again modified. All of the B5 was painted out and replaced with B20. In January 1944 she was sent out to the Pacific via the Panama Canal with a full load of mines aboard. She stopped off at Pearl Harbor, and while there the US Navy added two single 40mm guns in place of the twin 20mm mounts on each side of the foremast. She then proceeded to Australia, visiting several ports, and working with units of the British Pacific Fleet. On the night of 19/20 June she laid a minefield off Wewak, New Guinea, which was a cut-off Japanese base. She did the same again on 1 September and then acted as a troop carrier to land troops on Pegun Island on 15 November 1944. However, new, fast, coastal U-boats were causing problems off the UK, and it was decided that *Ariadne* was needed to assist in laying anti-submarine mines in home waters. The ship was ordered to proceed back to the UK as quickly as possible. At some time while in the Pacific, the ship had adopted a camouflage scheme for that area as shown in the next illustration.

HMS ARIADNE Pennant M65
Abdiel class minelayer (second group) November 1943

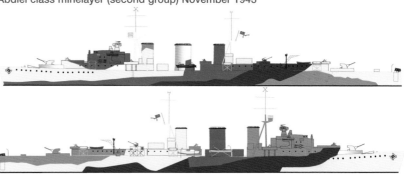

There were adjustments to the previous camouflage pattern, but it is uncertain when they occurred. Areas of B20 dark blue were added and the B6 and B5 also altered. In December 1943 she was sent to intercept the German blockade runner *Alsterufer*, ending up in action against German destroyers and torpedo boats in the Bay of Biscay. She was then prepared for transfer to the Pacific, having been offered to help the US Navy.

HMS ARIADNE Pennant M65
Abdiel class minelayer (second group) January 1945

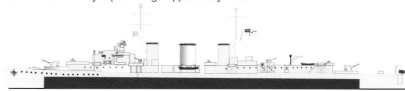

The Pacific scheme shown is how *Ariadne* appeared on return to the UK. During her time with the US fleet it is possible that the blue hull band extended the full length of the hull, like US ships. The hull panel was B20, the overall pale grey was 507c and the decks were 507b. This scheme was, of course, the same on both sides. Apart from her two new 40mm guns, the ship was little altered since she had left the UK at the start of 1944.

HMS ARIADNE Pennant M65
Abdiel class minelayer (second group) April 1945

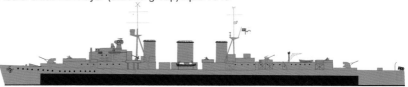

Ariadne was refitted on her return home and painted to the Admiralty standard scheme of MS3 and MS1. The decks presumably remained 507b. Some countermeasures were added, as I have shown. Protection against German guided bombs was particularly important.

HMS ARIADNE Pennant M65
Abdiel class minelayer (second group) 1946

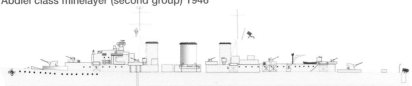

Ariadne is shown here in peacetime colours of overall 507c. The wood decks were returned to natural, but horizontal surfaces remained 507b. The boot topping was thickened to form a more distinct waterline. The armament changed, with twin 20mm being replaced by single 40mm Boffins. An additional twin 40mm Hazemeyer mount replaced the twin 20mm forward. Type 293Q radar was at the head of the foremast, with Type 277 radar on the foremast. There were directors with radar for each of the Boffin mounts. *Ariadne* was reduced to reserve in 1947 and finally scrapped in 1963, having seen no further service.

HMS APOLLO Pennant M01
Abdiel class minelayer (second group) June 1944

The camouflage worn by D-Day had changed to the light upper/dark lower style using MS3 and MS2. The decks remained dark grey. On the day after the landings, *Apollo* was conveying the senior commanders of the operation on an inspection along the beachheads. The senior commanders insisted that she sail as close to the beaches as possible, some of which were still under fire. During this she struck an uncharted shallow area and damaged her propellers. After transferring her important passengers to the destroyer *Undaunted*, she was able to limp from the area under her own power to be repaired. She was not able to return to service until September 1944.

HMS APOLLO Pennant M01
Abdiel class minelayer (second group) August 1945

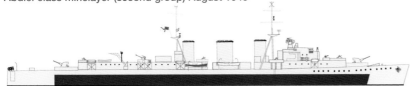

Apollo was sent to Australia to join the British Pacific Fleet for operations against Japan. Her scheme became 507c overall, with a hull panel of B20. The decks appear darker at this time, possibly 507a or B15. The ship was not involved in any offensive operations while in this theatre, having arrived too late.

HMS APOLLO Pennant M01
Abdiel class minelayer (second group) February 1944

The camouflage worn at completion comprised MS3 overall, with MS2, B20 and B30. Decks were dark grey, possibly 507a. The port side was very similar. Radar Type 276 radar was carried, but the others were as her sister ship. Light AA had two extra single 20mm guns mounts before the bridge, for anti E-boat work, as the ship regularly operated in coastal waters. She was heavily involved in the mining programme to protect the Normandy landing beaches. This often entailed sailing to within range of German patrols and coastal batteries while remaining unsighted, so that the location of the minefields laid would not be seen.

HMS APOLLO Pennant M01
Abdiel class minelayer (second group) September 1944

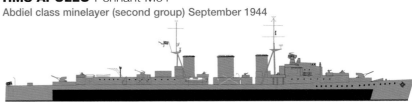

On return to service, *Apollo* adopted a standard Admiralty scheme, using MS3 with a hull panel of B15 blue-black. By this time the Allies were advancing through France, and the Germans were starting to employ small coastal U-boats in a new submarine offensive against Allied shipping. *Apollo* laid emergency anti-submarine minefields to counter them, often in company with her sister *Ariadne*. In April 1945 Apollo laid an anti-submarine minefield off the Kola Inlet near the coast of north Russia, as German U-boats had become very active attacking convoys in those waters. This was her last minelaying operation in European waters.

HMS APOLLO Pennant N01
Abdiel class minelayer (second group) 1957

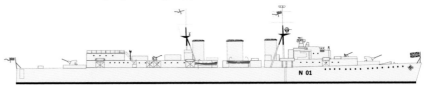

Apollo became a despatch vessel and Admiralty yacht for CinC Home Fleet. A cabin was added aft. Pennant number changed to N01 in 1948. Here she is in 507c with heavy black boot topping, as she was when CinC Home Fleet led the fleet past Queen Elizabeth II on Royal Yacht *Britannia* in 1957. A Union Jack is at the bow, White Ensigns on the foremast and the stern, and the admiral's flag on the mainmast. She was sold for scrap in 1962.

HMS ALCANTARA Pennant F88
Armed merchant cruiser
July 1940

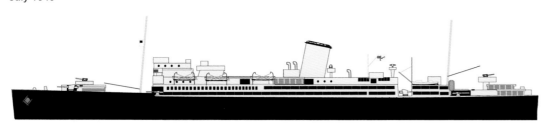

As requisitioned, *Alcantara* had a black hull/light grey upper works, was converted at Malta and mounted four 6in guns and four unshielded 6in casemate guns from old battleships and cruisers, with two 3in AA guns. All but the base of a dummy funnel forward was removed; accommodation was better than RN warships. A rangefinder was on the main structure, searchlights on each side of the funnel and a few Lewis guns were added. On 28 July 1940 she ran down German raider *Thor*: both had guns of similar age, but the enemy's had a higher elevation, outranging *Alcantara*, wreaking havoc among the unshielded gun crews. Hit in the engine room, she slowed almost to a stop. *Thor* also suffered hits and withdrew with a significant list. After seaworthy repairs at Rio de Janeiro, *Alcantara* went to Freetown, then for full repairs in the UK and more up-to-date 6in guns installed.

HMS ALCANTARA Pennant F88
Armed merchant cruiser
1943

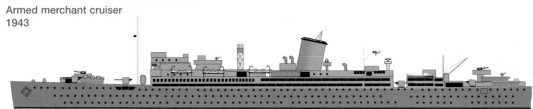

Alcantara is shown the year before conversion to a troopship. The base of the fore funnel was a platform for two 20mm AA guns in late 1941. A third 20mm was placed aft. By 1943 she had three more 20mm added, one right aft, and two behind the bridge. She was fitted with Type 271 radar on a tall lattice aft of the dummy funnel base. Her superstructure was in B55 and the hull 507b. The new guns were all shielded and had longer range. Had she met *Thor* again, she could have exceeded the raider's gun range. The mainmast was removed, but spreaders on the funnel enabled aerial wires to be rigged. She was refitted in 1948 and resumed passenger liner service until broken up in 1958.

HMS ANDANIA
Armed merchant cruiser
1940

Andania was completed in 1922 with strengthened areas for guns in the event of a war, for which her owners received a subsidy. She commissioned into the RN in November 1939 after conversion at the Cammell Laird, Birkenhead. She wore a camouflage of three colours: 507b, 507a and areas of MS4a. Wood decks were unpainted. She joined the Northern Patrol, to intercept German merchant ships or neutrals with cargo for Germany. On 16 June 1940 she was torpedoed by U-boat *U-A* and sank 200 miles south of Iceland seven hours later. *Andania* carried a standard AMC armament of eight 6in guns and two 3in AA guns. There were some machine guns as light AA.

HMS ARAWA Pennant F12
Armed merchant cruiser 1941

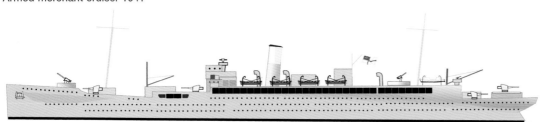

Built as *Esperance Bay* in 1921 for the Commonwealth & Government Line, her owners changed several times before World War II: the last ones pre-war renamed her *Arawa*. Hired for RN use in 1939, and converted at Sydney she had seven shielded 6in plus two 3in AA. Light machine guns were in tubs on the aft superstructure. Her duties were patrols on the China Station, then Freetown and the East Indies. On 18 January 1941 she sighted gun flashes from the German raider *Kormoran*, but was unable to catch her. She is shown here in grey, probably MS4a. Probably the wood decks were unpainted, but horizontal metal surfaces were most likely mid-grey by 1941. The top of the funnel was white and all masts were white above the level of the bridge. Later she was converted to a troopship.

HMS ASCANIA Pennant F68
Armed merchant cruiser 1940

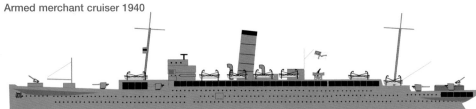

This ship was completed in 1925. Her peacetime route was between the UK and Canada. In 1939 she was hired by the RN as an AMC with an armament of eight 6in guns and two 3in AA. Light machine guns were added. She was painted in a very sombre 507b with a low black boot topping. She took part in the escort of convoys from Halifax to the UK. *Ascania* was sent to New Zealand waters in November 1941and remained there until September 1942, then converted to a troopship. While on the New Zealand station, it is probable she was painted in 507c. Her crow's nest was common to many Atlantic liners and more comfortable than those on regular warships.

HMS ASTURIAS Pennant F71
Armed merchant cruiser 1939

Completed in 1925, *Asturias* had a speed of 18 knots, 19 if pushed. She was called up when war broke out; her original armament comprised eight old pattern 6in guns and two 3in AA with added machine guns. Her colour was a black hull with 507c upper works. In 1940 she was painted in 507b overall. There was originally a dummy fore funnel, but only the base was retained. A simple gun director was placed there. Serving on the Northern Patrol and various convoy escort duties, she was damaged by fire in May 1940 at Gibraltar. She captured a Vichy French ship off Puerto Rico, and then went to the US for repairs and rebuilding. She emerged as in the lower image in camouflage of 507a on 507c. The wood decks were unpainted. An aircraft hangar was placed aft of the remaining funnel, and an athwartships catapult on top of the deckhouse, each carrying a Seafox aircraft. A centreline crane was added. A ramp from hangar to catapult spanned the gap across the superstructure. The mainmast was struck and the foremast used to carry aerials via various spreaders aft. Old model 6in were replaced by seven later, shielded guns. A second director was added on top of the aircraft hangar, plus a centreline 3in AA gun. Two 20mm guns were placed behind the aft 6in gun, with a good arc of fire. Single 20mm were also placed on the aft end of the hangar and two more on the forward deckhouse. Type 271 radar was added between the bridge and the aft funnel. This level of refit indicated the Admiralty had plans to use her as an AMC, although many were being converted to troopships. She went to the West Africa Command until July 1943, when she was damaged by a torpedo attack from the Italian submarine *Cagni* and had to be towed 400 miles to Freetown. The damage was so severe she was laid up with many compartments awash. At the end of the war she was purchased by the British government, repaired and converted as a troopship, then finally scrapped in 1957.

HMS ASTURIAS Pennant F71
Armed merchant cruiser 1941

HMS CALIFORNIA Pennant F55
Armed merchant cruiser 1941

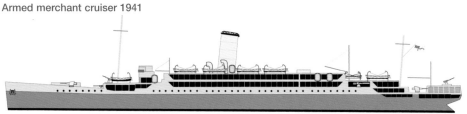

California was completed in 1923 with her deck strengthened for guns. In 1939 she was converted at Fairfield's to carry eight 6in and two 3in AA guns. Her first scheme was a black lower hull and 507c upper works, but by 1941 she had a lower hull of 507b and above that MS4a. On the Northern Patrol she captured two German ships, but one was sunk by *U-31*. California later served with the Northern and Western Patrol Groups, then the Western Patrol, the North Atlantic Escort Force and the South Atlantic Patrol. In March 1942 she was converted for service as a troopship and in July 1943 was bombed by German planes off the Bay of Biscay, caught fire and sank. Most of the troops on board were rescued.

HMS CANTON Pennant F97
Armed merchant cruiser 1942–3

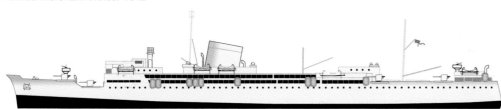

Built in 1938, *Canton* was hired as an AMC in 1939, with eight old pattern 6in and two 3in AA guns. After the Northern Patrol, she went to Western Approaches Command for convoy escort, then Freetown in August 1940. She was in 507b until early 1940, when she had dark hull/light upper works, then at Freetown, 507c overall. In early 1942 she was refitted. Camouflage illustrated is MS4a, 507b and B5. Both 3in AA were removed and the 6in replaced by newer models; an extra gun was added forward. There were two twin 4in AA amidships, sixteen single 20mm and two single 2pdrs. Type 271 and 79M radar were added, with NZ SW1 from the cruiser *Achilles* and an athwartships cata-pult for US-type Kingfisher aircraft. She was on the South Atlantic Station, then the Eastern Fleet; in April 1944 she became a troop transport, returned to her owners in 1946 to be scrapped at Hong Kong in 1962.

HMS CARINTHIA
Armed merchant cruiser
1940

Built in 1924–5 as *Servia*, she was purchased before completion by Cunard, as *Carinthia*. Her run was Liverpool to New York. Hired as an AMC in September 1940, she was hurriedly fitted for service on the Northern Patrol. The standard eight old 6in guns and two 3in AA made up her armament. She had a black hull and funnel, with MS4a elsewhere. This suited the dull conditions, enabling AMCs to close with a suspect ship. In bad weather she collided with another AMC, *Cilicia*, but was repaired. On 6 June 1940 she was torpedoed by *U-46* off Ireland. All power was lost to the engines and the pumps damaged. After a thirty-hour struggle, she sank, losing four men.

HMS CARNARVON CASTLE Pennant F25
Armed merchant cruiser 1942

Completed in 1926, this ship had beautiful lines after a 1938 modernisation. Her top speed of 19.5 knots was marginally faster than most German raiders. Because she was air-conditioned, the ship was mostly used in the South Atlantic and West Africa Commands, painted in overall 507c. Her peacetime arching black boot topping was retained. The foremast was struck and replaced with a light tripod mast. The boats carried were reduced but like most AMCs had a large motor launch, so suspect ships could be examined by a boarding party. Armament comprised the usual eight 6in guns in single mounts, plus two single 3in AA. By 1942 some 20mm guns were added, with Type 271 radar on the bridge, and Type 279 radar at the head of the tripod. Converted to a troopship in December 1943, she still operated mostly in African and Indian Ocean waters.

HMS CHESHIRE Pennant F18
Armed merchant cruiser 1942

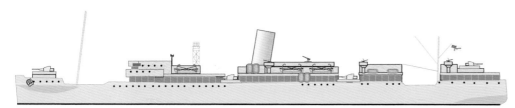

Cheshire was built in 1927 for the Bibby Line UK–Rangoon route, requisi-tioned in the Far East and converted at Rangoon with six old 6in, two 3in AA guns, and a few machine guns. Her scheme seems to have been MS4a, with a thin black boot topping. Wood decks were unpainted, and metal decks MS4a. Her foremast was retained, but the mainmast cut to a stump, and most derricks removed. She went to the South Atlantic, then North Atlantic, for patrol and convoy duty. On 14 October 1940 she was torpedoed by *U-137* off Ireland. With a hole 36ft long by 20ft deep, she was thought a total loss, but struggled slowly to Liverpool aided by tugs and salvage ship *Ranger*. In repair 20mm AA were added and in 1941 a Type 271 radar on a lattice. She again survived torpe-doing, by *U-214* in August 1942, and was converted to a troop transport.

HMS CHITRAL Pennant F57
Armed merchant cruiser October 1939

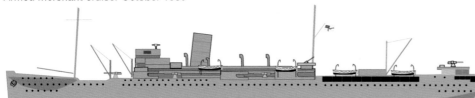

Chitral was built in 1925 for the UK–Australia service and could make 16 knots, receiving an Admiralty subsidy. In 1939 she received an 'emergency equipment' outfit, of 6in unshielded ex-casemate guns from old battleships and two 3in AA. An overall coat of a medium grey was almost certainly local procurement by the commercial yard Alexander Stephen & Sons, as it was darker than MS4a, but lighter than 507c. The second, dummy, funnel was removed. Machine guns were also added before the ship was sent to the Northern Patrol where on intercepting the German *Bertha Fisser*, the crew scuttled. She later rescued survivors of *Rawalpindi*. Sent to Bermuda then Halifax, she joined the North Atlantic Escort Force in 1941.

HMS CHITRAL Pennant F57
Armed merchant cruiser 1942

In 1941 *Chitral* was given 6in guns removed from 'C' class cruisers that had undergone AA conversion. The 3in AA were removed, replaced by three 4in AA guns and four single 20mm also added. Type 271 radar was placed on the forecastle, an unusual position. Type 291 radar was placed at the head of the foremast. Her camouflage was quite unique. The overall shade was MS4a, but there was a dark blue area along the waterline edged in a false white simulation of wave crests. The decks remained unpainted wood, but most horizontal metal surfaces were painted a bluish grey, possibly B5. She served on the East Indies Station and with the Eastern Fleet until April 1944, when converted to a troop transport with the false funnel reinstated. After the war she was used as a one-class emigrant ship until 1953, then broken up.

HMS CILICIA Pennant F54
Armed merchant cruiser 1942

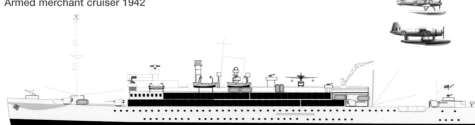

Built in 1938, *Cilicia* could make 16.5 knots, or more if pushed. She received an 'emergency' fit with unshielded 6in and two 3in AA. She patrolled the South Atlantic and West Africa. In a later refit, modern 6in guns with shields were supplied, one 3in AA gun moved forward and one removed. Single 2pdrs were placed on the bridge, and eight single 20mm added. A hangar was placed on the superstructure with an athwartships catapult, and a crane. She carried a Fairey Seafox, but later a US-type Kingfisher. The hull was 507c, the masts were white and the funnel also white, or very close. This seems to have applied to the bridge and upper works as well. She was returned to her owners, sold to a Netherlands company and scrapped in 1980.

HMS CIRCASSIA Pennant F91
Armed merchant cruiser 1939

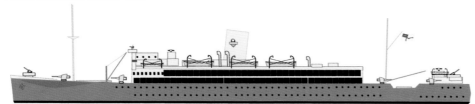

Circassia was a sister ship of *Cilicia*, but as AMCs they were fitted out differently. Armament was the standard eight 6in guns and two 3in AA guns, but she acquired a pair of single 20mm AA guns, which were placed on top of the bridge. The hull was 507b or a similar local procurement colour. The upper areas were light grey. The wood decks were not painted and horizontal decks were light grey. *Circassia* was converted to a troopship in 1942, owing to a shortage of such vessels.

HMS COMORIN Pennant F49
Armed merchant cruiser 1941

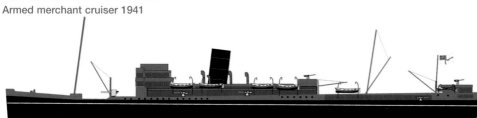

Comorin was completed in 1925 and could make 16 knots. In 1930 she caught fire while at Colombo. During repairs, new turbines were fitted, increasing her speed to 17 knots. As an AMC, the aft 6in were unshielded ex-casemate guns, while the forward guns were shielded and a more modern type. Two old 3in AA guns were fitted. The aft funnel was removed and she retained her mercantile colour scheme. *Comorin* was sent to Simonstown, then to the Halifax Escort Group, then Bermuda and back to Freetown. On 6 April 1941 she caught fire off Sierra Leone in heavy seas. The crew could not control the fire and had to abandon ship. All but twenty crew were saved. At the time of the fire, photographs show *Comorin* still wearing her peacetime colours.

HMS CORFU Pennant F86
Armed merchant cruiser 1941

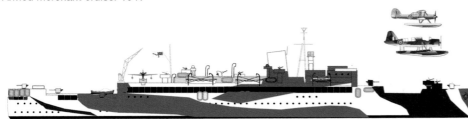

Built in 1931, this 18-knot liner was fitted as an AMC with one funnel removed, eight 6in and two 3in AA guns. After a 1941 refit, the armament was nine 6in on improved mounts and two twin 4in AA. Eleven 20mm were carried. Type 271 radar was on the bridge and Type 79M radar on the tripod foremast. An athwartships catapult was added. Two Seafox were originally carried, but later Kingfishers. Only one aircraft could fit in the hangar and the other stowed on the catapult. *Corfu* went to Freetown in 1941, then the East Indies and Eastern Fleet during 1942, the South Atlantic in 1943, and finally West Africa in 1944, then converted to a troopship. She continued in that role until 1949, when she was returned to P&O and was broken up in 1961.

HMS DERBYSHIRE Pennant F78
Armed merchant cruiser 1941

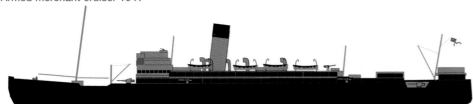

Derbyshire was built in 1935 but, with a 15-knot speed, was near the lower end of AMC requirements. After the usual 'emergency fitting' in December 1939, she went to the Northern Patrol. *Derbyshire* was painted in a dark, non-standard battleship grey of local procurement and had a black hull. There was a deep band of black at the top of the funnel. She originally had four tall masts, but after conversion the foremast remained the same, and the other three were reduced to stumps. She was typical of many vessels of her type that were called into service for the initial emergency of war. In February 1941 she was converted to a troopship and in 1943 to a Landing Ship Infantry (Large).

HMS JERVIS BAY Pennant F40
Armed merchant cruiser October 1939

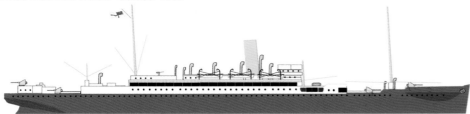

This 15-knot passenger liner was built in 1922, and already past her prime when called in for AMC duty. She was given eight old pattern 6in guns and two 3in AA guns. At first she wore her pre-war house colours of a mid-green hull, with a red boot topping, a white superstructure and pale yellow funnel, ventilators, masts and spars. Owing to the urgent need to get ships to sea to search out enemy raiders, several AMCs initially wore house colours in full, or at least partly. No doubt the paint lockers had sufficient paint to maintain this look for at least a few months, until the ship could go into yard and receive a coat of grey. *Jervis Bay* was on the South Atlantic Station in these colours and was not repainted until she went to Bermuda in May 1940.

HMS JERVIS BAY Pennant F40
Armed merchant cruiser November 1940

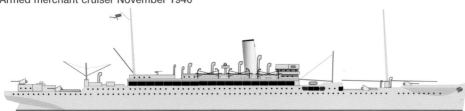

In 1940 *Jervis Bay* joined the Bermuda and Halifax Escort Squadron, convoying ships across the North Atlantic. On 5 November 1940 she was with convoy HX84, a convoy of thirty-seven merchant ships, when the German heavy cruiser *Admiral Scheer* fell in with them. Captain Edward Fegen immediately ordered the convoy to scatter and then turned to engage. It was a totally unequal fight, during which *Jervis Bay* found it hard to get within range, while being pounded by the 11in guns of the enemy ship. The selfless action delayed the enemy cruiser closing the ships of the convoy, allowing all but five to escape. Captain Fegen was awarded the Victoria Cross posthumously. The actual grey of *Jervis Bay* at the time of the battle is unclear. It was a few shades lighter than medium, and was probably a local procurement type.

HMS KANIMBLA Pennant F23
Armed merchant cruiser 1939

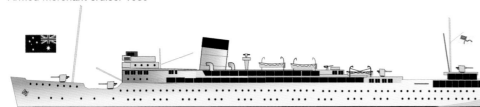

Kanimbla was commissioned as an HM ship and did not join the RAN until 1943, despite being crewed by Australians. She was dressed in what is believed to be 507c, but with her bridge still in polished wood. A black funnel top was retained until 1940, when it was painted out. Wood decks were unpainted and the colour of the horizontal metal decks is not known. She was fitted with seven 6in and two 3in AA guns. The aft guns may have been unshielded. She served on the China Station first. In 1941 she embarked 300 troops of an Indian regiment for a surprise attack on Bandar Shahpur in Persia, capturing several ships, including Axis vessels. *Kanimbla* performed duties in the South Pacific until 1943, then converted to a Landing Ship Infantry (Large) and commissioned as an HM Australian ship.

HMS LACONIA Pennant F42
Armed merchant cruiser 1939

Built in 1921 as a 16-knot passenger liner, *Laconia* was called up by the Admiralty and found to be poor condition, with her top speed obtained only with great effort and fuel consumption. She carried eight old 6in, of which six were unshielded ex-casemate guns, and two old 3in AA. She escorted convoys across the Atlantic, but as she was thought too vulnerable to act alone, *Laconia* was converted to a troopship in 1941. She was torpedoed on passage to Freetown in September 1942 by *U-156*. Of the 2,846 people aboard, half were Italian POWs. Only 1,111 survivors were picked up, 1,400 of the POWs perishing. Note that although painted grey of unknown origin, she retained a black funnel top, and all masts and spars were brown.

HMS LAURENTIC Pennant F51
Armed merchant cruiser 1939

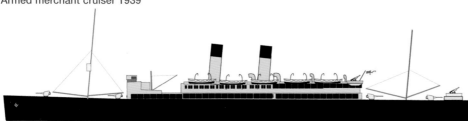

Laurentic was built in 1927 as a 16.5-knot liner. In 1935 she collided with *Napier Star* and after repair was laid up. She sailed once for a voyage as a troopship, then laid up again. In 1939 she was in poor condition, and it was October 1940 before she was ready, with the usual eight old 6in, four being ex-casemate weapons and four shielded. Best speed had fallen to 15 knots. She had a black hull and black funnel tops on the Northern Patrol, and sank the German merchant ship *Antiocha*. In 1940 she was rearmed with seven shielded 5.5in guns of more modern type and longer range. Three single 4in AA guns replaced the 3in AA. The illustration shows her appearance after this gunnery upgrade and at her loss. She was torpedoed by *U-99* off Bloody Foreland, Ireland, and sunk with the loss of forty-nine men.

HMS MALOJA Pennant F26
Armed merchant cruiser 1940

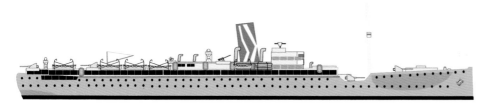

Completed in 1923, this ship could make 16 knots, but improvements made to her engines gave her 17 knots. In September 1939 she was armed at Bombay with eight 6in and two 3in AA. One funnel was removed. The mainmast remained stepped along with many derricks, but were removed in the UK. On the Northern Patrol, she intercepted the German merchant *La Corunna*, whose crew scuttled. In 1940, with the Western Approaches Command, the hull was MS4a and the upper works 507c. The funnel was dark grey with white vertical, but irregular, stripes. The paint may have been local procurement. A pair of quad 0.5in machine guns were added. At the end of 1941, she was converted to a troopship. *Maloja* survived the war, was given her second funnel back and served as an emigrant ship until 1954, then sold for scrap.

HMAS MANOORA Pennant F48
Armed merchant cruiser 1942

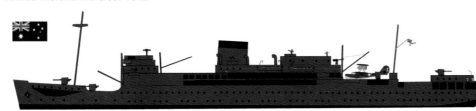

Although small, the Australian AMC *Manoora* packed more AA punch than most by 1942. Overall MS4a was worn for much of her career, but when first converted the hull was black. She later adopted overall USN blue. *Manoora* could make 16.5 knots and carried seven 6in, with the aft gun on the centreline, plus two 3in AA guns, but also carried six 20mm AA and two twin Lewis guns. A Walrus aircraft was shipped, but had to be lowered over the side for launch. Depth charges were carried for defensive reasons. *Manoora* was very useful, being built in 1934, with reliable machinery. The loss of regular cruisers had left a shortage of ships for patrol duty. In 1943 she was converted as a Landing Ship Infantry (Large) or LSI, serving until 1947. She was sold to Indonesia in 1961, but sank in 1972 while being towed to be scrapped.

HMNZS MONOWAI Pennant F59
Armed merchant cruiser 1942

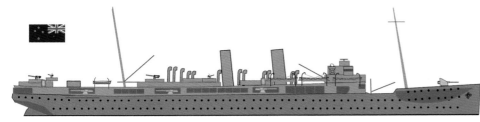

Monowai, built in 1925 to old-fashioned lines, was fast at 18 knots. She mounted eight 6in guns, of which six were old casemate guns on open mounts. Only the bow guns had shields. There were two 3in AA. There appear to have been four 20mm AA guns added. She patrolled the South Pacific and on January 1942 surprised the Japanese submarine *I20* while on the surface, forcing the enemy to crash dive. Subsequently it fired four torpedoes at *Monowai*, but all missed. Later in the same year she was sent to the UK for conversion into a Landing Ship Infantry (Large) and remained in service until 1946, when she was returned to her owners. *Monowai* served until 1960 and was scrapped in Hong Kong.

HMS MOOLTAN Pennant F75
Armed merchant cruiser 1941

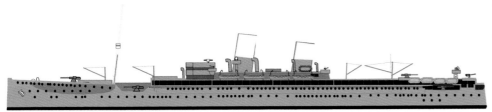

Mooltan was ordered in 1918, but not completed until 1923. Her 16 knots was unsatisfactory, and later new Bauer-Watch exhaust turbines were fitted, improving speed to 17 knots. AMC arming consisted of eight 6in, all having been casemate weapons. Two 3in AA guns were added. The aft funnel was removed, along with the mainmast and many derricks. Conversion was slow, taking until April 1940. The paint was apparently of local procurement, as the shade of grey fell between those of RN issue. As illustrated, she wore a dummy funnel for a time, with the fake and the real one painted white at the top. This could have been for a special operation, as when first converted *Mooltan* had only one funnel, the mainmast was in place and she was painted dark grey. She went to Freetown and the South Atlantic. In January 1941 she was converted to a troopship, remaining such until 1947. Post-war, *Mooltan* was an emigrant ship, and was scrapped in 1954.

HMCS PRINCE DAVID Pennant F89
Armed merchant cruiser 1941

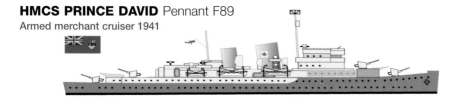

HMCS PRINCE HENRY Pennant F70
Armed merchant cruiser 1942

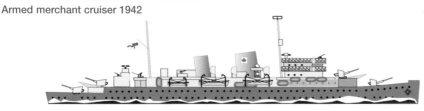

HMCS PRINCE ROBERT Pennant F56
Armed merchant cruiser 1940

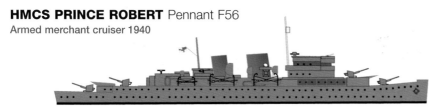

HMS QUEEN OF BERMUDA Pennant F73
Armed merchant cruiser
1942

HMS RAJPUTANA Pennant F35
Armed merchant cruiser April 1941

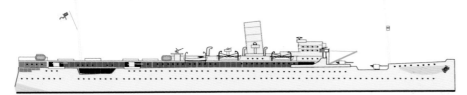

Prince David was a 22.5-knot coastal passenger ship built in 1930 for Canadian National Railways. All three ships in the class were purchased in 1940 for conversion into AMCs for the Royal Canadian Navy. Alterations were extensive. An original third funnel was removed and the others enlarged. They were quite small, but their design enabled a centreline armament to be fitted, giving them the same four-gun broadside as large eight-gun AMCs. Two 3in AA were added; twin Lewis guns were in the bridge wings. They were small cruisers, but without armour. The 6in guns had small shields, with a higher elevation to improve range. The long barrels suggest they were from late World War I. All carried depth charges and eventually had Asdic. I have illustrated them in the three most common camouflage schemes.

Prince David shows the fake destroyer outline, with dark grey hull/pale grey upper works. In photographs, the decks appear to be dark grey. She is illustrated with Canadian Type 2SW1C radar with a sixty-degree sweep ahead.

Prince Henry is shown in a dark hull/light upper works scheme, but she also had an elaborate fake waterline, including blue and white to give an impression of speed. I have depicted the ship in 1942. Machine guns of unknown type were on the bridge and aft superstructure, and single 20mm on each side behind the aft funnel; 3in AA guns had shields of a type similar to those usually on 12pdr AA. At the fore masthead she carries the later Canadian Type SW2C radar, which was a fully rotating, improved version. *Prince Henry* and *Prince David* were converted into fast Landing Ships Infantry (LSI) in 1943.

Prince Robert is illustrated as built, in an overall coat of dull 507b, possibly carried onto the decks. Armament was also four 6in guns and two 3in AA guns, but with twin Lewis guns in the bridge wings. Like her sisters, she was used on convoy escort, then converted to an AA cruiser, as illustrated in Book 1.

This was the largest liner taken into the RN as an AMC during World War II: she is shown late in her service. The aft funnel was removed and eight 6in guns, plus two 3in AA, added. She also had at least eight 20mm AA guns, possibly more. A large crane and hangar were placed aft for Seafox aircraft. However, she was altered for her to ship two US Kingfisher floatplanes. When first converted, her guns were of older type. The ship is shown in overall MS4a Home Fleet grey. However, her initial style was very dark, possibly 507a, until she moved to the South Atlantic. Wood decks were probably left unpainted and allowed to fade. This ship was too large and valuable for an AMC, so in 1943 she was converted to a troopship. Returned to her owners in 1946, the vessel was broken up in 1966.

Rajputana was a 17-knot steamship built in 1925. She was hired as an AMC and had her second funnel removed. The armament was the usual eight 6in guns, but all were shielded. The two 3in AA guns were placed amidships. She is shown here in overall 507c, which she wore while part of the Bermuda and Halifax Escort Force. Four single 20mm AA guns had been added since conversion. She was sunk by *U-108* on 13 April 1941.

HMS RANPURA Pennant F93
Armed merchant cruiser 1943

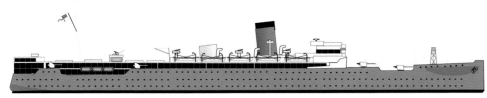

Ranpura was completed in 1925 and had a speed of 17 knots. In September 1939 she had the top of the aft funnel removed, but the lower part was left in place. Guns comprised eight 6in. Those forward were a later mark with longer range, while the four aft were older with different shields, remaining so during her service. Two 3in AA were added. By 1943 six single 20mm AA were carried. She had a lattice tower with Type 271 radar on the forecastle, with around seventy degrees of coverage. Although she used various schemes, by 1943 the hull was of a shade approximating 507b, the superstructure was white, the stump funnel and all masts where white, but the funnel was a darker shade of grey than 507b, probably local procurement. The funnel also had a black top added. This was unusual, as the dark funnel did not match the white superstructure. In 1944 this ship was purchased by the Admiralty for conversion into a Heavy Repair Ship.

HMS RAWALPINDI
Armed merchant cruiser 1939

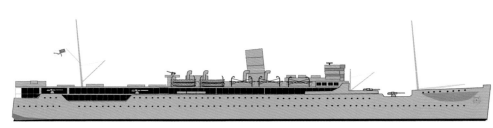

Rawalpindi was delivered in 1925 and capable of 17 knots. At the outbreak of World War II she became an AMC. The aft funnel plus her derricks and superfluous equipment were removed. She had eight old ex-casemate guns without shields and two 3in AA guns, and was painted overall in grey. Having been converted at a non-naval yard, the mix was something between MS4a and 507b. The decks were unpainted. On 19 November 1939 she stopped the German merchant *Gonzenheim*, but its crew scuttled it to avoid capture. Thirteen days later, she had the misfortune to run into the German battleships *Scharnhorst* and *Gneisenau*. Unable to evade these fast, powerful ships, she engaged them in a truly hopeless action. Although *Rawalpindi* scored one hit, the devastating fire of the two enemy battleships quickly overwhelmed her. Of her crew, 266 men lost their lives, twenty-six were picked up by the Germans, and the next day the AMC *Chitral* rescued another eleven.

HMS SALOPIAN Pennant F94
Armed merchant cruiser 1941

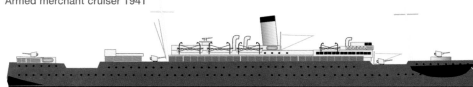

Built in 1926 as *Shropshire*, she could make 15.5 knots. In later years that fell to 15 or less. As the RN already had a cruiser named *Shropshire*, she was renamed *Salopian* when called up for service, although there were doubts about her speed. Six 6in were installed, two on the centreline, two on each side in front of the bridge, and two more on each side by the mainmast. She originally had four masts, but two were removed. Two 3in AA guns and twin Lewis guns were carried. She became an ocean escort in the North Atlantic. On 13 May 1941 she was escorting Convoy SC30 when she was hit by five torpedoes fired by *U-98* and sank almost instantly.

HMS VOLTAIRE Pennant F47
Armed merchant cruiser 1942

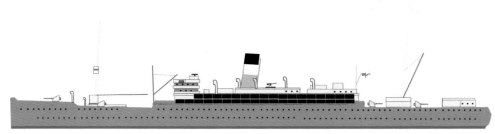

Voltaire completed in 1923 and could make 15 knots. At the start of the war she was operated by Lamport & Holt when taken up as an AMC. It was common for many crew to remain with their ship, becoming officers and ratings of the Royal Navy. Perhaps for pride, the funnel colours were retained, even after being painted drab grey. Paints were almost certainly local procurement, similar to 507c and 507b. The civil funnel colours of black, white and light blue and the red waterline were retained. She had the usual eight old 6in and two 3in AA guns. On 4 April 1941 she fell in with the German raider *Thor*. Accurate German fire shot away the radio aerials and *Voltaire* could not send a contact report. Her old 6in guns could not reach *Thor*, which used superior speed to stay out of range. Within thirty minutes *Voltaire* had been sunk. Of her crew, seventy-five were lost and 177 taken prisoner. Details of her sinking were not known to the RN until after the war when survivors were released from POW camps.

HMAS WESTRALIA Pennant F95
Armed merchant cruiser 1940

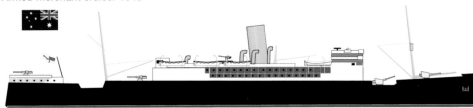

Westralia was built in 1929, and had a top speed of 15.5 knots. On the outbreak of World War II, the ship was requisitioned and given an emergency fitting. There were two guns with shields forward and three unshielded weapons aft. All were old guns. Two old 3in AA guns were also provided. There were many enemy merchant ships still trying to get home to Germany, as well as neutrals that could be carrying cargo for German ports, therefore *Westralia* could not even wait for the colours of the Huddard Parker Line to be painted over, before she sailed from Sydney on her first patrols into the Pacific. It was some months before she would change to a more naval appearance, at first by merely painting out the yellow and white with 507c, and removing the white band above the red waterline.

HMAS WESTRALIA Pennant F95
Armed merchant cruiser 1942

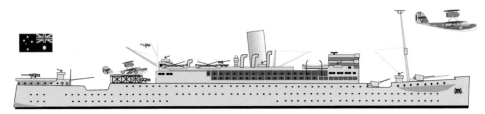

Westralia received her Seagull V, or Walrus, aircraft and platform while still in civilian colours. But she is illustrated here as she was early in 1942. The ship is shown in overall MS4a in this illustration, but wore 507c on other occasions. She may have been painted in dark blue while operating with the US Navy around the Solomon Islands. The ship had ten single 20mm guns added. Depth-charge throwers and a rack of spares were carried. At the head of the foremast is an aerial which was either Type 286 radar or the New Zealand Type SW1 radar. Several of the New Zealand sets were sent to Sydney in 1941 to make up for a shortage of other types. The aircraft was moved via a heavy derrick, requiring the ship to be stationary while the aircraft was being handled. During the Japanese advance, this ship transported garrisons and engineers to potentially threatened areas and evacuated troops and civilians from others. On one occasion a Japanese submarine was sighted in a surface attack position, but it was driven off by gunfire from the US cruiser *Chicago*. *Westralia* was converted into a Landing Ship Infantry for the island hopping campaigns that drove the Japanese back.

HMS WORCESTERSHIRE Pennant F29
Armed merchant cruiser 1942

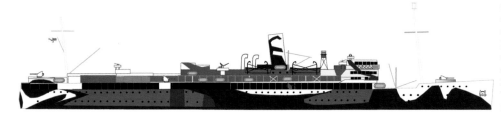

Worcestershire was a 15.5-knot small passenger and cargo liner built in 1930 for the Bibby Line. She became an AMC on 9 September 1939, with six 6in and two 3in AA guns. She was torpedoed by *U-74* while escorting Convoy SC-26, but was able to make it safely to port. In November 1941 she was sent to the East Indies Station, then joined the British Eastern Fleet, where she served until mid-1943. Conversion to a troop transport followed. She carried a very thorough camouflage of MS1, MS2, G10 and white. Deck colours are not known but, considering the thoroughness of her other camouflage, it is quite likely she had dark grey decks. She also carried four single 20mm AA and may have had several more, plus a pair of single 2pdr AA. Type 271 radar was carried on a tower between the bridge and funnel. Type 279 radar was carried on the foremast. She was returned after the war and was broken up in 1961.